Early in 1943 Robert J. C. Butow was called into active service and sent to the Army Intensive Japanese Language School at the University of Michigan and then to the Military Intelligence Service Japanese Language School at Fort Snelling, Minnesota. He was subsequently ordered to Tokyo in December of 1945 to serve as a Language-Intelligence Officer with the Civil Intelligence Section of GHQ, SCAP.

After his return from Japan, he earned his A.B. (*magna cum laude*) from Stanford University, and subsequently an A.M. in history. He then began work for his Ph.D., an undertaking which was to serve as the basis for *Japan's Decision to Surrender*.

Early in 1950 he was awarded a Rotary International Foundation Fellowship which enabled him to continue his studies in Japan. From October 1951 to January 1952 he served in a civilian capacity in Japan and Korea, working for the United Nations Command. This assignment resulted in a report to the U.N. General Assembly covering the UNC's civilian relief and economic aid program for Korea. As a reserve officer, he has also had short tours of duty with the Historical Division, War Department Special Staff, Washington, D.C., and with the Civil Historical Section, GHQ, Far East Command, Tokyo.

After receiving his Ph.D. at Stanford in 1953, Dr. Butow was awarded a postdoctoral fellowship at the Center of International Studies, Princeton University, where he continued his research on Japan. He is now an Assistant Professor of History at Princeton University and a Research Assistant at the Center of International Studies. tice: the rise and fall of cabinets, the interplay of power groups within the circle of the ruling elite, the activities of the senior statesmen, the machinations of the military services, and the role of the Emperor in affairs of state.

Hitherto untapped primary sources of information have been used by the author during three and a half years of original research in Japan and the United States. These include records, exhibits, and proceedings of the Tokyo Trial; documents in the possession of and investigations undertaken by the Japanese Ministry of Foreign Affairs; unclassified and unpublished interrogation files of the U.S. Army's Far East Command; and unpublished personal material (notes, diaries, letters) obtained by the author from a number of the participants in the events described.

THE HOOVER LIBRARY ON WAR, REVOLUTION, AND PEACE
——————————Publication No. 24——————————

JAPAN'S
Decision to Surrender

Published under the authority of the
Publication Committee of the Hoover Library
on War, Revolution, and Peace

JAPAN'S
Decision to Surrender

By ROBERT J. C. BUTOW

Foreword by Edwin O. Reischauer

STANFORD UNIVERSITY PRESS
STANFORD, CALIFORNIA

To LOUISE M. BUTOW
and IRENE ELKELES BUTOW

STANFORD UNIVERSITY PRESS, STANFORD, CALIFORNIA

London: Oxford University Press

Copyright 1954 by the Board of Trustees of the Leland Stanford Junior University
Printed in the United States of America

Library of Congress Catalog Card Number: 54-8145

First edition, 1954
Second printing, 1956
Third printing, 1959

FOREWORD

THE PACIFIC WAR, as the war against Japan is sometimes called with geographic accuracy but semantic incongruity, was won by the United States long before the Japanese acknowledged defeat. Certainly by the end of 1944, if not much earlier, the scales of war had been tipped so steeply against the Japanese that no counterweights at their disposal could possibly have balanced them. Germany, which for the Japanese had been a seemingly invincible first line of defense, was facing inevitable destruction; the defense perimeter that the Japanese had created far out beyond their island base had been cracked and deeply penetrated; worst of all, Japan's military potential was dropping rapidly with her industrial capacity, as American submarines and planes cut the last of her economic lifelines to the outside world and great aerial armadas began the methodical destruction of her cities. The Japanese, first and last, counted most heavily on "Japanese spirit," on their own firmness of purpose and determination. But Japanese will power had been matched by that of their opponents, and as had happened since time immemorial, determined men with more and better weapons were triumphing over their less well-armed adversaries.

It had taken the lives of many thousands of men and the devoted efforts of countless millions more to decide the outcome of the war, and even after the eventual defeat of Japan had become certain, this vast human sacrifice had to continue until the climactic moment of surrender. The crucial area of historical decision, however, had shifted from the far-flung battlefields and factories of the world to the narrow confines of the imperial palace and government buildings in Tokyo. Mass action on an unprecedented scale had determined that Japan would be defeated, but only a handful of men decided just when Japan would acknowledge defeat.

Conceivably the masters of Japan's fate might have surrendered when the inevitability of defeat had become clear to the few who were able and willing to be fully rational. More possibly they might have surrendered when Germany's collapse in May of 1945 offered some emotional justification for capitulation. On the other hand, they might much more probably have delayed surrender until the Japanese government itself had been engulfed by invasion, and the only surrender then would have been by scattered remnants of the Japanese population after the greatest slaughter of combatants and civilians in history. The postwar course of events in East Asia and perhaps in the rest of the world might have been far different than it has been, if the Japanese had surrendered before their industrial power had been so seriously crippled or they themselves had been so fully demoralized, or if, on the other hand, the destruction of Japan had continued through further bombardments and eventual invasion. Significant changes in the postwar world would have resulted even from a shift in the date of surrender by two weeks one way or the other—before the atom bombs and the Soviet entrance into the war or after the Russian armies had penetrated further into the Far East and Japan had been more irreparably destroyed.

In any country in wartime a few men inevitably must make grave decisions for all their countrymen, but for Japan the decisions were particularly crucial and the men participating in them unusually few. Because of the theory of imperial rule and still more because of the growing dictatorship of the military and the corresponding intellectual strait jacket into which the masses had been forced, there were not many Japanese who even thought of participating in Japan's great decision to surrender. Only a few score at most attempted to have any say in it, and still fewer had any effect. For some time there were vague gropings toward peace by some of the few civilians who still exercised any political influence. There were also some vain efforts at starting peace negotiations by minor Japanese officials whose perception and daring exceeded their authority. But ultimately the decision narrowed down to a mere handful of men. Naturally they were influenced by what they felt the Japanese public would understand and still more sharply limited by what the deeply indoctrinated and often bitterly fanatical professional soldiers of Japan would accept. But the final decision was essentially made by eight men—or perhaps it was only one, the Emperor himself. The mystical concept of the imperial will had been much used by military extremists in their drive toward dictatorial power in Japan. It is a strange irony of history that the one clear expression of a Japanese Emperor's will since ancient times sealed the doom of that dictatorship.

Japan's decision to surrender was a fateful turning point in history. The full record of that decision also makes one of those true stories that so effectively belittle fiction. It is this story that Dr. Butow has told in careful and scholarly detail but also with a verve that does justice to these dramatic events.

EDWIN O. REISCHAUER

CAMBRIDGE, MASSACHUSETTS
July 27, 1954

PREFACE

JAPAN's formal acceptance of the Potsdam ultimatum in August 1945 represented much more than just a hasty reaction to the atomic bomb and the Soviet Union's entry into the war. The capitulation was actually the climax of the behind-the-scenes activities of those Japanese whose thoughts and actions produced Japan's decision to surrender. This book is a history of those activities and a study of that decision.

The narrative begins with the early months of the military's gamble at conquest, keeps pace with the successive crises growing out of Japan's mounting defeats, and terminates with the unprecedented developments which keynote the last fateful days of Japan's tragedy.

The promotion of schemes to negotiate a settlement favorable to Japan, the launching of peace feelers in Sweden and Switzerland, the quest for Soviet aid and later for Soviet mediation, and the final reliance upon the influence of the Emperor and the Throne record the steps by which a small faction within the ruling elite committed the Japanese government to salvaging, through negotiation, a part at least of what the military could no longer maintain by force of arms. The internal obstacles encountered by the end-the-war advocates and the external problems posed by Allied policy pronouncements figure both as incidents in the story behind Japan's struggle to surrender and as explanations of why the surrender was a struggle.

The writing of "recent history" is difficult at best; at worst, it degenerates into a form of disguised fiction with little or no claim upon the *historical*. The years ahead may reveal new sources of untapped information or may seal into near oblivion a part, at least, of what is presented here. This is both the limitation and its justification. Had it not been for those who wrote of events close to themselves, who recorded the history of their own times, our present record of the past would be far less rich, far less intimate, than is generally admitted.

The author wishes to extend his sincere appreciation to Professors Claude A. Buss, Edgar E. Robinson, and James T. Watkins IV for the many hours they have spent reviewing his work and stimulating its development. Their advice and guidance have helped make the task an easier one. From Professor Bunshirō Satō, friend and tutor, the author received invaluable assistance and a broader understanding of things Japanese. Mrs. Hildegard R. Boeninger, Colonel Allison R. Hartman, Dr. Nobutaka Ike, Mr. Proctor Jones, Dr. Kazuo Kawai, Dr. Felix M. Keesing, Mr. Takahiko Kido, Mr. Ken Kurihara, Mr. Denver Lindley, Marquis Yasumasa Matsudaira, Dr. Kijirō Miyake, Mrs. Ruth R. Perry, Dr. Hubert G. Schenck, Mr. John T. Zatteau, Mr. Tomotake Teshima, and Dr. James B. Zischke have all been helpful in many ways.

Special thanks are due Professor Edwin O. Reischauer for the interest and encouragement he has expressed and for the Foreword he has written to this book.

A final debt of gratitude, by no means the least, is owed to the Rotary International Foundation, whose fellowship grant cut the trail to another year of research in Japan, and to Dr. C. Easton Rothwell, whose untiring efforts have made publication possible.

ROBERT J. C. BUTOW

STANFORD, CALIFORNIA
August 1954

EXPLANATORY NOTE

DIACRITIC marks have been used throughout—a concession to the numerous Japanese references which appear in the footnotes in Rōmaji. Only one exception occurs and that is in the geographical place name, Tokyo, which, according to the standard followed hereinafter, should have been written as Tōkyō.

The Japanese plural, which is the same as the singular, has been used in preference to the more common practice of adding an "s" to the Japanese word in question. Thus, more than one senior statesman (*jūshin*) is still *jūshin* and not *jūshins*.

Japanese proper names have been written to accord with English usage, that is, Kōichi (personal name), Kido (family name), and not Kido Kōichi, which would be the correct Japanese word order.

KEY TO ABBREVIATIONS USED IN THE FOOTNOTES

Aff.	Affidavit
Analyses	Analyses of Documentary Evidence (IMTFE)
ATIS transl.	Allied Translator and Interpreter Section translation
Ch.	Chapter
Def. Doc.	Defense Document
E	English
Exh.	Exhibit
FEQ	*Far Eastern Quarterly*
Govt.	Government
IMTFE	International Military Tribunal for the Far East
J	Japanese
JFO	Japanese Foreign Office
JFO MS	The form of reference used in citing the Japanese Foreign Office MS study entitled "Shūsen no keii to sono shiryō."
Statements	The form of reference used in citing the unpublished interrogation (and voluntary statement) material compiled by the Military History Section, Far East Command.

Translations	The form of reference used in citing cablegrams, minutes of conferences, official summaries of governmental and Supreme Command decisions, and other similar material compiled (in translation) by the Military History Section, Far East Command.
USAAF	United States Army Air Force
USFCC	United States Federal Communications Commission
USOSS	United States Office of Strategic Services
USSBS	United States Strategic Bombing Survey

Examples

IMTFE: Tōgō, 37541–42 is a reference to evidence offered by Tōgō in IMTFE: *Proceedings*, page 37541 to page 37542. The word *Proceedings* is used in the footnotes only when its absence might otherwise cause confusion. The abbreviations *Aff.*, Def. Doc., and Exh. appear from time to time, either for clarity's sake or because the material in question, having been rejected by the Tribunal, does not appear in the *Proceedings*. When Japanese originals existed for IMTFE translations, both the J and E texts were checked. The J text is cited in the footnotes whenever the E text contains an error in translation or whenever the J text is the only available text.

JFO MS: Ch. 56 (Gyokuon hōsō rokuon to Rengōkoku ate tsūkokubun no hatsuden) is a reference to Chapter 56 (J title as shown in parentheses) of the JFO manuscript study entitled "Shūsen no keii to sono shiryō" which was used by the author during the period of his research in Japan (February 1951–May 1952). This form of reference makes it possible for those who wish to do so to correlate the material presented here with that found in the published version of the MS study which appeared in May 1952 under the title, *Shūsen shiroku*.

Statements: Kido #61476 is a reference to a statement or "interrogation" of Kōichi Kido (document number: 61476) found in an unpublished compilation prepared by the Military History Section, Far East Command. Whenever a document number was missing, the author used the date of the statement or interrogation (e.g., *Statements:* Sakomizu 5/3/49).

Date references of the type shown above (5/3/49) have been written in the following order: month/day/year.

CONTENTS

PROLOGUE

Japan Accepts the Potsdam Ultimatum

EARLY in the morning on August 15, 1945, Radio Tokyo stunned its listeners with the announcement that His Imperial Majesty would broadcast a message to the nation at noon. The news spread rapidly, causing a flurry of activity. Individual radio owners arranged for friends, relatives, and neighbors to come in. Factories, schools, and offices hurriedly set up loud-speakers. Everywhere the excitement grew intense as people waited impatiently for noon.

In the three and a half years which had elapsed since the Tōjō regime had challenged destiny in early December 1941, the Island Empire of Japan had fanatically fought and utterly lost a major war. For months on end, B-29's and other raiders had struck at the industrial plants and strategic bases of the homeland with ever-mounting success. But even though the war had long since been carried to Japan's own doorstep, no visible breach had as yet occurred in the solid front of Japanese resistance. In spite of their bitter taste of war, the masses were still united in spirit— still prepared to defend to the death their most cherished possession, the Emperor and the Throne. Even the terrible destruction which had been visited upon their once impregnable shores had failed to dent the armor of their passivity and enforced ignorance.

Since the Emperor had never before turned to a microphone to address himself to his people, His Majesty's millions now assumed that they would be exhorted to redouble their efforts in support of Japan's holy war. Even among the few who did realize that the country was balancing on the brink of disaster, the feeling was generally the same: the time had apparently come to break out the bamboo spears.

As the fateful hour struck, technicians began spinning the imperial record which had been secretly cut inside the palace the previous evening. Traffic ground to a halt, and a deep stillness settled upon the land. As one man, the people of Japan arose and bowed: The Emperor was speaking.

To Our good and loyal subjects:

After pondering deeply the general trends of the world and the actual conditions obtaining in Our Empire today, We have decided to effect a settlement of the present situation by resorting to an extraordinary measure.

1

We have ordered Our Government to communicate to the Governments of the United States, Great Britain, China and the Soviet Union that Our Empire accepts the provisions of their Joint Declaration.[1]

Overwhelmed by the emotion of the moment, the masses could not grasp His Majesty's meaning—could not fathom the formal, classical style of expression in which the imperial rescript was couched. Their failure to understand was further magnified by the purposeful absence of concrete words and phrases which would have scuttled all doubt had they been used. In spite of the fact that a special daytime distribution of electricity had been authorized to ensure the largest possible audience, radio reception was poor, especially in the more distant reaches of the four main islands. Thus, in all that the Emperor said the unwelcome fact of Japan's *capitulation* remained hidden in the shadows.

The Emperor had not written the rescript himself; he was merely repeating words which the cabinet had placed in his hands. Though few of his listeners realized it, the rescript being read by their sovereign would one day stand in history as the final and ultimate justification for an act of aggression for which the people of Japan would now be forced to pay the price of failure.

Using the imperial "We" and "Our" which were then the standard pronouns, the man who sat "By the Grace of Heaven" upon "the Throne occupied by the same Dynasty changeless through ages eternal" spoke on:

To strive for the common prosperity and happiness of all nations as well as the security and well-being of Our subjects is the solemn obligation which has been handed down by Our Imperial Ancestors, and which We lay close to heart.

Indeed, We declared war on America and Britain out of Our sincere desire to ensure Japan's self-preservation and the stabilization of East Asia, it being far from Our thought either to infringe upon the sovereignty of other nations or to embark upon territorial aggrandizement.

Here was the rationalization for the wild gamble which had begun on December 7, 1941, and had lasted for nearly four years, thanks to the backbreaking efforts of a straining people. Every ounce of their energy had gone into the war effort, and with what result?

Despite the best that has been done by everyone—the gallant fighting of military and naval forces, the diligence and assiduity of Our servants of the State and the devoted service of Our one hundred million people, the war situation has developed not necessarily to Japan's advantage, while the general trends of the world have all turned against her interest.

The government was fighting the battle of nuances so as not to offend the imperial army and navy or the terrorists and the fanatics. There was

---

[1] A euphemism for the Potsdam ultimatum of July 26, 1945. See Appendix I for the English text of this rescript. For the Japanese text, see Japanese Govt., *Dai Tō-A sensō shūsen ni kan suru shiryō,* flyleaf opposite 1, or JFO MS: Ch. 56 (Gyokuon hōsō rokuon to Rengōkoku ate tsūkokubun no hatsuden).

compelling sense in this, since at various points throughout the country and especially in the capital there was a pulsing sore of discontent within the army that threatened to erupt at the slightest provocation.

True to the pattern set during Japan's wayward rise to power at the expense of her neighbors, the military had insisted that their damning failure be exonerated in terms of a war situation *that had not developed to Japan's interest.* The words "defeat," "surrender," and "capitulation" were taboo. They were harsh words, and His Majesty must not use them. Instead, he must make the people believe that even though the initiative still belonged to Japan she did not choose to continue the war because strategic factors were not in her favor. There was another reason as well:

. . . the enemy has begun to employ a new and most cruel bomb, the power of which to do damage is indeed incalculable, taking the toll of many innocent lives. Should We continue to fight, it would not only result in an ultimate collapse and obliteration of the Japanese nation, but also it would lead to the total extinction of human civilization.

Here was the first real admission of failure, yet the awful clarity of it was dulled by the ominous prediction that human civilization faced annihilation. The inference was that Japan, by her own act, was saving the rest of the world.[2] This was clever, but words were one thing and realities were another. The facts were stubborn.

For all their gems of euphemism, the ruling elite could not deny that Japan was at the end of the road. The survival of the nation and atonement before the hallowed spirits of the imperial ancestors dictated Japan's "acceptance of the provisions of the Joint Declaration of the Powers." This, the Emperor said, was why he had "decided" to end the war.

It was painfully obvious that Japan's boasts and promises to her "Allied nations of East Asia" were now just so much jetsam washed back on her own shores. The Emperor could do nothing "but express the deepest sense of regret to [the] Allied nations . . . who [had] consistently cooperated with the Empire towards the emancipation of East Asia."

It was difficult to explain defeat to one's allies, but more difficult still were the excuses which had to be given to the Japanese fighting man who had carried the banners of the Empire onto the continent of Asia

[2] The following quotations from an editorial in the *Nippon Times* for August 15, 1945, are typical: "It is only proper that the ultimate welfare of the people and the saving of human civilization from extinction should prevail over lesser considerations even if substantial sacrifices should be necessary."

"Out of the depths of her own experience of suffering, Japan has been moved to subordinate all lesser considerations to the advancement of the greater cause."

"There must be universal recognition of the seriousness with which Japan has made this decision which contributes so immeasurably to the future welfare of all humanity."

and across the wide Pacific. Here the past was now a heavy hand upon the present. Again there was little that could be said. Japan's obligations to her servicemen and their families added up to a prodigious total of unpaid and unpayable debts. The thought of fallen warriors and their bereaved families pained the Emperor's heart "night and day." To the survivors, the wounded, and the war-sufferers in general, His Majesty offered his "profound solicitude."

Having thus probed the depths of sorrow and bitterness, the Emperor approached the end of his historic pronouncement—and perhaps the most significant part of all:

We are keenly aware of the inmost feelings of all ye, Our subjects. However, it is according to the dictate of time and fate that We have resolved to pave the way for a grand peace for all the generations to come by enduring the unendurable and suffering what is insufferable. Having been able to safeguard and maintain the structure of the Imperial State, We are always with ye, Our good and loyal subjects, relying upon your sincerity and integrity.

The ring was familiar, or was it overtones from the past?

. . . We have decided . . . We have ordered . . . We are keenly aware . . . We have resolved . . .

. . . *We are always with ye, Our good and loyal subjects, relying upon your sincerity and integrity.*

In effect, the Emperor was repeating an exhortation of a great imperial prince of bygone days: "The Lord is Heaven, the Vassal is Earth. Heaven over-spreads, Earth up-bears. . . . Therefore the Imperial Commands must be obeyed, or ruin will ensue."[3]

Then came the final warning: all Japanese must "beware most strictly of any outbursts of emotion" that might engender "needless complications." They must not fall prey to "any fraternal contention and strife" that might create "confusion," lead them "astray," or cause them "to lose the confidence of the world."

Let the entire nation continue as one family from generation to generation, ever firm in its faith of the imperishableness of its divine land, and mindful of its heavy burden of responsibilities, and the long road before it. Unite your total strength to be devoted to the construction for the future. Cultivate the ways of rectitude; foster nobility of spirit; and work with resolution so as ye may enhance the innate glory of the Imperial State and keep pace with the progress of the world.[4]

It was all over in a matter of minutes. The people, at least those who

[3] From Article III of the "Constitution of 17 Articles" written by Shōtoku Taishi (*ca.* A.D. 572–621) as translated by Sansom, *The First Japanese Constitution*, 8.

[4] U.S. Government publications pertaining to the surrender contain only a **very** brief and innocuous rescript prepared by General MacArthur's headquarters in Manila and issued as a proclamation by the Japanese government on September 2, 1945 (see Appendix J). U.S. State Dept., *Occupation of Japan*, 64, carries this proclamation as "Imperial Rescript Announcing Surrender to the Japanese People." This designation should really be applied only to the rescript quoted here.

had understood, were left to weep in silence. In the metropolis of Tokyo, once a deafening melee of noise and activity, the inhabitants of the capital quietly trudged along bombed and gutted streets toward the imperial palace plaza to bow in the direction of the Emperor by whose command the war had been brought to an end. While they tearfully sang their national anthem and repeatedly shouted *"Banzai!"* in His Majesty's honor, others solemnly gathered at the Yasukuni Shrine to do obeisance before the spirits of their warrior dead. Still others flocked to the great shrine of the Emperor Meiji, the renowned grandfather of the man who now, in the twentieth year of his reign, presided over an Empire in ruin. What traffic there was moved smoothly. Martial law, which would have been a dangerous weapon in the hands of the military at this juncture, was not proclaimed.[5]

Tutored in a strict school, the people of Japan went on with the business of life as best they could. Shadows from the recent past lurked everywhere, recalling painful memories. Some of the Emperor's subjects broke under the impact of the national failure. A few sought compensation in open violence; others simply resigned themselves to death by suicide. The great majority, however, accepted the inevitable. The principle of unquestioning obedience was deeply inbred in them; resilience was one of their greatest assets.

Eighteen days later, on September 2, 1945, men in other lands dropped what they were doing to listen to another broadcast. This one, too, would figure large in history. Lying quietly at anchor in Tokyo Bay, the great battleship *Missouri* suddenly became the focus of attention throughout the world. The scene recalled the name and exploits of Commodore Matthew Calbraith Perry whose "black ships" had sailed into this same bay ninety-two years before to force Japan to discard her almost two-hundred-and-fifty-year-old policy of self-imposed seclusion. Now, a countryman of Perry's, General of the Army Douglas MacArthur, the Supreme Commander for the Allied Powers, had come to accept Japan's surrender and to direct the destiny of the nation against which he had played such an outstanding role in the march toward victory. It had been a hard road and a long road, but today the guns were silent and he could report to the American people,

A great tragedy has ended. A great victory has been won. The skies no longer rain death—the seas bear only commerce—men everywhere walk upright in the sunlight. The entire world is quietly at peace. The holy mission has been accomplished. . . .[6]

As the curtain fell at last on Japan's Greater East Asia War, the two

---

[5] See USFCC, *Radio Report Far East*, #80, B 4–B 5 and B 7; Shimomura, *Shūsen hishi*, 211.
[6] See U.S. Senate, *Surrender of Italy, Germany and Japan*, 96–99.

principal delegates who had signed the Instrument of Surrender on board the *Missouri* sped back to Tokyo to report to the Throne. The one, Mamoru Shigemitsu, was a diplomat. He had endeavored to clear a path that would lead to a termination of Japan's folly. The other, Yoshijirō Umezu, was a soldier. He had sought a continuation of the conflict in the hope of securing terms favorable to the nation and acceptable to the army. The group of which Shigemitsu was representative had at great length and with much difficulty won the behind-the-scenes struggle to decide the course of national policy. The ranks to which Umezu belonged had failed. It is the record of this fateful struggle between the contending groups—typified by the statesman and the soldier—which now unfolds.

1

BEHIND THE SCENES

Pearl Harbor to the Fall of Tōjō

OUT of the south and north they came—plane upon plane of the imperial Japanese navy—peeling off to strike the land, air, and naval forces of the United States at Pearl Harbor. It was 7:55 A.M. Honolulu time, Sunday, December 7, 1941. The war in the Pacific had begun.

As the smoke cleared from the wreckage at Oahu, only the foolish or misinformed still scoffed at Japanese capabilities. For most Americans, the mere fact of such an attack was sufficient reason to cache their complacency, at least for the duration. They were now committed to a war begun on the enemy's terms and at great disadvantage to themselves. After what had happened that morning, it did not take a statesman or a strategist to realize that the struggle which lay ahead would be long and bitter.

On the other side of the Pacific, the people of Japan were primarily concerned with the results of their hit-and-run raid upon America's island fortress. The "Rising Sun" navy had won a smashing victory and the masses, who constituted the base of the imperial pyramid and the foundation stone upon which the war effort would rest, were duly proud. For years they had been nurtured on the propaganda fed them by their military masters—men who purposefully suppressed any scrap of information which might challenge the view that Japan, in the twentieth century, was invincible. So misled and deceived were the people of Japan that they were quite incapable of understanding the magnitude of the task which lay before them. As they had been meticulously trained to do and as they had almost invariably done, the "one hundred million" simply turned unquestioningly to their leaders for guidance.

It was the latter, the ruling elite in the inner councils of the state, who, more than any of the others, had cause to take a lingering look behind. The great majority of this group was gratified by the success accruing from the labors of those responsible for planning and initiating the attack upon the American outpost. Now that Japan was at war, the key to victory lay in moving forward rapidly and in force. Since the horizons were beckoning, they hastened to answer the summons.

7

Yet there were a few, a mere handful among this ruling elite, who were still troubled by the somewhat vague misgivings which had persistently been shadowing their inmost thoughts for some time. Even the news of the tremendous damage inflicted at Pearl Harbor could not quite dispel their fears or soothe their exasperation at having now to participate in what they felt was the supreme folly for Japan. But patriotism was a stirring bugle call even for reluctant men, and so they, too, were soon following in the wake of bolder spirits.[1] Had they themselves been strong-willed and courageous leaders or had they been more fundamentally convinced of the impossibility of achieving victory against America and Britain, the nation might not have gone to war. Unfortunately for Japan, however, these men had long since lost their chance to shape the future or had let that chance pass them by.

The doubts which did exist in the minds of the minority were, in many instances, more the result of general impressions than of specific knowledge. Even if the dissidents had had the factual evidence to back up what they thought, they would not have spoken frankly or openly. Japan was a police state, and the punishments for any deviation from the norm as prescribed by the militarists and enforced by the secret police were severe.[2] Equally effective as a silencer, at least during the early months of the war, was the abundantly obvious fact of Japan's initial gains. There was no need to resort to coercion or false propaganda then, for the truth was the government's own best friend.

During the first three months of the fighting, Japan's sea-borne blitzkrieg netted her a land area roughly equal to one-half the area of the United States. The line on the Japanese map of expansion moved steadily eastward, southward, and westward until it contained great areas from which Japan could at last siphon the natural resources so vital to her war effort. By the time Americans were awake to the danger, Japan was at the gateways to India and Australia. It thus became forcefully apparent to every Japanese that the imperial army and navy had been highly successful.

While the victories stifled any tendency toward criticism that might

---

[1] In answer to a question on foreign policy posed in the Diet toward the end of January 1942, Foreign Minister Tōgō stated that it was necessary to work for peace and that he was fully prepared and resolved to do so. This created such a storm of protest that his remarks were stricken from the record. As a result, Tōgō decided that the circumstances prevailing at the moment made it impossible to do anything more than work toward individual or isolated opportunities for peace. It was his hope that these might later be developed into an over-all effort. *Statements*: Tōgō #50304.

Mr. Shigenori Tōgō, Japanese Foreign Minister in 1941 and again in 1945, should not be confused with General Hideki Tōjō, Japan's Premier from October 18, 1941, to July 21, 1944.

[2] See *Statements*: Kido #61541 and #61476; Shigemitsu, *Shōwa no dōran*, 186–88. "Secret police" is used here to refer to the *kempeitai* (military police corps), a branch of the army that was under the provost marshal general (an officer directly responsible to the Minister of War).

otherwise have appeared, especially within the inner councils, they also inspired confidence and lent support to a soothing delusion which had gained currency among many of the elite who were charged with the formulation of policy.[3] Japan's military plan, based on the arbitrary phases of offense, stabilization, and defense,[4] had been geared to the idea that the United States could be induced to abandon what threatened to be a long-drawn-out war in return for a compromise peace. Just what the compromise would be was not very clear since considerations relating to a termination of hostilities were not part of the military's puritan concepts. Although many officers may have hoped to overwhelm the United States by force of arms during the first or second year of the war, the weight of the evidence indicates that Japan's military authorities did not believe the American people would support a war in the Pacific when forced to fight in the Atlantic as well. While the leaders of Japan had not overlooked the possibility of an extended conflict, they had placed great emphasis upon the role Japan would play in defeating Britain and in wooing the two giants, Germany and the Soviet Union, into negotiating a settlement of their disturbingly dangerous war. It was felt that Japanese success in this regard, together with Japan's planned conquest of the Pacific and her destruction of the American fleet, would certainly undermine whatever fighting spirit the United States might initially possess.[5] Although they admitted that Americans were materially strong, Japan's militarists stoutly affirmed that morally and spiritually no American could begin to compare with a Japanese. This was axiomatic. Japan's strength lay in her spirit; America's weakness in her lack of it.

All Japan had to do was to establish an impregnable defense ring around the conquered territories and then set out to exploit, in safety and at leisure, the rich resources which would permit her to become self-sufficient and to maintain the war in the event that that proved necessary. At the same time, Japan would promote friendly relations with her Soviet neighbor and would do everything in her power to prevent the

[3] The outline of Japan's war strategy, which follows in the text above, is based upon the decisions of the Liaison Conference (an extraconstitutional, deliberative, and policy-forming organ established to maintain liaison between imperial headquarters and the government), which are appended in their final form to JFO MS: Ch. 2 (Sensō shoki ni okeru gumbu no sensō shidō yōkō). See also *Statements*: Tōjō 2/28/48, Suzuki #531, Hara #50140, Hattori and Tomioka #50612, Matsutani #51018, and Tōgō #50304.

[4] See USSBS, *Interrogations*, II, Fukudome (chief of staff of Japan's Combined Fleet), 529–30.

[5] "There was considerable opinion in very high places, both military and political, that a few powerful blows . . . might be sufficient to make you seek a way out of a [sic] war by negotiation. But, after Japan had committed itself to war it was extremely difficult to get out on terms other than our own because of the inherent policy of saving face." See USAAF, *Mission Accomplished*, 8 (quoting Prince Konoye). For similar remarks made by Admiral Soemu Toyoda (last wartime chief of the Naval General Staff) and Admiral Kichisaburō Nomura (Japan's ambassador in Washington at the time of Pearl Harbor), see USSBS, *Interrogations*, II, Toyoda, 326 and Nomura, 384.

consolidation of ties of amity and co-operation between the Soviet Union and the Anglo-American bloc. Japan would also endeavor, by political and military means, to undermine the Chungking government and cause its defection.[6] In this way, Japan would be able to destroy the American will to fight without becoming involved in the patently difficult task of reducing the United States to impotence. Subsequent offensive operations would be left to the future and would be devised in accordance with the demands created by circumstances and opportunities. The basic principle throughout this plan was "first things first."

Although the unexpectedly rapid and vigorous recovery of the United States eventually spelled ruin for Japan's enlightened scheme, the battle reports of the first six months of the war served to reinforce the conviction underlying the basic strategy portrayed in her war plans. Thus the scheme gained confirmation from Japan's initial successes and thereby derived a sustaining power which did not finally crumble until Japan's defeats at length outweighed her victories.[7] As a result, new policy decisions which should have been a natural consequence of the Allied refusal to accept the Japanese *dictat* in the Pacific were not speedily forthcoming.[8]

It was not just a matter of psychology; it was also a question of economics. Here, too, Japan's war planning and effort fell woefully short of the degree of achievement so vitally necessary if her gamble at conquest were to retain even some slight chance of success. Unless Japan could negotiate a settlement within the first or second year of the war, she would have to equal and even surpass the tremendous economic and industrial output of the United States. Capturing the resources to the south and maintaining her control over the conquered territories were only the first steps. To obtain the widest margin for success, Japan would have to channel her newly won resources into a huge industrial processing mill capable of producing the materials of war needed to sustain her fanatical effort. Her ability in this respect would, in turn, depend upon the maintenance of transportation facilities and lines of communication.

[6] The question of terminating the China Incident was discussed at a Liaison Conference meeting held toward the end of May 1942, but no agreement was reached as to concrete measures to be adopted. The matter was subsequently referred to the General Staff for study. *Statements*: Tōgō #50304.

[7] Although Japanese leaders had everything to gain by an early termination of the war through negotiations which would confirm their hold over the spoils of victory, many were quite prepared psychologically to wage a long war. Tōjō and others believed the fighting might last ten to twenty years and that the United States would require at least two years to build up her fighting power to the point where she could launch a counteroffensive. Ideas about the length of the war varied with the individual, and this divergence of views found expression in the decisions of the government. See IMTFE: Tōgō, 35741–42, and *Statements*: Tōgō #50304.

[8] As late as August 1944, Japan was still hoping to undermine the American and British will to fight and was still striving to mediate between Soviet Russia and Germany. *Statements*: Hattori #53074.

There would have to be a continuous flow of overseas resources to the home plant and of finished products from the homeland to Japan's military consumer at the front. If this two-way traffic were disrupted at any point and thereafter suspended completely as a result of enemy action, the country would face certain defeat.

In spite of the essential character of this question, Japan actually undertook hostilities without a war economy. Instead of attempting a rapid and substantial expansion of the entire level of production, Japanese leaders merely placed greater emphasis upon a more complete transfer of available resources from nonwar into war uses. The inadequacy of this approach to the problem became so apparent that by the end of the first year of fighting Japan's war leaders were forced to revise their initial concept of economic mobilization.[9]

From November 1942 until about the middle of fiscal year 1944, the Japanese put every effort into raising the whole level of output and into increasing even further the proportion of production utilized for war purposes. In the end, they failed. By the time 1944 had been reached, Allied air and naval attacks upon Japanese shipping, qualitative deficiencies in the Japanese labor force, dwindling stockpiles of raw materials, and an ill-conceived and poorly executed dispersal program had all contributed their deleterious effects to the economy, and a decline in production had inevitably set in.[10] Thus, long before Japan capitulated, she had already lost the war economically.

As time passed, more and more members of the ruling elite realized that the high tide of initial Japanese expansion had left the Empire aground in an overextended line incapable of defense against the forces being mustered by the Allies. Yet realization did not always spell acceptance of an apparently logical conclusion. Those who feared that Midway and Guadalcanal were turning points[11] and who perceived that

[9] In many vital industries, peak production had been reached by 1941. Nothing the Japanese did later was able to raise output any further in these industries.

[10] The text is based upon the analyses, quotations, and figures found in Cohen, *Japan's Economy in War and Reconstruction*, 48–58. Dr. Cohen uses the economic evidence he has accumulated to support the view that Japanese leaders did not plan to wage a long war but hoped instead to negotiate a peace on the basis of their initial gains. He lays their failure to broaden the base of the economy from the very beginning to their conviction that they could undermine the American will to fight.

For additional material relating to the gradual exhaustion of resources (especially oil) and to Japanese reasoning on this subject, see U.S. Congress, Joint Committee on the Investigation of the Pearl Harbor Attack, *Pearl Harbor Attack*, 4011–12.

[11] Interrogations of key personnel in the Japanese navy have revealed that they variously consider either Midway or Guadalcanal as *the* turning point. See USSBS, *Interrogations*, II, Toyoda, 316; Yonai, 331; Nagano, 356; and Nomura, 393. See also USAAF, *Mission Accomplished*, 47–53. The loss of Saipan, which is also mentioned from time to time, is generally considered to be several steps beyond the turning-point stage. Those who continued to hope, after Midway, for a favorable change in fortune knew, after Saipan, that their hopes had lost all meaning.

Japan had very probably already lost her chance to create an economy capable of challenging the resources of the United States were loath to face the unwelcome implications inherent in the facts. As the physical bases for predicting victory gradually disappeared, many of Japan's leaders—especially the vociferous exemplars of the military arts—began re-emphasizing the importance of *Nippon seishin*: the mind, the soul, the spirit of Japan. Their plea was simply this: "Japan may be weak in resources, but she is strong in *spirit*. This will lead the nation to victory!"

But *seishin*, no matter how fiery, was a wholly inadequate substitute for Japan's economic insufficiencies. *Seishin* could not produce arms or ammunition, planes or ships, steel or petroleum; nor could it provide any of the actual equipment and resources so desperately in demand by the fighting forces. While time was needed to strengthen impressions, the fact remains that Japan's comparative weakness in total war inevitably gave rise to the first serious reflection on the part of the few men whose patriotism or wishful thinking did not deny them the use of their reason.

Among the members of the ruling elite who tentatively approached the subject of Japan's prospects was the determined and powerful figure of Marquis Kōichi Kido, the Lord Keeper of the Privy Seal. It was he who had charge of the privy and state seals which were impressed upon imperial rescripts and upon the legislative acts and orders of the government following their approval by the appropriate organs of the state. Affixing the seals, of course, was a mere formality. Kido did not legally have either the duty or the authority to examine the documents which passed through his office, and there was no question of his bearing any responsibility for their contents. The real significance of his position of trust actually rested in an entirely different function, for it was the duty of the Privy Seal to render advice to the Throne and to be in constant attendance upon the Emperor.[12] In a sense, Kido was the eyes and ears of the Throne—a general clearinghouse of information in which rumor, fact, and fiction were duly processed with a view to providing the sovereign with a running account of the currents of opinion and activity sweeping the nation and the world at large at any given moment.

If the Emperor asked the Privy Seal a question, it was Kido's job to

---

[12] During the five and one-half years he served as Privy Seal it was customary for Kido to be received in audience by the Emperor for approximately one hour almost every day. When circumstances required, he saw the Emperor five or six times during the course of a day. Unless summoned by the Emperor, Kido normally did not report at the palace on Sundays. *Statements*: Kido #61541. Also interview with the former Privy Seal, Tokyo, May 1, 1952.

"Constant attendance" did not include either the right or the duty to be present at imperial audiences granted to state officials and others. Actually, many of the persons who were received in audience by the Emperor also called on Kido, sometimes both before and after their audiences. *Statements*: Kido #61476. In this connection, see footnote 50, Ch. 2, below.

supply the answer. Even if no questions were asked, it was Kido's duty to offer his advice to the Throne whenever he felt it was proper to do so, for how else could he fulfill the obligation with which he was charged?

While thus acting as the imperial weather vane, the Privy Seal was expected to remain above politics. He was not to use his office to further his own ambition or to promote the special cause of any pressure group from which he might derive personal advantage.[13]

Kido's assignment was obviously a difficult one. How could he effectively advise the Throne on political issues without taking sides at least some of the time? When he did take sides, was he then conducting secret politics without respect for regular channels or was he merely meeting the responsibilities of his office in good faith by giving free rein to the dictates of his conscience?

Whatever answer eventually emerges from the mountain of material pertaining to these questions, one thing seems clear. As the war passed from the first into the second year, and then into still another year, Kido became convinced that Japan could not win after all, and he therefore lent his support to the argument that Japan must salvage through negotiation what she could no longer hope to save by prolonging hostilities. Once Kido had discerned that the tide had turned against Japan and was unlikely to rise again in her favor, the responsibility of preserving Japan's polity based upon an "unbroken" line of emperors began to weigh heavily upon his shoulders, and he saw that he could ultimately meet this responsibility only by helping to bring the war to an end.

As early as the first week in February 1942, when hostilities were scarcely two months old and the Japanese were on the point of taking Singapore,[14] the realistic and well-informed Privy Seal was already thinking in terms of the day when the difference in strength between the United States and Japan would be a telling factor. Although the army and navy were proudly emphasizing the elaborate preparations and training through which they had put their men, Kido seriously doubted the ability of the military to maintain the supply of picked troops for very long in the future. As more and more replacements were needed, the standard would certainly fall. The Pearl Harbor attack, moreover, had signally served to unify American public opinion—not, as had been

[13] On the functions and duties of the Privy Seal, see IMTFE: Tōgō, 35789–99; Kido, 31208, 31266, 31295, 31583, 31608; IMTFE: Def. Doc. 2247, *Makino Aff.*, 2–4 (rejected: 31615–22); and IMTFE: Exh. 95, *Imperial Ordinance Relating to the Organization of the Office of the Lord Keeper of the Privy Seal* (J and E texts).

[14] Assertions have been made from time to time that England asked for peace when Singapore fell. (See, for instance, a passing mention of the possibility in Toyoda, *Saigo no teikoku kaigun*, 204–5.) When questioned about this, Tōgō (the then Foreign Minister) replied: "That is completely untrue . . . to conceive of the possibility of such a thing is to underestimate the perseverance of the British people. As a matter of fact, no such report ever came to my attention. . . . Such a thing is a logical impossibility." *Statements*: Tōgō #50304.

expected, to destroy the American will to fight. Kido therefore warned the Emperor that the war in the Pacific would not end either so quickly or so easily as the military and other leaders in the government believed.[15]

Some two months later, in April 1942, Kido received positive confirmation of his pessimistic views. Ambassador Shigemitsu, who had just returned from the Asian mainland, told the Privy Seal that the military situation in China was not nearly so splendid as the army authorities were claiming. He therefore advocated a fundamental change in Japan's continental policy that would provide for the recognition of China's sovereignty and independence and for the return of China to the Chinese.[16] Although this plan was broadly conceived out of a serious need, it was obviously anathema to the Japanese army and was consequently stillborn.

About the time of Shigemitsu's return, persons from the so-called intellectual class who were thinking in terms of promoting "peace" gradually appeared on the scene. One of these was former ambassador to England, Shigeru Yoshida, later to become Prime Minister of postwar Japan.[17] On June 11, just four days after the Japanese defeat at Midway—a setback now regarded as a turning point of the war—Yoshida called on Kido to discuss a scheme that involved sending Prince Konoye to Switzerland. The prince was to have no definite mission other than to keep in touch with influential leaders of various countries so as to ensure that Japan would not miss any opportunity which might lead to ending the war.[18] Like an earlier fiasco, a prewar proposal for a

[15] Kido expressed these views to the Emperor on February 5, 1942, at which time he states he also counseled His Majesty "to grasp any opportunity to bring about the earliest possible termination of the war." (The Kido "Nikki" is less specific on this point than Kido's IMTFE affidavit.) Because of the impending fall of Singapore, the Emperor seemed somewhat surprised by what Kido said. Deputy Grand Chamberlain Kanroji, who had heard about Kido's remarks from the Empress, called on Kido to discuss the matter. Several days later the Emperor informed Kido that he had admonished Premier Tōjō "not to lose an opportunity to end the war." Five months later, in July 1942, the Emperor mentioned his desire for an early termination of the war to Foreign Minister Tōgō and revealed to him that he had expressed the same sentiments to the Premier the previous February. See IMTFE: Kido, 31053–57; Tōgō, 35740, 35807, 31403; and Kido, "Nikki," 2/11/42.

In a postwar statement referring to February 5, 1942, Kido declared that he advised the Emperor of the necessity of ending the war speedily by taking advantage of Japan's capture of Singapore. As a result, the Emperor spoke to Premier Tōjō (on February 10) of the imperial desire for peace. *Statements*: Kido #61541 and #61476.

[16] IMTFE: Kido, 31061. Shigemitsu's earlier views have been described by Admiral Teijirō Toyoda, Foreign Minister in the Third Konoye Cabinet from July 18 to October 18, 1941, who testified that shortly after he became Foreign Minister he received an oral report from Ambassador Shigemitsu, who had just returned from London, in which Mr. Shigemitsu "emphasized . . . that Great Britain would never be defeated in the war with Germany . . . that Japan should in no case be involved in any war, and that the negotiations . . . with the United States should by all means be brought to a successful end." IMTFE: Toyoda (Teijirō), 34541.

[17] This Mr. Shigeru Yoshida should not be confused with the Shigeru Yoshida who became Munitions Minister in the Koiso Cabinet.

[18] See IMTFE: Kido, 31065–66. About this same time, Konoye was apparently

Konoye-Roosevelt meeting in the Pacific, the Yoshida suggestion fizzled into nothing more than a mutual pledge between himself and the Privy Seal to exert themselves for peace.

The first development to hold any long-range promise of action and accomplishment did not appear on the scene until after the initial months of the war lay forgotten in the crowded days of 1943. It was then that a few of the *jūshin*, or senior statesmen, slowly and belatedly began to stir.[19] Comprising the big names of the Japanese political world, the *jūshin* were simply those men who had once held the post of Premier.[20] Their position as senior statesmen found no legal expression either in the Japanese Constitution or in imperial decree. They had first met as a group long before the war began when they had been summoned, with imperial sanction, by Prince Saionji, the last of the *genrō*, an extremely privileged and powerful group of elders who had been especially designated "veteran statesmen" by imperial edict as a result of their great services to the nation. A cabinet had fallen, and Saionji had called the former Premiers together to obtain their views on a likely candidate to succeed the outgoing Premier. After having listened to what they had to say, Saionji had recommended a successor to the Throne "on his own responsibility."[21] Out of this modest beginning arose an institution destined to play a significant role in national life. There was, of course, no thought of the senior statesmen becoming a ruling oligarchy or a dictatorial council and, in truth, opportunities for asserting themselves proved to be rather limited. In theory, they functioned as an advisory body only when a change in cabinet occurred. To have functioned properly, even to this limited extent, they should have had access to information possessed

---

involved, together with Prince Higashikuni, in the intrigues of the *Shōwa kenkyūkai*, a so-called "research society" reputedly interested in negotiating for peace. The work of the society failed to produce concrete results.

During the tenure of the Koiso Cabinet (July 1944–April 1945), the Premier toyed with the idea of sending Prince Konoye to Switzerland, so that the prince would be in a position to open negotiations should a favorable opportunity present itself. It seems that Koiso had heard indirectly that the prince would be willing to go to a neutral nation for such a purpose. The plan never got beyond the idea stage. *Statements*: Koiso #55906.

[19] On the *jūshin*, see IMTFE: Okada, 29275; Kido, 31333–34; Tōjō, 36365; IMTFE: Def. Doc. 2247, *Makino Aff.*, 6 (rejected: 31615–22); and Wakatsuki, *Kofūan kaikoroku*, 397–98

[20] Wakatsuki, Okada, Hirota, Konoye, Hiranuma, Abe, and Yonai. Two other former Premiers, Kiyoura and Hayashi, died early in the war (November 1942 and February 1943, respectively). After their wartime cabinets collapsed, Tōjō and Koiso also joined the ranks of the *jūshin*.

[21] It is interesting to note that the outgoing Premier was included in this first senior statesmen's conference. This was the one exception, for thereafter the outgoing Premier was never permitted to attend the meeting which chose his own successor. At all subsequent meetings, of course, he was a member in good standing.

by the government, yet state secrets were not divulged to them and their requests for information were either refused or ignored.[22]

But the *jūshin* were the cream of Japan's officialdom, and some of them, at least, were not content to remain in the background until summoned by the Grand Chamberlain to a meeting called by the Emperor at the time of a cabinet change. Like the *genrō* before them, a few of the senior statesmen aspired to the task of overseeing the government of the country.[23] As the self-styled guardians of *kokutai*, Japan's peculiar national structure,[24] they could not help but be concerned when anything appeared on the horizon to threaten this way of life. And the war—or, more exactly, the manner in which the military were conducting it—soon gave them cause to be worried.

Early in 1943, Prince Konoye assumed the initiative, and thereafter four of the senior statesmen—Wakatsuki, Hiranuma, Okada, and Konoye—began meeting together frequently at the prince's residences in Mejiro and Ogikubo and somewhat later at the very Dai Ichi Building subsequently used by General MacArthur as his headquarters.[25] Many things were discussed at these meetings, but the primary emphasis was upon the war situation and Japan's prospects for the future.[26] The only course that seemed to offer any hope was to get someone into the Tōjō Cabinet who was opposed to the war. After careful consideration, the group decided that Admiral Mitsumasa Yonai was the logical man.

The admiral, who was a senior statesman himself, was a good choice. His cabinet had fallen in the summer of 1940 because of his reluctance to support the army's projected alliance with Germany. He had felt that the Nazis would not stand a chance against the likely combination of America and Britain and, by extension, neither would Japan. Now

---

[22] IMTFE: Okada, 29259–60, 29276–77, 29280; USSBS, *Interrogations*, II, Yonai, 327.

Admiral Yonai testified that the senior statesmen "are told nothing as to what is going on in the Government or the Supreme War Council" (Supreme Council for the Direction of the War). They constitute "merely an advisory council" with "no power of decisive action."

[23] On the *genrō* as the overseers of the government, see Sansom, *The Western World and Japan*, 364–65.

[24] *Kokutai* is variously translated as national structure, polity, or entity. Devotion to *kokutai* is synonymous with devotion to the imperial family. The term embraces a galaxy of meanings, both real and implied.

[25] See IMTFE: Okada, 29259–63. The group rented space in the Dai Ichi Seimei Hoken Sōgō Kaisha Building when the rising frequency of air raids rendered other sections of the city dangerous. Presumably this was sometime in late 1944 or early 1945.

[26] Okada generally kept Kido's private secretary and aide, Marquis Yasumasa Matsudaira, informed as to what went on at the meetings of the four senior statesmen. At times, Konoye also relayed information concerning the meetings. (IMTFE: Kido, 31110. The IMTFE record here contains a sentence which does not appear in the Japanese text of the affidavit presented to the Tribunal. The sentence is to the effect that the central point of discussion at these meetings was "how to terminate hostilities.") See also *Statements:* Kido #61541 and unpublished USSBS interrogation #489 (Hiranuma).

that Japan and America were both in the war and against each other, he was anxious to see Japan get out.[27]

Having once decided on Yonai, Konoye and his colleagues went to great pains to create opportunities to meet and talk with Premier General Tōjō.[28] In the end they failed to get their man into the cabinet. He was offered a post as Minister without Portfolio, but it was felt that he would be unable to accomplish anything in that capacity. The Konoye faction had wanted Yonai appointed Minister of the Navy to replace Admiral Shimada, a staunch Tōjō supporter, but the general, who at that time was still secure in his position of supreme power, had said "No."[29]

Japan had now been fighting her Greater East Asia War for some eighteen months. In that time her achievements in the field had failed to keep pace with the strenuous demands and desperate aspirations of her deskbound strategists at home. The war in Europe had not produced the results on which she had counted and the German and Soviet giants were still at each other's throats. In the Pacific, the United States gave no indication of a desire to do anything other than push hostilities to a successful conclusion. To men like Konoye, Kido, and Shigemitsu, who were in a position to know or at least to discern the truth behind the fiction of the military's mounting propaganda releases, the outlook, even at this early date, was exceedingly disturbing.

The entries in Kido's diary which relate to this period reveal that he knew the war was going against Japan and that Konoye and Shigemitsu shared this view. Early in February 1943, for instance, Kido had a three-hour discussion with Prince Konoye, who was extremely pessimistic about the war situation. During the course of this long conversation, which took place at the residence of Kido's aide and private secretary, Marquis Yasumasa Matsudaira,[30] Konoye repeatedly spoke of the

[27] See USSBS, *Interrogations*, II, Yonai, 330–32. For a fellow admiral's corroboration of Yonai's opposition to the war, see *Statements:* Hoshina #61978.

[28] At times the *jūshin* were forced to resort to stratagems in order to see Tōjō and his cabinet ministers. In a letter written to Konoye on August 13, 1943, Okada suggested inviting Premier Tōjō and several of his colleagues to a luncheon at the Peers' Club on August 30. The purpose of the invitation was to provide the senior statesmen with an opportunity to talk with the cabinet ministers. See IMTFE: Okada, 29273; *Statements:* Okada #61884 and #61307; Hiranuma #55127; and IMTFE: *Analyses*, #506 (Okada letter to Konoye). From the latter part of 1943 on, some of the *jūshin* met at the Premier's official residence about once a month, but they never obtained more than perfunctory information from Tōjō (Hiranuma #55127). When Koiso became Premier, he made a practice of inviting the *jūshin* to his residence regularly twice a month. *Statements:* Koiso #55906.

[29] See IMTFE: Okada, 29262–63.

[30] Care must be taken not to confuse Marquis Yasumasa Matsudaira, wartime private secretary and aide to the Lord Keeper of the Privy Seal, with Mr. Tsuneo Matsudaira, Minister of the Imperial Household (until June 1945). Kase's *Journey to the Missouri* is in error on this point in a number of places. Of the page references (in

necessity of terminating the conflict as soon as possible lest unsettled internal conditions lead to an intensification of Communist activity within Japan. The issue, in Konoye's mind, was clear-cut: end the war now or be prepared to see communism emerge as the ultimate victor.[31]

Not long after this conversation, Mamoru Shigemitsu, the man who had recommended giving China back to the Chinese, became Foreign Minister and immediately set to work on a "new policy toward China" which the Japanese Foreign Office hoped would lead to a "peaceful settlement" of Japan's war against the sprawling republic.[32] Marquis Kido, who considered Shigemitsu one of his most trusted friends, confided to his diary that now, for the first time since the outbreak of the war, he had found a companion with whom he could talk about his ideas for the restoration of peace.[33]

On May 13, some three weeks after Shigemitsu assumed the Foreign Minister's mantle, the two men discussed the war situation. Kido expressed the view that hostilities could not be ended until the military had been brought under control and that the only way this could be accomplished was through the imperial family. If a prince of the blood were to cast his influence in support of a termination of the war, even the opposition of the obstinate *gumbatsu* (military clique) might melt.[34] The

---

Kase's index) listed under the mistaken heading, "Matsudaira, Marquis Tsuneo" (Tsuneo was not a Marquis; Yasumasa was), those to pages 74, 75, 98, 130, 146, 147, 176, 180, and 236 are clearly references to Marquis Yasumasa Matsudaira. Those to pages 102 and 206 are references to Mr. Tsuneo Matsudaira.

Page 74 of Kase's text confuses Marquis (Yasumasa) Matsudaira with Mr. Tsuneo Matsudaira by introducing the former as "minister of the imperial household." In spite of this error, Kase is clearly referring to Yasumasa who, as Kase points out in the same sentence, was "private secretary to Marquis Kido." Footnote 6 (p. 74) should, therefore, have been a reference to Yasumasa Matsudaira and not to Tsuneo Matsudaira (erroneously called, as on page 102, a marquis) who had had, as the footnote correctly points out, "a distinguished diplomatic career."

The author has checked the above against the material contained in Japanese yearbooks and in the Japanese equivalent of *Who's Who*. He has also verified the facts pertaining to the lives of the two Matsudairas with Marquis Yasumasa Matsudaira, who is, at present (1952), the Emperor's Grand Master of Ceremonies.

[31] IMTFE: Kido, 31068. The Konoye-Kido conversation took place on February 4, 1943. Kido states that he and Matsudaira, who also participated in the discussion, shared Konoye's anxiety and promised not to let any opportunity slip by that might be utilized constructively in achieving the desired end.

[32] Shigemitsu states that he entered the Tōjō Cabinet on the condition that he would be permitted to inaugurate this new China policy. *Statements*: Shigemitsu 1/13/50. For Shigemitsu's account of the policy, see his *Shōwa no dōran*, 158–74. Kase, who worked with Shigemitsu on the policy, describes it as the first step in a broad plan designed to divert Japan's foreign policy from the channels of war into those of peace. See Kase, *op. cit.*, 69–70.

[33] IMTFE: Kido, 31069–70. In describing his meeting with Shigemitsu, Kido wrote that he "laid bare his heart" and that as a result of his discussion with the Foreign Minister he felt more and more the necessity of exerting himself to bring about a speedy termination of the war.

[34] *Ibid.* See also *Statements*: Shigemitsu 1/13/50 and Shigemitsu, *Shōwa no dōran*, 188. The latter citation, which deals with a "May 1943" meeting between Shigemitsu

next day, May 14, Kido carried this thought one step further by telling the Emperor's younger brother, Prince Takamatsu, that it would be necessary to request His Highness to exert himself to the fullest in the event of an effort to make peace. Without the prince's help, Kido declared, the whole issue would hang in a precarious balance while a struggle raged within the government to reconcile the demands of the Japanese military with the conditions laid down for peace.[35] This was mid-May 1943, a long way from the event, but an accurate prophecy of it, nonetheless.

While Shigemitsu was working out the "new policy toward China" and Kido was developing his own plan of action, an independent effort to secure peace with Chungking as the first step toward a general peace in the Pacific was being sponsored by a group of men around the indefatigable Prince Konoye.[36] The history of this bizarre and unauthorized venture into foreign policy covers the years 1941 to 1945 and centers upon the activities of a number of highly placed individuals known collectively as the *Itsuyūkai*, the "1945 Club." As the name suggests, the group seems to have aimed at achieving a general peace by 1945. Like an earlier Konoye organization, the so-called "Enlightened Peace Research Society" formed in 1942, the intrigue-bound and necessarily cautious *Itsuyūkai* failed to accomplish its purpose. In fact, the negotiations between the "nineteen forty-fivers" and their Chinese and Korean contacts were still in progress when the war suddenly ended without their efforts having contributed in the slightest.

In spite of their failure, Japanese moves toward China marked certain individuals as being inclined toward terminating hostilities or desirous of at least narrowing the scope of the fighting by reducing the number of enemies.[37] The approaches to China also helped create a habit of mind

---

and Kido at which the Privy Seal spoke of a compromise peace based upon Japanese concessions in the South Seas area, may not necessarily be a reference to the May 13 meeting mentioned in the text above.

[35] See IMTFE: Kido, 31069–70, and Kido, "Nikki," 5/14/43. Kido states that about this same time (May-June, 1943) he "counseled the Emperor as to the advisability of bringing the war to the speediest possible conclusion." (IMTFE: Kido, 31404.)

[36] See Fishel, "A Japanese Peace Maneuver in 1944," *FEQ*, VIII (August 1949), 387–97.

[37] In mid-September 1943 Premier Tōjō reported to the Emperor that Sun Fo of Chungking had asked for the good offices of Nanking's Wang Ching-wei in a move to negotiate a settlement between Japan and China. According to a report submitted by Ambassador Tani, who had just returned from China, Chiang Kai-shek wanted to abandon his wartime policy of co-operation with the Communists so that he could destroy the Chinese Communist party and bring its following under his control. To do this, he would have to stop fighting the Japanese, and so he wanted Japan to withdraw her troops from China. If Japan did this, Chiang might consider severing relations with the United States and Great Britain.

Within several days after this intelligence was received, Wang Ching-wei arrived

which perhaps made the final, bold decision more readily acceptable to the men who were responsible for its initiation and execution. The failure of these moves, however, and the progressive disintegration of Japan's front in China at length eliminated the Middle Kingdom as a decisive field for negotiating the end of the war.

While Allied leaders sat in Cairo in late November 1943 discussing their forthcoming policy declaration on Japan, a member of the ministerial secretariat of the Japanese Naval General Staff, Rear Admiral Sōkichi Takagi, was busily engaged in Tokyo in a secret study of the war—a study which went far beyond anything hitherto envisaged by either Konoye, Kido, or Shigemitsu.

The admiral's case was somewhat unusual, for throughout his career in the navy changes in assignment had brought very little change in emphasis. His duties, which had been concerned primarily with research, had projected him into political and economic affairs and had provided him with free access to the secret files and reports of the navy. This latter privilege, severely restricted even among top-ranking officers, had enabled him to form an adequate frame of reference against which to measure Japan's capabilities and prospects. Even before the conflict in the Pacific began, he was one of the very few people who enjoyed such a dangerous advantage.

Although the naval high command had estimated that Japan could not wage a successful war beyond the end of the second year, hostilities were actually only six months old when Admiral Takagi began feeling concerned about the situation in the field. He recognized that the battle of Midway was a turning point, but he felt that there was still some chance of mending the damage before it could spread into a general deterioration. The key seemed to lie in the unification of the army and navy, particularly in the amalgamation of their air arms. If the Supreme Command could consolidate and co-ordinate the efforts of the two branches, Japan might be able to turn the tide again in her favor. Feeling that such a solution offered the only hope, Takagi spent a great deal of time in promoting the idea, only to see his efforts fail. The army, which was especially jealous of its position, proved to be dead set against unification, and no argument could change its mind.

When the Allies stepped up their penetration of the Solomons on

---

in Tokyo for general consultations with the Japanese government. During the course of Wang's stay, Premier Tōjō revealed that he did not think Chiang would entrust peace negotiations to Sun Fo and Madame Sun Yat-sen because of their Communist affiliations. Tōjō also told Wang that he had no objections to his proceeding with peace talks but that Japan would not take part in them (at least for the time being). Furthermore, peace between Japan and China would be impossible unless Chungking severed relations with the United States and Britain. If Chiang did this, Japan might be able to consider withdrawing her troops from China. (Kido, "Nikki," 9/17–18/43 and 9/21–23/43.)

June 30, 1943, Takagi theorized that the outcome of this operation would decide the issue of the war. If Japan lost the Solomons (as she did), all roads, he feared, would lead to Tokyo. With this foregone conclusion secretly embedded in his thinking, Takagi answered a summons to the capital and there, on orders from the Navy Minister, began a study of the "war's lessons" to date.[38] Being capable and conscientious, he assiduously plunged into his new assignment and for the next three months carefully gathered data that in the end served as a sound basis for analysis and prediction of Japan's capabilities. Had the navy initially wanted anything more than a résumé of past errors, Takagi would have been so informed, but the navy had no reason to suspect that the admiral would step out of line. Hence the tone of the directive, so circumscribing for a literal-minded traditionalist, yet so open to interpretation by a man already committed to a disturbing idea. By the time Takagi had finished, he had gone well beyond the implied limits of his assignment and had purged his mind of any doubts he might originally have had about his theories. The idea had become a fixation: Japan could not possibly win the war; therefore, she must seek a compromise peace.

Clearly this would not be easy. Japan would have to make concessions, and she would have to decide just how she was going to initiate the compromise. The Soviet Union was neutral and might afford an avenue of approach, but it would be a dangerous avenue at best. At the same time, a direct feeler to the United States or Great Britain would almost inevitably cause trouble at home. The younger officers, in particular, would raise a hue and cry that might well result in violence.

As for the concessions, that was not easy either. Withdrawal from China, Manchuria, and southern Sakhalin might provide a basis acceptable to the Allies. Takagi hoped so, but he knew that the enemy would also have something to say about Formosa and Korea, and possibly the Kuriles as well. These areas were crucial. Formosa and Korea were essential from the standpoint of food supply, since Japan simply could not feed her people from what she could grow in the home islands. Takagi felt that Japan could relinquish her political overlordship but that she must maintain some type of economic control or arrangement which would ensure the flow of rice and other foodstuffs on which she depended.

The Kuriles were a slightly different matter. They were important strategically. The Chishima—or "Thousand Islands" as the Japanese call them—were the Empire's first line of defense against aggression

---

[38] The details relating to Takagi's study were obtained during a five-hour interview with Admiral Takagi in Tokyo on July 30, 1951. A portion of the text is also based upon material found in USSBS, *Japan's Struggle to End the War*, 3. Takagi began his work in September 1943 and completed it in February 1944. (USSBS is in error on Takagi's first name, which is Sōkichi, not Soichi.)

from the north and east. There seemed to be no question about their rightfully belonging to Japan, for that issue had been settled by a treaty with Russia well over a half-century before the Pacific war began. Takagi realized that it would be hard enough to convince the ruling elite to sign away China, Manchuria, and southern Sakhalin, but if he threw in Formosa, Korea, and the Kuriles as well, the elite's reluctance might be fanned into so stubborn a resistance that the negotiations would be sabotaged before they were even begun.[39]

Both in his research and in his conclusions, Takagi was on solid ground. His coverage had been comprehensive. He had analyzed the air, fleet, and merchant marine losses Japan had sustained to date. He had investigated the difficulties Japan was experiencing in acquiring essential imported materials. He had assayed the internal confusion in Japan and the growing feeling that Tōjō should be forced out.[40] The war's battle lessons and conditions within Japan had constituted his evidence, and he had interpreted the evidence correctly. Yet he was in a difficult position, for he had independently gone far beyond the point envisaged by Navy Minister Shimada, who had given him the assignment. If Takagi presented his views to Shimada, there was no telling what would happen to him personally, but it was almost certain that the results of his research would never reach anyone else. Shimada was not only a cabinet colleague of Premier General Tōjō; he was a real friend and supporter as well. Realizing that he was guilty of heresy, Takagi decided to take what seemed the only way out. He would not discuss his findings with Shimada. He would simply wait his chance. Little by little and cautiously, he would pass his ideas along to a few key men whom he knew to be of a similar frame of mind.[41] In this way, he hoped to make his study bear fruit.

By the time Takagi had made this decision, Japan was on the threshold of her third year of war, the year 1944. In the many months which had passed since Pearl Harbor, she had reaped a bitter harvest of defeats. With each new victory snatched by the enemy her problems of production and supply had so multiplied that a certain feeling of frustration in the face of the increasing pressure of uncontrollable events had begun to make itself felt among the minority who had read disaster in the

[39] There is a rather striking parallel between the concessions envisaged by Takagi and the terms of the Cairo Declaration of December 1, 1943 (Manchuria, Formosa, and the Pescadores shall be restored to the Republic of China; Japan shall be expelled from all territories she has taken "by violence and greed"; "in due course Korea shall become free and independent"). For the text of the Cairo Declaration, see Appendix A.

[40] The defeats Japan had sustained to date, the scarcity of commodities, the stagnation of industry, and the slackening of national morale constituted a grave warning. *Statements:* Kido #61541.

[41] In March 1944, Takagi verbally presented his conclusions to Admiral Mitsumasa Yonai and Vice-Admiral Seibi Inouye.

coming of the war. Although from the early months of 1942 on there had been some talk and a great deal of thinking with respect to peace-by-negotiation, the soil of independent judgment and personal initiative had been dormant too long. Thus, even at the beginning of 1944, it seemed that Japan would still have to experience much in the way of misery before any contemplated solution could promise a possibility of success.

Confiding his thoughts to his diary on January 1, Lord Keeper of the Privy Seal Kido, perhaps the best informed of all the elite, bluntly characterized the prospects for 1944 as precarious. That there would be changes in the months to come was obvious, yet what troubled Kido most was the thought that this might possibly be the year in which Germany would go under. The foremost question in his mind was far-reaching in its implications: in the event of Germany's unconditional surrender, should Japan endeavor to end the war in the Pacific at the same time?

Although Kido posed this question, he sidestepped the issue in answering it. Japan, he wrote, should follow a course of action based upon a decision independently determined through an appraisal of the conditions prevailing at the time.[42] In spite of this obliqueness, Kido was not content to let the matter rest in such an unsatisfactory way. Every problem had to have a solution, every eventuality a preconceived plan.

Kido realized that should events take the turn he envisaged the Tōjō Cabinet might find it extremely difficult to maintain itself in office. If Tōjō fell, a new Premier would have to be recommended to the Throne, but Kido wondered whether the usual practice of having the senior statesmen select a successor would suffice. Since the capitulation of Germany and the unseating of Japan's military strong man would create problems of fundamental importance, it might be necessary for the senior statesmen first to formulate Japan's future foreign policy and then to recommend a cabinet which would accept the responsibility of carrying out that policy.[43]

This was really a rather extraordinary idea, for the senior statesmen were not a policy-forming group. To ask them suddenly to assume such a function would be an unusual departure from standard operating procedure. The *jūshin*, who existed outside the constitutional fabric of political life, would in effect be taking over, without legal authority to do so, a task for which they possessed no responsibility in point of law.

In order to obtain a cabinet which would implement a predetermined foreign policy, the senior statesmen would have to hand-pick the more important cabinet ministers. Recommending a Premier alone, no matter how personally loyal to his sponsors he might be, would accomplish

---

[42] In this connection, see footnotes 7 and 8, Ch. 4, below, and the text corresponding thereto.

[43] See IMTFE: Kido, 11368–69 and 31071. Also, Kido, "Nikki," 1/6/44.

nothing, for the Premier would be helpless unless he had the support of the Ministers of Foreign Affairs, War, and the Navy.

Thus far, the senior statesmen had never done anything more than indicate their choice of a successor to the premiership. This had been handled through channels, that is, through the Privy Seal, who played an important role in aiding and advising the *jūshin* in their selection. There was no precedent for their recommending a whole cabinet and certainly none for their directing the nation's destiny by formulating its foreign policy. But Kido's musings along the lines of action open to Japan in the event of an Axis defeat in Europe had led him into a hitherto off-limits area of untried political practice. When the final test came, Kido did not plunge into the wholly unprecedented, but he did oversee the creation of a cabinet which was at least different from any of its predecessors. To this extent, his contemplation of the unusual on New Year's Day 1944 was not completely wasted.

The same is true of some other thoughts which kept him busy during the first week of January. Apparently the entries he had made in his diary would not let him rest. As he had looked ahead, he had realized that considerable concessions would be necessary if Japan were to be successful in ending the war in the Pacific. For Kido, the matter resolved itself quickly. Ink and paper translated the thoughts into a plan.[44]

The affairs of the Pacific, wrote Kido, shall be determined henceforth by the major powers: Japan, the Soviet Union, China, the United States, and Great Britain. These five nations shall organize, and contribute representatives to, a commission charged with administering the occupied areas. The latter, now in Japanese hands, together with the islands of the Pacific, shall become nonfortified zones. Those independent countries which do not rank as major powers shall, with the exception of Manchuria, become permanent neutrals like Switzerland. All economic policies shall be based on the principles of freedom, reciprocity, and equal opportunity.

Kido recognized that the timing of the release of his program would be as important as the content of the plan itself. If his remedy for Japan's growing ills were to succeed, it must not be proposed simultaneously with Germany's collapse. Of equal importance was the necessity of Japan's taking the lead before the United States, Great Britain, and the Soviet Union could unite against her. In fact, Kido thought the best approach might be to request the good offices of the Soviet Union.

When he subsequently discussed his ideas with Shigemitsu, Kido found that his own pessimistic outlook was fully shared by the Foreign Minister. Shigemitsu even spoke of a need for "great determination" and frankly declared "unconditional surrender, in essence, will be

---

[44] See IMTFE: Kido, 11370, 31072–73; and Kido, "Nikki," 1/6/44.

unavoidable."[45] As a result, Kido decided to lay his "peace proposal" aside.[46] Its scope was simply too narrow to make any impression upon the Allies, who were now in a dominant position with respect to their enemy, Japan.

In the silence kept by Kido lurked a latent danger. Those who knew the facts and were capable of taking action might keep silent too long. By the spring of 1944, certain highly placed individuals had come to believe that Japan could not win the war. This was a significant step forward, but even greater strides were necessary. The solution of the dilemma facing the nation hinged upon such persons' spreading what knowledge they possessed to everyone who was in any way connected with the formulation of policy. Obviously, this was easier said than done.

From the very beginning of the conflict, one of the most formidable obstacles in the path of realistic thinking and action had been the power concentrated in the hands of Japan's militarists.[47] The rigidity of the latter, together with their flair for patriotic and nationalistic sentiments which made any word of criticism an act of treason, served to perpetuate their monopoly of power beyond all reason. In spite of their obvious failures, the militarists continued to control the politics and policies of the country. In effect, they were being paid in full for the efforts they had expended in fostering an obedience-unto-death psychology in the minds of the people. Their well-developed propaganda and thought-control technique stood ready to shore up the bastions of this powerful defense against criticism and to pounce upon any possible psychological delinquent, regardless of his station in life.

---

[45] IMTFE: Kido, 31072–73. Mr. Shigemitsu has since declared that the Cairo Declaration made him realize "nothing but practically unconditional surrender could save the Country." (*Statements:* Shigemitsu 9/9/49.) Kido testified before the IMTFE that Shigemitsu told him "on several occasions" during the course of the war that unconditional surrender would be inescapable. (IMTFE: Kido, 31224.)

[46] Kido had not actually intended to make use of his plan until Japan's war aim of breaking the ABCD encirclement had been fulfilled. Although he did not officially submit his ideas to any government circles, his thoughts are interesting as an initial framework of reference against which to measure his meaning when he speaks of his "efforts for peace." Had the Japanese military become aware of Kido's plan, the Privy Seal might easily have been accused of interfering with the functions of the Supreme Command.

[47] So strong was the army's position that it was impossible for a cabinet to interfere effectively with any course of action followed by the army. The latter, however, could and did intrude upon general affairs of state on the grounds that they were matters pertaining to national defense. The navy possessed the same power as the army but did not abuse the privilege to the extent the army did.

Brigadier Nolan (IMTFE: *Proceedings*, 548) declared *the Prosecution* would show that the Supreme Command "when acting in its proper sphere, is supreme over the civil power, and that the right of direct access [to the Throne] of the military prevents the Cabinet from acting collectively at all times as a parliamentary body when an important segment of its function and administration is carved away."

Even such notables as Kido, Konoye, Shigemitsu, and Okada scarcely dared do anything more than clandestinely exchange opinions behind locked doors. Although these men had been discussing Japan's prospects for months, their talk had always ended in more talk. Thus, while Kido and Okada had delved into the question of terminating the war and had agreed that such a step should be taken as soon as possible, they had concluded that "extreme caution" was necessary and that they must wait for an opportunity to present itself. In other words, the time was not ripe.[48] Similarly, the results of the Kido-Shigemitsu conversations, although a little more promising, had still been far from a concrete plan. The Privy Seal and Foreign Minister had decided that neither the Tōjō government nor the army could be influenced and so an open approach toward either would result only in failure. Shigemitsu had favored encouraging the senior statesmen to play a more active role close to the Throne, but Kido had doubted that they could accomplish what was desired of them even if they served in the manner suggested. He had also expressed the fear that such a step would arouse the whole nation and would lay the senior statesmen open to the charge of being Japanese Badoglios.[49] After further consideration, the two men had at length agreed that there was really only one course they could follow. Should there be an opportunity to do anything, they must do it themselves. They would naturally depend upon an imperial decision for guidance, but each would accept the responsibility within his own sphere, that is, Kido for the court and Shigemitsu for the government.[50]

The atmosphere of the times is forcefully illustrated by the case of Colonel Makoto Matsutani, a farsighted officer whose estimate of Japan's prospects left him dissatisfied with the studiously cautious conversations and carefully secreted paper plans which had thus far constituted the only approach to Japan's increasing difficulties. Toward the spring of 1944, a group of General Staff officers with Matsutani in the forefront drafted what might be termed a thesis.[51] Entitled "Measures for the Termination of the Greater East Asia War" and classified as a state secret, this document made the rounds of the top officials in both the

[48] IMTFE: Okada, 38924–26.

[49] See IMTFE: Kido, 31074–75 and Shigemitsu, *Shōwa no dōran*, 189–90.

[50] *Ibid.* This agreement of views was reached on June 26, 1944. On June 29 Kido discussed the matter with his aide, Marquis Yasumasa Matsudaira, and with the Minister of the Imperial Household, Mr. Tsuneo Matsudaira. Kido states that his ideas at this time were generally the same as those which governed his actions at the war's end. IMTFE: Kido, 31076.

[51] See *Statements:* Tanemura #61977. Also, interview with Colonel Matsutani, Tokyo, March 7, 1952. In addition to Matsutani and Tanemura, the group (known as Group #20) included Colonel Tanaka and Lieutenant Colonel Hashimoto. In spite of Mr. Kase's implication to the contrary (*Journey to the Missouri,* 76) the Matsutani circle seems not to have been an informal, secret organization but rather a section of the Army General Staff charged with handling matters pertaining to war plans.

army and navy departments. Among other things, it preached that Japan should endeavor to end hostilities in the Pacific at the time of Germany's collapse in Europe. The reasoning here was that only harsher terms would result if Japan attempted to continue fighting once the forces of Hitler were brought to bay. The thesis also included several plans, all of which listed terms which might be sought in various eventualities. The so-called "Third Plan" expounded the minimum basis for ending the war in the event that Japan was in dire straits and had to choose between giving in or committing national suicide. This rock-bottom plan very simply proposed that under such circumstances Japan should be content to end the war with nothing more than an Allied guarantee that the national polity would be safeguarded and the imperial homeland preserved. Everything else, including the hotly disputed issue of territory, would have to go by the board.

Of those who saw the document prepared by Matsutani's group, no one raised any direct objections, but the colonel himself did not profit from his display of initiative and wisdom. Shortly after he had explained his thesis to the unresponsive Tōjō, Matsutani received orders reassigning him to Japan's expeditionary forces in China. The inference was clearly that the general had not appreciated the colonel's efforts.

But even a man of Tōjō's determination and shrewdness[52] could no longer stem the pressure which had been building up against his ironfisted regime. There was anxiety in various quarters and dissatisfaction with the cabinet, and this discontent appeared throughout Japan.[53] The cabinet had nearly fallen in June when two cabinet ministers[54] had threatened to resign. Tōjō had managed to counteract this move by reconstructing his cabinet, but the Saipan invasion, which came immediately afterward, was a crisis of much greater magnitude. The loss of this island lying far within Japan's defense perimeter, the disintegration of Japan's front in Burma, and the magnification and multiplication of problems on the home front proved to be too much for the cabinet to handle. While several ministers pooled their efforts to sabotage the cabinet from within, the senior statesmen worked to destroy it from

[52] In a mid-February 1944 talk with Kido, Tōjō had advocated moving Imperial General Headquarters inside the palace and holding important cabinet meetings in the presence of the Emperor. Tōjō's intention was to link the Emperor with the war effort by making the people believe His Majesty was personally attending to the affairs of state. Kido, "Nikki," 2/18/44. See also USOSS, *The Japanese Emperor and the War*, 1.

[53] IMTFE: Okada, 29263–65; *Statements:* Okada #61884 and #61307; and Kido, "Nikki," 7/13/44. Toward the latter part of May, Admiral Okada attempted to convey to Premier Tōjō the senior statesmen's concern over the war situation, but Tōjō angrily accused the *jūshin* of attempting to overthrow his cabinet. (*Statements:* Kido #61541 and interview with Marquis Matsudaira and Admiral Takagi, Tokyo, July 30, 1951.) In this connection, see also IMTFE: Kido, 31080, and Kido, "Nikki," 7/18/44.

[54] Foreign Minister Shigemitsu and Minister without Portfolio Kishi. See USSBS, *Japan's Struggle to End the War*, 3, and Shigemitsu, *Shōwa no dōran*, 225–31.

without.[55] Finally, on July 17, 1944, the intrigue came to a head.[56] Quite informally and on their own initiative, the former Premiers met at Baron Hiranuma's residence to clarify their stand and to forestall an attempt by Tōjō to maintain himself in office by resorting to another cabinet shuffle and reorganization.[57] After some discussion, the group[58] adopted a resolution:

New life must be injected into the minds and hearts of the people if the nation is to surmount the difficulties besetting it. The whole nation must join together and work together. A partial reorganization of the cabinet will serve no purpose whatsoever. A strong National Cabinet that will move forward unswervingly must be formed.[59]

This resolution was the culmination of weeks and even months of discussions and conversations which had ranged far and wide but had always revolved around a fixed nucleus, the problem of Japan's prospects. While this question of policy was being mooted, the Tōjō Cabinet had become increasingly unpopular, and it was this fact that had opened a somewhat devious but important avenue of approach. The July 17 resolution anticipated Tōjō's fall and indicated that in so far as the senior statesmen were concerned he was finished.[60]

Actually, more than a year was to pass before surrender was even

[55] Early in July Marquis Matsudaira informed Kido that some of the senior statesmen were working to overthrow the cabinet. Admiral Okada had visited Baron Hiranuma and had spoken about the necessity of changing the cabinet. Hiranuma had suggested submitting a memorial to the Throne. Okada had also discussed the same matters with Prince Konoye. IMTFE: Kido, 31076–78. There was also an anti-Tōjō plot under way among a number of civilians working in conjunction with a faction in the army (under the leadership of Lieutenant General Kanji Ishihara). Kido, "Nikki," 9/26/44.

[56] On this same day, an Associated Press dispatch reported that Ken Harada, Japan's ambassador to the Vatican, had told the Pope that Japan was ready for peace on certain conditions and that "Japanese leaders had no desire to carry on a long and inconclusive war, but were ready for any peace which would recognize Japan's right to national life and economy." This report was categorically denied by Katsuo Okazaki, acting spokesman of the Board of Information. See USFCC, *Radio Report Far East*, #50, AA 3.

[57] Tōjō had warned Kido that a political change would be extremely dangerous and that he intended to continue in office by petitioning the Emperor to excuse him from responsibility for the loss of Saipan. See Kido, "Nikki," 7/13/44.

[58] Wakatsuki (made chairman), Okada, Hiranuma, Hirota, Abe, Konoye, and Yonai. After the meeting, Okada went to the official residence of Privy Seal Kido and personally handed the resolution to him and explained the details of the meeting. Early the next morning, Kido informed the Emperor of what had occurred at Baron Hiranuma's. That same day (July 18) the Tōjō Cabinet resigned en bloc and the senior statesmen met to recommend a succeeding Premier. See Kido, "Nikki," 7/17–18/44.

[59] The text is reconstructed from material contained in the following: IMTFE: Okada, 29264–65, 29297; Kido, 31076–79, 11372, 11374; Kido, "Nikki," 7/17/44.

[60] Just before his cabinet fell, Tōjō made a belated attempt to win the *jūshin* to his side by indicating that he was prepared to consider the revival of the cabinet advisory system if the senior statesmen so desired. Tōjō also promised that his cabinet would always keep in close touch with the senior statesmen in the future and would fully reflect their wishes. He even offered cabinet posts to Yonai and Abe and tenta-

in sight, but Tōjō's enforced retirement from office was tremendously significant since it brought the possibility of a termination of hostilities closer to realization than even the most ardent end-the-war advocate had dared hope prior to this time.

It was the summer of 1944, and Japan had experienced some two and a half years of fighting the "decadent" West. If the lessons of those years could teach her anything, it was that Japan faced defeat. In the early months of the war, the people and their leaders had congratulated each other on the extensive accomplishments of their invincible army and navy. They had prided themselves on their peculiar national structure. Sitting within the inner keep of their vast empire, they had felt secure in the belief that they could surmount all obstacles in the accomplishment of their sacred mission. Japan was the Elder Brother; the peoples of the rest of Asia were the Younger Brothers. It was Japan's manifest destiny to rule all Asia. Some had even said, the world.

In spite of the fact that the war had already turned against Japan's "interests," the circumstances and attitudes of the period conspired against an easy cessation of hostilities. For those who possessed inside channels of information, the day of awakening had come relatively early in the war. They had then to adjust to their new and distasteful knowledge and to prepare for the time when they would have to act upon that knowledge. For the masses, however, it was not until the war had ended that they realized how completely they had been deceived. Only after they had re-experienced the security of bomb-free days and nights could they survey and comprehend the widespread destruction which lay in silent mockery of their wartime efforts to achieve victory.

The hindsight of 1944 sternly ridiculed the foresight of 1941, and by the time the end was near in 1945 both the apologist and the rationalist had agreed that the "bold beginning" made at Pearl Harbor had indeed been "a very unfortunate thing."[61]

---

tively approached Hirota as well. None of the three would agree to enter the cabinet. See Kido, "Nikki," 7/13/44 and 7/17/44.

[61] A quotation from Lieutenant General Torashirō Kawabe, vice-chief of the Army General Staff at the war's end. USSBS, *Interrogations*, II, Kawabe, 426.

2

STRESS AND STRAIN

The Koiso-Yonai Cabinet, July 1944–April 1945

IN the late afternoon of July 18, 1944, the senior statesmen met[1] at the Emperor's command to select a successor to Premier General Tōjō, whose regime had at length collapsed after a record thirty-three months in office—the longest tenure enjoyed by any cabinet in more than twenty years. Although on the surface Tōjō's political demise could have indicated that the army's monopoly of control over national affairs had at last been broken, this did not prove to be the case at all. In spite of the fact that Tōjō and the military clique which he represented had failed miserably in their prosecution of the war, the men behind the scenes knew that the army had by no means lost its grip. Some of the former Premiers had serious misgivings about the role the army had thus far played in the affairs of state and, therefore, felt deep concern over the future. Admiral Yonai, the moderate whom Konoye and others had tried to insinuate into the Tōjō Cabinet early in 1943, was perhaps the most outspoken. Military men were strong, he declared, because they received "a one-sided education," but for this very reason they were "unsuited for politics." If something were not done about this now, Japan would be "destroyed."[2] For the time and place, these remarks were unusual in the extreme, yet they went unheeded.

Like Yonai, Konoye also expressed his distrust of the military, but in a different, yet characteristic way. Referring to the existence, for over ten years, of leftist thoughts within a segment of the army, he warned of the danger of a left-wing revolution supported by the co-operative efforts of military men, officials, and the people. Such a revolution, he said, would be more dangerous than defeat itself. Even if Japan lost the war, she would be able to maintain the imperial house and her polity. In the

---

[1] For the details of the meeting, see IMTFE: Kido, 31087 ff. and Okada, 29265; JFO MS: Ch. 10 (Koiso-Yonai naikaku no seiritsu to rikugun no taido); Kido, "Nikki," 7/18/44; and citations listed in succeeding footnotes. In addition to the senior statesmen, the Privy Seal (Kido), the President of the Privy Council (Hara), and the Grand Chamberlain (Hyakutake) were also present.

[2] IMTFE: Kido, 31087.

event of a leftist revolution, however, both the Emperor and his Throne would be doomed to extinction.[3]

In spite of this rather bold beginning, the senior statesmen were already committed by their resolution of the preceding day to creating a strong national cabinet that would move forward unswervingly. While a few of the former Premiers were unwilling to accept the army's contention that a general in active service *had* to be chosen as Japan's next Premier, their attitude did not preclude the selection of a military man.[4] With the nation locked in war, there were all manner of military problems which made someone with more than just a passing knowledge of the military arts a virtual "must." A civilian Premier would stand little chance of maintaining the delicate balance toward the army without which no cabinet could long survive.

Faced with this contradiction between a certain desire for change and a real need not to go too far in that respect, the senior statesmen ranged back and forth over the field of eligibles, listening to various pro and con statements which were seldom, if ever, actual arguments. In the end the group finally decided to nominate a general after all.[5] There was no ready agreement, however, as to exactly who should be named, for of all the generals mentioned there was something about each one, either with respect to his position or with regard to his personality and orientation, that made him a questionable choice. After further discussion and considerable debate, the senior statesmen at length requested Lord Keeper of the Privy Seal Kido to forward the names of Terauchi, Koiso, and Hata to His Imperial Majesty, and with that the meeting adjourned. It was now up to those close to the Throne to decide which of the three candidates should be elevated to the premiership.[6]

[3] IMTFE: Kido, 31093–94. Konoye realized that the selection of a war minister was very important. He wanted a man who would be strong enough to control the leftist elements in the army.

[4] *Statements:* Hiranuma #55127.

[5] Before this decision was reached, Admiral Kantarō Suzuki's name was placed in nomination by Prince Konoye. Suzuki, being a navy man, lost out when the final selection was made. IMTFE: Okada, 29265, and Kido, 31095.

Kido declares that Konoye's recommendation was endorsed by Hiranuma but was opposed by Yonai, who said that it would be better for the country if Suzuki did not emerge. Yonai did not explain his meaning, but subsequent events seem to indicate that nothing personal was meant. If a navy man had become Premier at that time, he would have been very much under army domination. This may have been what Yonai wished to avoid. IMTFE: Kido, 31095.

Hiranuma (who says that he nominated Suzuki) recalls that President of the Privy Council Hara believed Suzuki should be retained as vice-president of the Privy Council. Hara stated that Suzuki had "constantly" said he "did not have the qualifications to become premier" and so Hara believed Suzuki would decline even if he were recommended. See *Statements:* Hiranuma #55127 and Kido #61476.

[6] The elevation of Terauchi, who was in command of the Southern Area Army with headquarters in Singapore, was subsequently blocked by outgoing Premier Tōjō on the grounds that the removal of Terauchi from his command would adversely affect troop morale and would endanger military operations. Kase, in his *Journey to the*

The next day, July 19, Prince Konoye unexpectedly visited Baron Hiranuma and Marquis Kido in order to suggest a co-premiership[7]—an idea which was apparently based on Konoye's certain knowledge that the imperial mandate would be granted to Koiso.[8] After obtaining their concurrence, the prince revealed his scheme to Admiral Yonai and urgently advised him that the nation would profit greatly if he would accept an appointment as co-Premier.[9] In the meantime, Marquis Matsudaira, Kido's aide and private secretary, hastily called upon the other senior statesmen to inform them of the plan. Only two of the former Premiers, Abe and Okada, had reservations, but even they withdrew their objections once they received more detailed information. When the senior statesmen once again met together in conference, on the afternoon of July 20, it was unanimously agreed to recommend Konoye's proposal to the Throne.[10] Thus, by the time General Koiso arrived in the capital from his post in Korea the Konoye plan had matured into a firm decision. It so happened, however, that no one had taken the trouble to enlighten the general. As the latter entered the waiting room adjoining the imperial chamber on July 20, he was quite surprised and somewhat at a loss when he suddenly came face to face with Admiral Yonai. Koiso's first thought was that possibly he had been wrong in supposing that the Emperor would command him to form a cabinet. The imperial summons could easily have been prompted by some other purpose. That would mean that Yonai, who was a former Premier, would emerge from

---

Missouri, 83, suggests that the real reason why Tōjō blocked the elevation of Terauchi lies in the fact that the two men were mortal enemies. Hata was passed over because a few of the senior statesmen remained opposed to appointing a general on the active service list. Presumably this was also a factor in the case of Terauchi. Hiranuma has stated that Koiso (a general on the reserve list) was finally chosen for want of someone better.

[7] When asked why the joint-premiership idea had not been broached at the conference on July 18, Hiranuma declared the regular procedure did not envisage recommending co-Premiers and the idea may not have occurred to anyone until Konoye suggested it. Hiranuma also reasoned that the *jūshin* may not have wished to disturb the regular procedure of the conference. *Statements:* Hiranuma #55127.

[8] On the evening of July 18, after he had heard that the Tōjō Cabinet had resigned en bloc, Koiso, who was serving as governor general in Korea, received a telephone call from Grand Chamberlain Hyakutake instructing him to proceed to Tokyo for an audience with the Emperor. See *Statements*: Koiso #55906 and IMTFE: Tanaka, 32532.

If Koiso's date is correct, it would seem that the decision to elevate Koiso rather than Terauchi or Hata had already been made on the evening of July 18, for there is no record of the two other candidates having been summoned. (This view is supported by IMTFE: Kido, 31102–5.)

[9] The details of the Konoye plan were obtained during the course of a three-and-one-half-hour interview with Marquis Matsudaira at the Tokyo Hotel on August 14, 1951. See also the material contained in JFO MS: Ch. 10 (Koiso-Yonai naikaku no seiritsu to rikugun no taido) ; IMTFE: Okada, 29265–66 (Okada's recollections differ slightly in so far as the details are concerned but the general outline is the same) ; *Statements*: Hiranuma #55127; Matsudaira #61636; and Kido, "Nikki," 7/19–20/44.

[10] IMTFE: Kido, 31102, and *Statements*: Hiranuma #55127.

the audience chamber as Japan's next wartime leader. Before Koiso had a chance to continue this train of thought, Marquis Kido entered the room and announced that the general and the admiral would be received by His Majesty. This immediately posed the problem of who should lead, and to this Kido replied, "Koiso, of course."[11]

When the audience was over and the two reappeared in the waiting room, the general was still confused. The Emperor had merely enjoined them, in co-operation with each other, to form a cabinet and to exert themselves to attain the objectives of the Greater East Asia War.[12] The Emperor had also warned against antagonizing the Soviet Union, but he had not said anything that could have indicated which of the two men would be Premier.[13] Again the Privy Seal, who was waiting in the ante-room, came to the rescue. Yonai put the question to him and Kido once more replied, "Koiso, of course." By this time the general was beside himself. "What a strange conversation," he thought.

Only later did it occur to Koiso that Yonai, who had been present at the senior statesmen's conference on July 18, must have known all along who was to be Premier. Not until he was on trial before the International Military Tribunal for the Far East did Koiso obtain confirmation of his supposition, and it was then that he decided that Kido and Yonai had merely been "putting on an act" in order to inform him that *he*, and no other, was expected to lead the government. At the time, however, Koiso simply turned to Yonai and asked, "Now what office are you going to fill? That of Navy Minister?" And to this the admiral replied, "That's the only post I am capable of filling."

Since it would have been awkward for Yonai to ask the navy to re-instate him in active service and designate him Navy Minister, Koiso personally raised the issue with the then Navy Minister, Admiral Naokuni Nomura. The latter, who had apparently hoped to stay on in the Koiso Cabinet, seemed rather "nonplussed," but Koiso presented the matter as stemming from the wishes of His Majesty. He told Nomura that he had not heard it directly from the Emperor but that he believed the Throne wanted Yonai appointed to the post. After verifying this at the palace, Nomura and the navy agreed. Thus it was that the so-called Koiso-Yonai

[11] *Statements:* Koiso #55906.

[12] Koiso regarded the Emperor's words as constituting an order to destroy America and Britain and to carry to completion Japan's objective of establishing a Greater East Asia empire. *Statements:* Koiso #55906.

[13] See *Statements:* Koiso #55906; Kido, "Nikki," 7/20/44 and 7/24/44; JFO MS: Ch. 10 (Koiso-Yonai naikaku no seiritsu to rikugun no taido).

There is no evidence to support the USSBS contention (*Japan's Struggle to End the War*, 3) that the Emperor admonished the co-Premiers to give Japan's situation a "fundamental reconsideration." When asked about this point, Koiso emphatically declared, "It is absolutely incorrect." *Statements:* Koiso #55906.

When asked whether the Emperor had specifically said anything to Koiso about terminating the war, Kido replied, "The Emperor might have said something to him; however, I have no clear recollection of it." *Statements:* Kido #61476.

Coalition Cabinet emerged with General Kuniaki Koiso as Premier and
Admiral Mitsumasa Yonai as Navy Minister and—in name at least—
co-Premier.[14]

The fact that Koiso and Yonai were received in audience together
and were commanded to form a cabinet in co-operation with each other
was so rare a departure from standard procedure[15] that it immediately
stimulated a great deal of speculation, especially abroad, as to exactly
why two men, instead of one, had been given the imperial mandate. Was
this just a bid for closer army-navy unity—an attempt to weld stronger
ties of co-operation between the government and the Supreme Command—or was it a realistic maneuver aimed at creating an atmosphere
conducive to a termination of the war within the very group which alone
possessed the authority and the responsibility to make such a decision?

Although the record is not entirely clear, the purpose behind Yonai's
appointment seems to have been an admixture of the two possibilities
with the idea of strength and solidarity rather than of peace predominat-
ing. Yonai was well informed and popular; he knew his way not only
around the navy but around political circles as well. Koiso, an army
man through and through, had been away in Korea serving as Japan's
Governor General; he did not have too clear a picture of either the domestic or international situation and his knowledge of developments
at the fighting fronts was equally restricted. So far as anyone could
determine, his opinions with respect to the war conformed to the usual
army line of reasoning, whereas Yonai appeared at least to be numbered
among the very few who had been against the venture from the beginning.[16] A great deal could be said either way, but only the developments of the future could provide an answer. As the Japanese man on
the street saw it, the cabinet's sole purpose was to fight through to victory
by achieving unity between the rival services and co-operation between
the government and the Supreme Command.[17]

To anyone who might have studied the composition of the cabinet
the outlook with respect to unity would undoubtedly have been encouraging. The new cabinet ministers were men of "long-term political and

[14] See *Statements*: Koiso #55906.

[15] The only precedent for such a co-premiership was the so-called "Waiban Naikaku" jointly formed by Ōkuma and Itagaki in June 1898. See the Tokyo *Asahi Shimbun* for July 21, 1944.

[16] Hiranuma has stated that Yonai was brought into the cabinet because the *jūshin*
"were not very familiar with KOISO's views." They knew, however, that Yonai "had
been opposed to the war from the very beginning." Hiranuma and Konoye felt that the
restoration of peace could be expedited by having Yonai in the cabinet. *Statements*:
Hiranuma #55127 and Toyoda #61340.
    See also IMTFE: Kido, 31243, and *Statements*: Kido #61541 and #61476.

[17] See Koiso's speech to the 85th session of the Diet, IMTFE: *Proceedings*, 3703–
18, especially 3706 (J text, 454/1–454/14, especially 454/3–454/4); IMTFE: Kido,
31104; Kuroki, "From War to Peace Cabinets," *Contemporary Japan*, XIV (April–
December 1945), 183; and Tokyo *Asahi Shimbun* for July 21, 22, and 23, 1944.

military leadership" with a "first hand knowledge of and interest in the China continent." Many were schooltime friends while still others had served together in earlier cabinets.[18] In fact, it would have been hard to find another group of men so obviously capable of becoming an effective working organization. But fate ruled otherwise, and from the day it assumed power to the day it relinquished control the new cabinet failed to achieve the very thing it needed most: co-operative and harmonious relations with the Supreme Command.

One of the keys to Premier Tōjō's success had been that he had concurrently held the posts of War Minister and Chief of the Army General Staff. With the strong backing he had enjoyed in the army itself, this arrangement had given him an almost limitless advantage in crushing opposition whenever it threatened to arise. In spite of the example set by his predecessor, Koiso decided against asking to be reinstated in active service—a necessary step to his becoming War Minister in his own cabinet.[19] He did suggest, however, that the army[20] assign the war portfolio to either General Yamashita or General Anami. To this he added a significant request for army approval of an innovation which he personally felt would have to be undertaken if his cabinet were to function properly. His proposal was in the form of alternatives which centered on one specific and crucial issue: permission for the Premier to participate, as a full-fledged member, in the activities and decisions of Imperial Headquarters.[21] Koiso knew that if he became War Minister in his own cabinet he would not only be a member of Imperial Headquarters but he would be in a position to control the very vital Munitions Ministry as well. In spite of this obvious incentive he believed that he could satisfactorily achieve the purpose of his plan without assuming any

[18] See USFCC, *Special Report*, #130 ("The Koiso-Yonai Cabinet"), 3–5 and 7.

[19] It has been said (e.g., Kase's *Journey to the Missouri*, 84) that Koiso exerted every effort to become War Minister in his own cabinet *at the time of its formation*. This view has been denounced by Koiso whose remarks are so well in accord with evidence uncovered elsewhere that they undermine any suggestion that the general is speaking to history rather than about it. Koiso does not deny his attempts to become War Minister but dates them after the Leyte fiasco (December 1944). See *Statements:* Koiso #55906 and IMTFE: Koiso, 32256 and 32266–67. That Koiso was not seeking to become War Minister in his own cabinet at the time of its formation (July 1944) receives confirmation from the Foreign Office compilers of the "Shūsen no keii to sono shiryō" (JFO MS) and from IMTFE: Tanaka, 32535 and 32539.

[20] The War and Navy Ministers are nominated by their respective services, not by the Premier. In the case of the army, the choice is made by the Big Three: the War Minister (Tōjō), the Chief of the Army General Staff (Umezu), and the Inspector General of Military Education (Sugiyama). In this connection, see IMTFE: *Proceedings*, 546–47 and 589–90; IMTFE: Def. Doc. 2247, *Makino Aff.*, 8 (rejected: 31615–22); and *Statements:* Koiso #55906.

[21] See *Statements:* Koiso #55906. It has been maintained (e.g., Kase, *Journey to the Missouri*, 84) that Koiso and Tōjō had a bitter argument at this time, but Koiso's own testimony is quite to the contrary. He discussed his proposal with Tōjō who expressed agreement and said that he himself had tried, unsuccessfully, to do the very same thing.

added and no doubt troublesome burdens. The War Minister, who was really only an administrative officer and hardly more than just an associate member of Imperial Headquarters, normally had no real voice in war policy formulation unless, as in the case of Tōjō, his personality, position in the army, and other duties gave him such power. Although, as War Minister, Koiso would have been charged with supervising both the military and civilian personnel of the army, he did not feel that it was necessary for him to exercise such control and he had no desire to do so. With respect to munitions, Koiso believed that he would be able to influence policy as he saw fit through the Munitions Minister. For these reasons, he was content to let someone else become War Minister, especially if the army made him a member of Imperial Headquarters anyway. But the problem, as Koiso soon learned, was not quite so simple or clear-cut. When the army's Big Three (the men actually responsible for nominating a war minister) sat down to discuss the Koiso plan, the Premier-designate suffered his first defeat—and a most serious one—at the hands of the very organization of which he himself was a general officer. Koiso had primarily wanted the Imperial Headquarters ordinance permanently revised to read that the Premier would henceforth be a member of this policy-making group, but if this could not be done he had suggested enacting a special ordinance whereby the Premier would be granted the said privilege for the duration of the war. To both of these suggestions the army, with navy concurrence, said, "No." The furthest anyone in the military would go was to sanction the establishment, through some other means, of a system that would permit the Premier to exercise some authority in the military field of war leadership.[22] Without a doubt, this was the third and least desirable of the alternatives. Not only that, but the Big Three also snubbed Koiso's suggestions for a war minister—ostensibly because both Yamashita and Anami were field commanders who could not be spared from their duties at the front. As a result, General Gen Sugiyama, Inspector General of Military Education and himself a member of the Big Three, was designated to fill the post.[23] This arrangement, which Koiso could not have rejected unless he had been prepared to give up the idea of forming a

[22] See *Statements:* Koiso #55906 and IMTFE: Tanaka, 32536. Koiso declares that the army reply to his plan contained one statement which bore no relationship to anything he had proposed. The statement was to the effect that regardless of what stand the navy would take the army would strongly oppose the appointment of General Koiso as War Minister in his own cabinet. (Although Koiso does not suggest it, this phraseology may be responsible for the confusion which exists on the question of whether or not Koiso attempted to become War Minister at the time his cabinet was formed.)

[23] See *Statements:* Koiso #55906 and IMTFE: Tanaka, 32536. Several days before this development, Koiso had advised Tōjō against endeavoring to stay on as War Minister. Chief of the Army General Staff Umezu concurred in this but warned the Premier-designate that difficulties would arise over the appointment of either Yamashita or Anami (Koiso's choices) since both were needed at the front. The references cited

cabinet, was a root cause of the uneasy relations with the army which marked his tenure in office.

Unfortunately for the success of his cabinet, Koiso had momentarily overlooked a salient feature of army practice that he had learned earlier in his military career. To his great regret, it was only when it was too late that he recalled how the Supreme Command frequently had to get in touch with and make inquiries of the War and Navy Ministries in order to bring its plans to working completion. If he had thought of this at the time he would have made a different decision, for he would then have realized that only as War Minister could he acquire *advance* information of Supreme Command plans and intentions and only with such prior knowledge in his grasp could there be any possibility of his co-ordinating the plans of the Supreme Command with the affairs of state.[24]

Thus, from the very moment he assumed office, Koiso was off to a false start. He not only had to fight a war which he personally feared was lost,[25] but he had also to maneuver constantly in what proved to be a fruitless effort to gain a position from which he might participate effectively in those functions of the Supreme Command pertaining to the direction of the war.

Although it was some time before Koiso appreciated how fundamental his initial failure had been, he did know enough of what was going on to anticipate trouble. He therefore set out to reinforce the foundations of his cabinet, as best he could, by launching a drive aimed at improving relations with the Supreme Command. After the outbreak of the China Incident, a special organ known as the Liaison Conference[26] had been established to co-ordinate the activities of the civilian and military branches of the government in their conduct of the war on the continent. Following the Japanese pattern of things, this Liaison Conference was another informal arrangement, not a legal entity. Its membership was such that the army found the conference very useful in obtaining the consent and co-operation of the government with respect to its plans. Within two weeks after the investiture of his cabinet, Koiso undertook to salvage what was left of his original scheme to gain a voice in the formulation of war policy by replacing the Liaison Conference with a simplified and more powerful, six-member "Supreme Council for the Direction of the War."[27] In theory, this Supreme Council was to be a liaison body between the cabinet and the military. In fact, it became in

---

elsewhere do not support the view that Sugiyama emerged as War Minister as a result of a bargain struck between Tōjō and Koiso.

[24] See *Statements:* Koiso #55906; IMTFE: Koiso, 32255–56; and IMTFE: *Analyses,* #2965 (notes prepared by Koiso ca. 1946).

[25] See *Statements:* Koiso #55906 and IMTFE: Tanaka, 32532–34.

[26] See IMTFE: *Proceedings,* 630–32.

[27] *Saikō senso shidō kaigi,* established August 8, 1944, with the following member-

time "an inner war cabinet" concerned with the highest policy formulation and planning.[28] Like its prototype, the Supreme Council worked on a basis of unanimity, not on a majority vote. No decision of the council could become final until ratified by the cabinet. When debating matters of particular importance, the council could request the Emperor to attend its deliberations. The sovereign could also initiate special sessions of the council whenever those close to the Throne deemed such action necessary.[29]

While the newly formed Supreme Council held meeting after meeting to explore such weighty problems as the prosecution of the war and the possibility of a rapprochement between Germany and the Soviet Union, two of its members, Foreign Minister Shigemitsu and Navy Minister Yonai, secretly and independently directed their thinking toward the more distant future and the "dangerous" idea of a general peace. Toward the latter part of September 1944, Yonai had orders cut attaching Rear Admiral Sōkichi Takagi to the Naval General Staff. With the full knowledge, consent, and encouragement of the Navy Minister and Vice-Minister, Takagi once again ranged over a wide field of inquiry.[30] He was no longer preoccupied with the lessons of battle since they already pointed toward impending disaster. His purpose now was to study the immensely difficult problem of easing Japan out of her ruinous entanglement in a conflict which she could no longer hope to win.

Two questions were of primary importance: (1) How could the government get the army to agree to ending the war? (2) What means could be found to give substance to an eventual decision by the Emperor to

---

ship: the Premier, War Minister, Navy Minister, Foreign Minister, Army Chief of Staff, and Navy Chief of Staff.

An erroneous impression is created when the Japanese characters are translated as Supreme War Direction Council since, in Japanese, the word Supreme (saikō) is an adjective modifying the word Council (kaigi) and not the word War (sensō). The term "War-Direction" (sensō shidō) is a direct translation from the German word, Kriegsführung (conduct of war). Great care must be taken not to confuse the Supreme Council for the Direction of the War with the group known as the gunji sangiin (military council), a term which is generally translated into English as Supreme War Council. Kase (op. cit.) frequently makes no distinction between the two.

[28] See IMTFE: Proceedings, 630–32; IMTFE: Tanaka, 32536–38, and Koiso, 32254; USFCC, Radio Report Far East, #52, A 1–A 10; Koiso's speech to the 85th session of the Diet, IMTFE: Proceedings, 3706 (J text, 454/3–454/4); and USSBS, Japan's Struggle to End the War, 4.

[29] See USSBS, Japan's Struggle to End the War, 4; IMTFE: Proceedings, 631–32; and USSBS, Interrogations, II, Yonai, 327–28.

A meeting of the Supreme Council for the Direction of the War in the presence of the Emperor is called an "imperial conference" (gozen kaigi). A meeting of the cabinet (or a joint session of the Supreme Council and the cabinet) in the presence of the Emperor is also called an "imperial conference."

[30] The details relating to Takagi's work are contained in a letter from Admiral Takagi to the author, dated Chigasaki City, August 7, 1951. See also USSBS, Japan's Struggle to End the War, 4.

wager the future of his Throne upon the single issue of terminating hostilities?

It was generally felt that the army could be controlled only through the Emperor, whose influence could deal a crushing blow to any would-be opposition. For this reason it was vital that the Emperor be enlightened concerning the situation facing the country and that whatever personal desire he had to end the war be reinforced and molded into an irrevocable resolution to throw the weight of his hypnotic and sanctified will behind those who sought to save the nation by negotiating a peace.

As far as the formulation of policy was concerned, public opinion meant very little, but the reaction of the masses to a sudden termination of a war they thought they were winning could not be ignored. It was difficult to predict how the people would respond but it was considered gospel that if the Emperor commanded them to surrender they would do so without question. At any rate, it was axiomatic that they would obey him when they would obey no other.

At the same time it would have been foolhardy, in view of the extent to which the masses had been propagandized by the army and the government, to have assumed that when the time came the people could be controlled through the Emperor on a moment's notice without any prior preparation or planning on the part of persons in positions of authority. Takagi therefore turned his attention to studying ways and means of directing public opinion to the point where the government could end the war without running the risk of internal chaos.

The admiral also realized that no Japanese overture could be successful unless the government had a clear understanding of the terms and conditions around which the proposed negotiations would revolve. Just what could Japan offer by way of inducement to a patently victorious enemy? Just how far would the Allies go in the way of demands toward a tottering empire? To what extent could the imperial government meet or even counter these demands?

As a step in the direction of providing a key to the whole complex of factors upon which the final policy decision would inevitably hinge, Takagi undertook a rigorous program of investigation in which he placed emphasis not only upon gaining an understanding of the situation within Japan but also upon interpreting the various trends in the world at large. With the estimates he subsequently formed of internal and external conditions as a general point of departure, Takagi turned his attention to the lines of action open to Japan. This naturally led to a thorough review of the demands the Allies had thus far lodged against the Island Empire. Foremost among these was the uncompromising issue of unconditional surrender. This "formula" for victory had made its appearance very early in the war but had not produced a marked reaction in Japan until after its formal reiteration in the joint declaration issued at Cairo in early December 1943. In Japanese eyes, this declaration took "the rather strained position" that Japan would be required to relinquish all the territories she had added to her dominion from as early as 1895 onward on the grounds that they were the spoils of *aggressive* war. This latter suggestion, as well as the tenor of the Cairo Declaration as a whole, was unacceptable to the Japanese and was considered by many as a purposeful distortion of historical fact. The net result was that the declaration immediately became a serious hindrance to those who wished to exert themselves toward bringing the war to an end.[31]

While Takagi was immersed in this highly secret study which he did not reveal even to his immediate associates,[32] the question of a negotiated peace was being considered in other quarters as well. One day in mid-September 1944, shortly before the admiral began his monumental project, Bunshirō Suzuki,[33] the managing director of the *Asahi* newspaper, brought a peace proposal to the attention of the Swedish Minister to Japan, Mr. Widar Bagge. Suzuki told the Minister that he was acting as a go-between for Prince Konoye, who headed a group which was prepared to surrender the conquered territories, and possibly even Manchuria, in an effort to end the war. According to Suzuki, Konoye wanted Mr. Bagge to forward the plan to the Swedish government with a request that a feeler be made in London through Swedish channels. The assumption was that "it might be easier to find understanding for such a plan in Great Britain than in the United States." The Swedish Minister reported everything to Stockholm and over the months which followed kept in touch with Suzuki and discussed the problem of peace with him from time to time. During this period, Bagge learned from Suzuki and others that the Allied demand for unconditional surrender was "one

[31] The discussion with respect to the Cairo Declaration is based on a comment by former Foreign Minister Tōgō which accords very well with observations made by other Japanese. The text may therefore be construed as representative of general rather than individual viewpoint.

When the Potsdam Proclamation was released in July 1945, Tōgō still regarded the Allied position "as illogical, unacceptable to the Japanese people, and a distortion of historical fact." He realized that he "could not get anywhere with that attitude" and so he "approached the problem from a different viewpoint." *Statements*: Tōgō #50304. See also IMTFE: *Analyses*, #541.

[32] As he got further along in his work, Takagi occasionally held private briefing sessions with Prince Konoye, Marquis Kido, Admiral Okada, and others. USSBS (*Japan's Struggle to End the War*, 4–5) declares that these men gradually reached the point where they were prepared to "carry through toward peace in the face of Army opposition . . . even to the point of withstanding an Army revolt." Actually, the USSBS view does not seem tenable unless applied only to "the last days"—the period from August 9, 1945, through September 2, 1945.

[33] Suzuki had "excellent connections" in the political world and "was very well informed" even though he was not a political figure himself. See IMTFE: Bagge, 34559–61.

Bunshirō Suzuki should not be confused with Admiral Kantarō Suzuki who became Japan's last wartime Premier (April 1945).

of the greatest obstacles to peace." Even those who wanted to end the war could not entertain the thought of unconditional surrender so long as they did not know what was in store for the nation. Everyone said it would be better to fight to the bitter end than to submit the Emperor to insult and the national pride to humiliation.

While the Suzuki-Bagge talks were in progress and the more rabid of Japan's leaders were sneering at the very thought of surrender, the country was suffering serious reverses on both its military and diplomatic fronts. As a result of the naval battles fought in the Philippine Sea in October 1944 under the misnomer of "Operation Victory," Japan no longer had a fleet that could mount an offensive. The overwhelming defeats to which the Japanese navy fell victim at this time stemmed from a lack of air cover. Japan could still build carriers but she could not man them with planes nor the planes with pilots. She was simply losing both faster than she could replace them.[34]

The memory of this naval disaster was still very much alive when a new misfortune struck: the first large-scale B-29 raid to be carried out against the Japanese homeland. This marked the beginning of a devastating air offensive which at its height claimed, in a single fire raid on Tokyo,[35] a heavier penalty in human lives than even the atomic attack upon Hiroshima. It was not long before the people of the capital had reason to recall a saying current in Tokugawa days: "Fires are the flowers of Yedo [Tokyo]"—a phrase which cryptically told of the frequency of conflagration and of the capital's vulnerability to flames. From November 1944 on, Allied sky-borne visitors of death exacted an ever increasing toll from the living until, in the end, the ashes of more than 2,300,000 homes lay strewn about the countryside, a lingering and forceful reminder of war's devastation.[36]

As if this were not enough, the situation on the diplomatic front was equally unsettling. Try as she might, Japan could not get the Soviet Union and Germany to stop fighting and begin negotiating.[37] Then suddenly, on November 7, the anniversary of the Red Revolution, Marshal Stalin openly denounced Japan as an aggressor on a plane with Ger-

[34] Toshikazu Kase of the Foreign Office obtained the above appraisal from Admiral Okada immediately after Japan's defeat in the Shō (victory) operation. See *Journey to the Missouri*, 94–95.

[35] This raid was carried out by approximately 130 B-29's between midnight and 2:40 A.M., March 10, 1945.

[36] See Japanese Govt., *Dai Tō-A sensō shūsen ni kan suru shiryō*, 7.

[37] For Japan's efforts in this direction, see IMTFE: Exh. 2745, *Stahmer Aide Mémoire*, 24485 ff. and Exh. 3557, *Document on Behalf of the Accused Shigemitsu*, 34551–58; *Statements*: Hattori #53074; JFO MS: Ch. 11 (Doku-So wahei mondai oyobi dai sankai tai-So tokushi haken mondai) and Ch. 13 (Shigemitsu gaishō ga shuki shita to iwareru "Waga Gaikō" to Sutārin seimei); and IMTFE: *Analyses*, #1988 and #4094.

many.[38] Although the Japanese ambassador in Moscow was subsequently assured that the marshal's words were not predicated upon a forthcoming change in Soviet policy toward Japan, such an assurance actually had very little meaning.[39] The bombshell that exploded on Red Revolution Day in Moscow only served to heighten further the growing feeling of uneasiness resulting from the failure which greeted all of Japan's efforts to inspire a rapprochement between Germany and the Soviet Union.

While trouble closed in on all sides, new and more threatening storm clouds loomed on the horizon. On Christmas Day 1944, the United States announced the successful completion of its Leyte operation and thereby scored a psychological victory against Japan commensurate with the physical advantage accruing from the capture and the possession of the island itself. Since early November, Premier Koiso had been emphasizing that the fighting taking place in the Philippines was equivalent in importance to a battle waged in 1582 at Tennōzan, a small mountain in the Kansai district where a rising general named Hideyoshi had won a victory which proved to be the decisive factor in his becoming the supreme lord of all Japan. In other words, Koiso had characterized the Philippine operations as *decisive* and had declared, in effect: "If Japan wins on Leyte, she wins the war!"[40] The American announcement of December 25 forced Koiso to face the very embarrassing fact that his historical precedent had backfired and had thus created an opportunity for the word to spread that Japan's failure on Leyte rendered her ultimate defeat a foregone conclusion.

Although the sharp edge of this irony was blunted somewhat by the manner in which the government later handled the news, the damage done to Koiso's hold upon the premiership proved more difficult to mend. This was especially true in view of the developments which had led to Koiso's categorical reference to Tennōzan.

It seems that shortly after the Supreme Council for the Direction of the War had been established (August 1944) its members had met in the presence of the Emperor and had there adopted the basic policy Japan was to follow in her future conduct of the war. The Philippines

---

[38] See JFO MS: Ch. 13 (Shigemitsu gaishō ga shuki shita to iwareru "Waga Gaikō" to Sutārin seimei) and Tokyo *Asahi Shimbun* for November 9, 1944.

[39] That Stalin was already planning the Soviet Union's entry into the war against Japan receives forceful confirmation from material contained in dispatches which arrived in Washington some three weeks before Stalin's denunciation of Japan on November 7. In these dispatches, Major General John R. Deane (chief of the U.S. Military Mission in Moscow) reported that Stalin was willing to begin planning for full Soviet participation in the war in the Pacific subject to the condition that he would require the build-up of certain air complements and a two months' stockpile for thirty additional divisions in Manchuria. See Millis (ed.), *The Forrestal Diaries*, 12–13.

[40] See the Tokyo *Asahi Shimbun*, November 9, 1944 ("Hitō shūhen no sensō koso senkyoku wo kessuru Tennōzan") ; *Statements*: Suzuki #531; and IMTFE: *Analyses*, #2965 (notes prepared by Koiso *ca.* 1946).

thus came to be earmarked as the scene of the first in a series of decisive battles which were slated to provide Japan ultimately with an overwhelming triumph. Although the Supreme Command's strategy was to deal a vital blow to the enemy even at the cost of an equally vital sacrifice on Japan's part, Koiso privately argued against trading Japan's hide for American flesh in so cavalier a manner. Koiso wanted more than just a Pyrrhic victory, and in time and with persistence he won over the Supreme Command—or so he thought.[41] When the army agreed to concentrate its forces at Leyte in a bold effort to put the enemy to rout, Koiso publicly went on record in terms of the Tennōzan allusion.

In spite of the fact that as the fighting progressed in the Philippines the situation went from bad to worse for Japan, Koiso apparently believed that the Supreme Command would still make good on its promise. Then, on December 20, just five days before the American announcement, Koiso was suddenly collared by War Minister Sugiyama and told that the Supreme Command had abandoned its original plan in favor of deferring the decisive battle to the coming encounter on Luzon.[42] This was the first the Premier had heard of any such change in strategy and he was "stunned." Since he was at that very moment hurrying to an audience with the Emperor, he had to leave the remonstrances to later and continue on his way. He had no sooner entered the imperial chamber than the Emperor asked him if he had heard of the change in plans. To this Koiso replied, "Frankly, I did not know about it until War Minister Sugiyama whispered the fact to me just before I came for this audience with Your Majesty." The sovereign then asked what policy the government would follow in order to counteract the adverse effect the news of the Leyte defeat would exert upon the people and the war effort. All Koiso could do was to shake his head and say he would have to think of some means to make the best of the situation, and with that he withdrew.[43]

Koiso's unsatisfactory reply and the realization that another and perhaps *the* decisive battle, so far as America and Britain were con-concerned, was about to begin in the troubled Philippines only served to

[41] See *Statements:* Koiso #55906. According to Koiso, Japan could have sued for peace right after the fall of Saipan (July 1944) but she would have had to accept "merciless terms" and run the risk of a serious internal crisis. His desire to throw all of Japan's effort into winning at least one major victory was aimed at providing Japan with the opportunity to negotiate peace on terms which would be more favorable than those she might otherwise obtain.

[42] See *Statements:* Koiso #55906. Koiso stated that "it probably would have been advisable" for him to have resigned at this juncture, but he refrained from doing so in view of the Supreme Command's promise to concentrate all of its available forces in an endeavor to win a decisive victory at Luzon. (The Supreme Command later reneged on this promise, also.)

At this time Koiso launched what was possibly his first real bid to become War Minister in his own cabinet, but the Big Three refused to bestow the office upon him.

[43] *Ibid.* and Kido, "Nikki," 1/4/45.

increase the Emperor's anxiety. On January 6, just three days before the United States Sixth Army penetrated Lingayen Gulf in the first wave of the assault upon Luzon, the Emperor called in Marquis Kido and declared that it might be necessary for the Throne to consult the senior statesmen about the war situation.[44] Although the *jūshin* officially did not have access to the secret files and documents of the government, the Emperor apparently considered their advice, if not their information, sufficiently worth while to merit obtaining their opinions.

The imperial suggestion was, in itself, something of a departure from the strictly narrow path along which the Emperor normally moved. The former Premiers were not general consultants to either the Emperor or the government, and the army, in particular, looked with disfavor upon any interference by the senior statesmen in the affairs of the nation.[45] Had the army felt it could trust the senior statesmen, the group would undoubtedly have been used as an ultra rubber stamp, but many of the former Premiers were men whose cabinets had fallen as a result of the intrigues and machinations of the military. It was rather obvious that such men would hardly turn the other cheek.

When the Emperor suddenly suggested that he might call upon the senior statesmen, Kido, who feared the possible repercussions such a move might provoke, advised the sovereign to watch developments for a few days before taking any action. Then, depending on what happened, the Emperor might find it advantageous to question the army and navy chiefs of staff informally about the war situation and their plans for the future. Such an off-the-record chat with the two chiefs would be better than a formal audience which would tend to be stiff and conventional and would probably fail to produce the information desired by the Throne.[46] Once he had listened to the views of the army and navy, His Majesty could summon various members of the cabinet and put questions to them. Finally, if the situation were then such that a policy decision of the utmost importance had to be formulated, a joint conference

[44] See IMTFE: Kido, 31110–11, and Kido, "Nikki," 1/6/45.

[45] Only once in their history had the *jūshin* been summoned to consider a question which was not concerned with the selection of a Premier. That had been on November 29, 1941, when Premier Tōjō told them that an impasse had been reached in the negotiations between Japan and the United States. Tōjō seems to have been concerned lest the *jūshin* should go over his head by offering the Throne advice which might be antagonistic to policies envisaged by his cabinet. See IMTFE: Okada, 29259–61, 29278, and 29280; Kido, "Nikki," 11/26/41 and 11/29/41; and *Statements:* Matsudaira #61636.

[46] The chief aide-de-camp, who attends audiences granted to the War and Navy Ministers and to the chiefs of the Army and Navy General Staffs, withdraws from the imperial chamber after scheduled matters are formally reported to the Throne—thus permitting informal conversation to take place privately. The chief aide-de-camp may be informed later of what occurred, but he is not necessarily so informed. It was during the informal chats that the Emperor, as a result of his direct questions, occasionally received information which was more detailed than anything contained in the formal reports. *Statements:* Hasunuma (chief aide-de-camp) #58225.

of senior statesmen and cabinet ministers could be held in the imperial presence.[47]

In keeping with the Privy Seal's advice, the Emperor agreed to bide his time for several days before deciding whether to summon the former Premiers. By January 13, however, he had determined to go ahead with his original idea. In response to an imperial command, Kido discussed the matter with the Imperial Household Minister and then formulated a plan whereby the senior statesmen would be received individually in audience on different days in February rather than all together as a group on a single, specified day. This was apparently a concession to a certain fear that the military might step in if they knew what was going on.[48] Of course, even these individual visits could not be kept secret, so the word was spread that the senior statesmen would call upon the Emperor during February to pay their respects to the sovereign and to inquire after his health. Although the army probably saw through this explanation, it did not do anything drastic. Between February 7 and February 26, the *jūshin* proceeded to the palace according to a pre-arranged schedule.[49] Each had an audience with the Emperor, inquired after his health, and then discussed the situation facing Japan.[50] If the

[47] See IMTFE: Kido, 31110–12; Kido, "Nikki," 1/6/45; *Statements:* Matsudaira #61636 and #60745. The anomalous position of the senior statesmen, the fact that none of the *jūshin* had been received in audience during the preceding three years of the war, and the Privy Seal's primary concern with safeguarding the Throne by keeping the Emperor from taking any action not considered standard procedure explain Kido's advice to the Emperor at this time.

[48] See IMTFE: Kido, 32113.

[49] Hiranuma saw the Emperor on February 7, Hirota on the 9th, Konoye on the 14th, Wakatsuki on the 19th, Okada on the 23d, and Tōjō on the 26th. Abe, governor general of Korea, and Yonai, co-Premier and Navy Minister in the Koiso Cabinet, were prevented by virtue of their official positions from paying their respects to the Emperor in their capacity as *jūshin*. Although he was not a senior statesman, Count Makino, a former Lord Keeper of the Privy Seal who had a record of many years of service close to the Throne, was also received by the Emperor at this time (February 19). IMTFE: Kido, 31114, and Kido, "Nikki," 2/7/45, 2/9/45, 2/14/45, 2/19/45, 2/23/45, and 2/26/45.

[50] In the case of audiences granted to persons other than Ministers of State, it was customary for the Grand Chamberlain or his deputy to be present. This practice came into being as a result of the adverse criticism which occurred when a certain Railway Ministry official was accused, during the Hamaguchi Cabinet's tenure in office, of having taken the improper liberty of submitting his views to the Throne (during a *private* audience) with respect to the question of reducing the salaries of government officials. Kido, "Nikki," 7/12/45; interview with Grand Master of Ceremonies Matsudaira, Tokyo, August 14, 1951; and IMTFE: Kido, 31608, and Tōgō, 35885. Kido seems to suggest that the Privy Seal could request the Emperor's permission to attend audiences if there were any special reason for his doing so.

In the case of audiences granted to the War and Navy Ministers, to the army and navy chiefs of staff, and to officers of the rank of general and admiral, the Emperor's chief aide-de-camp (himself a general) was always present (instead of the Grand Chamberlain). Whenever military personnel matters came up for discussion, the chief aide-de-camp would always withdraw from the audience chamber. This practice arose as a result of a report, dating from the Russo-Japanese War (1904–5), to the effect

senior statesmen had gone as a group, "Tōjō the Razor" would have been among them, and his edge was keen. This way, the opportunity at least existed to forsake circuitous phraseology and cautious hedging. Each man could, if he so wished, speak his mind.[51] The records pertaining to these audiences, however, are disappointing in this respect,[52] for they reveal that, with one outstanding exception, the views submitted to the Throne in February 1945 did not point up the fact so many of these men had supposedly privately come to accept—the fact of Japan's impending defeat.[53] While Wakatsuki, for instance, declared that Japanese leaders must think about ending the war before the issue of victory or defeat became clear, he also stated practically in the same breath that under the circumstances then prevailing Japan's only course was to fight on until the enemy realized the disadvantages of continuing hostilities. Considerably more novel than this, but no less unsatisfactory, was the attitude of Hirota who told the Emperor that Roosevelt must certainly want to end the war, otherwise why would he have given positions of importance to Stettinius, whose grandfather was a German, and to Grew, a known friend of Japan.

In contrast to this type of advice, the remarks of General Tōjō were very much more to the point and essentially more realistic even though they were based on incorrect facts and figures. As Tōjō saw it, America's war aims in February 1945 were primarily political, not strategic, and were designed to prove to the nations scheduled to assemble at the United Nations Conference in San Francisco in April that Japan was powerless

---

that the chief aide-de-camp to the Tsar had interfered, to the detriment of the Russian war effort, with military personnel matters. *Statements:* Hasunuma #58225. See also footnote 46 above.

[51] With the exception of Grand Chamberlain Fujita, no one else was present at any of these audiences. On February 14, when Konoye saw the Emperor, Fujita was ill and so Privy Seal Kido was present. (Interview with Marquis Matsudaira, Tokyo, August 14, 1951; Imperial Household Document: "Shōwa nijūnen nigatsu, jikyoku ni kan suru jūshin hōtōroku"; and Okada, *Kaikoroku*, 233–34.) Both Fujita and Kido were completely trusted by the Emperor. Had they ever been so indiscreet as to reveal damaging confidences, they would have been forced to resign.

[52] USSBS states the concensus was "that Japan faced certain defeat and should seek peace at once" (*Japan's Struggle to End the War*, 5), but this is not borne out by the notes taken by Grand Chamberlain Fujita at the time (Imperial Household Document cited in the preceding footnote).

[53] Hirota, Konoye, Makino, and Tōjō all discussed the role of the Soviet Union. Makino described American "co-operation" with the Soviet Union and with the Yenan Chinese Communists as a marriage of convenience but one, nevertheless, which was fatefully laden with implications for Japan. Hiranuma spoke of the food problem and hinted at the existence of dangerous thoughts among the people. He emphasized the need to stress Japan's strong points as a step toward bettering the war situation. Although Okada decried expressions of defeatism, he did say that Japan's leaders should secretly give thought to the question of ending the war. At the same time, he called for the utilization of the special attack (*kamikaze*) corps. See Imperial Household Document cited in footnote 51 above; Wakatsuki, *Kofūan kaikoroku*, 441–44; Okada, *Kaikoroku*, 233–34; and *Statements:* Okada #61307.

to do anything. He did not believe that the United States could increase her air striking power or even continue the then current rate of attack. He felt that Japan's tactics to date had half succeeded and half failed and that the United States had fallen far short of its objectives. He estimated that Japan had a "fifty-fifty" chance of keeping the Soviet Union out of the war. Even if the Soviets did come in, Tōjō did not believe they would be able to commit sufficiently large forces to achieve any success. The most formidable enemy was defeatism, and the most pressing need a direct imperial command to the people to give their all to the war effort. "With determination," he declared, "we can win!"

The only former Premier who did present an exceptional point of view was that man about whom all manner of controversy exists—the imperial favorite among the senior statesmen, Prince Konoye. His so-called Memorial to the Throne is as interesting as it was, at that time, at least partially prophetic. In essence, Konoye's remarks[54] ran as follows:

Sad though it is, I believe that Japan has already lost the war. Although defeat will be a great stain upon our polity, it need not necessarily occasion undue concern especially since public opinion in America and Britain, on the whole, has not yet gone so far as to demand a fundamental change in our national structure. There are those, of course, who hold extreme views with respect to this question, and it is difficult to predict what changes may take place in public opinion as time passes. From the standpoint of maintaining Japan's imperial system, that which we have most to fear is not defeat itself but, rather, the threat inherent in the possibility that a Communist revolution may accompany defeat. The more I think about it the more I feel that conditions within Japan and those prevailing abroad are rapidly progressing toward such an eventuality.

In the world at large, for instance, there is the prodigious debouchment of the Soviet Union—a development which our people have shallowly tended to underestimate because of the recent dissolution of the Comintern and the earlier adoption by the USSR of a popular front, or two-stage-revolution, strategem. That the Soviet Union has not abandoned her plan to bolshevize the world, however, is manifestly clear from the undisguised mischief-making in which she has recently been engaged in a number of European countries. The fact of the matter is that the Soviet Union has been at pains to establish Soviet regimes in the countries contiguous to her borders and to promote the creation of at least pro-Soviet governments throughout the rest of Europe. In this task, it may be said that she has by and large succeeded.[55]

[54] In reconstructing the text of the Memorial, which was prepared at the home of Shigeru Yoshida (postwar Prime Minister of Japan), the author drew upon the following: Imperial Household Document cited in footnote 51 above; Iwabuchi, "Konoye kō no jōsōbun," appended to JFO MS: Ch. 14 (Tennō jūshin no iken wo go chōshu); IMTFE: *Analyses*, #572; and a draft translation of the Memorial prepared toward the latter part of 1945 by Mr. Tomohiko Ushiba, secretary and aide to Prince Konoye. This translation, which was lent to the author by Mr. Ushiba, is the original of the revised and partial translation which appears in USSBS, *Japan's Struggle to End the War*, 21-22.

[55] At this point, Konoye mentioned the activities of the Soviet Union with respect to Yugoslavia (which he called the most typical case); Poland; Rumania; Hungary; Finland; Iran (where the Soviet Union forced a cabinet to resign over the oil issue); Switzerland (where Soviet accusations that the government was pro-Axis resulted in

Although on the surface the Soviet Union stands for the principle of non-intervention in the internal affairs of a state, in actuality she is bent upon the most intensive intervention conceivable in her effort to draw the rest of the world into her orbit. Her goal in the Far East, moreover, is no more nor less than that toward which she is striving in Europe. In Yenan, a Japan Liberation League has been organized around Okano,[56] a Moscow-trained Japanese Communist. This League is collaborating with the Korean Independence Confederation, the Korean Volunteer Army, the Formosan Spearhead Corps, and similar groups in a verbal campaign of propaganda and revolutionary incitement directed at Japan. Such being the case, the danger of Soviet intervention[57] in our own internal affairs in the near future is abundantly great.

The situation within Japan is such that every possible factor favorable to the accomplishment of a Communist revolution is on hand. There is poverty in the life of the people, a rise in the voice of labor, and an expansion of pro-Soviet feeling growing out of an increase in enmity against America and Britain. In addition, there are the actions of the national renovationists—a movement championed by a certain faction within the military, the activities of the so-called "new bureaucrats"—the "fellow-travelers" of this movement, and the secret machinations of the leftists who are pulling the strings from behind.

Of the foregoing factors, that which we have most to fear is the national renovation movement of the militarists.[58] A great number of young military men seem to think that Communism is compatible with Japan's imperial system—a view which, I believe, constitutes the keynote of their renovation argument. I have heard that there are even some members of the imperial family who might lend an ear to their contentions.[59]

Since Japan's professional military men—at least a majority—hail from families below the middle class, their whole environment of life has been such that it is easy for them to fall prey to Communist doctrine. At the same time, however, their military education has thoroughly inculcated them with the spirit of our national polity. The Communist element, therefore, is endeavoring to captivate these militarists with the claim that the national polity and Communism can stand side by side.

I believe that it has at length become clear that the Manchurian Incident, the China Incident, and the Greater East Asia War were all perpetrated by the aforementioned national renovation faction of the militarists as part of a purposeful plan. It is a well-known fact that at the time of the trouble in Manchuria the military declared the purpose of the Incident to be internal reform here in Japan. Later on, when the China Incident occurred, one of the central figures of the renovation faction publicly declared, "the longer the Incident lasts, the better, for if a settlement is reached we shall be unable to bring about domestic reform." Although the aim of this national renovation faction within the mili-

---

the resignation of the Foreign Minister); France; Belgium; Holland; and Germany (where the Kremlin would attempt to establish a new Soviet regime).

[56] A pseudonym used by the Japanese Communist leader, Sanzō Nozaka.

[57] Konoye mentioned the following possible demands as the manner in which Soviet intervention might occur: official recognition of a Japanese Communist party; inclusion of Communists in the Japanese cabinet; repeal of the law relating to the maintenance of public order; abrogation of the Anti-Comintern Pact.

[58] This sentence does not appear in the Imperial Household Document but does appear in both the Iwabuchi text and Mr. Ushiba's penciled translation. It is clear from what follows that the sentence represents Konoye's conviction.

[59] This sentence appears in the Imperial Household Document but does not appear in the Iwabuchi text.

tary may not necessarily be a Communist revolution, I believe that I am not far wrong in saying that the "new bureaucrats" and the sympathizers among the people—who jointly fawn upon these militarists—are consciously harboring the intention of bringing about a Red revolution. It is immaterial whether we call this revolution-minded group right-wing or left-wing, for in reality the right-wingers are nothing more than Communists masquerading in the dress of the national polity-ists. Our ignorant and simple-minded military men are putty in their hands.[60]

What I have said represents the conclusions I have recently reached as a result of having quietly reflected upon the events of the past ten years—years during which I had acquaintances in various quarters: the military, the bureaucracy, the right-wing, and the left-wing. In the light of this conclusion, I now realize that there were a great many things during those years the true meaning of which I have only now come to grasp. Having been honored twice during that period with Your Majesty's command to form a cabinet,[61] I was so eager to do away with friction and conflict within Japan that I acceded to the demands of the national renovationists as much as I could. In my desire to achieve national unity I failed to perceive the real purpose hidden behind the contentions of the extremists. Since there is absolutely no excuse for my lack of foresight, I can only say that I feel gravely responsible for my failure in this respect.

The more critical the war situation becomes, the louder we hear the cry, "One hundred million die together!" Although the so-called right-wingers are the ones who shout the loudest, it is the Communists, in my opinion, who are the instigators of it all, for they hope to achieve their revolutionary aim by taking advantage of the confusion that will arise out of defeat.

While on the one hand there are those who clamor for the utter destruction of America and Britain, an atmosphere seems to be developing, on the other hand, that is favorably disposed toward the Soviet Union. I have been informed that there is even one group of militarists sponsoring a rapprochement with the USSR—a rapprochement at any cost, while others are thinking in terms of an alliance with the Yenan Chinese Communist regime.

Thus, with each passing day the internal and external scene is becoming increasingly favorable to the success of a Communist revolution. If the war situation deteriorates still further, this state of affairs will develop by leaps and bounds.

The question would be different if there were even some slight hope of the fighting taking a turn for the better, but with defeat staring us in the face we shall simply be playing into the hands of the Communists if we elect to continue a war wherein there is no prospect of victory. From the standpoint of preserving the national polity, therefore, I am firmly convinced that we should seek to end the war as speedily as possible.

The greatest obstacle to a termination of the conflict is the existence of that group within the military which ever since the Manchurian Incident has driven the country to its present plight. Although the military men have already lost confidence in their ability to prosecute the war to a successful conclusion, they are likely to continue fighting to the very end merely to save face.

Should we endeavor to stop the war abruptly without first rooting out the

---

[60] More literally, "Our ignorant and simple-minded militarists will be made to dance by them."

[61] Konoye actually held the premiership three times though his third cabinet was simply a reorganization of the second. This may explain why he speaks of having received the imperial mandate twice.

extremists, I fear that they—supported by sympathizers within both the right-
and left-wings—might perpetrate internal disorder thus making it difficult for us
to achieve our desired goal. The prerequisite to a termination of the war is therefore the elimination of this extremist element within the military. Once this is
done, their followers among the bureaucrats and right- and left-wing segments
of the people will also fade away, for the latter have not as yet attained an independent influence of their own but have merely tried to achieve their aims by
marching behind the militarists and using the latter to their advantage. Thus,
if the tree is struck at the roots, its leaves and branches will wither and die of their
own accord.

This may be slightly wishful thinking but, if the extremist group is purged,
is it not possible that the character of the army will so change that the atmosphere
in America, Britain, and Chungking may improve somewhat? The Allied war
aim is the overthrow of Japan's military clique, but if the character and policy
of our military undergo a fundamental change the Allies may be moved to give
careful consideration to the question of continuing the war.

At any rate, the reconstruction of the military through the elimination of the
extremists is the prerequisite to saving Japan from a Communist revolution. I must
therefore urge Your Majesty to make a bold decision toward that end.[62]

Although Konoye's emphasis may have been stronger than his evidence,[63] he had at least probed to the very core of the problem. In terms
of physical accomplishment, the Japanese military had already lost
the war, but *spiritually* they were still indestructible. For want of a
better solution they now insisted that, if given the chance to concentrate
their forces against the invader when he came, they could win a decision
on the battlefield of the homeland that would permit Japan to end the
war on favorable terms. To men like Konoye and others, this could mean
only one thing: It was too late for an ounce of prevention and it would
take more than a pound of cure. The problem was no longer how to deal
with the situation but rather how to deal with the situation so as to bring
it to an end.

[62] When Konoye had finished speaking, an exchange of questions and answers took
place. It was at this time that Konoye mentioned the following men (each representative of certain currents of thought within the military) as possible leaders of the
"purge" he envisaged: Ugaki, Mazaki, Ishihara, Kōzuki, or Obata. Since it was possible that the choice of one of these figures would lead to "confusion," he also added
the names of Anami, Yamashita, or Minami (men who were less controversial and more
likely to command greater support). The Emperor noted that unless Japan achieved
a military success, a purge of the type urged by Konoye would prove difficult. Konoye
agreed but rhetorically asked whether or not Japan would be able to snatch a victory.
"If it comes six months or a year from now," he concluded, "it'll be too late." (Imperial Household Document: "Shōwa nijūnen nigatsu, jikyoku ni kan suru jūshin
hōtōroku.")

[63] Kido does not believe there was any concrete evidence behind Konoye's fear of
a leftist revolution, and he personally would not go so far as to say the army was plot-
ting such a revolution. At the same time, Kido notes that an atmosphere sympathetic
to the leftists did prevail "to a surprising degree" within the army, particularly toward
the end of the war when men were being drafted into the services in a rather wholesale
manner. *Statements:* Kido #61476 and interview with the former Privy Seal, Tokyo,
May 1, 1952.

One possible answer, as Konoye had suggested, was to use the influence of the Emperor to undermine the power of the fanatics among the military. Another was to seek mediation of the conflict through a neutral nation. A possibly more definitive yet essentially more difficult approach was to stage a coup d'état and then negotiate directly with the United States and Great Britain. In spite of the number of possibilities,[64] there was really no single solution uncontaminated by all manner of dangers, both real and apparent. Since no one knew exactly where to turn, the aimless wandering among alternatives continued and the issue upon which the opinions of the senior statesmen had been sought was left undecided.

Shortly after Prince Konoye and the other former Premiers had paid their respects to the Throne in February 1945, Premier Koiso had become involved, partially by chance and partially by intention, in an interesting but essentially insignificant "peace" maneuver[65] which helped seal his doom. It seems that there was a certain Miao Pin,[66] an official of the Nanking puppet regime and a man of very doubtful character,[67] who was reputedly in radio communication with Chungking and supposedly desirous of serving as a mediator in order to negotiate peace between Japan and China. The matter was brought to Koiso's attention by Minister of State Ogata who in turn had his information from an *Asahi* newspaperman then in Shanghai, Miao's base of operations. Although

---

[64] Mr. Shigemitsu has stated that on March 23, 1945, he reported to Konoye, Wakatsuki, Okada, and Hiranuma that a peace overture could be launched at any time if the government would decide on such a policy. He affirms that he even hinted at the necessity of changing the cabinet (by constitutional means) in order to permit the organization of a new peace cabinet capable of supporting the desired policy without reservation. See *Statements:* Shigemitsu 9/9/49. Also, interview with Mr. Shigemitsu, Kamakura, March 5, 1952, and Shigemitsu, *Shōwa no dōran,* 258–62 (which deals, also, with the views expressed by Mr. Shigemitsu on March 30, 1945, at a meeting of the Privy Council).

[65] See *Statements:* Koiso #55906 and Shigemitsu 1/13/50; IMTFE: Tanaka, 32540–42; Kido, 31115 ff., 31245–48; Koiso, 32257–63, 32268–72; Kido, "Nikki," 3/27/45 and 4/3–4/45; Higashikuni, *Watakushi no kiroku,* 75–90; Nakamura, *Nagatachō ichibanchi,* 124–26; and JFO MS: Ch. 16 (Ryōhin kōsaku to sono ta tai-Shi wahei kōsaku). See also USSBS, *Japan's Struggle to End the War,* 5; Fishel, "A Japanese Peace Maneuver in 1944," *FEQ,* VIII (August 1949), 390–91; and IMTFE: *Analyses,* #2965.

[66] Miao's name has frequently been transliterated in rather unusual ways. According to the Who's Who section of *The Japan-Manchoukuo Year Book* (1941) and to the *Saishin Shina yōjin den* (1941), "Miao Pin" is correct.

[67] The then Foreign Minister, Shigemitsu, has characterized Miao as one of those "peace-brokers" who sought, through so-called peace efforts, to balance out the questionable portions of their past and thus save themselves from personal "difficulties" in the postwar period. To believe in Miao as a potential mediator, Shigemitsu said, was "childish naïveté" and betrayed "ignorance" with respect to Chinese politics. *Statements:* Shigemitsu 1/13/50. For a more favorable characterization of Miao, see IMTFE: Koiso, 32257–58 and 32268–72. After the war Miao was executed by the Chinese Nationalists, the very people he supposedly represented.

Koiso had met Miao Pin only once some years earlier (1939),[68] his interest was stimulated by the reports he received from Ogata and by an article written by Miao on the subject of Sino-Japanese peace. In order to make sure that this possibly renegade Chinese was really in a position to effect liaison between Chungking and Tokyo, Koiso finally sent an old friend and classmate, a retired colonel by the name of Yamagata, to Shanghai to investigate. The colonel spent some time in scrounging for useful information and in checking up on Miao.[69] He subsequently not only reported back in favorable terms but also suggested inviting Miao to Tokyo for consultations. Up to that point, Koiso had handled the affair on his own responsibility. He had not processed anything through the Foreign Office because he had heard that Miao Pin had had no use for Foreign Minister Shigemitsu ever since the latter had served as Japan's ambassador to China. Similarly, he had not broached the matter to the Japanese army because Miao's relations with Japan's military occupation authorities in China were hardly cordial, to say the least. When Yamagata suggested inviting the man to Japan, however, Koiso was forced to lay the question before his cabinet colleagues since there obviously was no point in sending for Miao unless the government as a whole would listen to what he had to say. Koiso now experienced a reaction which, though perhaps not unexpected, did not contain much promise for the success of his proposed venture. When Koiso approached Shigemitsu, the Foreign Minister flatly declared that he would concur only if the War and Navy Ministers were favorably disposed.[70] When Koiso called on Admiral Yonai, the latter said he would not give his approval unless the army had no objections. Not until the Premier found himself at War Minister Sugiyama's door did he finally and rather surprisingly obtain the necessary sanction.[71] As a result, arrangements were hastily made to permit Miao to travel to Tokyo on board a Japanese military plane and to bring with him his own radio receiving and transmitting set, a radio operator, a cryptographer, and a special representative from Chungking. Just as the arch schemer was to take off from Shanghai, however, the Japanese military police swooped down upon the field and refused passage to everyone and everything except the dis-

[68] "Once," according to *Statements*: Koiso #55906; "twice," according to IMTFE: Koiso, 32257. Whichever is correct, Koiso cannot have learned very much about Miao and his loyalties.

[69] As another means of maintaining a check upon Miao's activities, Koiso planned concurrently to negotiate through an agent in Peiping. When the proper moment presented itself, Koiso intended to send a Japanese emissary (Minister of State Ogata) to Chungking. In this connection, see IMTFE: Koiso, 32268–72, and *Statements*: Shigemitsu 1/13/50.

[70] It should be emphasized that Shigemitsu did not object to negotiating for peace, but he did—and for good reasons—oppose the manner in which Koiso proposed to handle the negotiations.

[71] See IMTFE: Kido, 31245–46, and Koiso, 32260–61.

gruntled Miao. Thus, when he arrived in Tokyo, he was very much alone and quite empty-handed. Koiso and his small coterie of Miao supporters were "thunderstruck."

Nor was this all. The first thing Miao did was to ignore the government by concentrating his efforts upon Imperial Prince Higashikuni, a man who had been an active participant in various other China moves. At a tête-à-tête which took place on March 17, 1945, the prince endeavored to get a clear idea of Miao's motives and whether or not there was any basis for undertaking negotiations which had already met with opposition not only from Koiso's cabinet colleagues but from the Japanese high command in China as well. In essence, the conversation ran as follows:

Higashikuni: Will Chungking recognize and acknowledge the Emperor?
Miao Pin: Yes.
Higashikuni: Why does Chungking want to make peace with Japan?
Miao Pin: Chungking has no desire to see Japan utterly destroyed, since China's self-preservation depends upon Japan's continued existence. Japan is China's breakwater. If peace is concluded now, we can also prevent the debouchment of the Soviet Union.
Higashikuni: In view of the fact that you were invited to Japan by Premier Koiso, why did you desire to see me before talking with anyone else?
Miao Pin: Because no one in Japan can be trusted, except the Emperor. His Majesty is the only one on whom we can rely. Since it is impossible for me to see the Emperor personally, I wish to present the question to Your Highness and to request you to convey my message to His Imperial Majesty.

In reply, the prince indicated that notwithstanding his personal relationship to the Emperor he could not, under Japan's constitutional system, bypass the cabinet and go directly to the Throne on such a matter. Before Miao took his leave, however, the prince expressed a number of warm sentiments with respect to Generalissimo Chiang and said that he hoped Miao's mission would be successful and would lead not only to peace with China but also to peace with America and the world at large.[72]

During the next two weeks, Miao was shown every hospitality but, for one reason or another, he was received by Premier Koiso only once. The rest of the time he had to content himself with negotiating with the Vice-Minister of War through whom he made no progress whatsoever in spite of the private representations made on his behalf by Prince Higashikuni. The difficulty lay partially in the nature of the proposals which Miao offered as representing the attitude of Chungking. His whole bargaining position rested upon a rather stiff *quid pro quo*: Chungking would give favorable consideration to the question of peace if Japan would undertake to (1) terminate hostilities and withdraw all of her troops from China, (2) dissolve the Nanking puppet regime and permit Chiang to resume control over the whole of China with his seat of govern-

---

[72] See Higashikuni, *Watakushi no kiroku*, 75–90.

ment at Nanking,[73] (3) open separate negotiations with respect to the question of Manchuria, and (4) make peace with the United States and Great Britain. Although positive evidence is lacking, it is just possible that instead of a general peace in the Pacific Miao's fourth and final point was an insinuation to the effect that if Japan agreed to points one through three Chungking, for its part, would not be unfavorably disposed toward severing its ties with the Allies in order to prevent America and Britain from using China as a base of operations against Japan. This would not have been a new idea but simply an amplification by Miao of a stipulation discussed by Tōjō and Wang Ching-wei in mid-September 1943 at a time when Sun Fo was reportedly seeking Nanking's good offices in an effort to negotiate a settlement between Tokyo and Chungking.[74] At any rate, the nature of the *quid pro quo* and the fact that almost everyone in the government except Koiso regarded Miao in the light of a political mercenary, who not only could not be trusted personally but who also did not actually represent Chiang at all, brought the negotiations to an abrupt halt. Upon receiving an indication from the Throne that key members of the government felt the circumstances of the case rendered a continuation of the negotiations most improper,[75] Koiso had no other choice than to send Miao Pin back to China as empty-handed as he had come.

Essentially more important than the questionable Miao Pin venture was the concurrent revival of interest, among a few Foreign Office people, in the possibility of achieving peace with the aid of Sweden. The Swedish Minister to Japan, Mr. Bagge, who had first been approached on the matter in September 1944, was preparing to return to Sweden. Since he had seen some twenty years' service in Japan, he felt that he could at least offer his good offices. Toward the end of March 1945, shortly before he was scheduled to leave, Bagge told the former Japanese Minister to Helsingfors, Tadashi Sakaya, that he did not believe the Allies would adhere to their unconditional surrender demand if Japan would only propose making peace. Should Japan take the initiative, Bagge declared, the imperial house would probably be permitted to remain.[76] Sakaya immediately reported the Swedish Minister's remarks to Foreign Minister Shigemitsu, and the result was a meeting between the latter and Mr. Bagge. At this meeting, Shigemitsu spoke

---

[73] It was envisaged that Chiang would establish himself in Nanking within three months after Japan had ceased hostilities and had dissolved her puppet government. Until Chiang appeared, a provisional government composed of Chungking personnel was to operate in Nanking. Miao's proposals also called upon Japan to give asylum to the principal members of her Nanking regime.

[74] See footnote 37, Ch. 1, above.

[75] The Ministers of War, Navy, and Foreign Affairs individually expressed their disapproval to the Emperor who, in turn, passed the information on to Koiso.

[76] See IMTFE: Bagge, 34561–64, and Shigemitsu, *Shōwa no dōran*, 262–63.

very frankly. He blamed the military for the bad war situation and declared that it was now up to the diplomats to get the country out of the conflict. He "spoke at length about the Emperor as a peace-loving man who had always been against the war"[77] and he asserted that most of the Japanese diplomatic corps, including himself, had shared the Emperor's feelings. He concluded by requesting Bagge "very earnestly" to do whatever he could to determine Japan's chances of obtaining "a negotiated peace." Bagge left Shigemitsu, convinced that the Foreign Minister was sincere in his desire "to do everything in his power to end the war as soon as possible, even at great sacrifice to his country."[78]

Before Bagge could leave for Stockholm, the Koiso Cabinet fell and with it went Foreign Minister Shigemitsu. On April 11, however, Sakaya—again acting as a go-between—undertook to inform Shigemitsu's successor, Mr. Tōgō, of Bagge's intentions.[79] The impression Tōgō got was that the Swedish Minister planned to sound out the views of the United States *on his own volition* without a formal request from the Japanese government. Since he was one of the few people who recognized the necessity of terminating the war, Tōgō responded warmly and indicated that he would like to see Mr. Bagge personally. Sakaya immediately conveyed this message to the Swedish Minister but the latter was unable to accept Tōgō's invitation since the departure of his plane

[77] During the course of the Tokyo trial, former Premier Tōjō was asked if it had been the "will" of the Emperor that war be instituted against the United States in 1941. In reply, Tōjō emphasized that the question of imperial will was beside the point. The fact was that the Emperor had "consented, though reluctantly, to the war" as a result of the advice which he, Premier Tōjō, and the Supreme Command had given. According to Tōjō, the Emperor's "love for and desire for peace remained the same" right up to the very moment hostilities began and "even during the war his feelings remained the same." The imperial rescript declaring war, Tōjō said, contains words to this effect: "This war is indeed unavoidable and is against my own desires." ["It has been truly unavoidable and far from Our wishes that Our Empire has now been brought to cross swords with America and Britain."] This passage was included in the rescript, Tōjō declared, because the Emperor wanted his own feelings and the responsibility of the government to be a matter of record. IMTFE: Tōjō, 36780–81.

[78] See IMTFE: Bagge, 34561–64. Shigemitsu requested Bagge to get in touch with Suemasa Okamoto, the Japanese Minister in Stockholm. Several days after this conversation, Sakaya again called on the Swedish Minister to express the Foreign Minister's hope that Mr. Bagge would leave for Stockholm as soon as possible so as to lay the matter before the Swedish government.

[79] On the Tōgō-Bagge and Bagge-Okamoto phases described in the text which follows, see IMTFE: Bagge, 34561–64; Sakaya, 35455–57; and Tōgō, 35780. See also JFO MS: Ch. 17 (Bagge kōsaku), especially Mr. Okamoto's recollections entitled "Suēden ni okeru wahei dashin kōsaku no keii"; *Statements*: Tōgō #61672 and Okamoto #61477.

Tōgō has stated that he was never informed about the Shigemitsu-Bagge talks by either Shigemitsu or Premier Suzuki. This remark is a reference to the fact that Tōgō entered the Suzuki Cabinet several days after its formation. It was Suzuki, therefore, and not Tōgō, who inherited the Foreign Minister's portfolio from Shigemitsu.

Sakaya recalls that Tōgō said, on April 11, that he had not received a report on the matter as yet but that he personally desired the prompt return of peace. Tōgō asked Sakaya to request the Swedish Minister to bring his plan to realization.

was expected momentarily. Two days later, on April 13, the plane took off for Manchuria whence Mr. Bagge entrained for Europe via Siberia. It was thus early May before he arrived in Sweden and actually May 10 before he was able to take the next logical step in the negotiations which he hoped would lead to peace. On that day he paid a visit to the Japanese Minister in Stockholm, Mr. Suemasa Okamoto, and soon learned—much to his surprise—that no instructions had been received from Tokyo. Under the circumstances, Okamoto was powerless to do anything but cable the Foreign Office for information and guidance.[80] When this cable arrived in Tokyo, Foreign Minister Tōgō was immediately faced with a contradiction, for it quoted Mr. Bagge as saying that the Swedish government would be glad to sound out American intentions *if formally requested to do so* by the Japanese government. This struck the new Foreign Minister as being rather odd since his own understanding, based on what he had heard from Sakaya, was quite the opposite. This, plus the fact that Tōgō was in the dark as to how far the preceding cabinet had gone in the negotiations, resulted in a cable being sent to the effect that the Japanese government could not take any action until it had investigated the matter thoroughly.[81] When Okamoto relayed this reply to Bagge, the latter was very much disappointed but was forced to agree that there was nothing either he or Okamoto could do except stand by and watch the situation a while longer.

In the meantime, an incident had occurred in Stockholm that throws some light on why Tōgō took the cautious attitude he did. Some time before Tōgō's answer had arrived, Bagge had called on Okamoto with a rather disturbing bit of information and with an off-the-record but nonetheless formal request from Swedish Foreign Minister Günther. It seems that without Okamoto's knowledge the Japanese military attaché[82] assigned to Okamoto's legation had plunged into a so-called peace effort quite on his own initiative. The result was that a certain German, who was at that time the director of a petroleum company, had undertaken on behalf of the military attaché to request Prince Carl of the Swedish royal family to sponsor a peace-through-mediation move aimed at saving the Japanese army from the postwar abolition with which it was threatened by the Allies.[83] The prince had immediately

---

[80] Shortly after his return to Stockholm, Bagge had a "long talk" with American Ambassador Herschel V. Johnson. Bagge described what had taken place in Tokyo and "gave a comprehensive account of the whole peace problem" against the background of his experience in the Far East. IMTFE: Exh. 3558, *Bagge Aff.*, 3. (This portion of the affidavit was not read before the Tribunal.)

[81] By this time, military, political, and court circles had more or less agreed that only mediation by the Soviet Union could save Japan from unconditional surrender. Tōgō was therefore of the opinion that the Foreign Office would not have pursued the matter further even if it had had more information.

[82] Major General Makoto Ono.

[83] Although there is no mention of this, the assumption is that the Ono move also envisaged the *sine qua non*: preservation of Japan's imperial system.

informed the Foreign Office, and the Foreign Minister, in turn, had asked Bagge to request Minister Okamoto to put a stop to this independent and potentially disruptive venture. The matter was hurriedly cabled to Tōgō, who replied at once that the chief of the Army General Staff had promised to warn the officer in question to lay his unauthorized activities aside.

In the end, considerable uncertainty, a few definite obstacles, and another—and it was thought more positive—plan all conspired to shove the Bagge overture off the stage and into the wings. In short, by the time the Okamoto-Tōgō exchange had taken place, the Japanese government had already been committed to concentrating its efforts in another quarter and to trimming sail on a diplomatic course charted toward an uncertain but enticing port of call—the giant of the neutrals and Japan's unshakable shadow in Asia, the Soviet Union.

The day of reckoning was drawing near.

3

INVISIBLE TECHNIQUE

The Role of Suzuki and the Concept of Haragei

At 8:30 in the morning, on Easter Sunday, April 1, 1945, thousands of Allied fighting men hit the west coast beaches of Okinawa, teeing off the costly invasion offensive which was to result in the capture of this strategic gateway to the Japanese heartland. Four days later, in Tokyo, the Koiso Cabinet collapsed,[1] and on that same day, in Moscow, the Soviet government announced that it would not renew its Neutrality Pact with Japan.[2]

Unaware of the secret provisions of the agreement which had been signed at Yalta in February,[3] Japan's leaders were scarcely in position to fathom conclusively the ulterior purpose behind the Soviet announcement.[4] Molotov had issued only a very brief statement, and it had contained nothing they did not already know: The four-year-old Pact had been signed on April 13, 1941, before either the German invasion of the Soviet Union or the Japanese attack upon the United States and Britain. Since that time the situation had "basically altered." The re-

---

[1] Toward the latter part of March, Koiso realized that he would either have to reconstruct his cabinet or resign. When he raised the question in an audience with the Emperor, the latter properly replied that the Premier himself should give the matter careful consideration. Koiso's failure to obtain a voice in the direction of the war, the Miao Pin fiasco, and opposition on the part of his cabinet colleagues contributed to the fall of his cabinet. See Kido, "Nikki," 3/26–28/45 and 4/3–4/45; JFO MS: Ch. 11 (Doku-So wahei mondai . . .); Ch. 16 (Ryōhin kōsaku to sono ta no tai-Shi wahei kōsaku); Ch. 18 (Koiso naikaku no taijin to jūshin kaigi); and *Statements*: Suzuki #531, Yoshizumi #54484, Koiso #55906, Hiranuma #55127, and Shigemitsu 1/13/50.

[2] For the terms of the Neutrality Pact and for Molotov's statement of denunciation, see U.S. State Dept., *Bulletin*, XII (April 29, 1945), 811–12. See also JFO MS: Ch. 19 (Nichi-So chūritsu jōyaku no haiki tsūkoku) and Satō, *Futatsu no Roshia*, 201.

[3] For the text of the Yalta Agreement, see Appendix B. See also Stettinius, *Roosevelt and the Russians*, 92–93. Tōgō states that the Soviet Union had naturally never given "the slightest indication" that she had promised at Yalta to enter the war. In fact, Molotov had emphatically denied that Japan had been discussed at Yalta. *Statements*: Tōgō #50304.

[4] They were aware, of course, of the possibility that the Soviet Union might commit herself to entering the war at any time. See *Statements*: Tōgō #50304 and Shigemitsu 9/9/49; Millis (ed.), *The Forrestal Diaries*, 20.

sulting change in circumstances over the years had now made a prolongation of the Pact "impossible."[5]

In spite of the ominous undertones, a rereading of the Neutrality Pact and assurances obtained from Molotov encouraged the Japanese Foreign Office to believe that there was no reason for immediate worry.[6] By its terms the Pact was to remain in effect until April 1946. The arrangement would then automatically be renewed for another five-year period unless either of the parties thereto had given a full year's notice that it did not desire renewal.[7] Although the Soviet Union had now done just that, the Pact would clearly still be valid for another year.

Here were apparently twelve months of grace—certainly enough time for the experts to devise some means of mending Japan's diplomatic fences. Perhaps the Soviet Union was scheming to obtain greater concessions from Japan. A new pact, satisfying Soviet desires, might be the answer. At any rate, the most pressing problem at the moment—and one which required immediate attention—was the question of internal politics.

On April 4, the day before the formal resignation of his cabinet, Premier Koiso had gone to Marquis Kido with advance notice of his intention to give up the thankless task of heading His Majesty's govern-

[5] In addition to the references cited in footnote 2 above, see the *Nippon Times* for April 7, 1945 (announcement, 1), April 8, 1945 ("Press Comments," 3), and April 8, 1945 (editorial, 4).

[6] In response to an inquiry from Ambassador Satō toward the latter part of April 1945, Molotov affirmed that in spite of the Soviet Union's announcement of April 5 his government would continue to abide by the provision of the Neutrality Pact under which the two countries would enjoy neutral relations for the duration of the Pact's validity (expiration date: April 1946). See *Statements*: Tōgō #50304 and JFO MS: Ch. 19 (Nichi-So chūritsu jōyaku no haiki tsūkoku). See also the assurances made on June 24, 1945, by Soviet Ambassador Malik to former Premier Hirota (discussed in Ch. 6, below).

At the very time Molotov made the assurances (or immediately thereafter) Lieutenant General Kuzma Derevyanko was attached to Major General Charles A. Willoughby's G-2 staff in Manila in order to co-ordinate the pending Soviet operations in Manchuria with American plans for an invasion of Japan. See *Pacific Stars and Stripes* for May 29, 1950.

[7] Article III of the Neutrality Pact (signed April 13, 1941) reads as follows: "The present Pact comes into force from the day of its ratification by both Contracting Parties and remains valid for five years. In case neither of the Contracting Parties denounces the Pact one year before the expiration of the term, it will be considered automatically prolonged for the next five years." See U.S. State Dept., *Bulletin*, XII (April 29, 1945), 812.

Since the Pact was ratified by Japan on April 24, 1941 (*Facts on File*, 1941, 204 C), and by the Presidium of the Supreme Soviet on April 25, 1941 (*Keesing's Contemporary Archives*, 1940–43, 4604 D), the Pact's five-year period of validity extended from April 25, 1941, through April 25, 1946. The Soviet notice of nonintention to renew, given on April 5, 1945, made it known that the Soviet Union did not desire to extend the Pact for another five-year-period—a period which would have begun April 25, 1946, and would have extended through April 25, 1951.

ment. The day had been rainy and in the afternoon a three-and-a-half-hour air raid had littered the capital with fresh piles of rubble. In this setting the harassed Koiso had discussed his formula for the future. His cabinet had failed, he said, because of the differences which existed between the home front and the war front, between the government and the Supreme Command. To remedy the situation it would be necessary to revamp the existing organization and framework of government. What the country needed, he felt, was an Imperial Headquarters cabinet, an innovation which would permit the Premier and his colleagues to participate directly in the conduct of the war. Only thus, he emphasized, could there be any hope of coping with the crisis facing the nation.[8]

Although the senior statesmen would normally have been summoned to the palace at once to recommend a successor to the outgoing Premier, the problem posed by Koiso involved considerations of a broader nature. If the initiative behind Koiso's proposal rested with Imperial Headquarters, an unwise choice by the senior statesmen would create great difficulties for the new Premier and would probably result in an early collapse of his cabinet. Marquis Kido therefore took the "unprecedented action" of conferring with the War and Navy Ministers and the chiefs of the Army and Navy General Staffs in order to determine where they stood with respect to the so-called Koiso plan. Their reaction proved to be immediate and precise. The idea of establishing an Imperial Headquarters cabinet was unacceptable to the military authorities,[9] and so the question of who should become Japan's next Premier reached the senior statesmen after all.[10]

The record of their conference, which took place in the imperial audience chamber on April 5, 1945, portrays an atmosphere of tenseness.[11] Tōjō was attending his first meeting as a member of this distinguished group of former Premiers, and throughout the long session he was sharp and aggressive. The new cabinet, he said, must be the final cabinet. Frequent changes during wartime were not good. There were two contrary opinions current at the moment. One favored fighting to the end in order to enhance the nation's future; the other sponsored a restoration of peace by submitting to unconditional surrender. This ques-

---

[8] See IMTFE: Kido, 11385–87, 31118–21; *Statements*: Kido #61476; Kido, "Nikki," 4/3–5/45; and JFO MS: Ch. 18 (Koiso naikaku no taijin to jūshin kaigi).

[9] See *Statements*: Kido #61476.

[10] Kido told the IMTFE that Koiso's resignation made him realize the necessity of taking the first step toward ending the war. He felt the opportunity provided by the cabinet's collapse should not be lost under any circumstances since it was the chance of a lifetime. See IMTFE: Kido, 31118, and *Statements*: Kido #61476.

[11] The senior statesmen present were Konoye, Hiranuma, Hirota, Wakatsuki, Okada, and Tōjō. Kido, as Lord Keeper of the Privy Seal, and Baron Suzuki, as president of the Privy Council, also attended. The conference took place between 5:00 and 8:00 P.M. As usual, the Emperor was not present. IMTFE: Kido, 31122, and Kido, "Nikki," 4/5/45.

tion would have to be settled first. Then they could recommend a new Premier.[12]

Aroused by several remarks of Kido to the effect that there were antimilitarist feelings among the people and a tendency on their part to withhold their wholehearted co-operation and "to turn the other way," Tōjō struck back in bold terms. Unless care is taken, he said, "there is danger that the army will look the other way. If the army does that, the cabinet will collapse."[13] This reminder of the military's power to make or break a cabinet was a poignant warning.

In line with what Tōjō had said, a few of the senior statesmen contended that the alternatives, fighting on or seeking peace, should be discussed first, but others argued that that issue was really outside their authority. The question was simply who should be Japan's next, and it was hoped last, wartime Premier. Taken as a whole, the discussion which now followed was a muddle of many voices and many different points of view, but in the end—as always in the past—a specific criterion of selection[14] eventually emerged. Thus it was decided that the new cabinet must be one which would enjoy the confidence of the people.[15] Koiso's successor would have to be a man of courage who could comprehend the whole picture without being encumbered by commitments or alignments formulated in the past.[16] He need not necessarily be a military man on the active service list. He could be a retired general or admiral.

It so happened that in addition to the Lord Keeper of the Privy Seal there was one other person present at this conference who was not a senior statesman at all. This was Admiral Kantarō Suzuki, the president of the Privy Council, who had been invited to attend in accordance with a precedent set the year before at the time of Tōjō's collapse. The

[12] See IMTFE: Kido, 31122–23.

[13] IMTFE: Kido, 31132, 31141–42, 31271–73; *Statements*: Kido #61541. Kido has defined Tōjō's use of the phrase "turn the other way" as meaning an army coup d'état. IMTFE: Kido, 31121–22.

When asked if there were any indications that the army might do what he had implied, Tōjō said: "I cannot say there are none." Kido, "Nikki," 4/5/45.

Kido states that no one touched explicitly upon peace moves because a careless word spoken in Tōjō's presence would have aroused the army, which would then have taken countermeasures. He claims, however, that the senior statesmen had a tacit understanding with respect to peace moves (discussed at length in the text which follows). IMTFE: Kido, 31121–22, and *Statements*: Kido #61476.

[14] See IMTFE: Kido, 31120–21 and 31132.

[15] The English translation in the *Proceedings* errs in stating "the incoming Cabinet must be one that will place confidence in the people." (See the citation listed in the preceding footnote.)

[16] Incorporated into the criterion of selection upon the insistence of Prince Konoye. The purpose was to get a man who could act as a "free agent," someone who would not be bound, by virtue of his past service or associations, to promote the cause of a single group such as the army. The idea may possibly have been to exclude any former Premier from becoming Japan's last wartime Premier. See also footnote 18 below.

Privy Council, which had once wielded considerable power in advising the Throne, had failed to maintain its position of importance following the meteoric rise of the military in Japanese political life. The inclusion of Suzuki in the deliberations over a successor to Koiso thus partially revived the influence of the council and gave it, in effect, a new grasp upon its traditional role.

Suzuki, who had hovered on the point of death in 1936 after having been shot by a military fanatic, was universally respected for his personal courage and integrity and for his loyalty to the Throne. His name was synonymous with all those high virtues attributed to the best among the feudal retainers and *samurai* of old. As the senior statesmen now turned to the specific purpose of their meeting, the admiral ventured to suggest that since all of the former Premiers had both the responsibility and the resolution to die for their country, Koiso's successor should be chosen from among the senior statesmen. "Since the physical strain is great," Suzuki said, "I should like to ask Prince Konoye, who is the youngest, to step forward."

The result was far from Suzuki's expectations and desires, for neither the prince nor any of the others rose to the occasion. It had been Konoye, in fact, who had introduced the idea that the new Premier should be a man who would not be encumbered by commitments or alignments formulated in the past. Since Konoye had already headed three different cabinets, he could scarcely be considered a "free agent." The obvious answer was the one immediately offered by Baron Hiranuma who chose this opportunity to nominate Admiral Suzuki,[17] the only man present who could truly qualify under the criterion of selection established earlier in the conference.[18]

While on the surface there was nothing extraordinary about this seemingly haphazard development, the nomination of Suzuki actually represented a rather nebulous decision which had been taking shape in the minds of several of the senior statesmen for some time. Hiranuma's endorsement of Suzuki was openly contrary to the army's long-standing insistence upon the Premier's being a general in active service and was

[17] See IMTFE: Okada, 29266; Kido, "Nikki," 4/5/45; Uchida, *Fūsetsu gojūnen*, 355; and JFO MS: Ch. 18 (Koiso naikaku no taijin to jūshin kaigi). On page 235 of his *Kaikoroku*, Admiral Okada states that he nominated Suzuki, but according to his IMTFE affidavit and Kido's diary this was actually not the case. Konoye and Wakatsuki "seconded" the nomination. Kido says he also lent his support since it was his opinion that a cabinet headed by Suzuki would enjoy the confidence of the people. See IMTFE: Kido, 31121–22, 31138, 31141; *Statements*: Kido #61541; and IMTFE: Tanaka, 2083–84.

[18] According to Hiranuma, some of the *jūshin* may have emphasized the "free agent" concept as a means of furthering Suzuki's nomination. (*Statements*: #55127.) Kido states that Konoye's insistence upon a man like Suzuki was aimed at making it possible to end the war. Be that as it may, it is obvious that Japan would have found it immensely more difficult to terminate hostilities had an army general on active service become Premier.

therefore consistent with the movement away from army domination
that had been launched the year before when the Koiso-Yonai coalition
had been formed. Thus, in spite of Suzuki's own *vigorous* objections[19]
and Tōjō's vain attempt to turn the tide in favor of a general on the
active service list,[20] the senior statesmen voted to support the nomination
of Admiral Baron Kantarō Suzuki, Imperial Japanese Navy, Retired.

Following their adjournment, the former Premiers proceeded to a
near-by room in the palace where a dinner had been prepared for their
pleasure.[21] Toward the end of the meal, Marquis Kido led Suzuki back
to the conference chamber for a brief and somewhat cryptic private
talk.[22] Without wasting words, Kido urged the admiral to lay his reluctance aside and to organize a cabinet at once. Suzuki referred again
to his own lack of confidence in his ability to undertake the duties of
the premiership, but Kido persisted. "Japan's situation has become so
critical," he declared, "that I, as Lord Keeper of the Privy Seal, must
implore you to make a firm decision to save the nation." These words
so impressed Suzuki that he promised to assume the burden of the
premiership in the event of an imperial mandate to form a cabinet.[23]

Kido readily admits that he did not say to Suzuki in so many words:
"Your mission is to terminate the war and lead Japan back to peace,"

[19] IMTFE: Kido, 31138–39. See also Okada, *Kaikoroku*, 235, for a description
of Suzuki's feelings with respect to politics.

[20] Field Marshal Hata was the man Tōjō had in mind.

[21] On page 11391 of IMTFE: *Proceedings* (Prosecution Exh. 1282, *Extract from
the Kido Diary*, as corrected), Kido is quoted as follows: "At the conclusion of the
meeting, the Senior Statesmen were asked to affix their private seals." Some 20,000
mimeographed pages later (IMTFE: *Proceedings*, 31142), Kido, speaking through his
affidavit (Item 286), makes the following statement: "The prosecution exhibit 1282
as corrected says: 'At the conclusion of the meeting, the senior statesmen were asked
to affix their private seals.' This is not translated properly. The correct translation
is 'At the conclusion of the meeting the senior statesmen were given a dinner by the
Emperor.'" (His Majesty did not attend—an impression one might not obtain from
the statement just quoted.)

Although the author found Kido to be correct and found the statement in his diary
("Nikki," 4/5/45) to be substantially the same as that presented in Item 286, the
author also discovered that the error made by the Prosecution appeared, in even
grosser form, in one of the partial translations (of the "Nikki") in the possession of
the Kido family. In the latter document, Kido is represented as having said, "Following the close of the conference, the minutes of the conference were initialled by His
Majesty."

The two errors cited here command careful consideration, for both fit perfectly
into the context of Kido's other remarks. Only when the diary is brought to light is
it clear that all Kido really said was that following the conference the *jūshin* were
favored with an imperial banquet which His Majesty did not attend.

[22] See IMTFE: Kido, 31143, and *Statements*: Kido #62131, #61541, and #61476.

[23] Kido has stated that he also suggested the retention of Shigemitsu as Foreign
Minister since the latter was a peace advocate and very well informed. Suzuki was
amenable but later found that outgoing Premier Koiso was opposed to the idea. Suzuki
explained the circumstances to Kido and said that he planned to ask Tōgō to accept
the post. Kido did not raise any objections since Tōgō was not considered a war
advocate. See the citations in the preceding footnote.

but he cites two reasons for his vagueness. In the first place, it was strictly contrary to custom for the Privy Seal to lay down conditions relative to the formation of a cabinet, thereby creating a situation where the candidate would either have to accept the conditions or resign himself to the fact that he probably would not be recommended to the Throne.[24] Kido therefore portrays his tête-à-tête with Suzuki as nothing more than an informal discussion in which their exchange of words simply reflected a mutual expression of their respective views and feelings. In the second place, Kido reasons that since Suzuki's frame of mind was the same as his own there was really no need for him to speak openly of peace as the desired goal. Suzuki, in other words, would *intuitively* understand[25] what was in the Privy Seal's mind and what his own mission should be once he became Premier.

Shortly after the Kido-Suzuki conversation took place, the mandate came and the old admiral bowed to the imperial will—but not without the ultimate in appeals.[26] When he was received by the Emperor at 10:00 P.M. that same evening (April 5) and commanded to form a cabinet, Suzuki tried in vain to convince the sovereign that his complete lack of experience in political affairs, his advanced age, and his deafness—so acute that he feared occasions might arise when he would fail to comprehend His Majesty's own words—all rendered him unfit for the post to which he had been recommended. But again his protests missed their mark. The Emperor, who was particularly fond of the venerable Suzuki, merely replied, "Your unfamiliarity with politics is of no concern, nor does it matter that you are hard of hearing. Therefore, accept this command."[27] Under the circumstances Suzuki could do nothing but accede to the imperial wishes.[28]

Within hours after receiving the imperial mandate, Suzuki consulted a number of senior statesmen[29] to obtain their advice on whom he should

[24] Kido notes that his conversation with Suzuki was unusual in the extreme and that his action at this time was prompted by the crisis facing the nation. Had he employed such tactics at any time prior to the period in question he "would have been criticized very severely" and his action would have been denounced as an unconstitutional exercise of authority. See *Statements*: Kido #61476.

[25] A reference to *haragei*. See footnotes 48 and 49 below and the text corresponding thereto.

[26] See JFO MS: Ch. 20 (Suzuki naikaku no seiritsu), especially the memorandum written by Suzuki's eldest son (Hajime Suzuki) entitled "Shūsen to chichi."

[27] "Seiji ni keiken ga nakutomo yoroshii, mimi ga kikoenakutomo yoroshii kara, yare."

[28] "When I was called upon to take over as PREMIER, I myself had been opposed to ever becoming PREMIER; I had never wanted to be PREMIER but under the circumstances I felt there was nothing I could do but accept the post." *Statements*: Suzuki #531 (ATIS transl.).

[29] Okada, Konoye, Hiranuma, and Wakatsuki. The fact that Suzuki's cabinet was supported by the senior statesmen resulted in its being called the "senior statesmen's cabinet." Of those consulted by Suzuki, Okada played the most prominent role in advising the new Premier. Okada's son-in-law, Hisatsune Sakomizu, became Suzuki's chief cabinet secretary.

Hiranuma felt that a powerful cabinet would emerge only if the senior statesmen

include in his cabinet.[30] He did this because he considered himself an "amateur in politics." Yet when it came to the important post of Foreign Minister, Suzuki made up his own mind.[31] According to his postwar testimony, he personally selected Shigenori Tōgō, not because he knew the man intimately but because he felt that Tōgō, Foreign Minister at the time of Pearl Harbor, "had been opposed to the war from the very beginning and . . . had resigned from the Tōjō Cabinet as a measure of opposition to Tōjō's dictatorial and high-handed policies."[32] In view of his own long-standing belief that Japan "could not be successful in a war against the United States and England," he considered it his "duty," Suzuki said, to exert himself to bring hostilities to an end and for that reason chose "a man who was clearly opposed to the war" to become Foreign Minister in his cabinet.[33]

But the Premier-designate had trouble convincing "his man" to join

---

took a hand in recommending the more important ministers. See IMTFE: Suzuki, 35590–91; Kido, "Nikki," 4/5/45; *Statements*: Sakomizu #62004; JFO MS: Ch. 20 (Suzuki naikaku no seiritsu); Okada, *Kaikoroku*, 237; and USAAF, *Mission Accomplished*, 36. For Kido's earlier views on the role the *jūshin* might play in the event of a cabinet change, see the text corresponding to footnote 43, Ch. 1, above.

[30] Needless to say, the Japanese army was the decisive factor and it was not until army approval had been received that Suzuki was able to complete the formation of his cabinet. For a rare public admission of the army's role, see the *Nippon Times* for April 9, 1945.

According to army testimony, outgoing War Minister Sugiyama recommended General Anami for the post of War Minister *after* Suzuki had endorsed the following army conditions: The cabinet will (1) prosecute the war to the bitter end, (2) effect a settlement of the problem of army-navy unification, and (3) exert every effort toward the complete reorganization of the nation for the prosecution of the war. See *Statements*: Nagai #61885, Hayashi #61436, Sakomizu #62004, Shirai #54472, and Yoshizumi #54484.

[31] Okada states that Suzuki wanted Hirota to become Foreign Minister but that Hirota recommended Tōgō instead. (Okada, *Kaikoroku*, 237.) See also footnote 23 above (the possible retention of Shigemitsu as Foreign Minister).

Since the three candidates were all former ambassadors to Moscow, it is quite possible (in view of the developments which had already occurred or which were even then looming on the horizon) that Suzuki was looking for a man with knowledge of Soviet affairs and past experience in the Soviet Union. All of the evidence available points to the conclusion that once the Suzuki Cabinet began functioning a rapprochement with the Soviet Union would be attempted.

[32] See IMTFE: Suzuki, 35590–91, and USAAF, *Mission Accomplished*, 36. According to Tōgō, a disagreement of views developed early in the war between himself and Premier Tōjō over the role of diplomacy and the conduct of the war. He also disagreed with Tōjō on China policy. Finally, these differences came to a head and Tōgō resigned (on September 1, 1942) over the Greater East Asia Ministry question. See IMTFE: Tōgō, 35740–42; Kido, "Nikki," 9/1/42; and IMTFE: Exh. 127, *Cabinet Secretariat Personnel Record of Shigenori Tōgō*, 787–91.

[33] Tōgō testified before the IMTFE that he had been opposed to the war before its outbreak and that his 1945 efforts to end the conflict were an extension of his earlier views. He also declared that on New Year's Day 1942 he had instructed his staff to study ways and means of ending the war so that the Foreign Office would not fail "to seize the chance" when it came. See IMTFE: Tōgō, 35776–77, and JFO MS: Ch. 3 (Sensō shidō ni kan shi Tōgō gaishō to Tōjō shushō to no shōtotsu). For statements in corroboration of Tōgō's testimony, see IMTFE: Sakomizu, 35604–6 and 35609–10; Matsudaira, 35597; and Suzuki, 35591–92.

the cabinet.[34] Tōgō had rushed to Tokyo from the mountain resort town of Karuizawa with Suzuki's telephoned request that he become Foreign Minister still ringing in his ears. As soon as he was closeted alone with the new Premier, Tōgō began asking a lot of questions. He was primarily interested in Suzuki's opinions on Japan's capabilities, for these, he felt, would inevitably provide a clue to Suzuki's intentions. If he were going to assume the heavy responsibilities of diplomacy, Tōgō wanted to be sure that the Premier would support an effort on his part to end the war. Although the two men talked for a long time, Tōgō at length refused to join the cabinet.[35] Suzuki, taken aback by Tōgō's stand, proposed that they discuss the matter again the following day. During the next twenty-four hours, Tōgō received representations from various quarters[36] urging him to enter the cabinet so as to "enlighten" the Premier: Suzuki, so the argument went, was an old man who needed guidance; he could not possibly know all of the details of Japan's critical military situation. Whatever warlike views he might hold at the moment could be changed once he learned the facts. Suzuki, in other words, would listen to reason.

One of Tōgō's callers said, in effect, that Suzuki could not just openly declare he was going to end the war, but (and it was a significant "but") that was clearly his intention.[37] Coming from the new chief cabinet secretary, this was a fairly reliable and convincing statement. All in all, the views expressed by his callers had their effect, and the somewhat reluctant Tōgō agreed to meet with Suzuki once more. During the course of a long conversation, Suzuki ultimately accepted, without reservation, Tōgō's position with respect to Japan's prospects and indicated that, as Foreign Minister, Tōgō would be free to act in accordance with the opinions he had expressed at their meeting the previous day.[38] As a

[34] For the details which are described in the text which follows, see IMTFE: Tōgō, 35778–80; Sakomizu, 35604–5; Suzuki, 35591–92; Matsudaira, 35595–97; *Statements:* Tōgō #50304 and Sakomizu #62004; Okada, *Kaikoroku,* 237; and JFO MS: Ch. 20 (Suzuki naikaku no seiritsu).

[35] Suzuki had told Tōgō that he believed the war could be continued two or three years more. Since Tōgō felt it was "imperative to end the war at once," he refused to join the cabinet.

[36] Tōgō's callers included the senior statesmen Okada and Hirota, Minister of the Imperial Household Tsuneo Matsudaira, Chief Cabinet Secretary Sakomizu, and Marquis Yasumasa Matsudaira, the aide and private secretary to Marquis Kido. See *Statements:* Tōgō #50304.

[37] In recalling the difficulties he had had convincing Tōgō to enter his cabinet, Suzuki declared that the conditions prevailing at the time had prevented him from speaking openly of ending the war. Consequently, he felt that Tōgō might not have realized, from their conversations, that their opinions and diagnoses were the same. IMTFE: Suzuki, 35591–92.

[38] On June 7, 1945, Tōgō told Admiral Sōkichi Takagi that he had agreed to enter the Suzuki Cabinet only after he had reached an understanding with the new Premier that henceforth the Supreme Council for the Direction of the War would (1) attack the problem of the war's prospects and (2) would formulate a counterplan (i.e., a plan to terminate the war) if it found that hostilities could not be continued at least

result, Tōgō submitted to Suzuki's request for his services and immediately assumed, once again, the duties with which he had been charged at the time of Pearl Harbor.

Months later, when Japan's surrender on board the *Missouri* was already "dead news," Suzuki had occasion to recall the circumstances surrounding the formation of his cabinet. When asked about the imperial mandate, the admiral declared he "did not receive any direct order from the EMPEROR" with respect to terminating the war, yet he clearly comprehended from what the Emperor did say that His Majesty was very much concerned over the plight of Japan and her people. The death of civilians due to bombing and the great losses on the battlefields of the Pacific and of Asia weighed heavily on the Emperor's mind. As Premier-designate, he was therefore "given to understand" that the Emperor desired him to make every effort to bring the war to a conclusion (i.e., make peace) as quickly as possible. And that, he affirmed, represented his purpose from the very beginning.[39]

Actually, the trail along which Suzuki moved as Premier is not so clearly blazed as one would suppose. Immediately before his elevation to the premiership Suzuki's frame of mind, which was being subjected to a good deal of probing by various interested parties, was quite contrary to a termination of the war—at least to a termination which envisaged a voluntary cessation of hostilities and an outright acceptance of Allied terms. In talking with Prince Konoye and others toward the latter part of March 1945, Suzuki had frankly indicated what he apparently considered was Japan's best, or only, course. The revelation was in the form of an anecdote which had as its hero the greatest of all the Tokugawa clan, Iyeyasu. It seems that toward the end of the sixteenth century, during one of the numerous wars of the period, the forces under Iyeyasu were defeated at Mikata-ga-hara by the army of a rival lord named Takeda. Although his top retainers crowded around their chagrined leader to urge him to save the day by asking for terms and concluding peace, Iyeyasu refused to listen to their counsel and immediately issued the order to withdraw to his castle. Once there, he amazed his followers and Takeda's pursuing army by throwing open the gates. Taking a defiant stand in front of the main approach to the castle, the unpredictable Tokugawa lord taunted the confused Takeda: "If you want to come, *come!*" Knowing that his adversary was adept at craft

---

three more years (Suzuki's contention). See "Takagi hiroku: Tōgō gaishō dan" in JFO MS: Ch. 28 (Sensō kansui yōkō no kettei). See also *Statements*: Tōgō #50304.

[39] See *Statements*: Suzuki #531 and JFO MS: Ch. 20 (Suzuki naikaku no seiritsu), especially "Shūsen no hyōjō" (Suzuki Kantarō kōjutsu). Suzuki's testimony makes it clear that USSBS (*Japan's Struggle to End the War*, 12–13) is incorrect in stating that "*in extremis* the peace-makers would have peace, and peace on any terms. This was the specific injunction of the Emperor to Suzuki on becoming premier which was known to all members of the Cabinet."

and trickery, Takeda reluctantly signaled for his men to withdraw, leaving the defeated Iyeyasu untouched. Only when it was too late did Takeda learn that Iyeyasu had indeed tricked him—but with nothing more than Tokugawa daring. Had Takeda attacked, Iyeyasu and his retainers would have been slaughtered. The castle had been empty.[40]

This story, to which Suzuki was particularly partial, convinced many who heard it from his lips that the old admiral favored trying Iyeyasu's sham tactics on America and Britain when they came knocking at the gates of Japan.[41] Here was a rather different Suzuki from the one described in the *Nippon Times* on April 7, 1945, as a man who would be "a pillar of tested stability and soundness, of judicious orthodoxy and sanity, amidst the storm of any emergency."

The very senior statesmen's conference at which Suzuki was nominated is another case in point, for throughout the session Suzuki said nothing which could lead anyone to believe that he might have been thinking in terms of ending the war. He even seems to have exceeded the possible requirements of "strategy" by telling the former Premiers that they must first decide to prosecute the war to the fullest and only then pick a successor to Koiso, for their choice could not be suitable unless it fell upon a man who was willing to go all the way.

Somewhat prior to the "secret arrangement" which brought Shigenori Tōgō into the cabinet, the new Premier issued a statement to the press that was as picturesque as it was sincere. Making no attempt to gloss over the crisis threatening the nation, Suzuki patriotically promised that he would give his all to the state and would himself take up a stand in the foremost line of her defenders. Should death be his reward, he expected Japan's "one hundred million" people, acting as the shield of the state, to surge forward across his prostrate body to protect and preserve the Emperor and the imperial land![42]

In his opening speech to the 87th Extraordinary Session of the Diet, which convened on June 9,[43] Suzuki went perhaps even further than he

[40] See Uchida, *Fūsetsu gojūnen*, 355–56. It would appear that both Konoye and Tōgō (who heard Suzuki repeat the Iyeyasu story in early June) discounted this excess on Suzuki's part on the assumption that once the Premier learned the facts he would listen to reason. They may also have felt that only a man of Suzuki's character (and there were very few so bold) could execute the *volte-face* which would permit Japan to escape the ruin toward which the military were driving the country. See Tōgō, "Shūsen gaikō," in *Kaizō*, XXXI (November 1950), 128.

[41] Another interpretation is that Suzuki merely repeated the story by way of saying that Japan's leaders, while secretly engaged in seeking a termination of the war, should follow Iyeyasu's strategy, that is, they should not reveal Japan's weakness to the enemy.

[42] For the English text of the Suzuki statement (issued following the investiture of his cabinet on Saturday, April 7, 1945), see the *Nippon Times* for April 9, 1945. For the Japanese text, see the Tokyo *Asahi Shimbun* for April 8, 1945.

[43] See JFO MS: Ch. 29 (Dai hachijūnana rinji gikai). The Diet was in session from June 9 through June 13, 1945. This is the same Diet which is erroneously cited

had in any of his earlier pronouncements. He pictured the war as having been forced upon an unwilling Japan by an enemy who threatened the very existence, the basic polity, and the national aim of the Japanese Empire (peace in the world through the universal acceptance of the principles of moral justice). As long as the threat remained, Japan would have no choice other than to continue to defend herself to the last. Unconditional surrender was out of the question. It would result in the "destruction" of the national polity and the "ruin" of the Japanese race. There was only one path Japan could follow and that was "to fight to the very end."[44]

These sentiments were as clearly in tune with Suzuki's earlier statements as they were wholly out of line with the goal toward which he supposedly bent every effort from the moment he became Premier. Although Konoye, Okada, Wakatsuki, Yonai, and Hiranuma were all involved in Suzuki's elevation to the premiership, there seems to have been hardly more than a tacit agreement among them to support the aging admiral.[45] Indeed, it is difficult to see how there could have been much more than just that. Whereas Konoye, Okada, Wakatsuki, and Yonai were committed in varying degrees to an early termination of the war, Baron Hiranuma was of a different orientation entirely. During the conference on April 5, Hiranuma did nothing but gush the nationalistic and jingoistic sentiments typical of the times: There was no other way than to fight to the very end . . . Japan must have a man who would fight it out . . . The senior statesmen could not recommend a peace advocate . . . He was strongly opposed to the peace argument that called for a cessation of hostilities.[46] In other words, it would appear

---

as having met in early April (Kase, *Journey to the Missouri*, 150) and as having convened in late June (Zacharias, *Secret Missions*, 369).

[44] For the Japanese text, see the Tokyo *Asahi Shimbun* for June 10, 1945. See also the *Nippon Times* for June 14, 1945 (editorial) and June 16, 1945 (p. 1). As a consequence of the error noted in the preceding footnote, Mr. Kase has presented the above speech as having been made a full two months before it was delivered and Admiral Zacharias has implied that the speech was given a full month later than it was.

[45] See IMTFE: Kido, 31120; Okada, 29270–71; and Exh. 3229, *Okada Aff.*, J text, 7 (this section of the affidavit was rejected by the Tribunal); JFO MS: Ch. 18 (Koiso naikaku no taijin to jūshin kaigi); *Statements:* Hiranuma #55127, Kido #61476 and #62131; and Uchida, *Fūsetsu gojūnen*, 355. Disregarding his objections of the year before (see footnote 5, Ch. 2, above), Yonai endorsed the proposal to nominate Suzuki when the matter was presented to him prior to the conference. (As outgoing co-Premier and Navy Minister in the Koiso Cabinet, Yonai was ineligible to attend the *jūshin* conference in his capacity as a senior statesman.)

[46] Hiranuma has stated that his views at this time were based on his belief that Koiso's successor must be a man capable of continuing the war if continuation proved necessary. In other words, his statements "did not mean that we positively had to continue the war." (Hiranuma's position should be measured against the concept of *haragei*, which is discussed at length in the text which follows.) See *Statements:* Hiranuma #55127; IMTFE: Kido, 31123, 31127, 31134; Okada, 29270–71; and Exh. 3229, *Okada Aff.*, J text, 7–9 (submitted in evidence but rejected by the Tribunal).

that Hiranuma recommended Suzuki for a purpose clearly different from that foremost in the minds of the men who belonged to what might be called the Konoye faction.

One possible explanation of this obvious contradiction is that both Hiranuma and Konoye were essentially concerned with choosing a man of character—a man of sincerity and integrity—a man of courage and conviction. In this sense the two protagonists could easily have agreed that only a man of Suzuki's stature could possibly cope with the problems facing Japan. Such an agreement need not have precluded a difference of opinion on their part with respect to the manner in which Suzuki should face the crisis which was rapidly taking shape at this time.

Additional light is thrown on the contradiction behind his nomination in a statement made by Suzuki some months after the war was finally brought to an end. The imperial desire to see hostilities terminated as quickly as possible, Suzuki explained, had put him in a "very difficult position," since an open and aboveboard endeavor on his part to carry out the Emperor's wishes would probably have invited assassination from those opposed to any movement directed at negotiating peace. He had thus been forced to play a deceptive and often inconsistent role. On the one hand, he had found it necessary to promote an "increase in the war effort" and "a determination to fight on" while, on the other hand, he had simultaneously tried to exploit diplomatic channels in an attempt "to negotiate with other countries" to end the fighting.[47]

To a certain extent, Suzuki's quandary as Premier is linked with a skeleton in the closet of Japanese history that pops out time and again to confuse the issue and play havoc with the ledger of events. This is the concept of *haragei*,[48] the art of the hidden and invisible technique— the wary and prudent approach—against which the historian must judge a man's character and intentions.[49]

"To say what we thought would have been to cut off our noses to spite our faces."

[47] See USAAF, *Mission Accomplished*, 36; USSBS, *Japan's Struggle to End the War*, 6; *Statements*: Suzuki #531 and Sakomizu 5/3/49. Suzuki's remarks may explain why he inserted a passage in his Diet speech to the effect that, years earlier, while on a visit to San Francisco with the fleet, he had said the United States and Japan would incur the "wrath of the gods" if they ever went to war with each other. (It has been suggested that Suzuki was here hinting that the time had come to make peace.) See *Statements*: Sakonji #58226 and #61339; JFO MS: Ch. 29 (Dai hachijūnana rinji gikai).

[48] The word is a compound composed of two characters: *hara* (stomach—in this case, mind, intention, spirit) and *gei* (art, accomplishments). A man who "uses" *haragei* is a man who says one thing but means another.

[49] Chief Cabinet Secretary Sakomizu has described the relationship between Premier Suzuki and War Minister Anami as one in which each man, at the bottom of his heart, understood the other's mind most sympathetically. Neither spoke his true thoughts more frankly because that form of directness is "not the Oriental way." If the political stage is regarded in terms of the drama, both Suzuki and Anami were "consummate actors." (This is *haragei*.) *Statements*: Sakomizu 5/3/49. For another example of *haragei*, see Toyoda, *Saigo no teikoku kaigun*, 214–15.

"Our mouths could not speak what our 'stomachs' felt."

Why?

"Had we laid bare our hearts and revealed our firm beliefs, we would never have been able to achieve our goal."

This is the rationale behind the practice of *haragei*, an approach to action that derides as it damns any dissection aimed at establishing truth. Yet, here, in essence, is the one explanation which fits any case and covers every seeming contradiction. The obvious question is simply this: "If so many of those who moved within the circle of the ruling elite were addicted to practicing *haragei*, just how could there ever have been any confidence or understanding among them?"

When someone said, "Let us stand together and die together to the last man," did he mean what he said or was he trying to indicate to a possibly sympathetic listener that he really wanted to see the war ended without delay? If this were the case and if the listener inwardly agreed with the idea, there would somehow be a meeting of minds in spite of the contradiction posed by the speaker's words. At least, that was the assumption.

When someone said, "The sooner we terminate the conflict the better," did he really want to help end the war or was he treacherously inviting an unwary suspect to write his own one-way ticket to prison merely by dropping his guard?

Since September 2, 1945, the day on which Japan formally surrendered, the behavioristic pattern called *haragei* has ever more frequently been cited in explanation of the lengths to which the members of the so-called peace party were forced to go to promote their purpose. The concept has also been offered as an excuse by those whose wartime utterances belie what they now say were their real feelings and intentions at the time.

When a man defends himself by "standing" on his *haragei*, his explanation is perhaps good enough and correct enough and not necessarily damaging to his character, but beyond a point evaluation inevitably becomes a question of degree. What are the limits of camouflage beyond which no man can go, no matter how noble his ultimate aim, and still remain a man of integrity and courage? How consistently and for how long can a man say one thing and mean another and still not compromise his position? Where does the feint end and the thrust begin?

In the light of *haragei*, the efforts of a number of end-the-war advocates defy easy analysis. Because of its very ambiguity, a plea of *haragei* invites the suspicion that in questions of politics and diplomacy a conscious reliance upon this "art of bluff" may have constituted a purposeful deception predicated upon a desire to play both ends against the middle. While this judgment does not accord with the much-lauded character of Admiral Suzuki, the fact remains that from the moment he became Premier until the day he resigned no one could ever be quite sure of what Suzuki would do or say next.

Perhaps the old Premier was really an end-the-war advocate who was simply misunderstood, even by some of his closest associates,[50] because of the indirect and seemingly inconsistent approach he was forced to take. Perhaps Suzuki's interpretation of the Emperor's desire to see the war ended was warped by his outlook as a *samurai*. He might very well have been working for a termination of the war—a termination of the war which would grow out of a telling victory of the kind the military promised to achieve on Japan's very shores—a termination of the war which would be far different from the one envisaged by the enemy. Perhaps the passage of time further erased the already dimming clarity of this old man's memory, thus causing him—in later months—to disregard the very real possibility that he had only gradually acknowledged the necessity of ending the war after he had been in office long enough to gain a thorough understanding of the seriousness of the crisis facing the nation.[51] This, in fact, would seem to be the case, for shortly after Suzuki assumed office various studies were undertaken to ascertain Japan's prospects. The results, which clearly showed Japan's impossible position, are known to have made a deep impression upon the Premier. Although the solution to the riddle of Suzuki remains a matter of personal choice, one thing is certain. Whatever his personal motives may have been, the new Premier—to the frequent despair of his colleagues and to his own subsequent embarrassment—very largely succeeded in "fooling" a number of people.[52]

[50] In mid-June 1945, while discussing a plan to negotiate peace through the good offices of the Soviet Union, Navy Minister Yonai expressed his doubts to Marquis Kido concerning Suzuki's intentions. Yonai, who belonged to the end-the-war faction, felt that Suzuki fully intended to continue the war. Kido later took the matter up with the Premier who "laughingly replied that he had the same idea about Yonai." Kido reports that it was in this way that he discovered the two men were of the same mind, that is, they both wanted to end the war. Kido considered this a piece of good fortune for the accomplishment of the task which lay ahead and managed to allay the doubts Suzuki and Yonai entertained with respect to each other. (Here is an example of what can result when two men use *haragei*, for this seems to be the most likely explanation of the misunderstanding between the Premier and his Navy Minister.) See IMTFE: Kido, 31153–54; *Statements:* Kido #61476; Shigemitsu, *Shōwa no dōran*, 281.

[51] A reliable source who held an important position at the time has confidentially stated to the author that it was only after these studies were completed (*ca.* early June) that Suzuki at last realized that the responsibility of ending the war rested on his shoulders. In this connection, see Okada, *Kaikoroku*, 237; *Statements:* Sakonji #61339 and #58226; and the Tōgō statement quoted in footnote 52 below.

That Suzuki was not committed to ending the war from the moment he entered office gains support from a slip of the tongue made by a person (name withheld) who served in the cabinet: "it would be difficult to explain how the Premier came to feel the necessity of terminating the war."

As late as June 8, 1945, a full two months after Suzuki had assumed the premiership, Marquis Kido was still unable to discern any trend on the cabinet's part leading to a termination of the war. *Statements:* Kido #61541.

[52] In spite of the Premier's statements to the contrary, Tōgō believes that Suzuki *felt* the war had to be ended as quickly as possible, but Tōgō does not think that Suzuki realized the extent to which Japan's war potential had deteriorated. He also

As the Suzuki Cabinet entered office in the spring of 1945, the war in Europe was in its final stages. For Japan both time and space had long since run out. The hammer blows delivered by the Allied military forces in the Pacific had completely chiseled away the outer walls of Japan's island outposts of defense, leaving nothing between the victors and near-vanquished except short reaches of sea and sky. Both these routes to final victory were thoroughly controlled by Allied air and naval arms. Imperial General Headquarters was powerless to do anything except continue to ride roughshod over the minds of the multitude. The little lie gave way to the big lie, and the people of Japan—ever loyal and obedient—were led to believe that the rapidly worsening situation was in reality merely part of a grand plan conceived and regulated by their own invincible army and navy. It was the old story all over again. Like the inveterate gambler who always *knows* he is going to turn his luck with the next bet, so too did Imperial Headquarters proclaim that the "decisive battle" to be fought on Japan's shores would bring the nation its long-sought victory. There was no denial of what lay in store but rather a firm prophecy of a grand and glorious triumph for "Great Japan" when the "golden opportunity" should at last be at hand.

Although Imperial Headquarters continued to enjoy success in deceiving the masses, the propagandists failed to confuse the more informed of the ruling elite—men whose understanding of the actual situation was now so well founded that they could not be fooled any longer, if, indeed, they ever had been. The difficulty was that those who held official positions were fighting not only the battle of the homeland but also the battle of their individual destinies. To save the nation they would very likely bring ruin to their own doorsteps, for at least a few of the key figures at this time were the same men who had been in power prior to and at the time of Pearl Harbor. Although they may have been opposed to the war from the very beginning and may have been clandestinely planning to terminate the conflict at the earliest opportunity, not one of them had ever resigned his position of responsibility in protest over the actions of his government to which he supposedly inwardly took exception.[53]

---

does not believe that Suzuki anticipated such a rapid development of the military crisis. According to Tōgō, "there is much evidence to show that the majority of senior statesmen shared his opinion—at least up until July. Also, a premier has many delicate matters to handle. It may be that occasionally he was obliged to say things he did not mean. Although he may have been vacillating at times, I believe, I can safely say that his determination to conclude an early peace remained unchanged." *Statements:* Tōgō #50304 (ATIS transl.). For the opposite point of view, see *Statements:* Amano #54480 and Takeshita #50025-A.

[53] Tōgō told the IMTFE that after he became Foreign Minister in the Tōjō Cabinet he gave thought to the question of whether he could stop the march toward war by resigning but that by the end of October or early November (1941) he came to the conclusion that he "could not save the situation then by resigning." In retrospect, Tōgō

This issue, like that of *haragei*, is fettered to individual bias.[54] Study and analysis seldom produce satisfaction, for the explanation which is commonly offered can scarcely be supported with more than circumstantial evidence. Many of the ruling elite who might have resigned and might thereby have removed themselves from a postwar taint of guilt felt that such action on their part would have served no useful purpose. Resignation could have brought on assassination, a loss with no equivalent gain. Their idea, so they say, was to stay in office against the day when they could do some good.[55] In office, they had access to the highly classified material and confidential information without which they could never have given stature to their opposition to the war. Their plan was thus to remain in the center of things as long as they could in the hope of being able to make their influence felt and, if a favorable opportunity presented itself, of being able to end the war as quickly as possible. A few now realize that their resignations might have given them a clear record in the eyes of the Allies, but at the time they felt that by resigning they would have been running away from their true beliefs, thereby defeating their purpose. They do not see that a "clear record" would have done them or their country any good. They judge that they traveled a wiser path and made a more courageous choice, even though their continuance in office rendered them suspect and forced them, at times, to bow to the demands of the Japanese military.

This explanation must either be accepted on intuition or be rejected without proof. The arguments for it are as convincing as those against it. To attack the problem is to retreat before it, for the minds of the men behind the explanation are impenetrable.

---

could not conceive that his resignation at that time would have kept Japan out of war. See IMTFE: Tōgō, 36106–9.

Although it is impossible to say what might have happened, it is probable that Tōgō's resignation would have been little more than merely "embarrassing" to the government. Even if his resignation had caused Tōjō's cabinet to collapse, it is likely that the cabinet would immediately have been re-formed with a new Foreign Minister amenable to the army's wishes.

[54] For a Prosecution point of view on resignations, see IMTFE: *Proceedings*, 16794–98; for a Defense answer (as applied to a specific case), see IMTFE: Def. Doc. 3108, *Defense Summation for Hiranuma*, 58–59.

[55] There is also the argument that once the war began even those who were opposed to it had—as patriotic Japanese—the primary responsibility of performing their individual duties to the best of their ability. A resignation, according to this reasoning, would have helped create the possibility of defeat because it would have destroyed the confidence of the people and would have undermined the people's morale. See, for instance, IMTFE: Kaya, 30656 (as amended, 36996). This idea has been expressed in another way by former Premier Koiso: "The way of we Japanese is that no matter what our own personal opinions and our own personal arguments may be, once a policy of State has been decided upon, it is our duty to bend all our efforts for the prosecution of such policy. This has been the traditional custom in our country." IMTFE: Koiso, 32431.

Throughout the movement to end the war, a movement which did not really take definite shape or grow apace until after Suzuki became Premier, the activities of the officeholders were tantamount to treasonous intrigue covertly formulated and implemented behind the backs of a hostile military. The danger was real[56] and the reward, although commensurable with the aim of preserving Japan's polity, certainly did not contain the promise of personal salvation. On the other hand, the non-officeholders had perhaps more to fear from the wrath of their own people than from the postwar judgments of the victors. Their machinations, being harder for the military authorities to control, were more likely to produce once again that ugly scar of violence which mars the historical record of Japanese political practice for the ten-year period preceding the outbreak of the war.

The inner conflicts to which the end-the-war advocates fell victim and their fear of swift and violent retaliation from the military inevitably produced, on their part, a tardy reaction to events and robbed them of the effectiveness so vital to the consummation of their secret plan. Not until after Suzuki became Premier did the proponents of peace at length realize that the time was upon them when only bold action, not wary maneuvering, could save the day for Japan's "Son of Heaven." With the imperial structure hanging in the balance and with the trend of the war going daily from bad to worse, they had finally to attempt to preserve the state even though it might mean sacrificing themselves. While the goal naturally demanded discretion, and reason necessarily dictated patience, it was clear that continued wavering and circumspection would merely produce a point in time beyond which there could be only dangerously diminishing returns.

[56] On April 15, 1945, War Minister Anami ordered the arrest of some 400 persons suspected of harboring end-the-war sentiments. Included among these was former Ambassador to England Shigeru Yoshida (postwar Prime Minister) who was arrested in connection with the "Memorial" Konoye had presented orally to the Emperor in February 1945. (In this connection, see IMTFE: *Defense Summation for Hirota*, 182.)

According to the then chief cabinet secretary (Sakomizu), Judge Takejirō Sawada of the Court of Administrative Litigation was also arrested at this time for having "talked peace" to a naval officer. Since the judge was an official of *chokunin* rank, "imperial sanction" was required before the arrest could be made. *At a cabinet meeting held to discuss whether the sanction should be given*, the arrest was approved by a unanimous vote in spite of the fact that "every member" regarded the incident as ridiculous. The cabinet ministers were afraid to oppose the arrest for fear that they themselves would be suspected of being peace sympathizers. See *Statements*: Sakomizu 5/3/49.

The italicized phrase in the preceding paragraph indicates that it is quite misleading to assume that what is called "imperial sanction" emanates from the person of the Emperor. Although the cabinet's unanimous decision probably crossed the Emperor's desk, Japanese political practice was such that it would have been "unthinkable" for the Emperor to have reversed the decision. This point will be reviewed in the Epilogue.

4

EVERYONE IS AGREED

Japan Will Fight to the Bitter End

ABOUT the time Admiral Suzuki began feeling his way around the puzzling complex of duties and demands he had inherited with his new office, His Imperial Majesty, the Emperor of Japan, became fully aware of a state of affairs so seriously compromising to the nation's future that even the Japanese military could no longer provide adequate explanations. As if from some hitherto dormant spring of crisis, a veritable flood of disturbing information suddenly poured into the inner precincts of the imperial palace.[1] In rapid succession, the Emperor learned that the forces being readied for the expected Allied invasion of Japan were insufficiently equipped, that the situation on Okinawa was hopeless, and that the whole superstructure of Japan's war effort was in imminent danger of collapse. To this fateful pattern was added the continuing damage being inflicted upon Japan's helpless fleet, the growing scarcity of food throughout the country, and the appearance of antiwar sentiments among the people. His Majesty also learned that the hated B-29's were intensifying their activities, spreading out like an opening fan to cast their shadows, and bombs, on an ever increasing number of cities and towns across his narrow Empire.

The weight of this shocking evidence of failure was so overwhelming that the Emperor, whom everyone had tried to shelter from the disturbing and the distasteful, came to realize that each passing day was merely helping to compound further the unwanted interest already earned on Japan's mistaken calculations.[2]

Although an objective appraisal of the situation would have forced the admission that neither a military nor a diplomatic victory was at all likely at this late stage, Japan's military authorities chose to ignore such

---

[1] See IMTFE: Kido, 31145.

[2] In this connection, see also USSBS, *Japan's Struggle to End the War*, 6; *Statements*: Hasunuma #58225, Toyoda #61340, and Sakomizu 4/21/49. Toyoda noted that by early June 1945 the navy had lost virtually all of its surface forces and had no more oil. The training of recruits as aviators had been suspended at the end of March for want of aviation fuel.

implications even when they understood the facts. They thus continued to preach that the day of national redemption would come when they could at last meet the enemy on Japan's own shores. At the same time, these men did not entirely close their eyes to the possibilities of diplomacy. Regarding this art of foreign relations as a useful reserve to be employed here and there as it was needed, the military saw in Japan's mounting difficulties an opportunity to bring the diplomats into play.[3] So far as the army and navy high command was concerned the solution was simple. To fill the vacuum created by the Kremlin's denunciation of the Neutrality Pact the Foreign Office should negotiate a new arrangement with the Soviet Union. The better the arrangement, the better Japan's chances of continuing the war.[4]

Although the army placed primary emphasis upon preventing a possible Soviet entry into the conflict on the side of the Allies, the navy called for a more ambitious program. The admirals wanted the diplomats to negotiate a *quid pro quo,* preferably a coalition or alliance, whereby Japan would exchange naval cruisers and some resources in return for Soviet oil and aircraft. The planners in the navy apparently also hoped eventually to draw the Soviet Union into the Japanese war effort as a fighting member in good standing.

Foreign Minister Tōgō, who had once served in Moscow as Japan's ambassador, took a dour view of the army-navy attitude. He emphasized that the effectiveness of wartime diplomacy depended entirely upon the military situation and that barring an immediate Japanese victory no diplomatic overture would stand a chance of success. He further judged that it was already too late for the Foreign Office to repair the damage, and he even warned that the Soviet Union might already have reached some type of agreement with America and Britain regarding a division of the spoils after Japan's defeat. He therefore urged the military to concentrate their efforts upon the prosecution of the war or else face the fact that diplomacy could not restore peace to Japan on the basis they envisaged.

In reality, Tōgō had guessed correctly. A detailed settlement of the spoils had been written into the agreements undertaken at Yalta in

---

[3] Tōgō declared that diplomacy was not only expected to play a secondary role but was generally wholly neglected by the military, who refrained from informing the Foreign Office about matters directly concerned with foreign affairs. IMTFE: Tōgō, 35739–40. For a Prosecution statement describing the manner in which the army could present the cabinet with a *fait accompli* which the Foreign Office would then have to explain to the world, see IMTFE: *Proceedings,* 585–86.

[4] The request to commence overtures toward the Soviet Union was initially lodged by Umezu and Kawabe (chief and vice-chief, respectively, of the Army General Staff) and was later taken up by Ozawa (vice-chief of the Naval General Staff) and others. A few of the senior statesmen also began calling for new arrangements and agreements with the Soviet Union. See IMTFE: Tōgō, 35739–40, 35777, 35780–81; *Statements:* Tōgō #50304; JFO MS: Ch. 25 (Saikō sensō shidō kaigi kōseiin kaigi no seiritsu).

February 1945. The difficulty was that Tōgō lacked the one thing he needed to be convincing: he lacked *concrete evidence*. He was thus caught between his own desire to see the war terminated as soon as possible[5] and the army's insistent demand that he undertake immediately to court the Soviet Union. Burdened with this pressure for doing something and doing it right away, Tōgō acceded to the army's wishes and began devoting considerable time and energy to a program which contained only slight chance of success.

While these developments were taking place in Tokyo, "a solemn . . . but glorious hour"[6] had come for the Allies in Europe: their eleven-month-old invasion had at length raced to a victorious conclusion and had carried them to the point where they could bring the full force of their fighting strength to bear upon the now isolated Island Empire of Japan. Had the end-the-war argument within the inner circle of the ruling elite been more than embryonic, there can be little doubt that the so-called pro-peace faction would have tried to utilize this very moment to write "finis" across the record of Japan's war gamble. The European debacle had been developing for some months, and anyone who was thoroughly committed to leading His Majesty's government out of the war should have seen in Germany's impending collapse a tremendous opportunity not only to achieve peace but also to obtain a termination of the conflict on a basis at least partially favorable to Japan. Although the Allies were psychologically pledged to securing a victory so compelling that it could not later be denied, there seems little possibility that Washington and London either would or could have ignored any reasonable Japanese peace overture at this time.

Some Japanese have argued that Japan's treaty obligations to Germany and Italy prevented her from concluding a separate peace as long as the Axis powers remained in the war. Although the nominal reference in this connection is usually the Tripartite Pact of September 27, 1940, it would appear that the actual reference is Article II of the December 11, 1941, Agreement between Germany, Italy, and Japan whereby each of the three contracting powers undertook not to conclude an armistice or make peace with America and Britain without the consent of the other two powers.[7] While this article might be cited as a reason why Japan did not conclude peace prior to Germany's capitulation in May 1945, the Agreement of December 11 cannot possibly serve as an excuse for the failure of the Japanese to lay the groundwork

[5] See footnote 33, Ch. 3, above.

[6] A quotation from a presidential radio address to the nation (May 8, 1945) announcing Germany's defeat. See U.S. Senate, *Surrender of Italy, Germany and Japan*, 46–49.

[7] For the German texts of the Tripartite Pact and the Agreement of December 11, 1941, see *Jahrbuch für Auswärtige Politik*, IX (Jahrgang 1943), 80–84.

(within Japan) which would have permitted them to terminate the war in the Pacific immediately following a cessation of hostilities in Europe. Preparations undertaken with a view to negotiating a settlement or suing for peace at the moment of a German collapse could not have been construed by anyone as being contrary to either the spirit or the letter of Japan's obligations to her allies. An attempt on the part of the peace party to ring down the curtain in the Pacific at the same time that it fell in Europe would not have been easy; it might even have failed. But the opportunity was there, and the first and perhaps greatest chance for success, yet for one reason or another both were ignored.[8] By the time Hitler's aggressions had resulted in his ruin, it was too late for the end-the-war cadre within the government to act, even if it had wanted to do so.

On May 3, 1945, in anticipation of the German capitulation, Premier Suzuki issued a statement in which he emphasized that the changing situation in Europe would merely result in a further intensification of the Japanese government's determination to prosecute the War of Greater East Asia to a successful conclusion:

. . . we firmly believe that there will surely come in our grasp a golden chance.
Although the present changing situation in Europe has in no respect been unexpected on our part, I want to take this opportunity to make known once again at home and abroad our faith in certain victory.[9]

Six days later, on May 9, the government followed the Premier's lead by declaring that Germany's surrender would not cause "the slightest change" in national policy since Japan's war aims were based on "self-existence and self-defence."[10] But even with such pronouncements as these the government could not completely ignore the catastrophe which had overtaken its European counterpart. The masses were therefore told that the Germans had suffered defeat because they lacked the spiritual stamina possessed by His Majesty's subjects. It was also emphasized that Hitler had failed on the psychological level and had blundered into self-destruction because he had attempted what was purely

[8] Kido felt "that so long as Germany remained in the war Japan would be in danger of a military coup in the event firm and positive steps were taken immediately to end the war." (See USSBS, *Japan's Struggle to End the War*, 6.) Although this argument is stronger than the one referring to Japan's treaty obligations, Kido's remarks merely explain why Japan did not seek a termination of the war *prior to* Germany's collapse but do not explain Japan's failure to be prepared to end the war *at the time of the German capitulation.*

[9] See *Contemporary Japan*, XIV (April–December 1945), 273–74.

[10] *Ibid.* The phrase, "self-existence and self-defence," which also appeared in the Suzuki statement of May 3, is a recapitulation of an idea expressed in the December 8, 1941, imperial rescript declaring war: "Our Empire for its existence and self-defence has no other recourse but to appeal to arms to crush every obstacle in its path." See *Contemporary Japan*, XI (January 1942), 158–59.

suicide, a two-front war. Nothing was said of the overwhelming forces which had been marshaled by the Allies or of the devastation wrought by bombing.[11]

Surprising as it may seem, the man in the street generally accepted the government's sugar-coating of unpalatable facts. Even though the fighting perimeter had been relentlessly closing in on the home islands in an ever tightening ring, the literal-minded masses had largely missed the point of this fateful development. Kept ignorant, as they were, of the depth of Japan's plight, the people of the Island Empire were slow to react against the threat of annihilation contained in the refusal of their leaders to acknowledge defeat. Not until the air raids of the spring and summer of 1945 began to impress themselves upon the consciousness of even the humblest peasant did the first signs appear of possible future danger on the civilian morale front.[12] Even then, little fundamental consideration was given by the common man to matters which his well-indoctrinated instinct told him were outside his ken and purview.

The details of the government's masterful accomplishment of mass delusion are another story, but the fact of that accomplishment explains, in part, why the people themselves did not force a termination of the conflict. It also illustrates why the intrigue of those who sought a solution through negotiation was so long in taking shape and was so completely unsupported by any pressure from the outside.

A man of Foreign Minister Tōgō's astuteness, for instance, knew that the government was telling the people a lot of nonsense, but he found it difficult to make his knowledge serve any useful purpose. The people simply did not count. They would do what they were told, and they would obey to the letter. Some care might have to be taken in the event of a governmental *volte-face*, but not nearly so much care as was continually necessary in dealing with the Japanese military.

The crushing control exerted by the militarists over all forms of national life and thought made them resentful of criticism and even quite unwilling to listen to well-meant suggestions. From his own personal experience, Tōgō appreciated how sensitive and temperamental the military could be, but he also knew that the government, especially

---

[11] See USFCC, *Radio Report Far East*, #72, AAA 1–AAA 6. Foreign Minister Tōgō, however, drew the obvious parallel with Japan's own situation and therefore told the Emperor that the government would now have to formulate its policy with the knowledge that Allied raids had so curtailed strategic production that Japan would find it virtually impossible to continue the war. In reply, the Emperor said that he would like to see the war ended soon. *Statements:* Tōgō #50304 and IMTFE: Tōgō, 35780–82.

[12] For material on the civilian morale factor, see USFCC, *Radio Report Far East*, #72, Section AA, and unpublished USSBS interrogations #109 (Akabane), #157 and #158 (Koizumi), #175 (Hayashi), #176 (Nambara), and #458 (Nishizawa).

its civilian leaders, would have to act or else stand silently by and see Japan destroyed. If the military could be cajoled into co-operating, so much the better. If not, he and others like him would have to go it alone.[13]

With Germany's capitulation, an opportunity at last presented itself, and Tōgō, treading cautiously but with a purpose, strove to provide the leadership which was so necessary to a reorientation of national policy.[14] Beginning on May 11 and continuing through May 14, the Supreme Council for the Direction of the War, Japan's "inner cabinet," met to discuss the war situation.[15] Actually, it was not quite the same Supreme Council as before. The advent of the Suzuki Cabinet had of course brought in new faces, but the telling difference was that these particular meetings were attended by only the "constituent" or charter members of the council, that is, by the Big Six: the Premier, Foreign Minister, War Minister, Navy Minister, and the chiefs of the Army and Navy General Staffs.[16]

Prior to this innovation, the Supreme Council meetings had been little more than a dress parade of bureaucracy at work, for from the moment the council had been organized in the late summer of 1944 the fundamental drive had come not from the Big Six but from a group of

[13] That there were others within the cabinet who realized the need for action and who hoped to work out a decision acceptable to all is clear from the efforts exerted by Sakonji and Shimomura at the time of the "Six Ministers' Conference" of May 31, 1945. See JFO MS: Ch. 26 (Kakunai rokushō kondankai) and *Statements*: Sakonji #61339 and #58226.

[14] The details presented in the text which follows are found in IMTFE: Tōgō, 35780–82; Suzuki, 35592; *Statements*: Tōgō #50304, Tanemura #61977, Oikawa #61341; Toyoda, *Saigo no teikoku kaigun*, 213–15; Tōgō, "Shūsen gaikō," in *Kaizō*, XXXI (November 1950), 122; and JFO MS: Ch. 25 (Saikō sensō shidō kaigi kōseiin kaigi no seiritsu). See also the references cited in succeeding footnotes.

[15] At about this same time in Washington, Secretary of the Navy Forrestal and U.S. Ambassador to Moscow W. Averell Harriman raised the issue of American political objectives in the Far East. Among the questions posed by Forrestal were the following: "What is our policy on Russian influence in the Far East? Do we desire a counterweight to that influence? And should it be China or should it be Japan? . . . Have we given careful thought to the question of how far this country will go toward the complete defeat of Japan—the quick, costly assault versus a long, drawn-out siege?"

Harriman also expressed his concern in a number of questions: Should the Yalta Agreement "be re-examined in the light of the fact that Russia has not observed its part of that contract, and also in the light of the cessation of hostilities in Europe, which have changed the pattern of fact on which that agreement was drawn? How urgent is the necessity for quick Russian participation in the war against Japan? . . . What is our objective as regards the future of Japan? Destruction? Retention as a power?" See Millis (ed.), *The Forrestal Diaries*, 52–53 and 55–56.

[16] Suzuki, Tōgō, Anami, Yonai, Umezu, and Oikawa, respectively. Admiral Soemu Toyoda succeeded Oikawa toward the latter part of May. This change was sponsored by Yonai who felt that Toyoda, who came from the same clan as Anami and Umezu, might be of more help than Oikawa in persuading the army leaders to place their support behind a termination of the war. See Toyoda, *Saigo no teikoku kaigun*, 213, and *Statements*: Oikawa #61341.

eleven military and civilian aides known as secretaries and assistant secretaries.[17] Before very long it had become standard procedure for the assistant secretaries, who met regularly twice a week, to discuss and draft all policy decisions required to meet the exigencies arising out of the developing war situation. When an agreement of views was reached among the members of this "third string," each would report that fact to the secretary to whom he was attached. If no objections were encountered at this level, the particular policy decision being formulated in this bureaucratic mill would come up for discussion at one of the regular weekly meetings of the second string. The secretaries would then rehash the work of their assistants, make whatever changes they saw fit, and finally pass the decision-in-embryo to the first string, the Supreme Council itself.[18]

Since the Big Six had not always been able to keep abreast of the work which had been going on behind the scenes, they had found it to their advantage to bring their aides to the meetings. In very short order, however, it had become apparent that at least the military members of the secretary and assistant secretary group were committed to furthering the views of the fanatical younger officer element to which a few even personally belonged. Not only did their policies reflect the do-or-die attitude typical of Japan's field-grade, self-styled strategists, but their very presence also served as a further incentive to their superiors to follow the lead they so nimbly provided. The net result was that the Big Six had found it increasingly difficult to speak their minds freely. Rather than run the risk of a leakage of compromising information to the fanatics in the army and navy, the Big Six had soon taken refuge in the firm pronouncements and uncompromising arguments the younger officers expected of them. This situation, which had continued from August 1944 until May 1945, was finally brought under control by Foreign Minister Tōgō's insistence[19] that the Supreme Council meet from time to time in closed sessions at which all matters for discussion would

[17] This was both a holdover and an extension of a system which had grown up under the Liaison Conference. See *Statements:* Tōgō #50304.

[18] See *Statements:* Suezawa #62051 and Sakomizu #61979. Suezawa seems to suggest that, if any secretary objected to a decision reached by the assistant secretaries, the decision would go back to the latter before coming up for discussion at a meeting of the secretaries.

[19] Tōgō credits Chief of the Army General Staff Umezu with helping him inaugurate these closed meetings of the Supreme Council. While Tōgō recommended the innovation to Premier Suzuki and Navy Minister Yonai, Umezu broached the matter to War Minister Anami.

Umezu and Anami apparently supported the idea of closed meetings for fear of the effect the matters under discussion would have upon troop morale if leakages occurred. They may also have desired to eliminate the secretary group so as to be able more effectively to control their own subordinates, especially the fanatical younger officer element. See *Statements:* Tanemura #61977 and Toyoda, *Saigo no teikoku kaigun,* 213–15.

be initiated by the Big Six without the knowledge or participation of their Peeping Tom staff.[20]

In spite of the fact that this chance to speak freely coincided with a mute prophecy of impending disaster, the Foreign Minister proved to be the only one of the Big Six who was willing to square up to realities and to argue emphatically that Japan was no longer in the running either economically, militarily, or diplomatically. Tōgō, who had a reputation for being an outspoken individualist, reminded his colleagues that he had always warned the government that it would have to act before Russia, America, and Britain got together, otherwise Japan's whole program of utilizing the Soviet Union, of effecting a general rapprochement with her, and of encouraging the Russians and the Germans to lay down their arms would end in failure. Instead of following his advice, however, the government had merely stood around watching while the Allies and the Soviet Union had held one major conference after another and had forged a coalition incapable of being rent asunder. So far as Tōgō could determine, it was now too late and quite useless to expect any military or economic aid whatsoever from the Soviet Union.

Although these were strong words for the time, they failed to produce any startling results.[21] Instead of redirecting the course of national policy so as to provide for the earliest possible termination of the war, the Big Six continued to search for the mythical key that would unlock the doors which America and Britain had already slammed on Japan's future. The immediate upshot of this approach to the problem was the emergence of a somewhat halfhearted agreement whereby Japan was committed to extending a hand to her backyard neighbor, the Soviet Union.[22] That this decision was in itself the product of the desperate

[20] It was from about this time on that the Matsudaira (Yasumasa), Matsutani (Makoto), Takagi (Sōkichi), Kase (Toshikazu) circle assumed importance. Early in January 1945, the four, who theretofore had worked independently of each other, began meeting together frequently so as to co-ordinate their activities and concentrate their efforts. After May 1945 their liaison work became especially important. Their advice as well as their information seems to have confirmed and strengthened the end-the-war sentiment of their superiors (Kido, Suzuki, Yonai, and Tōgō)—the men on whom the fate of the nation rested. Interview with Marquis Matsudaira and Admiral Takagi, Tokyo, July 30, 1951; interview with Colonel Matsutani, Tokyo, March 10, 1952; IMTFE: Kido, 31224–26; Statements: Matsudaira #61636; and Kase, Journey to the Missouri, 146–47.

[21] Tōgō, however, had this to say: "Unless the leaders, at least, could be persuaded to listen to reason, the result would be domestic turmoil of such major proportions as to endanger any peace negotiations we might undertake. My basic idea in suggesting these meetings was that it was absolutely essential to create an opportunity for general discussion and for the development of an over-all attitude favorable to peace."

Tōgō also declared that in the general agreement reached at this time War Minister Anami and Chief of Staff Umezu accepted, in principle, the idea of terminating hostilities. In spite of this, they continued to insist upon not ending the war in defeat. See Statements: Tōgō #50304 and #61672, Oikawa #61341.

[22] In the weeks which followed, Radio Tokyo's propaganda efforts on the inter-

circumstances in which the nation was mired down is amply illustrated by the "plan" which served as a guide to the Foreign Office in launching Japan's Kremlin-bound overture. Listed in the order of priority and preference, the following points of the plan were crucial:

Point I: The Soviet Union must be prevented from entering the war in the Pacific.

Point II: The Kremlin must be "enticed" into an attitude of friendliness toward Japan.

Point III: Mediation of the conflict on terms favorable to Japan should be sought through Soviet good offices.[23]

Foreign Minister Tōgō warned that in order to be successful in this venture Japan would have to be prepared to make substantial concessions.[24] He even went so far as to suggest that the Empire might have to return to its pre-Russo-Japanese War (1904–5) boundaries—a retrogression which would have amounted to a cancellation of the Treaty of Portsmouth (1905) and of the economic concessions which were subsequently negotiated on the basis of that treaty. Since it was probable that Moscow would lodge a claim to North Manchuria, Tōgō openly spoke of relinquishing that area to the Soviet giant. He also envisaged making South Manchuria into a buffer state in order to forestall its becoming a new source of Soviet-Japanese friction, intrigue, and conflict.

Since the Big Six knew that Japan would have to pay some price for a peace with honor, no one took particular exception to Tōgō's remarks. The real argument, therefore, was not over the objectives as a whole or the price of the negotiations but over the issue of Japan's ability to continue the war, the manner in which the three-pronged plan should be implemented, and the nature of the eventual "truce."[25] The golden mean of Japanese political practice thus came into play and eventually produced, in the absence of unanimity, the only other realistic alternative: a compromise.

Navy Minister Yonai, who had earlier suggested that an attempt be

---

national level were largely devoted to "wooing" the Soviet Union. At the same time all rumors concerning Japanese peace feelers were denied. USFCC, *Radio Report Far East*, #74, BA 21–BA 25.

[23] See *Statements:* Tōgō #50304 and #61672.

[24] Tōgō also saw the danger that large-scale concessions would convince the Soviet Union that Japan had become desperate and would therefore encourage the Kremlin to move in a direction quite opposite to that desired by Japan. *Statements:* Tōgō #61672.

[25] Two separate arguments arose, one between Tōgō and Yonai (over the cruisers-for-oil issue) and one between Tōgō and Anami (over Japan's war capabilities and the terms relative to peace). See JFO MS: Ch. 25 (Saikō sensō shidō kaigi kōseiin kaigi no seiritsu); IMTFE: Suzuki, 35592; Tōgō, 35782; *Statements:* Tōgō #50304 and #61672; and Tōgō, "Shūsen gaikō" in *Kaizō*, XXXI (November 1950), 122–25.

made to obtain Soviet oil and aircraft in exchange for Japanese warships, now assumed the role of mediator.[26] Referring to the fact that the views of the War and Foreign Ministers could not be reconciled, Yonai proposed opening negotiations with the Soviet Union on the basis of Points I and II, with Point III being shelved at least for the time being. And this, indeed, became the decision which finally prevailed. The question of terminating the war—a question which had never previously been concretely or formally discussed by both the leaders of the government and the leaders of the fighting services—was thus shoved into the background. In the light of later developments, it would appear that the proposal to end the war through the good offices of a third power was pigeonholed not for the sake of compromise but for the benefit of those who were eager to negotiate a rapprochement with the Soviet Union that would permit Japan to continue the war in the Pacific.

Except for the fact that the ruling elite felt there was nowhere else to turn, Japan's decision to seek Soviet aid in one form or another seems, at first sight, difficult to understand and even quite unreasonable. The historical record of Russo-Japanese relations in the Far East places the two nations more in the role of enemies than in that of friends. For years on end, each had had aspirations in Asia, and each had stood in the other's way. The part played by Tsarist Russia in forcing Japan to re-cede the Liaotung Peninsula to China in 1895 had not been forgotten in spite of Japan's victory over Russia in 1904–5 and in spite of the period of rapprochement which preceded World War I. The Russo-Japanese War had, in fact, created new enmities which were still a factor in both Russian and Japanese thinking when the war in the Pacific began. The Siberian Intervention of 1918–22, border disputes and economic rivalries in Manchuria during the 'thirties, and continual haggling over fishing rights and other concessions in the Soviet Far East had all added their fuel to the fire. Even the negotiation of a Neutrality Pact in the spring of 1941 had not really cemented strong ties of friendship and good will between the two countries. Although the Pact did serve its

[26] See the citations listed in footnote 25 above. The proposal to exchange oil for ships may not necessarily have represented Yonai's own views, but it very definitely did represent the navy point of view. After the war, Yonai declared that by May 1945 he personally felt that Japan "had come to the end of the road," and by early June he felt that there "was absolutely no sense in continuing any longer." The apparent contradiction between this appraisal of the situation and the role played by Yonai at the meetings discussed in the text has been explained in terms of pressure from hothead elements in the navy and the consequent need to resort to *haragei*. See USSBS, *Interrogations*, II, Yonai, 332. For testimony in support of Yonai's opposition to the war, see *Statements:* Oikawa #61241 and Toyoda #61340 and #57669. See also footnote 27, Ch. 1, and footnote 16, Ch. 2, above.

purpose for four years and a temporary improvement in Soviet-Japanese relations did result from concessions made by Japan in the spring of 1944, the hidden threat of possible duplicity by either side at a moment's notice caused both parties to continue regarding each other with an almost traditional air of suspicion. As has already been seen, little more than a month before the Big Six began their closed meetings, the Soviet Union announced that it would not renew the Neutrality Pact when it expired in April 1946. Much earlier still, on November 7, 1944, Stalin had publicly denounced Japan as an aggressor. Since all this did not augur well for the success of the decision formulated by the Big Six, just why did the Japanese government turn to the Soviet Union at all?

The answer has already been given. The military's determination to continue the war rather than submit to unconditional surrender and the absence, so far as the government was concerned, of any other acceptable or workable alternative misled Japan into turning to her Soviet neighbor. In the spring of 1945 Japan was literally losing the war faster than the United States and her Allies were winning it. Japan either had to continue fighting on a shoestring, obtain Soviet aid in the form of oil and other war materials, or terminate the conflict on whatever basis the Allies demanded. Since the first and last possibilities were as unattractive as they were undesirable, the middle course was the only choice left.

Did Japan have any concrete basis for expecting Soviet co-operation in her plan? Apparently none at all, at least nothing so strong as the numerous indications that argued against placing even moderate hope or faith in the approach to Moscow. There were, however, a few interesting assumptions which were applicable not only to Points I and II of the plan but to Point III as well.

In Japanese eyes, the Soviet Union's participation in the Anglo-American grand alliance was nothing more than a marriage of convenience consummated out of Hitler's own madness. Since the war in Europe had ended and the Soviet Union had acquired all that she could in that part of the world, Japan might be able to arrange a new match by offering an enticing dowry. There was the whole of Northeast Asia where Japan, for all of her failures to date, was still in a position to consign vast economic, political, and territorial servitudes as the purchase price of Soviet assistance. Only if the Soviet Union refused to join forces with Japan would the government seek mediation. In view of the concessions she would still be able to offer for good offices, Japan felt that a possible Soviet rebuff with respect to Points I and II need not necessarily indicate a cool reception for Point III. Why should the Soviet Union fight in the Far East if she could gain a dominant position there merely by acting as Japan's diplomatic broker? Apparently no one in office at the time, with the exception of Foreign Minister Tōgō, ever seriously considered the possibility that the Soviet Union had already sold out to a higher bidder.[27]

In the event that Moscow did not show any interest in Points I and II, exactly why should Point III be attempted *through the Soviet Union?* Again the leaders in Tokyo had their reasons: a direct approach to the United States or Great Britain, aside from being difficult in view of the connotations it would have for the Japanese military, would probably produce an inalterable Allied demand for unconditional surrender, and Japan's leaders did not have it in their minds to accept such a demand as a basis for ending the war. Unconditional surrender was anathema to these men because their understanding of the formula would not permit them to accept its premises or face its implications.[28] As a result, they were thoroughly and primarily concerned with obtaining suitable conditions, that is, with opening a path which would lead to a negotiated peace.[29] The question of how to do this contained a natural answer: through a neutral nation.

The Vatican was the first to be considered, but "in view of the Pope's negative attitude toward the war" it was deemed virtually impossible to look for any aid from that quarter. Although China was mentioned, Japan's earlier maneuvers toward Chungking had not only ended in failure but had also resulted in serious repercussions within Japan itself. Furthermore, Chiang Kai-shek, as a signatory of the Cairo Declaration, had committed himself to the unconditional surrender

---

[27] Tōgō's postwar recapitulation is interesting: "It was my opinion . . . that the attitude of the SOVIET UNION was highly questionable; nor . . . did I consider our relations with her to be friendly. I felt that we would have to pay a high price for Russian mediation and that we would do well to sound out her intentions first. Accordingly, I hesitated for some time before agreeing to approach RUSSIA. However, the Supreme Council for the Direction of the War, Government and civilian circles, and the Lord Keeper of the Privy Seal all regarded the selection of RUSSIA as a foregone conclusion, and in the end it was decided to seek her good offices." *Statements*: Tōgō #50304 (ATIS transl.). In this connection, see footnote 32 below.

There were those who felt that the Soviet Union would want to see Japan retain a fairly important international position so that the two countries could ally themselves in the future against America and Britain. *Translations*: Doc. #62048.

[28] During the war Dr. Ladislas Farago, chief of a secret research and planning section of the Navy Department, found that in most instances when Japanese had fought among themselves their campaigns had ended in surrender and not in the mass suicide of the vanquished. (Zacharias, *Secret Missions*, 334–35.) This interesting revelation could have had value in the American psychological offensive only if Washington had been willing to make a positive commitment on the future status of the Emperor.

[29] See *Statements*: Tōgō #50304. When asked, after the war, why he had "avoided" direct negotiations with the United States and Great Britain, Tōgō replied: "At no time did I avoid direct negotiations with BRITAIN and AMERICA. It was BRITAIN and AMERICA who avoided negotiating for peace. First of all, we must remember that JAPAN was in no position to accept unconditional surrender at that time. This is fundamental. . . . there was no thought of unconditional surrender in this country. We were concerned with the steps to be taken to obtain suitable conditions; in other words, with how we could obtain a negotiated peace." (ATIS transl.)

formula. So far as Sweden or Switzerland were concerned there was some question as to whether either of these countries would make "a serious effort" to arrange a conditional peace for Japan. In addition, they did not have the influence with the Allies that the Soviet Union had. Their weak, off-stage whisper of mediation would probably only serve to produce an adamant Allied stand. It would also have been awkward and possibly dangerous for Japan to ask either country for its good offices while blandly ignoring the one major power, the Soviet Union, with which she still enjoyed ostensibly neutral relations.[30]

A few civilian members of the ruling elite may also have hoped to entice a faction of the Japanese army oriented toward Russia into at least playing along with, and later actually supporting, a peace-by-negotiation overture processed through what they considered to be a "favorably disposed" Moscow. Conceivably, the long-silent and rather inevident pro-America faction of the army and navy would also join the move even though there would be misgivings with respect to the manner in which the overture was to be implemented.[31] The general situation, and its critique as well, thus seemed to call for Soviet good offices or for no mediation at all.[32]

Just how far Japan's leaders would actually have been willing to go in their proposed horse-trading venture cannot definitely be established,[33] but the outline contained in an earlier plan[34] suggests that the concessions

[30] *Statements:* Tōgō #50304 and Kido #61476.

[31] Interview with Mr. Tomohiko Ushiba (former secretary to the late Prince Konoye), Tokyo, February 6, 1952; *Statements*: Kido #61476; and JFO MS: Ch. 19 (Nichi-So chūritsu jōyaku no haiki tsūkoku).

[32] As early as July 1943 Privy Seal Kido spoke to Tōgō of the necessity of improving relations with the Soviet Union without delay and of the advisability, should occasion demand, of seeking a settlement in the Pacific through the good offices of the Soviet Union. Kido, "Nikki," 7/26/43. (Kido made these remarks upon hearing from Tōgō that Badoglio had just assumed control in Italy.)

Early in 1944 Kido again mulled over the problem of engineering a closer alignment between Japan and the Soviet Union. He felt there was some hope of doing this since he considered the Soviet Union "Oriental" in outlook. In May 1945, as Japan was once again preparing to make overtures to the Soviet Union, Kido personally believed that an approach through Moscow would permit greater "elbowroom" in the negotiations than an approach to London or Washington. IMTFE: Kido, 11370 and 31150. In this connection, see also the text corresponding to footnote 5, Ch. 6, below.

[33] On June 15, 1945, Kido spoke to Foreign Minister Tōgō of the necessity of obtaining an honorable peace through Soviet mediation *regardless of the price* Japan would have to pay. IMTFE: Tōgō, 35783.

The material contained in *Translations*: Doc. #62048 indicates that, if forced by circumstances, the Big Six would ultimately have been willing to strip Japan of practically all of the territories and servitudes she had acquired since 1904–5.

[34] Colonel Tanemura has stated that at the time in question there was no need to discuss the conditions on which diplomatic negotiations with Moscow would be based since an informal agreement on this matter had already been reached at a Supreme Council meeting held in September 1944. (This was the meeting at which Shigemitsu presented the plan to be discussed in the text which follows.) On or about May 10, 1945, Chief of the Army General Staff Umezu asked Tanemura for a copy of this agreement. When Tanemura brought the document, Umezu put it in his

might well have exceeded the stakes won by the Soviet Union at Yalta. As early as September 1944, before the battles of the Philippine Sea and the landings on Leyte, the then Foreign Minister, Mamoru Shigemitsu, had had the Foreign Office prepare a draft of "Diplomatic Measures to be taken vis-à-vis the Soviet Union" in which both the demands which were anticipated from the Soviet Union and the concessions Japan might be willing to make were clearly enumerated.[35] The over-all purpose of this plan had been to maintain neutrality between Japan and the Soviet Union, to promote peace between Germany and the Soviet Union, and to utilize Soviet assistance in improving Japan's situation in the event of a German collapse in Europe. Should Germany capitulate or negotiate a separate peace or should a general peace be achieved through Soviet good offices, Japan would have "no objection" to acceding to all of the envisaged demands. Should a deterioration occur in Soviet-Japanese relations and should Japan wish to guard against a Soviet attack, the government would have "no objection" to acceding to each and every item in the list of demands.

In other words, in September 1944 Foreign Minister Shigemitsu was suggesting that the Japanese government should be prepared, upon Soviet insistence, to recognize a sphere of interest for the Soviet Union in Manchuria and Inner Mongolia; to give the Kremlin title to southern Sakhalin, the northern Kuriles, and the North Manchurian Railway; to acquiesce in the "peaceful activities" of the Soviet Union in China, Inner Mongolia, Manchuria, and other parts of Greater East Asia; and to accept an abrogation of Japanese fishing rights in Soviet Far Eastern waters.

Shigemitsu also felt that his government should be prepared to make whatever other sacrifices were necessary to ensure success. Thus, he threw in the following: abrogation of the Anti-Comintern Pact and of the Tripartite Pact and Agreement, revision of the Soviet-Japanese Neutrality Pact, and permission for Soviet vessels to pass through the territorial and strategic waters of the Tsugaru Straits which lie between the main Japanese islands of Honshū and Hokkaidō. All this, he had reasoned, Japan should be secretly willing to condone should events conspire to force Germany out of the war (and thus make a general peace

---

brief case without further comment. (See *Statements*: Tanemura #61977.) The material contained in *Translations*: Doc. #62048 supports the view that the discussions held by the Big Six at this time were based upon the Shigemitsu plan of September 1944.

[35] See IMTFE: Exh. 3557, *Document on Behalf of the Accused Shigemitsu*, 34551-58, and Exh. 2745, *Stahmer Aide Mémoire*, 24485 ff. For background material on the Shigemitsu draft plan, including several Japanese attempts to mediate the Soviet-German war, see JFO MS: Ch. 6 (Shigemitsu gaishō to dai Tō-A kaigi narabi ni dai ikkai dai nikai tai-So tokushi haken mōshi-ire); Ch. 11 (Doku-So wahei mondai oyobi dai sankai tai-So tokushi haken mondai); and Ch. 13 (Shigemitsu gaishō ga shuki shita to iwareru "Waga Gaikō" to Sutārin seimei).

possible through Soviet good offices) or should Soviet-Japanese relations deteriorate to the point where Japan might be in danger of attack from the Soviet Union.[36]

Although these "Diplomatic Measures" had never progressed beyond the draft-plan stage and had even now served merely as a basis for discussion, it is possible that had the Kremlin subsequently shown any interest in Japan's proposals the Big Six might eventually have dangled the full range of these concessions before Soviet eyes in exchange for the active assistance, the continued neutrality, or even the good offices of the Soviet state.

If the ruling elite had known, in the spring of 1945, that the Soviet government had promised, in February, to enter the war in the Pacific within two to three months after the German defeat in Europe, the Big Six might have turned directly to the United States or Great Britain in spite of the current belief that such a step could only result in unconditional surrender. Secure in their ignorance of the provisions of the Yalta Agreement and in their assumption that the Soviet Union would not enter the war because of the year of grace remaining under the terms of the Neutrality Pact, Japanese leaders fell prey to the hope that they would be able to barter the rich resources of the southern regions of the Pacific for precious Soviet oil and that, if they were frustrated in this respect, they would still be able, through Soviet mediation, to negotiate some kind of settlement short of unconditional surrender.

The immediate result of the decisions reached by the Big Six in mid-May was that Foreign Minister Tōgō requested a former Premier and one-time ambassador to Moscow, Kōki Hirota, to approach the Soviet ambassador to Japan, Jacob A. Malik, who happened to be staying, at that time, at the Gōra Hotel in the Hakone Mountains near Tokyo.[37] Hirota's mission was to improve the very poor and unstable relations then existing between the Empire of Japan and the USSR and to lay the groundwork for a diplomatic arrangement powerful enough to keep the Soviets from entering the war against Japan. If Hirota could convince the Soviet Union to renew the Soviet-Japanese Neutrality Pact beyond its expiration date in April 1946 or if he could negotiate a new pact, Japan would at least be able to go about her task of fighting or ending the war with a feeling of greater security. Hirota was even to try for a nonaggression treaty and actual Soviet aid since such arrangements would obviously be the best answer to Japan's problems. If everything else failed, he was to reach far down into his diplomatic pouch and come

---

[36] See the first two citations listed in the preceding footnote.

[37] Hirota had once told Foreign Minister Tōgō that he would be glad to do anything he could to improve relations between Japan and the Soviet Union. This statement, plus the fact that he was "the best man available," made Hirota a natural choice for the negotiations with Malik. See *Statements: Tōgō #50304.*

up with a request for the good offices of the Soviet Union in ending the Pacific war. This would clearly be the last resort.

The pressure of events in the capital and the need to prepare Hirota for his mission resulted in some delay so that it was not until June 3 that Hirota was ready. That evening, Japan's unofficial ambassador of good will[38] took a stroll around Hakone and on the way "dropped in" on Malik for a chat. The next evening he stopped at the hotel again, this time as Malik's dinner guest, and the sparring began.

As Hirota warmed to his task, he grew somewhat expansive.[39] Speaking confidentially of his pro-Russian sympathies and of his personal concern with furthering Soviet-Japanese friendship for the sake of the security of Asia, Hirota strove to convince Malik that the universal desire of the Japanese people was to promote friendly relations with their Soviet neighbor. But Malik proved hard to convince. He simply countered what Hirota had said by declaring that although the Kremlin's policy toward Japan was one of peace his government found it difficult to trust Japan since many Japanese harbored unfriendly feelings toward the Soviet Union. This was an issue that had to be settled first. He would like to know, Malik said, what Japan proposed to do about the anti-Soviet feeling within the country and whether Mr. Hirota's remarks represented merely his own private opinions or whether they possibly reflected the views of his government as well.

In reply, Hirota assured Malik that his opinions were those of the government and *the people*, and he emphasized that the Japanese Foreign Office earnestly desired the betterment of relations between their respective countries. Such an achievement would put an end to whatever other feelings might exist among a segment of the population, particularly since the number of Japanese who understood the true attitude of the Soviet Union was steadily growing. The points of similarity in the outlook of the two countries should be stressed. If this were done, an improvement in relations would naturally result. It was for these reasons, Hirota concluded, that he had come seeking the opinions of the Soviet Union through its representative in Japan. But Malik remained noncommittal. The whole question, he said, would have to be studied before an answer could be given and this would take time. Meanwhile, he would have to ask Mr. Hirota to wait upon his government's reply.[40]

---

[38] Tōgō has declared that, in his talks with Malik, Hirota was not acting either as an adviser to or as a representative of the Foreign Minister. "If you want a name for the talks," Tōgō said, "you might call them unofficial conversations." At the same time, Hirota was instructed to tell Malik that he was "acting with the knowledge of the Government." *Statements:* Tōgō #50304 (ATIS transl.).

[39] For the details of the Hirota-Malik conversations outlined in the text which follows, see JFO MS: Ch. 27 (Hirota-Mariku kaidan no kaishi); IMTFE: Tōgō, 35782–83, and Kido, 31164; *Statements:* Tōgō #50304; and USSBS, *Japan's Struggle to End the War*, 6–7.

[40] See the citations listed in the preceding footnote.

The preliminaries were over and Hirota took his leave. All that he had accomplished was to get his foot in the door, and there was nothing that either he or the Foreign Office could do now but wait. The matter was out of their hands.

While Hirota had been exploring the Soviet mind at Hakone and the Big Six had been meeting *in camera* in Tokyo to map out Japan's diplomatic strategy, a strangely threatening development had taken place around the policy-making tables of the very men whom Foreign Minister Tōgō and others had decided to exclude, or at least bypass, during their current discussions. In spite of the fact that at the time in question the Supreme Councilors were personally initiating all of the matters under consideration without any preparatory consultations at the lower level, the second and third echelons did actually continue to function as before so as to lay the groundwork for the decisions which they felt would be necessary in order to prosecute the war.[41] As the Big Six were arguing over the three-point plan, therefore, the assistant secretaries[42] were beginning to turn their attention to the very same problem which was serving as a basis for discussion at the closed meetings of their superiors.

As a result of Germany's collapse and the rapidly worsening situation on Okinawa, the army had been calling for the establishment of a national policy for the future direction of the war—a policy which would be in accord with the principle of carrying out a decisive battle in the homeland[43] even at the cost of the self-destruction of the entire Japanese race. Since a matter of this kind was within the recognized responsibility of the assistant secretaries, it was not very long before a draft plan representing the army's views appeared on their agenda.[44] While this draft was being discussed by the assistant secretaries, various quarters began pressing for an extraordinary session of the Diet.[45] The idea here was to provide a stage from which His Majesty's subjects could be exhorted to rededicate themselves to a fighting spirit sure of ultimate triumph. It was also anticipated that the Diet would vote such extensive emergency powers to the cabinet that Suzuki and his colleagues would

[41] See *Statements:* Tanemura #61977.

[42] Mr. Hideoto Mori of the Plans Co-ordination Bureau (Cabinet); Captain Yatsuji Nagai, chief of the Naval Affairs Division of the Naval Affairs Bureau of the Navy Ministry; Mr. Masaru Sone, chief of the 1st Division of the Political Affairs Bureau of the Foreign Ministry; Mr. Arata Sugihara, chief of the General Affairs Division of the Greater East Asia Ministry; and Colonel Sakō Tanemura of the Army General Staff. See *Statements:* Sone #60999 and Sakomizu 4/21/49.

[43] According to Colonel Tanemura, the "homeland battle" strategy was first officially adopted on February 25, 1945, at a meeting between War Ministry and Army General Staff officers. *Statements:* Tanemura #61977.

[44] See *Statements:* Suezawa #62051; Sakomizu #61979, #62003, and #62016.

[45] See *Statements:* Sakomizu #62003, Sakonji #61339; JFO MS: Ch. 29 (Dai hachijūnana rinji gikai).

at last be able to deal effectively with the problems besetting the nation.[46] At the same time, arrangements were made to have the final decision with respect to the new war policy sanctioned at a meeting held in the presence of the Emperor—a move which would lend an "indisputable dignity" to the army's plan for victory.[47]

On June 6, just two days after Hirota's tête-à-tête with Malik, the army suddenly called a full-dress meeting[48] of the Supreme Council for the Direction of the War, thus broadening once again the attendance which had only so recently been restricted.[49] The sole item of business on the agenda was a document rather typically entitled "The Fundamental Policy to Be Followed Henceforth in the Conduct of the War," the very same which the assistant secretaries had speedily drafted to meet the need envisaged by the Supreme Command. Here was nothing less than the army's final, comprehensive demand that the nation engage the enemy on Japan's own shores, for only thus, said the military, could the imperial land be preserved and the national polity maintained. As they saw it, Japan's "one hundred million" people, ever steadfast in their loyalty to their imperial father through all eternity, would arise together from the vantage ground of their sacred land to strike the invaders dead![50]

[46] The 87th Extraordinary Session of the Diet convened on June 9 (the day following the imperial conference to be discussed in the text above) and adjourned on June 13. The cabinet encountered a great deal of difficulty in trying to press its legislation through the Diet but finally won its point by compromise. In addition to a volunteer military service (corps) law, a "Wartime Emergency Measure" was passed conferring extensive emergency powers on the government. See the citations in the preceding footnote and Statements: Sakonji #58226, Hayashi #54482, Shirai #54472, Yoshizumi #54484 and #54485.

[47] See Statements: Sakomizu #62003 and Tanemura #61977.

[48] See the voluminous documents and memoirs found in JFO MS: Ch. 28 (Sensō kansui yōkō no kettei). The more important of these which have direct bearing upon the June 6 meeting of the Supreme Council are: "Kongo torubeki sensō shidō no kihon taikō," "Kokuryoku no genjō," "Sekai jōsei handan," "Tōgō gaishō kōjutsu hikki," "Tōgō gaishō shuki," and "Takagi hiroku (Tōgō gaishō dan)." See also Statements: Hoshina #61978, Matsudaira #60745, Sone #60999, Yoshizumi #54484, Sakomizu 4/21/49; Toyoda, Saigo no teikoku kaigun, 193–94; USSBS, Japan's Struggle to End the War, 7, 16–18; USSBS, Interrogations, II, Toyoda, 319, and Yonai, 328.

[49] In addition to the Big Six, the following persons (the secretary group) were present: Chief Cabinet Secretary Sakomizu, Chief of the Plans Co-ordination Bureau Akinaga, Chief of the Military Affairs Bureau Yoshizumi, and Chief of the Naval Affairs Bureau Hoshina. Two cabinet ministers were also present: Munitions Minister Teijirō Toyoda and Minister for Agriculture and Commerce Ishiguro. At the time in question, Chief of the Army General Staff Umezu (one of the Big Six) was away on an inspection trip so his place was taken by the vice-chief, Lieutenant General Torashirō Kawabe.

Since the Foreign Office was not represented by a "secretary," Sakomizu, who represented the cabinet, delved into matters of diplomacy from time to time. This led to friction between Sakomizu and the Foreign Office people who felt that Sakomizu was not any more capable of discussing foreign policy than were the military representatives in the secretary group (name of source withheld by request).

[50] The "vantage ground" phrase in the "Fundamental Policy" referred to a key

In order to provide a basis of reference for its grandiose scheme, the army also submitted two documentary appraisals entitled "Estimate of the World Situation" and "The Present State of National Power,"[51] but here fate played a most ironical prank upon Japan's stalwart warriors. Since both documents had been prepared *prior* to the army's demand for a basic policy decision relating to the future conduct of the war, neither the one nor the other properly served the purpose for which the army was now using them.[52] The appraisal of conditions within the homeland, in particular, contained astounding evidence of a general and irremediable deterioration.

The ominous turn of the war, so the document began, and the increasing tempo of Allied air raids have resulted in a serious disruption of land and sea communications and essential war production. The food situation has worsened and "it has become increasingly difficult to meet the requirements of total war." Although morale is high, there is dissatisfaction with the present regime, and criticism of the government and the military is on the ascendancy. "The people are losing confidence in their leaders, and the gloomy omen of deterioration of public morale is present. The spirit of public sacrifice is lacking and among leading intellectuals there are some who advocate peace negotiations as a way out." We are faced, the appraisal continued, with insurmountable difficulties in the field of transportation and communication, and if we lose Okinawa (which they did) we cannot hope to maintain planned communication with the Asian mainland after the end of this month (June 1945). Our total production of steel, at present, is about one-fourth of our output during the same period last year. The construction of steel ships, therefore, cannot be expected to continue after the middle of this year. There is also a strong possibility that a considerable portion of Japan's various industrial areas will soon have to suspend operations for want of coal. From midyear on, there will be a shortage of basic industrial salts, making it difficult for us to produce light metals, synthetic oil, and explosives. Henceforth, prices will rise sharply—bringing on inflation. This, in turn, will seriously undermine our wartime economy.[53]

And so it went, facts and figures and cold calculations which should,

---

point which had been expressed by an Army General Staff officer, namely, that the closer to home the Japanese fought the greater would be their advantage. In view of the facts, this was either a surprisingly naïve assertion or an open and cunning distortion. Japan simply did not have the weapons of war with which to back up the moral (and other) advantages of fighting within the homeland. In addition to the citations listed in footnote 48 above, see *Statements:* Amano #54480.

[51] "Sekai jōsei handan" and "Kokuryoku no genjō," for the texts of which, see JFO MS: Ch. 28 (Sensō kansui yōkō no kettei).

[52] See *Statements:* Sakomizu #62003, Suezawa #62051, Matsudaira #60745, and Sone #60999.

[53] See USSBS, *Japan's Struggle to End the War*, 16–18, and "Kokuryoku no genjō" in JFO MS: Ch. 28 (Sensō kansui yōkō no kettei).

without any stretch of the imagination, have cast derision on the army's theory and bespoken the impracticability of its plan, yet which, in reality, did neither the one nor the other.

The military, of course, had not gone into this matter nonchalantly, nor were they unprepared. Some time prior to the opening of the conference in question, one of the assistant secretaries representing the army had suggested that the damaging contents of both appraisals be revised so that the tenor of the documents as a whole would come into line with the recommendations contained in the "Fundamental Policy." The official who would have had to make the changes at first refused to countenance any such flagrant falsification of statistics, but on June 6, the very day on which the Supreme Council met, he suddenly experienced a mild change of heart. In a great rush, he composed two "explanations" and attached one to each appraisal in the form of a paragraph entitled "Conclusions."[54] Although these appendages helped blur the patent contradiction existing between the "Fundamental Policy" and its "supporting" documents, the "Conclusions" could neither destroy the contradiction nor suppress the later suspicion that the army had flown into the face of reason because it was psychologically unprepared to accept the fact of its failure.

Not all the militarists were blind. Many of them, in fact, knew that there was little or no chance of their achieving so smashing a success that the Pacific war would end gloriously for Japan, but they were confident of at least winning an operational victory in the decisive battle for the homeland. One important section of the Japanese military argued that no matter through what neutral power Japan might seek peace the world at large would assume that Japan was *surrendering* and a complete split in the national unity and polity would result. The alternative, they said, was to open peace negotiations *after* a success on the field of battle had been achieved. Only a very few of those who supported this view really believed that Japan could turn the impending Allied invasion back completely; the rest merely hoped to inflict so much damage initially that the enemy would be forced to regroup before renewing the attack. In the interim, Japan—on the basis of the decision she had won—might be able to negotiate a settlement on favorable terms.[55] Although they naturally

---

[54] It is impossible to determine whether the "Conclusions" were written by the chief of the Plans Co-ordination Bureau or by an assistant secretary representing the cabinet. To what extent the person who drafted the "Conclusions" was coerced into doing so—and to what extent he was a free agent—is also open to question. There can be no doubt, however, that the "Conclusions" were an afterthought, written in order to reconcile the trouble-laden content of the two appraisals with the recommendations set forth in the "Fundamental Policy." See *Statements:* Suezawa #62051, Matsudaira #60745, Sone #60999, Toyoda #57669, Sakomizu #62003 and #62016.

[55] The possibility of winning an operational victory and of thereby obtaining terms favorable to Japan became a key point in the military's demand to continue the war through an Allied invasion of the home islands. In this connection, see *Statements:* Suezawa #62051, Amano #54480, and Toyoda #61340.

did not say so, these same men, under such circumstances, might also have called for an all-out drive aimed at exploiting their initial and temporary success into a resounding victory for Great Japan. Who could be sure, in other words, that their argument did not just represent a clever plot on the part of the bitter-enders to ensnare the government into committing the nation to suicide? There were, after all, many persons who sincerely felt it would be far better to die fighting in battle than to seek an ignominious survival by surrendering the nation and acknowledging defeat.

As they had been able to do often in the past, so now at this conference, the Japanese military adroitly launched a psychological offensive sure of hitting its mark. Japan, they declared, had come to the fork in the road of destiny. The life or death of the nation was at stake! The traditional loyalty of the people to their imperial land must be enhanced beyond measure. Japan must embrace a fighting spirit bred of conviction in certain victory. She must leave no stone unturned to seize the divine opportunity to triumph![56]

Here were drowning men grasping at the proverbial straw, bamboo warriors bending beneath the weight of uncontrollable events, yet never toppling to the ground. Here was yet another case of spirit feeding upon spirit, while the decisive material considerations were ignored or left to the future.[57]

In all, the conference of June 6 consumed hours of explanations and reports. Morning passed into afternoon, and the final decision became a foregone conclusion. Of those present, all except the Foreign Minister were either ardent supporters of the army's plan[58] or, like Yonai, ap-

---

[56] See "Kokuryoku no genjō" and "Sekai jōsei handan" in JFO MS: Ch. 28 (Sensō kansui yōkō no kettei) and IMTFE: Kido, 31146.

[57] Suezawa, who helped draft the "Fundamental Policy," clearly realized that while it called for a fight to the bitter end there was nothing definite in the policy so far as practical measures were concerned. Even so, he felt he had no other course open to him than the one he followed at the time. *Statements:* Suezawa #62051.

[58] Chief Cabinet Secretary Sakomizu, who was called upon at the beginning of the conference to read and explain the "Fundamental Policy," has stated that he endeavored to convey the interpretation that the war could be ended by diplomatic or other means if it became clear that Japan's polity could be preserved and the imperial homeland safeguarded. When two of the Big Six were asked about this after the war, they replied that they could not remember any such interpretation having been made. They considered the policy to be "a strong emphasis upon persistent continuation of the war" but did not regard it as a manifestation of the true intentions of the Big Six since the latter had been discussing a move to end the war (a reference to Point III of the plan of May 14) and had been keeping this absolutely secret from their subordinates (the men responsible for the "Fundamental Policy"). In reply to this, Sakomizu subsequently declared that since he had had to take great care in choosing his words the others had probably failed to understand what he had really intended to say. (In either case, this is still *haragei*—in one form or another.) See *Statements:* Sakomizu #61979, #62003, #62004, #62006, #62016; Suezawa #62051; and Tanemura #61977.

parently cautious devotees of the obscurity of silence.[59] Tōgō, who had entered the conference room completely in the dark as to what was on the agenda,[60] vainly endeavored to counter the explanations offered in support of the "Fundamental Policy" by declaring that Japan's failing strength was a development which ought to occasion grave concern, that increased production would be extremely difficult to attain in view of the mounting intensity of the enemy's air offensive, and that so long as Japan lacked adequate air power he could not endorse the view that the situation would improve the closer the enemy penetrated to the Japanese home islands.[61]

In response to a request lodged by the secretaries to the effect that the Foreign Minister endeavor to improve relations with the Soviets to the point where they would supply Japan with war materials, Tōgō flatly declared that such a maneuver was out of the question. So far as he could see, the Soviet Union was not then, and would not later become, Japan's ally.[62]

Here, at least, was a whisper of actuality in a wilderness of make-believe, but as in the case of the closed meetings held in mid-May the Foreign Minister's views, although overburdeningly sound, failed to turn the tide of general agreement, which swept all else before it and even carried on its crest the enigmatic figure of the Premier himself.

The charitable view is that the story of the monkey and the trainer, which someone had related to Suzuki prior to the meeting, had made an impression. It seems that there was a certain monkey trainer in ancient

[59] Tōgō has stated that after the meeting of June 6 he expressed his surprise to Yonai that the latter had not come to his assistance but had maintained silence throughout. Yonai merely replied that it was useless to oppose a document like the "Fundamental Policy." It would appear from other evidence that both he and Premier Suzuki did not feel that any harm was being done.

Toyoda also says he did not take the meeting seriously and he does not think Suzuki, Yonai, or Tōgō did. There was such a "crowd" present that frank discussion was out of the question. In other words, the decision represented the will of their subordinates but not that of the Big Six who had already decided on the course to follow in May. See *Statements:* Toyoda #57669.

[60] Unlike the army, the navy, and the cabinet, the Foreign Office did not have a representative in the secretary group (the Foreign Office was represented in the assistant secretary group—see footnote 42 above). This may explain why Tōgō was unaware of what lay in store when he entered the conference room on June 6. It is also possible that the military had taken special pains to keep the Foreign Office in the dark. See *Statements:* Sone #60999 and Tōgō #50304.

[61] In addition to the references cited previously in connection with the Supreme Council meeting of June 6, see *Statements:* Tōgō #50304; Yoshizumi #54484; and Sakomizu #61969, #62003, #62004, and #62006.

[62] While the secretaries were urging Tōgō to improve relations with the Soviet Union, Ambassador Harriman in Moscow was cabling Washington that Stalin's armies would be deployed on the Manchurian frontier by August 8—ready to launch their attack upon Japan's Kwantung army. See Millis (ed.), *The Forrestal Diaries*, 67, and Leahy, *I Was There*, 383.

China whose monkey was not at all pleased when offered three acorns in the morning and four in the evening as the reward for the tricks it performed. The trainer, determined not to be outsmarted by the monkey, thereupon suggested four acorns in the morning and three in the evening instead. To this the monkey readily agreed and ever after performed its feats willingly when the trainer gave his commands. The story had been aimed at convincing Suzuki that so long as he did not forsake the goal (presumably a termination of the war) he "might as well carry things along smoothly for the time being without offending the army."[63]

The stand taken by Suzuki is as tantalizing as it in interesting. His position as Premier made his performance the most inimical to the nation's interest and the most unsatisfactory from the point of view of the purpose for which he supposedly had been elevated to the premiership. The question is, why did he carry the army's banner not only in this conference but also in those which immediately followed?

As has already been indicated, some say that Suzuki lent his support to the army's plan with the intention of later turning the tables on the military when an opportunity presented itself. This would be a type of *haragei* which theoretically could have been fathomed by the end-the-war advocates but not by the military. Yet the fact is that those who really wanted to end the war were sorely distressed by Suzuki's attitude. They did not know what to think. Was Suzuki an opportunist—a man of dual personality—or were his remarks and actions the result of subtle coercion applied by the military?[64] The one explanation which is rarely given, yet seems closer to the truth, is that Premier Suzuki supported the army's plan because he personally felt that it was a good one or, at least, that it could do no harm. In other words, Suzuki himself desired to continue the war as long as humanly possible in the belief that Japan might still inflict such heavy casualties on the invading forces that the Allies would finally be willing to discuss terms. Apparently the only limitation so far as he was concerned was the status of the Emperor. If it became clear that a continuation of the war through an invasion would stiffen the Allied attitude toward the Throne and thereby produce a situation where the United States and Britain might decide to abolish the imperial institution, then, and only then, would the Admiral Baron Premier step forth with the courage he possessed to announce that the war must stop and Japan must surrender. Barring such a development, Suzuki would be content to prosecute the war with every means at his command, for that, after all, was the way of the warrior and the path of the patriot. Thus,

---

[63] Source withheld by request.

[64] Sakomizu, Shimomura, Wakatsuki, and Kase support Suzuki on the basis of coercion by the military, enforced use of *haragei*, or Suzuki's intention of turning the tables on the military. Takagi and Tōgō are more critical of Suzuki, considering him either an opportunist or a man of dual personality. See JFO MS: Ch. 28 (Sensō kansui yōkō no kettei). For another (and rather different) characterization of Suzuki by Tōgō, see footnote 52, Ch. 3, above.

even in the absence of the actual physical wherewithal to repel the invaders, Suzuki was, at this time, still anxious to give Iyeyasu's Mikataga-hara strategy a try. Put up a bold front, in other words, and taunt the enemy to his face: "If you want to come, *come!*"

At any rate, by the time the conference had adjourned at 5:00 P.M., the die had been cast.[65] What followed over the next two days was anticlimactic. On June 7 Premier Suzuki carried the Supreme Council's decision to the cabinet and there portrayed the bloodletting which lay in the offing in terms of *human* explosives who would throw themselves beneath the enemy's tanks and of *training planes* (the only type Japan had left to send aloft)[66] which would hurl themselves at the enemy's war fleet and transports. In the end, Suzuki called upon the government to enhance its efforts and strengthen its resolution so as to keep pace with the onward march of the Supreme Command. "There is only one way to win," he declared, "and that is by determination. When the whole nation possesses this will, then we shall be able to achieve victory!"[67]

With the cabinet's rubber-stamped approval on the "Fundamental Policy" the stage was now set for the last act. On June 8 thirteen officials of state,[68] including the Big Six members of the Supreme Council, gathered in the front audience chamber of Building No. 2 of the Imperial Household Ministry, and there, in the presence of the Emperor, again proposed the plans[69] and recapitulated the discussions of June 6–7.

---

[65] As if to confirm the decision to fight to the last man, the Supreme Councilors agreed that the capital should not be evacuated, that is, that the government and the court should not remove to the underground redoubt being readied in the mountains. See the JFO MS citation listed in the preceding footnote, especially "'Senso shido no kihon taiko' kakugi kettei ni tai suru sori no shoken." See also *Statements:* Inaba #61148, Suzuki #531, and Yoshizumi #54484.

[66] In this connection, see *Statements:* Toyoda #61340.

[67] At the Supreme Council meeting on June 6, Vice-Admiral Hoshina had said that each person present should put forth his best efforts and that if anyone failed he should be prepared to commit suicide. Although Suzuki repeated this thought to the cabinet on June 7, he was forced to retract his statements after Minister of Agriculture and Commerce Ishiguro vigorously protested. See *Statements:* Hoshina #61978; JFO MS: Ch. 28 (Senso kansui yoko no kettei), especially "'Senso shido no kihon taiko' kakugi kettei ni tai suru sori no shoken" and "Shimomura, *Shusenki*"; and *Translations:* Doc. #53440-F.

[68] In addition to the Emperor, the following persons were present: the Big Six: Suzuki, Togo, Anami, Yonai, Kawabe (substituting for Chief of the Army General Staff Umezu), Toyoda (Soemu); President of the Privy Council Hiranuma; Munitions Minister Toyoda (Teijiro); Agriculture and Commerce Minister Ishiguro; and the four members of the secretary group: Sakomizu, Akinaga, Yoshizumi, and Hoshina.

Admiral Soemu Toyoda, Japan's last wartime chief of the Naval General Staff, should not be confused with Admiral Teijiro Toyoda, who served in several cabinets but principally as Foreign Minister in the third Konoye Cabinet and as Munitions Minister in the Suzuki Cabinet. See Foreign Affairs Association, *The Japan Year Book, 1946–48*, section entitled "Change of Cabinets."

[69] The key point of the "Fundamental Policy," as expressed on June 6, was as follows: "With a faith born of eternal loyalty as our inspiration, we shall—through

This was nothing more than a glorified form of play-acting since the real decision had already been made and a reversal at this point was almost out of the question.[70] In the event that there had not been unanimity on June 6 and 7, the imperial conference would not have been held, for it was standard procedure not to trouble the "August Mind" of His Majesty with the various details and the pro and con arguments underlying the formulation of state policy. Only when there was agreement in the Supreme Council and the cabinet did such a conference convene, for in matters of grave importance it was desirable to record the final decision in the presence of the Emperor. Although the sovereign usually merely listened to the discussion and generally never said anything, a decision adopted by a conference of this type was considered to be endowed by the imperial presence with imperial sanction. Such a decision, therefore, could normally be superseded only at the instance of the original sponsor (in this case, the Supreme Council) acting with the concurrence of the cabinet and the sanction of the Throne.[71]

Although some new opinions were expressed at the imperial conference of June 8, they all fell into line with the army's plan and pur-

---

the unity of our nation and the advantages of our terrain—prosecute the war to the bitter end in order to uphold the national polity, protect the imperial land, and assure a basis for the future development of the nation." The policy, as adopted on June 8, was the same except for the last phrase, "and assure a basis for the future development of the nation," which was changed to read "and accomplish the objectives for which we went to war [seisen]." (It is possible that a mistake—careless or willful—in characters has occurred and that seisen is not the objectives "for which we went to war" but the more common phrase, the objectives of the "holy war.")

Tōgō believed that the change was made to eliminate the possibility of the original phrase being interpreted to mean that Japan must retain the occupied territories. He therefore regarded the change as an indication of Japan's willingness to scale down her war aims. See Statements: Tōgō #50304 and JFO MS: Ch. 28 (Sensō kansui yōkō no kettei), especially "Kongo torubeki sensō shidō no kihon taikō."

[70] In addition to the documents already cited in reference to the discussions held on June 6, see JFO MS: Ch. 28 (Sensō kansui yōkō no kettei), especially the following: "Gozen kaigi keika," "Gozen kaigi ni okeru gunju daijin hatsugen yōshi," "Rokugatsu yōka gozen kaigi ni okeru sūmitsuin gichō no hatsugen," "Gozen kaigi ni okeru gaimu daijin ken dai Tō-A daijin hatsugen yōshi," "Gozen kaigi ni okeru naikaku sōri daijin hatsugen yōshi," "Gozen kaigi ni okeru sambō sōchō [sic, but actually jichō since Kawabe was substituting for Umezu] hatsugen yōshi," and "Gozen kaigi ni okeru gunreibu sōchō hatsugen yōshi." See also Translations: Doc. #53440, Doc. #53440-D, and Doc. #53440-E.

Kase, Journey to the Missouri, 173, is in error in stating that the imperial conference of June 8 "lasted only a little over fifteen minutes." The basic Foreign Office documents cited herein affirm that the conference lasted one hour and fifty minutes, from 10:05 to 11:55 A.M.

[71] The evolution of policy and the part played by the cabinet, the Supreme Council, the imperial conference, and the Throne find expression in Statements: Kido #61476, Suzuki #531, Hasunuma #58225, Matsudaira #60745, and Sakomizu 5/3/49. See also unpublished USSBS interrogation #507 (Hyakutake) and IMTFE: Proceedings, 663–64.

pose.[72] Only Foreign Minister Tōgō again sounded a note of warning. Drawing attention to the fact that world conditions were very unfavorable to Japan and that wartime diplomacy was fundamentally influenced by changes in the war situation, Tōgō emphasized that it would be impossible to obtain outside aid. Unless the war took a turn for the better and Japan's fighting power was enhanced, all Japan could expect, he said, was a further deterioration of her international position. He consequently implied that in view of the improbability of any such change taking place the nation would undoubtedly encounter very severe difficulties in the near future.[73]

In spite of the Foreign Minister's remarks, the result anticipated by the military was obtained. When Suzuki called upon those present to offer their opinions on the "Fundamental Policy," everyone remained silent. In the face of the obvious, the Premier asked whether he might assume that everyone was in agreement. Again there was silence, so Suzuki simply declared, "Well then, I conclude that no one has any particular objection to the plan."[74]

The assembled ministers and councilors arose and bowed, and the Emperor, who had not uttered a single word the whole time,[75] solemnly withdrew from the chamber.

The imperial conference of Friday, June 8, 1945, was over. The

[72] President of the Privy Council Hiranuma, for instance, gave his full support and encouragement and asked everyone present to take care to suppress the propagation of peace sentiments among the people. In a postwar response to a leading question about his role at this time, Hiranuma declared that in speaking of the need to guard against crying for peace ("heiwa wo tonauru ga gotoki wa mottomo imashimu beshi") he did not mean that Japan's leaders should not *think* about peace. The documents submitted on June 8, he said, convinced him that the war could not be continued and that a decision to end the war should be formulated as national policy. Until this happened, however, it would be improper "to cry for peace" since "crying for peace would defeat its own purpose." (*Statements:* Hiranuma #55127.) The manner in which this explanation was solicited and the evidence as a whole does much to destroy the significance of the statement, yet in the light of *haragei* it cannot be completely ignored.

[73] See "Gozen kaigi ni okeru gaimu daijin ken dai Tō-A daijin hatsugen yōshi" in JFO MS: Ch. 28 (Sensō kansui yōkō no kettei); IMTFE: Tōgō, 35783; and *Statements:* Tōgō #50304.

A careful comparison of the remarks made by Tōgō on June 6 with those made by him on June 8 reveals that on the latter date he presented a slightly less pessimistic view of the possibility of an improvement in Soviet-Japanese relations. Whether this was because of the Emperor's presence or because of a change in Tōgō's own thinking is difficult to say. (Interview with Atsushi Ōi and *Statements:* Yoshizumi #54484.)

[74] See "Gozen kaigi keika" in JFO MS: Ch. 28 (Sensō kansui yōkō no kettei). Suzuki also made a brief closing statement which is notable only for his promise that the government would work hand in hand with the Supreme Command.

[75] If this seems strange, it should be remembered that the Emperor was not expected to say anything and that the imperial conference had been convened in His Majesty's presence to lend an "indisputable dignity" to the proceedings—not to ask the Emperor's wishes or even to listen to his opinion. See the citations listed in footnote 71 above.

"highest authority"[76] had spoken in unmistakable terms. The nation would, fight to the bitter end.[77]

[76] Since cabinet approval had been obtained on June 7 for the "Fundamental Policy" adopted by the Supreme Council on June 6 and since the "Fundamental Policy" adopted by the imperial conference on June 8 was, in essence, the same as that adopted by the Supreme Council on June 6, the imperial conference decision represented, in this particular instance, the "highest authority." In practice, it would have been *unprecedented* to have had a policy broached at an imperial conference unless that policy had first received the unanimous support of the cabinet, for if the cabinet ministers later refused to endorse the action of the imperial conference the said policy could not become a decision of state. This, coming after a conference attended by the Emperor, would have been considered an affront to His Majesty's person.

[77] Although Tōgō and several others interpreted the action taken by the imperial conference as a decision to continue the war only if certain conditions could be met, this view was not shared by the military. According to the latter, the "Fundamental Policy" committed the nation, without reservation, compromise, or quarter, to a fight to the finish. See IMTFE: Tōgō, 36110–11, and *Statements:* Tōgō #50304.

5

INTERLUDE IN SWITZERLAND

Peace Feelers Through the Dulles Organization

JUST one month before the imperial conference of June 8, 1945, unanimously endorsed "The Fundamental Policy to Be Followed Henceforth in the Conduct of the War," a Japanese naval attaché at Berne, Commander Yoshirō Fujimura, dispatched the first in a series of urgent and secret cables in which he attempted to convince his superiors at home that Japan should negotiate for peace through the medium of the American OSS organization in Switzerland.[1]

This somewhat unusual suggestion was the outgrowth of months of discussion—months during which Fujimura, who was then stationed in Germany, had traded views and shared opinions with others of a similar mind among the naval personnel attached to the Japanese Embassy in Berlin. Although these representatives of Japan abroad had come to realize that their once powerful ally was nearing the end of the road, they had despaired of doing anything to help their own country. They were shackled to their posts in Germany, and Tokyo, where any real or final decision would have to be made, was thousands of miles away. Even if their cables got through, there was no certainty that the unwelcome warnings in them would be given more than passing notice. The men of rank and power within the navy, like their colleagues in the army and in the civil branches of the government, were not prone to listen to subordinates who failed to support the view that only victory or death could satisfy the national honor.

About the time the group in Germany had all but given up hope, fate suddenly intervened and a transfer of personnel took place. Almost overnight, Fujimura found himself in Switzerland, an ideal springboard from which to launch a movement aimed at achieving the purposes of the men from whom he had drawn his inspiration.

---

[1] Unless otherwise indicated, the details of Fujimura's negotiations with the Dulles organization are from an account written by Commander Yoshirō Fujimura entitled "Tsūkon! Daresu dai-ichi den" which appeared in *Bungei Shunjū*, XXIX (May 1951), 106–18, and from an unabridged version of the same found in *Statements: Fujimura* #46118. See also JFO MS: Ch. 23 (Daresu kōsaku).

103

Within a very short time after his arrival at his new post in Berne, Fujimura took two nonofficial Japanese civilians[2] into his confidence and together they approached Dr. Friedrich Hack,[3] a German national with a rather bizarre background. It seems that Hack, whose connections with the Japanese navy went back more than twenty years, had once enjoyed the confidence of von Ribbentrop, the German Foreign Minister. In fact, during the negotiations which culminated in the Anti-Comintern Pact of 1936 Hack had occasionally had the opportunity of playing host to the then Ambassador von Ribbentrop and his Japanese counterpart, Major General Ōshima.[4] Later on, after the Nazis had begun in earnest to proclaim their "World Dictatorship" doctrine and their "Master Race" theory, Hack had risen in open opposition to their wild schemes. The immediate result of this action had been arrest and imprisonment.

Fortunately for Hack, his friends in the Japanese navy had subsequently interceded in his behalf and had managed to get him released into their custody. Although they had spirited him off to Japan, he had found it continually necessary to dodge the efforts of Nazi Ambassador Ott to have him returned to Germany. After having spent some time in Japan, therefore, Hack had proceeded to Switzerland where, as a purchasing agent for the Japanese navy, he had dedicated himself to serving the cause of those who had given him a new lease on life. Thus, when Fujimura arrived in Berne, Hack was a natural choice as a co-conspirator.

On April 23, 1945, while the battle for Okinawa was still raging in the Pacific, Dr. Hack, acting as an intermediary for Fujimura, paid his first visit to the so-called Dulles organization,[5] a group of OSS agents whose political warfare activities reached out across Europe under the direction of Allen Dulles, the younger brother of the man who was later

[2] Mr. Shigeyoshi Tsuyama (an executive of the Ōsaka Shōsen Kabushiki Kaisha) and Mr. Shintarō Ryū (correspondent for the Tokyo *Asahi Shimbun*).

[3] Although the IMTFE material uses the spelling, "Hack," employed in this study, it is possible that the IMTFE translator did not have anything more definite than the author's own Japanese source, "Hakku." In spite of countless hours spent in attempts to trace the man and the name (and the possible variations such as Haak, Haag, Hoch, and Hock), the author has not been able to come to a firm conclusion other than that "Dr. Hack" (who is said to have died in Zurich in March 1949) either was not well known or was masquerading behind a pseudonym.

References to a "Haak" or "Haag" in Willoughby, *Shanghai Conspiracy*, 69 and 216, are apparently references to the Dr. Hack mentioned in this chapter. This is not to suggest that Hack was connected with the Sorge ring. In fact, the Willoughby references imply that "Haak" or "Haag" met Sorge in the latter's capacity as a journalist, not in his role as a spy.

[4] See IMTFE: Ōshima, 5913–16 and 33984–85. See also Willoughby, *Shanghai Conspiracy*, 69.

[5] Fujimura's decision to initiate negotiations through Mr. Dulles stemmed from a feeling that the latter's efforts and activities with regard to the peace negotiations in northern Italy invited trust and respect. The Fujimura group also knew, or at least suspected, the true nature of the Dulles organization and assumed that any feelers directed through Mr. Dulles would receive serious and careful consideration.

to draft the Japanese Peace Treaty. Three days after this initial meeting,[6] Hack and Fujimura received word from the Dulles group that it desired their personal history statements and a point-by-point written outline of Japan's position and intentions. A hastily convened meeting of the Fujimura "circle" was immediately held and a reply was drafted to the following effect: Commander Yoshirō Fujimura, Japanese naval attaché in Switzerland, wishing to exert himself to the utmost to bring about direct negotiations between Japan and the United States, is desirous of obtaining the views of the government of the United States with respect to this question.[7]

This evasion of the issue and clumsy attempt to place the burden of initiative and responsibility upon the United States would probably not have been accepted by the Dulles group had it not understood the difficult role Fujimura was attempting to play. The remarks made by Dr. Hack, who presented the above statement along with Fujimura's personal history file, indicated that Fujimura was in reality speaking out of turn and as yet had no authority to undertake any negotiations whatsoever.[8] At the same time, Hack promised that Fujimura would do everything in his power to win over the naval authorities in Tokyo and to convince the Japanese government to dedicate itself to ending the war promptly

The Dulles organization immediately informed Washington and requested instructions. On May 3 a reply arrived from the State Department authorizing Mr. Dulles' agents to receive whatever representations Fujimura wished to make but warning them not to commit the United States in any way. Washington's willingness to hear what he had to say was relayed to Fujimura that same day, but it was not until five days later, May 8, that the commander's consultations with his confidants produced results. It was then that he decided to send an urgent telegram

[6] Present at the April 23 meeting in addition to Hack were Mr. White (of the American Bank in Zurich), Dulles' American secretary (Mr. von Gaevernitz), and Dulles' adviser on Japanese problems (name withheld by request). Fujimura never actually dealt with Dulles directly. In fact, Mr. Dulles did not personally take an active part in the negotiations.

[7] Although the key to the problem of ending the war lay in the hands of the military in Tokyo, Fujimura reasoned that the distrust with which the United States regarded the Japanese army invited him, as a loyal servant of the Throne, *to act on his own initiative.* Since he was a navy man and since the navy had always been considered more liberal and less chauvinistic than the army, Fujimura—with Hack's concurrence—concluded that the Japanese navy offered the only channel through which an approach to peace could be made. It was his hope that the navy authorities in Tokyo would back him to the limit on whatever he might be able to arrange in Switzerland.

[8] Some time after Fujimura made his first overture through Hack, Mr. Dulles' adviser on Japanese affairs requested Fujimura to produce concrete evidence that would show that he had the authority to undertake negotiations and the backing necessary to carry them through to completion. Since Fujimura was acting solely on his own initiative and without any authority from home, he was unable to comply with this request.

addressed directly to the Minister of the Navy and to the chief of the Naval General Staff. Late that night, in the utmost secrecy, Fujimura began the intricate coding process using a cryptographic device which, along with many others, had been transported to Europe from Japan by submarine. Early the next morning, a bare twenty-four hours after Germany capitulated, Fujimura at last sent his message on its way to Japan's all but beleaguered capital. His cable bristled with practically every classification possible: Urgent, Personal, Secret, Code. Not only that, but it went out as an operational dispatch. This meant that it would end up on the desks occupied by the Navy Minister and the chief of the Naval General Staff without being held indefinitely in the in-baskets of subordinate officials.

In opening his "attack" upon the authorities in Tokyo, Fujimura was careful to be selective in dealing with the truth. He thus made it appear that he had been nothing more than the passive recipient of a proposal made by Mr. Dulles through Dr. Hack.[9] According to Fujimura, the American agent had declared that if Japan desired an early termination of the war he would be pleased to inform Washington to that effect and to exert himself toward the realization of Japan's wish.[10]

In fairness to Fujimura, it must be said that had he told Tokyo the untampered truth he would very likely have done irreparable damage to his cause and might even have found himself placed under arrest on orders from the naval authorities at home. At any rate, he did at least include a statement to the effect that he personally believed Japan had no course open to her other than to plan for an immediate peace with the United States.

On May 10, 13, 14, 16, 18, and 20, the impatient Fujimura sent follow-up cables to his initial one of May 9. All of them, addressed as before, dealt with the proposed negotiations by implication while studiously avoiding, for security reasons, any direct mention of them by name. The second cable conveyed the details of the German surrender

---

[9] The cable described Mr. Dulles as a leading American political figure and as the head of the United States' political warfare activities for nearly all of Europe. Some time after Fujimura's cables began arriving in Japan, Navy Minister Yonai asked Foreign Minister Tōgō who Dulles was. Tōgō, who apparently did not know the answer, expressed more interest in the American position than in the American agent. He therefore asked Yonai to cable Fujimura that Japan could not accept unconditional surrender, that she must have some conditions, and that Japan wanted to know what she should do. Two or three weeks later Tōgō learned from Yonai that the navy had not sent the cable. See Tōgō, "Shūsen gaikō," *Kaizō*, XXXI (November 1950), 128–29, and *Statements*: Tōgō #50304.

[10] Fujimura emphasized that the Dulles "offer" was addressed specifically and solely to the Japanese navy. The naval authorities in Tokyo never really learned that the initiative had been Fujimura's. One of the admirals concerned with the negotiations on the Tokyo end thought that the American "offer" might be a reaction to Japan's peace feelers through the Soviet Union.

and laid the blame for Germany's "tragic end" on a group of reckless Nazi die-hards comparable to the faction in Japan which was planning to fight to the death—with bamboo spears if necessary. The cable warned of the utter folly of such a policy and exhorted Fujimura's superiors to profit by the lesson of Germany. The third and fourth cables reported that the American and British forces which were then concentrated in Europe and the Soviet armies stationed on the eastern front would soon be transported to the Far East where they would attack and lay siege to the Japanese homeland. This report, moreover, was supported with details. The fifth cable, dispatched on May 16, discussed the role Dulles and his organization had played in effecting a separate truce in northern Italy and compared the good fortune which had thereafter accrued to the Italians with the misery inherited by the Germans as a result of their stubborn resistance to the bitter end.

Not until almost two weeks after Fujimura's first message did the naval authorities in Tokyo deign to reply. The chief of the Naval Affairs Bureau, speaking for the policy makers, instructed Fujimura to take the utmost care lest he fall into an enemy trap. The proposed negotiations, the cable warned, seemed to be an enemy scheme to undermine Japan's will to fight by creating a split between the imperial army and navy.[11]

Needless to say, this cable was most unwelcome in Berne where Fujimura and his fellow conspirators feared the negotiations would break down completely if they could not soon convey something positive to the Dulles group. Bedeviled by Tokyo's disinterested attitude,[12] Fujimura decided there was only one way out. When he could delay no longer, he reported to the Americans, through Hack, that Tokyo had not as yet replied. At the same time, he sent still another cable to the navy people at home in which he asked them, in the absence of concrete evidence about an enemy plot, to accept his view that their suspicions were unfounded and to authorize him to open negotiations at once so as to

[11] In addition to the citations listed in footnote 1 above, see Toyoda, *Saigo no teikoku kaigun*, 203–4; *Statements:* Toyoda #61340, Suezawa #62051; and Takagi, *Shūsen oboegaki*, 38–39. The policy makers in Tokyo were also suspicious because Fujimura was a "mere" naval commander. Since the "American offer" had not been made to a person of rank and authority, they doubted its "sincerity" and authenticity.

[12] After his return to Japan in 1946, Fujimura "learned" that Navy Minister Yonai had been in favor of pursuing the negotiations and that Chief of the Naval Affairs Bureau Hoshina, Chief of Naval Operations (IGHQ) Tomioka, and Chief of the Training Bureau Takagi (also cabinet liaison officer to IGHQ) had all concurred. Opposition had arisen, however, on the part of the chief and vice-chief of the Naval General Staff (Toyoda and Ōnishi, respectively).

Toyoda has since stated that his unwillingness to permit his subordinates to dabble in peace negotiations sprang from the danger that any such activity on their part would cause the fanatical younger officer element in the army and navy to resort to violence. In other words, the domestic situation at the time demanded that any strong arguments favoring peace be restrained.

save Japan from a fate like Germany's. By the end of May, Fujimura had sent four more cables[13] but to none did he receive even the slightest reply.

While they anxiously awaited instructions which they hoped would give them full powers to negotiate a termination of the war, the members of the Fujimura group endeavored indirectly to discover the probable American attitude toward the conditions on which they felt the negotiations would have to be based. Of primary importance was the question of Japan's sovereignty: the retention of the Emperor and the perpetuation of the national polity were essential. Next in importance was the preservation of Japan's merchant marine and last, but by no means least, was the disposition of Korea and Formosa. The unofficial reactions they obtained indicated that they might stand a chance of keeping the Emperor and the merchant marine but would get absolutely nowhere if they attempted to hold onto Korea and Formosa.

When still no answer came, the group rather excitedly decided that Fujimura should return to Japan and present his case on the spot. When the matter was discussed with Mr. Dulles' adviser on Japanese affairs, he did not exactly oppose the idea but he did suggest that Fujimura might only be asking for trouble by returning home. It would be more to the point, he said, if Tokyo were to dispatch a man of rank—a general, admiral, or cabinet minister—to Switzerland. Should the Japanese government desire to do this, the United States would guarantee a safe conduct for the emissary and would make it possible for him to reach Switzerland.[14]

By the time the negotiations had progressed this far, however, the Navy Ministry had decided to refer the whole matter to the Foreign Ministry and so a telegram went out to Fujimura instructing him to work with Minister Shunichi Kase and his staff in Berne.[15] So far as the imperial Japanese navy was concerned the issue was closed, and this, in

---

[13] These cables dealt primarily with the anticipated transfer of the American forces in Europe to the Far East and with the concentration of Soviet forces along the Manchurian border.

[14] Fujimura immediately cabled this proposal to Navy Minister Yonai. Somewhat earlier in the negotiations, Admiral Takagi, who had long realized the need for direct negotiations, had strongly recommended to Navy Minister Yonai that Japan use this opportunity to approach the United States directly. Takagi had even requested that he personally be sent to Switzerland to open negotiations, but the opposition of the Naval General Staff had rendered this impossible (Takagi letter to the author, dated Chigasaki City, August 7, 1951).

[15] These instructions were received by Fujimura on June 20 (in a cable from Navy Minister Yonai). The next day Fujimura met with Minister Kase and explained the negotiations to date.

The names Shunichi Kase and Toshikazu Kase are written with exactly the same characters. Anyone using Japanese material relating to this period should take care not to confuse the two men. Shunichi was the Japanese Minister to Switzerland; Toshikazu was a section chief in the Foreign Office in Tokyo who also served, at one time or another, as secretary to several Foreign Ministers.

fact, proved to be the case from the point of view of the Dulles organization as well.[16]

While these developments were taking place in Berne, a parallel but independent effort to obtain a negotiated peace was being launched in Zurich and Basel by Japan's military attaché, Lieutenant General Seigo Okamoto[17]—a man who had apparently grown so deeply concerned over the war situation that by the spring of 1945 he could no longer remain silent.[18] Early in May, Okamoto began comparing notes with Messrs. Yoshimura and Kitamura, officials of the Bank for International Settlements in Basel, and, together, these three secretly laid plans which were essentially similar in their purpose and execution to those adopted by Fujimura and his group.

After a thorough discussion of the prospects and issues involved, it was decided that Mr. Kitamura should first inform Minister Kase of Okamoto's intentions and should then endeavor to communicate with the United States government through Mr. Dulles. In order to reach the Dulles organization, Mr. Kitamura would request the good offices of a Swedish adviser to the International Settlements Bank, a certain Mr. Jacobsson, who was known to be on friendly terms with members of the American Consulate in Basel.[19] At the same time General Okamoto would cable his views and intentions to army Chief of Staff Umezu in order to obtain the necessary backing that would spell the difference between success and failure.[20]

[16] About mid-June 1945 Admiral Leahy questioned Mr. Dulles about rumors to the effect that some OSS agents in Switzerland were trying to arrange for conversations regarding peace terms with Japan. Leahy states that Dulles said "he had no knowledge of any such activity and did not believe the OSS was involved." (See Leahy, *I Was There*, 384.) Mr. Dulles' remarks, if correctly quoted, are difficult to reconcile with the facts. Although he did not personally take part in the negotiations, he was kept posted on developments.

[17] Lieutenant General Seigo Okamoto should not be confused with Mr. Suemasa Okamoto, Japan's Minister to Sweden, who was mentioned in connection with the Baggë negotiations (see Ch. 2 above).

[18] Except as specifically indicated, the details in the text are from an account of the negotiations written by Messrs. Kase (Shunichi), Yoshimura, and Kitamura which is appended to JFO MS: Ch. 23 (Daresu kōsaku). The author also discussed the negotiations with Shunichi Kase during an interview in Tokyo on March 7, 1952.

[19] At first, Kitamura and Yoshimura were uncertain whether it would be better to seek Mr. Jacobsson's good offices or the help of the American president of the Bank for International Settlements, Thomas H. McKittrick. They finally decided on Mr. Jacobsson (possibly because his wife's uncle was the vice-chief of the British Naval General Staff).

[20] In the event that the negotiations progressed favorably in Switzerland, Okamoto hoped that a delegation would be sent from Tokyo to Guam to open direct negotiations with the United States.

The Okamoto group apparently used the same strategy as Fujimura in reporting to Tokyo, for the then Foreign Minister, Shigenori Tōgō, was under the impression that the initiative in both the Fujimura and the Okamoto negotiations had come from Mr. Dulles. See *Statements:* Tōgō #50304.

While this decision was being made, Mr. Jacobsson was in Finland, rendering his services to that country in its peace negotiations with the Soviet Union, but as soon as he returned to Switzerland the matter was broached and his good offices were requested. In talking with Jacobsson, Yoshimura and Kitamura frankly sketched the range of their "desires," namely, preservation of the imperial system, nonrevision of the Japanese Constitution, internationalization of Manchuria, and retention by Japan of Korea and Formosa. Whatever Jacobsson thought of this ambitious overture is not known, but he did agree to render what assistance he could.

The problem was slightly complicated by the fact that Mr. Dulles was in Frankfurt am Main, but thanks to his American consular connections Mr. Jacobsson soon found himself in an auto sent to convey him to Wiesbaden, where Dulles had proposed they should meet. After spending some thirty-six hours with the OSS chief, Jacobsson returned to Basel and laid Dulles' answer before the Okamoto group. The picture Jacobsson painted was not encouraging. Although Dulles had said that the United States itself was not opposed to preserving the imperial institution, he had made it clear that Washington would have to give consideration to the objections which had been raised in the past by various other powers at war with Japan. For the time being, therefore, the United States could not make any firm commitments. All it could do was state its *understanding* that the imperial institution would be maintained *if Japan surrendered*. So far as the Constitution was concerned, it would have to be changed. With respect to the disposition of Korea and Formosa, "no comment."

Although this was all Dulles had offered at the moment, he had advised Jacobsson to inform the Japanese that their venture would end in failure unless they initiated negotiations in advance of a possible Soviet entry into the war.

By the time Jacobsson had reported on his meeting with Dulles it was already July and the stage was being set for the impending Allied conference at Potsdam. Okamoto was busily cabling Tokyo, but silence was his only answer. About ten days before the Big Three held their first meeting at Sans Souci, Minister Kase began an intensive campaign to gain the support of the Japanese Foreign Office for the negotiations, but all he received in reply was a request from the Foreign Minister for more information.[21] In this thoroughly unsatisfactory and frustrating way, the negotiations ground to a decided halt.

[21] Tōgō says, in effect, that by the time he became fully aware of the negotiations in Switzerland it was too late to take advantage of them. He makes it quite clear that his impression was that Dulles had recommended unconditional surrender, which was not an acceptable basis for terminating the war as far as Japan was concerned. Tōgō also states that the "strained relations" existing between the Japanese Minister in Switzerland and the military attachés there "made it unwise to entrust them with such a delicate matter." *Statements:* Tōgō #50304.

In spite of the unusual opportunity which existed in Switzerland during the spring and summer of 1945, the Japanese government was too involved in trying to find a way out of its difficulties through the Soviet Union to heed the warnings or exploit the efforts of either Fujimura or Okamoto. At the same time the United States and its Allies were too concerned with winning the Soviets to their side to pay more than cursory attention to the unauthorized feelers being set in motion in far-off Berne, Zurich, and Basel.

In Washington there was also the feeling that it was not the responsibility of the Allied Powers to plead with the Japanese to lay down their arms or in other ways to cajole the children of the land of the gods into acting sensibly. The important thing was ". . . to exert maximum force with maximum speed."[22] Peace overtures of the type undertaken by Fujimura and Okamoto were not interpreted as Japanese offers to capitulate. In a long statement released to the press on July 10, 1945, for instance, Acting Secretary of State Grew declared,

We have received no peace offer from the Japanese Government, either through official or unofficial channels. Conversations relating to peace have been reported to the Department from various parts of the world, but in no case has an approach been made to this Government, directly or indirectly, by a person who could establish his authority to speak for the Japanese Government, and in no case has an offer to surrender been made. In no case has this Government been presented with a statement purporting to define the basis upon which the Japanese Government would be prepared to conclude peace. . . .[23]

The nature of the purported "peace feelers" must be clear to everyone. They are the usual moves in the conduct of psychological warfare by a defeated enemy. No thinking American, recalling Pearl Harbor, Wake, Manila, Japanese ruthless aggression elsewhere, will give them credence.

Japanese militarism must and will be crushed. . . . The policy of this Government has been, is, and will continue to be unconditional surrender. . . .[24]

When the fateful day of capitulation came at last, Commander Yoshirō Fujimura recalled with chagrin the blindness which had contributed toward his government's failure to follow the path of negotiation he had endeavored to use to good advantage. In Zurich, meanwhile, Lieutenant General Seigo Okamoto, burdened by a defeat greater than his own, indelibly inscribed his name upon the sacred registers of the *samurai* by taking his life with his own hand.

[22] See Stimson and Bundy, *On Active Service*, 628–29. In Stimson's opinion, "reports of a weakening will to resist and of 'feelers' for peace terms . . . merely stimulated the American leaders in their desire to press home on *all* Japanese leaders the hopelessness of their cause; this was the nature of warmaking."

[23] Although this paragraph accurately describes the facts of the matter, the words and phrases employed are of particular interest in the light of what is now known about the Fujimura-Okamoto negotiations.

[24] See U.S. State Dept., *Bulletin*, XIII (July 15, 1945), 84–85.

6

LOOKING TO MOSCOW

Japanese Overtures to the Kremlin

ALTHOUGH the Emperor had maintained a sphinxlike silence throughout the imperial conference of June 8, Lord Keeper of the Privy Seal Kido was struck by the shadows of deep concern which he found lingering in the imperial countenance when he was received in audience shortly after the fateful meeting adjourned.[1]

This somewhat vague clue to His Majesty's true feelings[2] and the realization that the opportunity to achieve peace would now inevitably be delayed and possibly even lost altogether stirred Kido into action in a rather typical way. Upon leaving the imperial presence, Kido immediately began drafting a counterplan designed to invalidate the decision which had just been sanctioned by the "highest authority" in the land.[3]

A hasty review of the situation facing Japan convinced the sorely pressed Privy Seal that His Majesty's millions would soon be licking the wounds of a new defeat—the loss of Okinawa, and that from the second half of the year on, that is, *in less than a month*, the nation's ability to prosecute the war would be almost completely gone. In view of the enemy's overwhelming air superiority, there would be an intensification of air activity to include small towns and villages throughout the coun-

---

[1] See USSBS, *Interrogations*, II, Toyoda, 320, and IMTFE: Kido, 31146. Toyoda has noted that although the Emperor said nothing throughout the conference, "discontent was written all over him." (*Statements*: Toyoda #57669.)

[2] Kido has stated that the Emperor's desire to see the war terminated became "particularly intensified" at the time of the American landing on Luzon in January 1945 and that by June the Emperor was firm in his determination that the war must be brought to a close no matter what happened to him personally. See *Statements*: Kido #61541 and #61476, Hasunuma #58225.

[3] Kido's fear that the June 8 decision would ultimately result in the collapse of the national polity, the situation on Okinawa, the decline in Japan's fighting strength, and the "complete failure" of Japanese strategy and tactics served to strengthen Kido's determination to draft a counterplan aimed at setting peace talks in motion. See *Statements*: Kido #61541 and #61476, Matsudaira #60745; and IMTFE: Ishiwata, 38931–33.

try. The resulting losses and suffering, made more unbearable by the coming of winter, would cause unrest which the government might find itself unable to control.[4]

The enemy's major objective, Kido reasoned, was to overthrow Japan's powerful *gumbatsu*, or military clique. It therefore made sense that the militarists should be the ones to advocate peace, thus giving the government an opportunity to develop a plan and to open negotiations. But the *gumbatsu* would never co-operate and Kido knew it. The "high aim" of getting Japan out of the war was to preserve the imperial house and to maintain the national polity, yet if Japan waited for the supreme moment much longer—for the "favorable opportunity" which somehow was never quite within reach—she would probably miss it altogether and would meet the same fate as Germany. How could Kido, or anyone else, then achieve the nation's high aim?

No matter how he approached the problem, Kido could find only one solution which held even a slight promise of success. In spite of obvious dangers, he would have to turn to the unprecedented by requesting the Emperor personally to render the bold decision that would permit the government to take steps to end the war. Once the Emperor had spoken, the government could open negotiations by means of a "letter" from the sovereign. This document, to be based on the content of the December 1941 imperial rescript declaring war, would emphasize His Majesty's constant and long-standing concern for peace and his determination, in view of the terrible ravages wrought by the continuation of the struggle, to serve the cause of international peace and understanding by seeking a termination of the conflict on the broadest possible terms of compromise. Although Kido would personally have preferred to approach the United States and Great Britain directly, he believed the ready objections of the military would render such a choice impossible. Since Japan's radio and other communications were under military control, there would scarcely be any chance of bypassing the censors through normal communication channels. The fact that the so-called pro-Soviet group within the Japanese army was secretly willing to support a peace overture through the good offices of the Soviet Union encouraged Kido to hope that the army as a whole might be induced to join in his plan if that plan were initiated through the Kremlin. It was also clear that because of her vital interest in the Pacific the Soviet Union would eventually participate in whatever negotiations Japan attempted. The desirability of having as much "elbowroom" as possible in these negotiations thus convinced Kido that it would be to Japan's advantage to request the good offices of her Neutrality Pact partner, especially since the latter was the only nation among the countries entertaining neutral

---

[4] See IMTFE: Kido, 31146–51; Kido, "Nikki," 6/8/45; and *Statements:* Kido #61541 and #61476. See also *Statements:* Matsudaira #60745 and #61636.

relations with Japan that was powerful enough to influence the world situation.[5]

As Kido saw it, Japan's outstanding requirement would be a "peace with honor," but he realized that this high-sounding phrase might merely signify a termination of the war on a basis *only very slightly removed from unconditional surrender*. Japan would thus have to be prepared to relinquish her role of leadership in and her control over the occupied areas of the Pacific. She would also have to withdraw her armed forces from those areas and would have to reduce her own armaments to a standard which would provide only the minimum requirements for defense. In Kido's eyes, these were the fundamentals; the detailed terms around which any specific negotiations would eventually revolve would have to be drafted by the experts.[6]

Within twenty-four hours after completing his plan, Kido carried his ideas directly to the Emperor for the latter's sanction.[7] He then spent the next ten days (June 9–19, 1945) in approaching key personnel in the government in order to obtain their concurrence and backing.[8] The results were encouraging. Premier Suzuki, Foreign Minister Tōgō, and Navy Minister Yonai all pledged their support, and even War Minister Anami indicated that he would go along with the plan although he personally believed that steps should not be taken to end the war until after the army had had an opportunity to deal a severe blow to the enemy.[9] Foreign Minister Tōgō reminded Kido that from a practical point of view it would be very difficult for the Foreign Office to implement his plan in the face of the agreement which had been reached by the imperial conference of June 8, but Kido replied that he would exert himself to make the Foreign Minister's task an easier one. Although he did not say so, it was obvious that, with the tide of the war rapidly washing away the military's position of hitherto supreme and unchallengeable power, Kido now dared to assume the right to advise the Emperor "to command" the Big Six to set aside their "death to the last man" decision of early June.

Ever since the beginning of the 1930's "imperial decisions" had been forced to fit the pattern of army supremacy in the affairs of state. Had

[5] *Ibid.*

[6] See the citations listed in footnote 4 above.

[7] IMTFE: Kido, 31151–52. Kido judged that the Emperor was "deeply satisfied" with his recommendations.

[8] For the details of these conversations, see IMTFE: Kido, 31151–58, and Tōgō, 35783–85; *Statements:* Tōgō #50304, Kido #61476 and #61541. See also IMTFE: Def. Doc. 3074, *Yonai Aff.*, J text (rejected: 38919–21).

[9] Kido states that he and War Minister Anami also discussed the army's desire to force him out of the Privy Seal's office—a desire which was based, according to Kido, on the fact that his "peace movements" had become known in spite of his efforts to work in strictest secrecy. IMTFE: Kido, 31158; Kido, "Nikki," 6/18/45; *Statements*: Kido #61476 and #61541 (in which Kido states that Anami discussed with him rumors to the effect that he would resign as Lord Keeper of the Privy Seal).

victory and not defeat been in the air, Kido would not have dared even
to think about tampering with the well-entrenched monopoly of the
militarists. The very fact that the Privy Seal was planning to invoke
His Majesty's sanction at this juncture suggests, more forcefully than
any other evidence, that the time was drawing close when it would be
possible for the civil arm of the government to apply this extraordinary
use of imperial *influence* against the army and all others who still opposed a cessation of hostilities.

While Marquis Kido was busy with his "measures for dealing with
the situation," a former governor general of Formosa, Admiral Kiyoshi
Hasegawa, was meticulously checking and rechecking the content of a
report which he was about to submit to the Throne.[10] Toward the end of
February 1945, right after the senior statesmen had individually visited
the palace to inquire after His Majesty's health and to offer their respective views on what lay ahead, the admiral had received an imperial command directing him to investigate the navy's war potential from the
point of view of both morale and material strength.[11] As a result, he had
spent March, April, and May in visiting and inspecting the various naval
districts, ammunition arsenals, and special attack (*kamikaze*) units scattered throughout Japan. On June 12, just four days after the imperial
conference decision to fight to the bitter end and at the very time when
Kido was tapping the opinions of his colleagues, Admiral Hasegawa
proceeded to the palace to report directly to the Throne on his findings.
Standing solemnly before the Emperor, the admiral carefully read the
formal report which he and his subordinates had prepared in anticipation
of this day. Here was shocking confirmation of what many had already
suspected. Although Hasegawa avowed that there was no problem with
respect to navy morale, he emphasized that there was much to be desired from the standpoint of material strength. Not only was production
low as a result of inadequate facilities and a shortage of raw materials, but also what did roll off the assembly line was frequently de-
fective because of hasty production and careless inspection. In spite of
the fact that the morale of those engaged in war industry was high, they
were constantly overworked and generally hampered by insufficient technical knowledge and training. As a result, their output was continually
falling far short of expectations. The unsatisfactory conditions existing
with respect to the material strength of the Japanese navy, Hasegawa
warned, invited serious reflection.

[10] Hasegawa subsequently also reported his findings to Navy Minister Yonai
and Chief of the Naval General Staff Toyoda. Later that same month (on June 28,
1945) Admiral Sōkichi Takagi submitted a report to Admiral Yonai based upon the
findings of his "second" study (discussed in Ch. 3). Takagi's report (like Hasegawa's) pointed up the hopelessness of continuing the struggle.
[11] The details with respect to Hasegawa's assignment and subsequent report to
the Throne are found in *Statements:* Hasegawa #57667 and Tōgō #50304.

As soon as the admiral had run through his unusual report, the Emperor assumed the initiative by pointedly probing here and there among the various matters Hasegawa had described. The latter grasped this opportunity to go into detail, stating candidly and straightforwardly what he had seen and what he had found.[12] Some of the instances of failure and incompetency which he cited were fundamental in their importance: the Naval General Staff's "plan for coping with the situation" was still unexecuted; considerable waste and duplication were arising from the failure of the mobilization program to come into line with the actual circumstances then prevailing; operation strength and transport capability were being decreased with each new bombing. The special attack units were inadequately trained and their complement of weapons was as yet incomplete. Some units were even scrounging for used automobile engines with which to rig up makeshift *kamikaze* launches to be used against Allied transports and vessels of war when the expected invasion became a reality. Except for morale, the over-all situation in the special attack corps was so bad that it seemed probable that the corps would be unable to cope with the demands an enemy D-day would create.

While the militarists were committing Japan to national suicide and the Privy Seal and Admiral Hasegawa were warning the Emperor of the dangers ahead,[13] American war leaders in Washington were putting the finishing touches on the final invasion plans which would at length bring the Japanese military face to face with the very "golden opportunity," "the divine chance," for which they had been waiting and clamoring so long. On June 18 these plans were approved at the White House and Operation Olympic then awaited only the coming of November.[14] On that same date Premier Suzuki returned to Tokyo from Ise,

---

[12] Confirmation of the fact that Hasegawa had the courage to report the actual conditions prevailing in the navy is found in *Statements*: Matsudaira #60745.

[13] Hasegawa's report and one submitted about the same time by Chief of the Army General Staff Umezu convinced the Emperor that Japan's preparations, both at home and abroad (China), "were so extremely inadequate as to render it absolutely essential to end the war without delay." See *Statements:* Tōgō #50304 and Hasegawa #57667.

Umezu's report stated that Japanese troops in China and Manchuria would together equal only about eight American divisions and that their ammunition stocks would be sufficient for only one battle. Some time prior to this report the Emperor had asked Umezu about the army's preparations for the defense of the Kantō Plain (Tokyo area) and Umezu had been unable to give a definite reply (thus indicating that the army was encountering serious difficulties in carrying out even this basic defense measure). See JFO MS: Ch. 31 (Tennō no shūsen hōsaku suishin kata ni kan suru go shiji), especially "Matsudaira hishokanchō kōjutsu"; *Statements:* Tōgō #50304 and Matsudaira #60745.

[14] See Stimson and Bundy, *On Active Service*, 619-20, and Leahy, *I Was There*, 383-85.

where he had visited the Grand Shrine of the Sun Goddess,[15] and that evening called a meeting of the constituent members of the Supreme Council, the Big Six.

Although the decision of the imperial conference of June 8 was very fresh in the minds of these men, the discussion seems to have taken a turn for the better. While the War Minister and the army and navy chiefs of staff still had their eyes fastened on the day when they would meet the enemy on Japanese soil, they did not voice any serious objections to efforts being made *to find an opportunity* that would lead to peace. At the same time they did oppose undertaking any direct negotiations until after the initial invasion battle had been fought, for they believed the engagement would go in their favor and that this would be a tremendous advantage in the negotiations.[16] In spite of this "on the one hand—on the other hand" treatment of a pressing problem, an agreement did emerge to the effect that the time had come when Japan would have to seek Soviet mediation without necessarily holding out for a non-aggression treaty or even a new and more adequate neutrality pact.[17] In this the Big Six were anticipated by the Japanese ambassador in Moscow, Naotake Satō, who had already divined that the most his country could possibly hope to achieve was to keep the Soviet giant out of the Pacific war; and even that, he had warned, would be no minor miracle.

On June 19, the day after the Big Six decision, Foreign MinisterTōgō called at Kōki Hirota's home in Kugenuma to request this former Premier to press forward his talks with Malik in accordance with the new emphasis of approach envisaged by the Supreme Council. The following day, June 20, Tōgō was received in audience by the Emperor to whom he explained Hirota's mission and the course of the negotiations to date. Surprisingly enough, this was apparently the first the Emperor

---

[15] See IMTFE: Kido, 31160. Before Suzuki had left for Ise, Navy Minister Yonai had advised him to commune with the Sun Goddess in order to derive the determination necessary to bring the war to an end. See IMTFE: Kido, 31155, and *Statements*: Kido #61476.

[16] See IMTFE: Kido, 31160, and Tōgō, 35783–85.

[17] See JFO MS: Ch. 32 (Hirota-Mariku kaidan no saikai); *Statements*: Toyoda #61340; and Tōgō, "Shūsen gaikō," *Kaizō*, XXXI (November 1950), 127. Tōgō suggested that Japan should plumb Soviet intentions by the beginning of July so as to bring the war to an end at least by the latter part of September. To this there was general agreement, but the feeling was that a continuation of the war would be inevitable if the Allies remained firm in their demand for unconditional surrender. This attitude was based on the assumption that the Allied demand encompassed a decision to destroy the imperial framework of the Japanese state.

Toyoda (*Saigo no teikoku kaigun*, 196–97) declares that the question of who should be sent to Moscow was raised but that no names were proposed. It was agreed, however, that no matter who went, he could not go empty-handed. According to Toyoda, Foreign Minister Tōgō felt that a solution might be obtained if Japan would revert to the position she had occupied prior to the Russo-Japanese War. (In view of the other evidence, it seems probable that Toyoda has confused the discussions of a later conference with what occurred at the meeting on June 18.)

had heard not only of Hirota's endeavors but also of the three-point plan the Big Six had formulated in mid-May. At the time the closed meetings had been held, it had been agreed that Premier Suzuki should report to the Throne on what had transpired. Everyone had naturally assumed that this had been done, but a month later and just five days before the audience in question Foreign Minister Tōgō suddenly learned that Suzuki had never said anything to the Emperor at all.[18] When Tōgō questioned his chief, the old Premier simply replied that he had not got around to doing it yet. It was primarily for this reason that Tōgō spoke at considerable length about the Hirota-Malik affair. In reply the Emperor told his Foreign Minister that the reports he had received from special investigator Hasegawa and from Chief of the Army General Staff Umezu had convinced him that the military's preparations, in both China and Japan, were so extremely inadequate as to make it necessary to end the war without delay. It was his hope, therefore, that the Hirota talks could be expedited and a general peace achieved quickly. He understood, the Emperor continued, that this would be far from easy but he personally desired the government to do all in its power to stop the fighting as soon as possible. Although Tōgō warned the Emperor that Japan was in such an unfavorable military position that it would be all but impossible to obtain advantageous terms, he did promise to devote himself "heart and soul" to the realization of His Majesty's fervent desire for an early conclusion of hostilities.[19]

In the meantime the discussions Marquis Kido had had with various government leaders concerning his "measures for dealing with the situation" had convinced the Privy Seal that in view of the imperial conference decision of June 8 an indirect indication from himself to the effect that the Emperor desired peace would not be sufficient and that only a direct statement from the Emperor to the Supreme Councilors could make the Big Six press on with negotiations for a termination of the war. When Premier Suzuki reported the details of the Supreme Council meeting of June 18 to Kido, the Privy Seal recognized in the decision formulated on that date the opportunity for which he had been waiting. He therefore immediately counseled the Emperor to utilize this favorable moment to urge the Big Six to seek a way out of the war through diplomatic channels. Several days later, on June 22, the day on which the United States announced the successful completion of its Okinawa campaign, the Emperor—acting on Kido's advice—suddenly summoned

---

[18] Tōgō learned this from Marquis Kido on June 15; on June 20 Tōgō decided to rectify the matter by bringing the Emperor up to date. See the citations in footnote 19 below.

[19] See *Statements:* Tōgō #50304; IMTFE: Tōgō, 35783–85; JFO MS: Ch. 32 (Hirota-Mariku kaidan no saikai); and Tōgō, "Shūsen gaikō," *Kaizō,* XXXI (November 1950), 127–28.

the Big Six to their second imperial conference in two weeks.[20] Departing from the usual, His Majesty personally opened the proceedings with what might have been a bombshell had the wording been more positive. Rather simply and in carefully chosen phrases, the sovereign declared that although the decision of June 8 had established the principle that the war would be fought to the end, it was necessary to consider other methods of coping with the crisis facing the nation. He wanted to know if the cabinet or the Supreme Command had given any thought to this matter.[21]

In reply to the imperial query, Foreign Minister Tōgō[22] reiterated what he had said at the various meetings which had taken place earlier in the month and also what he had privately told the Emperor on June 20. When Tōgō had finished, the Emperor inquired when an envoy could be sent to the USSR and what the prospects for success were. Tōgō again took the floor and said that Japan's representatives should be in Moscow before the Russian delegation left for Potsdam. In other words, the matter should be decided and the envoy sent by the early part of July. He then warned that the negotiations with the Soviet Union contained an element of great danger and that Japan must be prepared to pay a substantial price in order to achieve success. The Japanese government must also offer to make peace, Tōgō said, while it still had the power to fight, or else it would certainly fail.[23]

[20] See *Statements*: Kido #61541 and #61476; Kido, "Nikki," 6/21/45; *Statements:* Tōgō #50304 and Matsudaira #60745. On June 21, the day before the imperial conference, the Privy Seal submitted his advice to the Emperor with respect to what the latter should say at the conference.
    USSBS, *Japan's Struggle to End the War*, 7; USSBS, *Interrogations*, II, Toyoda, 319; and Katō, *The Lost War*, 323, all confuse the date of the imperial conference—giving it either as June 20 or June 26. The correct date is June 22. (See Kido, "Nikki," 6/22/45, and JFO MS citation in footnote 21 below.)
[21] For the Emperor's remarks and other details of the imperial conference of June 22, see JFO MS: Ch. 31 (Tennō no shūsen hōsaku suishin kata ni kan suru go shiji); Toyoda, *Saigo no teikoku kaigun*, 198–99; IMTFE: Suzuki, 35593; Tōgō, 35783–85; Kido, 31160–63; Sakomizu, 35607; *Statements:* Tōgō #50304 and Toyoda #61340; Kido, "Nikki," 6/22/45; and the references in footnote 20 above and footnote 23 below.
[22] Suzuki, who was the first to reply to the Emperor, hastily affirmed that the government had been giving thought to the question of negotiating a settlement. He then called upon Navy Minister Yonai to report on developments to date. Since Yonai did not feel it was within his competence to discuss matters of diplomacy, he passed the task to Foreign Minister Tōgō. When the latter had finished speaking, Yonai said, "I agree with the views of the Foreign Minister."
    Why Suzuki did not call on Tōgō in the first place is not known. Toyoda speculates that it may have been because Yonai exerted great influence over the other cabinet members and belonged to the group that wanted to see the war ended. It may also have been a matter of seniority, for Yonai's court rank was second only to Suzuki's. See Toyoda, *Saigo no teikoku kaigun*, 198.
[23] See "Tōgō gaishō kōjutsu shuki" in JFO MS: Ch. 31 (Tennō no shūsen hōsaku suishin kata ni kan suru go shiji) and Tōgō, "Shūsen gaikō," *Kaizō*, XXXI

When Tōgō sat down, the Emperor turned to the others and asked them to express their opinions. War Minister Anami characteristically declared that he did not object to attempts being made "to save the situation" but he did feel Japan should not be overanxious to end the war at any price and thus expose her weakness to the enemy. Chief of Staff Umezu seconded Anami's stand and expressed the view that caution was of paramount importance and that Japan should not rush blindly into such negotiations. This caused the Emperor to ask if an excess of caution might not result in Japan's losing the right moment altogether. This mild rebuke brought Umezu into line immediately. Without further argument he concurred with the view that the negotiations should be pushed at once. With that, the Emperor arose and left the chamber. The meeting had lasted thirty-five minutes and had produced a new decision. The overtures toward Moscow would be carried forward with a view to obtaining a negotiated peace.[24]

Paradoxical as it may seem, this was not the first time the Emperor had asked the government not to be limited by a policy established at an earlier imperial conference. It had happened once before, in the autumn of the year the war began. The Konoye Cabinet had fallen as a result of a decision made at an imperial conference held on September 6, 1941.[25] This decision had recognized the inevitability of armed conflict in the Pacific unless the Hull-Nomura negotiations produced a friendly settlement by the beginning of October. The razor-sharp General Hideki Tōjō had emerged out of Konoye's fall to become Premier. On the day he assumed power, Tōjō was urged by the Emperor to disregard the decision of September 6, but from what followed it would appear that it was the Emperor who was disregarded instead.[26]

Now, four years later, the precedent was repeated. Success or failure would depend on the reactions of those at whom the imperial admoni-

---

(November 1950), 128. Mr. Shigemitsu, Tōgō's predecessor as Foreign Minister, has since stated that as a result of the changing emphasis which had occurred in the Soviet attitude toward Japan from August 1944 onward he had come to the conclusion that any attempt to ask the Kremlin to bring about peace would contain "great danger" for Japan. *Statements*: Shigemitsu 9/9/49.

[24] See the citations in footnote 21 above. On June 23, 1945, the Emperor addressed a personal message to his people in which he said, "the present crisis is unprecedented in scope in our national history." In a broadcast to the people that same day, War Minister Anami reported that enforcement of the volunteer military service corps act would lay the "foundation for sure victory" in the battle of Japan. See *Facts on File*, 1945, 200 M. It would appear that Anami was endeavoring to counter the effect the imperial message might have upon the people.

[25] There is a rather interesting point of comparison between the decision of September 6, 1941, and that of June 22, 1945. By the former, Japan elected to prepare for war while continuing negotiations for peace; by the latter, she elected to prepare for peace while continuing the war.

[26] For a summary of events concerned with the imperial conference decision of September 6, 1941, see IMTFE: *Decisions of Conferences*, 13–17. See also Kido, "Nikki," 9/6/41, 10/16/41, 10/20/41, and 9/26/45.

tion was directed. If the Big Six unanimously supported the reorientation of national policy implied in the Emperor's remarks, the war could
possibly be ended relatively soon and without any new or major en-
counters. If the military representatives on the Supreme Council remained obstinate, however, it was equally possible that there would be
bloodshed within the capital as well as on the invasion beaches.

On the day following the second conference in the imperial presence,
Foreign Minister Tōgō informed former Premier Hirota of what had
transpired and once again requested him to press on with the Malik negotiations which had been left pending since early June.[27] Hirota was at
first disposed to remonstrate that it would be a bad idea to give the
Soviets the impression that Japan was in a great hurry, but Tōgō managed to convince him that while what he said accorded with normal diplomatic procedure the current circumstances made haste an absolute
necessity. If the Russians were not interested, in other words, Japan
would speedily have to consider other measures.[28]

As a result of this conversation, Hirota called on Malik on June 24
and very frankly declared that Japan wanted to negotiate a strong agreement to take the place of the Neutrality Pact which the Soviet Union had
recently announced it would not extend beyond April 1946.[29] Malik
appeared neither impressed nor interested. He told Hirota that the
Soviet announcement did not mean that his government had broken the
Pact. So far as Moscow was concerned, the arrangement was still in effect
and its terms were being honored. Consequently, the Soviet government
could see no need to negotiate a new and stronger agreement of the type
apparently desired by Japan.

Balked in this direction, Hirota tried a different approach, the diplomat's ace in the hole, a *quid pro quo*: Japan would like to trade the
rubber, tin, lead, and tungsten of the southern regions in return for Soviet
oil![30] And on top of this—somewhat wistfully perhaps—Hirota de-

[27] Tōgō visited Hirota on June 19 (after the Big Six meeting of June 18) and
saw him again on June 23 (after the imperial conference of June 22). This point is
not always made clear in the documents cited previously in connection with the
Hirota-Malik talks.

[28] See *Statements:* Tōgō #50304.

[29] Hirota's proposal indicates that in spite of the decisions of June 18 and June 22
Japan could not quite close her eyes to Points I and II of the plan of mid-May 1945
(discussed in Ch. 4 above).

[30] Hirota's statement forms an interesting comparison with Yonai's mid-May
1945 remarks about trading Japanese warships for Soviet oil and aircraft (see Ch. 4).

In proposing to trade the resources of the southern regions for Soviet oil, Hirota
suggested that the resources be transported from the south in Soviet vessels. This
would obviously have been necessary since Japanese shipping had long since been
swept from the seas.

On April 5, 1945, at the time of Koiso's resignation, both the army and navy chiefs
of staff had expressed deep concern over Japan's lack of oil. According to their testimony, Japan's oil stocks would last only until June 1945. After that the only indige-

clared, "If the Soviet army and the Japanese navy were to join forces, Japan and the Soviet Union together would become the strongest powers in the world!"[31]

Whatever Malik really thought is not known. He seems not to have paid more than passing attention to anything Hirota had to say in spite of the fact that the latter was in dead earnest. In this particular instance (as with all the other proposals Hirota made), Malik simply dismissed the suggestion by declaring that Mr. Hirota was apparently expressing just the navy's point of view. The Japanese army might have a different opinion. As for oil—it would be impossible for his government to aid Japan in that respect since the Soviet Union herself did not have a great deal.

Malik's response effectively cut the ground out from under Hirota, and so he took his leave without having obtained any satisfaction whatsoever. In fact, Malik had even implied that he saw no point in further discussions unless Mr. Hirota could present Japan's "concrete plan."

Five days later, on June 29, Hirota made one final, vain attempt to solicit the interest of the Soviet Union.[32] This time he did indeed submit concrete proposals, and not verbally but in writing: If the Soviet Union would enter into a nonaggression treaty with Japan, Mr. Hirota's government would grant Manchuria her independence,[33] would relinquish Japanese fishing concessions in Soviet Far Eastern waters (in return for oil from the Soviet Union), and would be willing to consider any other matters the Soviet government might wish to place on the agenda. After a short discussion,[34] Hirota departed with a promise from Malik that these proposals would be reported to Moscow and that further negotiations would be resumed as soon as an answer had arrived. Although

---

nous source of oil would be pine roots. See Kido, "Nikki," 4/5/45, and unpublished USSBS interrogation #136 (Mori).

[31] For the details of the Hirota-Malik conversation of June 24, see JFO MS: Ch. 32 (Hirota-Mariku kaidan no saikai); Statements: Tōgō #50304; and IMTFE: Analyses, #492.

[32] For the details of the June 29 conversation, see the citations in footnote 31 above, especially the section of JFO MS: Ch. 32 entitled "Nisso gaikō kōshō kiroku."

[33] The Japanese proposal with respect to Manchuria envisaged a postwar withdrawal of Japanese troops, a mutual undertaking by Japan and the Soviet Union to guarantee the sovereignty and territorial integrity of Manchuria, and a Soviet-Japanese accord not to interfere in the internal affairs of the country.

About this same time (the date is not clear), Colonel Tanemura of the Military Affairs Section personally drafted a plan which he submitted to War Minister Anami through the chief of the Military Affairs Bureau, Lieutenant General Yoshizumi. The plan envisaged surrendering Manchuria and Korea to the Soviet Union in return for a Soviet undertaking not to enter the war against Japan. Anami returned the plan to Yoshizumi with the admonition that he was not to let junior officers "worry" about such things. See Statements: Yoshizumi #61338.

[34] Malik inquired whether it was true that Japan and the United States were conducting peace negotiations in Sweden. Hirota replied, "That's impossible," and assured Malik that Japan would first consult the Soviet Union before attempting any negotiations elsewhere.

this was the first and only commitment Malik ever made, it proved to be an empty gesture. In spite of the fact that Hirota tried time and again during the next two weeks to obtain another meeting with the Soviet ambassador, Malik refused to see him on the grounds of illness. When every approach failed, Hirota conveyed his condolences for the ambassador's ill health, and with that the negotiations ceased.[35]

It had now become clear to the Japanese Foreign Office that new and more drastic steps would have to be taken or else Japan's efforts to obtain Soviet good offices would certainly fail. Since a conference of the Big Three was to take place at Potsdam during the latter part of July,[36] it was imperative that Japan notify the Soviet government, *prior to the conference*, that the Emperor desired the war to be brought to an end. His Majesty, too, was growing impatient. On July 7 he personally informed Premier Suzuki that he felt Japan was losing valuable time by attempting to fathom the Kremlin's intentions through its ambassador to Japan. After listening to Suzuki's report on the progress of the negotiations to date, the Emperor requested the Premier to seek Soviet mediation outright by dispatching a special envoy to Moscow bearing a personal message from the Throne.[37] That very same day Foreign Minister Tōgō left for the mountain resort town of Karuizawa for an unofficial talk with Prince Konoye.[38] After bringing Konoye up to date on developments in the capital, Tōgō specifically asked him to undertake the mission to Moscow. The prince replied that he would go if the Emperor bestowed the command but added that he must be given carte blanche[39] since he would be unable to accomplish anything unless he had

[35] See JFO MS: Ch. 32 (Hirota-Mariku kaidan no saikai). Mr. Hirota conveyed his condolences on July 14, 1945.

Mr. Andō of the Foreign Office learned from the Soviet Embassy that Japan's proposals had been sent to Moscow by courier and not by cable (as the Foreign Office had naturally supposed). This inevitably forced the assumption that the Soviet Union was not sincerely interested in furthering the negotiations. Mr. Naotake Satō, Japan's ambassador in Moscow, received the same information from Molotov, who treated the matter very lightly and said no answer could be given until the courier had arrived with Malik's report. (Satō, *Futatsu no Roshia*, 205, and interview with Mr. Satō, Tokyo, January 31, 1952.)

When asked, after the war, about his negotiations with Malik, Hirota replied, "We acted too late. We should have begun negotiating earlier; only the Government dillydallied so much." (Hanayama, *The Way of Deliverance*, 233.)

[36] Tōgō has stated that prior to the meeting at Potsdam it had been his intention to inform the United States and the United Kingdom of Japan's desire to end the war. He had hoped thereby to dissuade the Allied powers from demanding unconditional surrender for he believed the government would find it impossible to conclude peace unless it could obtain some terms. Unfortunately, the Potsdam Proclamation of July 26, 1945, came before he had time to pursue this course. See *Statements:* Tōgō #50304.

[37] See IMTFE: Tōgō, 35783–85, and Kido, 31164–65; Kido, "Nikki," 7/7/45; *Statements:* Tōgō #50304; and Toyoda, *Saigo no teikoku kaigun*, 199–200.

[38] Tōgō left Tokyo on July 7 and met with Konoye the next day, July 8.

[39] See *Statements:* Tōgō #50304 and JFO MS: Ch. 33 (Konoye kō ni tokuha

a free hand. Tōgō agreed to this, and when the two men parted each harbored the knowledge that the sole purpose of the mission would be to get Japan out of the war on any basis whatsoever—short of unconditional surrender.[40]

Several days later, on July 12, Foreign Minister Tōgō instructed the Japanese ambassador in Moscow, Naotake Satō, to inform Foreign Commissar Molotov that the Emperor wanted the war ended immediately and wished to send Prince Fumimaro Konoye[41] to Moscow as a special envoy. The prince would bear a personal letter from the Emperor embodying the imperial views and would also be empowered to discuss any and all issues pertaining to Soviet-Japanese relations—especially the Manchurian question. Satō was to obtain Soviet permission for the entry of the Konoye party and was to ask the Soviet government to send an airplane as far as Manchouli or Tsitsihar to facilitate the party's travel to the capital. Since it would be impossible for the prince to reach Moscow before Stalin and Molotov left for Potsdam, Satō was directed to arrange a meeting for Konoye to coincide with the return of the Soviet delegation from Germany. In all this there was no mention of mediation. In fact, the cable even stressed that so long as the United States and Great Britain adhered to their unconditional surrender demand the Japanese government would have no choice other than to fight on in order to maintain the honor and existence of the nation.[42]

At three o'clock in the afternoon on July 12, the same day on which the above cable left Japan, Prince Konoye was received by the Emperor in a strictly private audience[43] which lasted a bare fifteen minutes. Com-

---

shisetsu go kamei). It has been suggested that Konoye subsequently obtained a commitment from the Emperor giving him full power to accept whatever terms the Allies might demand as long as the terms were ones which His Majesty himself could accept. It has also been suggested that Konoye was instructed (by the Emperor) to cable the conditions of peace directly to the Emperor. (This latter point is very much open to question.)

[40] See *Statements:* Tōgō #50304.

[41] The question of sending an envoy to the Soviet Union was discussed by the Big Six on July 10 and July 14. (Toyoda, *Saigo no teikoku kaigun*, 199–202.)

According to Kido, Konoye was chosen as the special envoy by Premier Suzuki after consultations with Foreign Minister Tōgō. Suzuki then suggested (to Kido and possibly to the Big Six as well) that the Emperor be petitioned to command the prince to accept the assignment.

[42] See IMTFE: Cable #893: Tōgō to Satō, 23591–92; Satō, *Futatsu no Roshia*, 205; *Statements:* Tōgō #50304; JFO MS: Ch. 33 (Konoye kō ni tokuha shisetsu go kamei) and Ch. 34 (Konoye tokushi ni kan suru Nichi-So kōshō). The text is also based on information obtained during an interview with Mr. Satō in Tokyo, January 31, 1952. The Tōgō-Satō exchange of cables for the period discussed in the text which follows may also be found in *Translations:* Doc. #57938.

[43] A strictly private audience was unusual in the extreme (see footnote 50, Ch. 2, above). According to Kido, it was he who was responsible for the rule being broken in this instance—a move which made it possible for both the Emperor and Konoye to speak their minds freely, without inhibitions of any kind. See Kido, "Nikki," 7/12/45; JFO MS: Ch. 33 (Konoye kō ni tokuha shisetsu go kamei) ; and *Statements:* Tōgō #50304. Shigemitsu (*Shōwa no dōran*, 282) is in error in saying the audience

ing directly to the point, the Emperor asked Konoye for his views on the "current state of affairs." Speaking in much the same vein as he had during his audience with the Emperor in February, Konoye frankly replied that the great disparity between the estimates of the army and those of the navy concerning Japan's ability to continue the war did not inspire confidence. The morale of the people was not particularly high, there being even a few among them who were going so far as to speak ill of the Emperor. By and large, however, the only thing that sustained the majority at all was the hope that a way out of Japan's difficulties would be found through the Throne. It was his opinion, therefore, that the war should be terminated without delay.

Taking this as his cue, the Emperor informed the prince that he might be asked to go to the Soviet Union as a special envoy from the Throne. Konoye, who had been thoroughly briefed by Foreign Minister Tōgō during their tête-à-tête in Karuizawa, replied without a moment's hesitation that he would accept such an assignment if it were given. Recalling that at the time of the formation of the second Konoye Cabinet the Emperor had enjoined him to share the imperial joys and sorrows, the prince firmly declared that he would undertake any command His Majesty chose to bestow even if it entailed risking his own life. When Konoye withdrew from the audience chamber at 3:15, the Emperor was left with the impression that *this time* the prince had resolutely made up his mind to be of service, come what may.[44]

The need for haste which was behind the developments taking place in Tokyo in rapid succession was well understood by Ambassador Satō in Moscow. Immediately after the arrival of Tōgō's cable, Satō requested an interview with Molotov in the hope of being able to carry Japan's proposal straight to the man through whose hands all foreign policy decisions could be expected to pass. Because of his impending departure for Berlin, Molotov was too busy to see Satō, but the ambas-

---

took place on July 11. Kido's diary and the material contained in JFO MS: Ch. 33 leave no doubt that the correct date is July 12.

[44] See Kido, "Nikki," 7/12/45; IMTFE: Kido, 31166–71; and JFO MS: Ch. 33 (Konoye kō ni tokuha shisetsu go kamei).

At a meeting of the Supreme Council held on July 14, it was decided that the Konoye entourage should include the Vice-Minister of Foreign Affairs (Shunichi Matsumoto), one general, and one admiral. When the question of terms arose, a very heated argument developed between Anami on the one hand and Tōgō and Yonai on the other. The issue was finally postponed to a later date for fear that the council meeting would break up if the matter were pushed too far. (*Statements:* Tōgō #50304.)

Konoye personally asked General Kōji Sakai (retired) and Mr. Shigeharu Matsumoto (not to be confused with Shunichi Matsumoto) to accompany him to Moscow and, together with them, began drafting a plan to be followed in the negotiations. (Interview with Mr. Ushiba, former secretary to the late Prince Konoye, Tokyo, February 6, 1952.) Kase (*Journey to the Missouri*, 189) states that he was one of those asked by Konoye to go to Moscow.

sador was able to arrange an interview with Vice Foreign Commissar Lozovsky[45] instead. At their meeting, which took place at 5:00 P.M., Moscow time, on Friday, July 13,[46] Satō handed Lozovsky a Russian translation of the imperial wishes, as they had been outlined in the cablegram from Tokyo, together with a confidential letter (addressed to Molotov) in which he personally explained the proposed Konoye visit. Satō emphasized that he was anxious to obtain the Soviet government's consent to the Konoye mission, in principle at least, before Molotov left for Potsdam. He also stressed that he would like to make arrangements for Konoye to meet with Molotov as soon as the latter returned to Moscow. When Lozovsky asked Satō to whom the imperial message was directed, the ambassador replied that since it was a message conveying the imperial wishes it was not addressed to any one person in particular but that he hoped it would be transmitted to Kalinin, Stalin, and Molotov. Although Lozovsky assured Satō that he understood the position of the Japanese government and its desire for haste, he declared that his government would find it impossible to reply prior to Molotov's departure since the foreign commissar was leaving that very evening. Satō, who was well versed in Soviet methods, then suggested that a reply be obtained from Molotov in Berlin by telephone or some other means that would give the Japanese government the time it would need to complete preparations for the Konoye mission. The interview finally ended with an indication from Lozovsky that he would do as Satō wished and a promise that he would immediately give Molotov the documents Satō had brought.[47] At midnight, however, Lozovsky phoned to say that the Soviet reply would be delayed several days, and this was the last the ambassador heard until July 18. On the evening of that day Satō received a confidential letter from Lozovsky in which the latter stated that the Kremlin found the imperial message general in form and lacking in any concrete proposals. The purpose of the Konoye mission, moreover, was not clear to his government. Under the circumstances the Soviet Union did not feel that it could give a definite reply either to the imperial message or to Japan's desire to send a special envoy to Moscow.[48]

[45] The vice-commissar in question is Alexander Lozovsky (pseudonym of A. S. Dridso). See International Who's Who, 1945–46. Kase (Journey to the Missouri, 194, 205, 222) is in error in calling the man "Rozovsky."

[46] On July 13 the Japanese Foreign Office also informed Soviet Ambassador Malik of Japan's request for good offices and asked him to cable his government. Malik promised to do so immediately. See IMTFE: Cable #898: Tōgō to Satō, 23592–93.

[47] See IMTFE: Cable #1385: Satō to Tōgō, 23594–96, and Satō, Futatsu no Roshia, 205–6.

[48] See IMTFE: Cable #1417: Satō to Tōgō, 23596–97, and Satō, Futatsu no Roshia, 206. At their first meeting at Potsdam on July 17, 1945 (the day before the July 18 Lozovsky letter to Satō), President Truman and Marshal Stalin discussed the question of the Soviet Union's entry into the war in the Pacific. See Byrnes, Speaking Frankly, 205.

In his Cable #483 (dated Stockholm, July 18, 1945, and addressed to Tōgō), Minister Okamoto drew attention to the following report from a London dispatch

On July 21, in response to a communication from Satō containing the text of Lozovsky's letter, Foreign Minister Tōgō dispatched yet another cable[49] to Japan's ambassador in Moscow in which he endeavored to define the Konoye mission in terms which could leave no doubt in Soviet minds as to Japan's purpose. He thus clearly emphasized that the prince, acting in accordance with the wishes of His Imperial Majesty, would respectfully request the Soviet government to use its good offices in bringing the war to an end.[50] The prince would reveal the concrete intentions of the Japanese government and would also discuss matters relating to the establishment of co-operative relations between Japan and the Soviet Union.

In a second cable,[51] sent the same day, Tōgō further spelled out for Satō's benefit the position of the government in Tokyo. Japan could not accept unconditional surrender, he declared, under any circumstances. As long as such a demand remained, the Japanese people would fight on as one man. At the same time, in accordance with the wishes of the Emperor, Japan hoped through the good offices of the Soviet Union to bring about peace on terms other than unconditional surrender. It was highly important that Satō make every effort to ensure that the United States and Great Britain understood this point.

Tōgō further explained that, while the Japanese government could not ask the Soviet Union to use its good offices on the basis of Japan's laying down no conditions whatsoever, the situation both at home and abroad made it similarly impossible for Tokyo to set forth actual peace terms.[52] In view of these delicate circumstances, Japan was sending

---

which had appeared in the July 18 issue of the Stockholm newspaper *Tidningen*: (1) The Soviet Embassy is not in a position to confirm or deny rumors that Stalin brought to Potsdam a peace proposal made by the Japanese government. (2) It is not against Soviet policy to act as a mediator if Japan makes a concrete proposal. (See IMTFE: *Analyses*, #941.)

[49] See IMTFE: Cable #931: Tōgō to Satō, 23597–98, and Satō, *Futatsu no Roshia*, 206–7.

[50] The July 21 cable constituted the first time Satō was given instructions permitting him to ask for Soviet *mediation* outright. The telegram dispatched on July 12 had merely stated that the Japanese government, in accordance with the Emperor's wishes, desired to discuss with the Soviet government ways and means of bringing the war to an end. (Based on information obtained during an interview with Mr. Satō in Tokyo on January 31, 1952.)

Statements to the effect that Japan requested Soviet mediation as early as February 1945 (e.g., Baldwin, *Great Mistakes of the War*, 96) are apparently based on erroneous evidence. To the author's knowledge, Japanese Foreign Office records, which constitute the "authority" in this matter, do not contain any documents which would support the view that Japan sought Soviet mediation prior to June or July 1945.

[51] See IMTFE: Cable #931: Tōgō to Satō, 23597–98; Cable #932: Tōgō to Satō, 23599–601; Satō, *Futatsu no Roshia*, 206–7.

[52] In this connection it should be noted that throughout May, June, and July (and even into August) the army insisted that mediation must not be based on the assumption that Japan was proposing peace because she was beaten. Since the army maintained that Japan was not defeated, it was impossible to reach any agreement on peace terms. It was for this reason that Tōgō was unable to forward Japan's concrete position to Moscow. See *Statements*: Tōgō #61672 and #50304.

Prince Konoye to the Soviet Union to present the concrete intentions of the Japanese government. After consideration had been given to Soviet demands in East Asia, Japan would ask the Soviet Union to approach the United States and Great Britain with a view to negotiating a settlement. Tōgō also instructed Satō to emphasize that, although the Japanese government bore the *responsibility* for sending Prince Konoye, the prince was being dispatched at the *wish* of the Emperor. Satō should make it clear that Konoye enjoyed the confidence of the Throne and held a distinguished place in Japanese political circles. Finally, the Foreign Minister instructed his ambassador to ascertain the true attitude of the Soviet Union but not to put the proposals contained in his earlier telegram of that same day (July 21) into writing "unless absolutely necessary."

This cable arrived in Moscow on July 24, and the very next day Satō managed to see Lozovsky again. At their previous meeting on July 13, the ambassador had had to talk in rather general terms but this time his instructions made it possible for him specifically to state that Japan was seeking the good offices of the Soviet Union in order to bring the war to an end. It was for this reason, he declared, that Japan desired to send one of her most renowned statesmen, Prince Konoye, to Moscow. The prince's visit would have a twofold purpose: to obtain Soviet mediation and to improve and strengthen Russo-Japanese relations.

In only one respect did Satō depart from his instructions. In spite of the Foreign Minister's injunction, he did give Lozovsky the written text of his statements. Although this may not have been "absolutely necessary," Satō apparently believed that the circumstances warranted his taking the responsibility. The ambassador also stressed the urgency of the matter and asked Lozovsky to communicate with Molotov in Berlin so that an answer could be obtained as soon as possible. The Vice Foreign Commissar again promised to take immediate action, and Satō left the Kremlin hoping but not daring to believe that there might now be some chance of success.[53]

Although Moscow's real attitude toward Japan's overture is a matter for speculation, it would appear that the excessively valuable territorial gains and other concessions promised to the Soviet Union at Yalta pro-

---

[53] See IMTFE: Cable #1449: Satō to Tōgō, 23602–7; Cable #1450: Satō to Tōgō, 23608; Satō, *Futatsu no Roshia*, 206–7.

From the very moment Foreign Minister Tōgō's first cable reached Moscow, Ambassador Satō resigned himself to attempting the impossible. In a series of courageous cables he warned the government in Tokyo that its approach to the problem would fail to produce the desired results. His arguments and views, which were both sound and blunt, would probably not have been tolerated had it not been for the very serious situation in which Japan found herself. Satō undoubtedly deserves great praise and credit for the forthright manner in which he cabled his unpopular opinions to Tokyo during the last weeks of the war.

vided Soviet leaders with whatever incentive they may have needed to undermine Japan's efforts to obtain mediation. The Yalta Agreement envisaged the participation of the Soviet Union in the war. If Stalin chose not to commence hostilities or if circumstances conspired to prevent a Soviet declaration of war, there would clearly be no moral obligation or legal necessity for the United States and Great Britain to implement their half of the bargain. Unless the Soviet Union entered the conflict, therefore, she would not be in a position to claim her share of the spoils. Undoubtedly, this reasoning, or at least considerations of a similar nature, can explain the circumspection and reluctance Ambassador Satō encountered in Moscow whenever he tried to get a Soviet answer to Japan's request. Measured in these terms, the issue of helping Japan get out of the war before the Soviet Union could get into it must have seemed ludicrous to the Kremlin.[54]

At Potsdam, to be sure, Stalin did not attempt to keep the Japanese overture a secret, but he did take the precaution of ascribing to His Majesty's government the least praiseworthy of motives. On July 28, two days after the now-famous proclamation on Japan had been released, Stalin personally told President Truman, Secretary of State Byrnes, and Prime Minister Attlee that the Japanese had requested Soviet mediation and had proposed sending Prince Konoye to Moscow. As if to allay any misgivings which might otherwise have appeared, the master of the Kremlin quickly explained that Japan's approach did not show a willingness to surrender unconditionally but was, instead, a calculated endeavor to obtain Soviet collaboration in the furtherance of Japanese policy. The Japanese had even indicated, Stalin said, that although they wanted to end the war they would fight on with all their strength as long as the Allies continued to adhere to the unconditional surrender formula. As a result, the Soviet government had unhesitatingly informed Japan that it could not give a definite reply to her request in view of the fact that the imperial message was general in form and lacking in any concrete proposals.[55]

What Stalin apparently did not know was that President Truman

[54] In early May 1945 Ambassador Harriman told Navy Secretary Forrestal and others that the Soviets were determined to enter the war in the Pacific because of their requirements in the Far East. He said the Russian fear of a separate peace between Japan and the United States was much greater than any American fear that some arrangement might be concluded between Japan and the Soviet Union. See Millis (ed.), *The Forrestal Diaries*, 55.

Toward the latter part of May or the first part of June (1945), Stalin indicated to Harry Hopkins that he was "disposed to favor" a continuation of the emphasis upon unconditional surrender even though he realized this might lead the Japanese to commit themselves to a fight to the finish. Stalin also said, in effect: "Perhaps we can get a surrender without using the words 'unconditional surrender,' but give them 'the works' once we get to Japan." See Millis (ed.), *The Forrestal Diaries*, 68; Leahy, *I Was There*, 383; and Sherwood, *Roosevelt and Hopkins*, 902–4.

[55] See Byrnes, *Speaking Frankly*, 205; Churchill, *Triumph and Tragedy*, 641–42;

and Secretary of State Byrnes had every reason already to be familiar with the details of what he was presenting by way of news. Some fifteen days before the marshal's "revelation," official Washington had again come face to face with a rare opportunity to capitalize politically and strategically upon its ability to intercept and decipher Japanese messages. As in the case of the Tōgō-Nomura-Kurusu exchanges of late 1941, so now in mid-1945, American leaders were once again probing the enemy's most secret thoughts—reading, with bated breath perhaps, the vital exchange of cables between Tōgō in Tokyo and Satō in Moscow.[56] It was all there, as clear as crystal:

Tōgō to Satō: . . . See Molotov before his departure for Potsdam. . . . Convey His Majesty's strong desire to secure a termination of the war. . . . Unconditional surrender is the only obstacle to peace. . . .

Satō to Tōgō: . . . There is no chance whatever of winning the Soviet Union to our side and of obtaining her support on the basis set forth in your cables. . . . Japan is defeated. . . . We must face that fact and act accordingly. . . .

Tōgō to Satō: . . . In spite of your views, you are to carry out your instructions. . . . Endeavor to obtain the good offices of the Soviet Union in ending the war short of unconditional surrender. . . .

Although the first of these intercepted messages was received and decoded in Washington on July 13, only four days before the Potsdam Conference began, it seems fair to say that even so short a period provided enough time for someone to take advantage of this unusual information about which there could not have been the slightest doubt as to authenticity. The record of what occurred during the next two weeks, however, indicates that Washington failed to turn this newly won and unquestionably vital intelligence data to active and good account.

It has been argued in defense of the policy which did prevail that the Japanese approach to Moscow was "[no] proof that Japan would surrender unconditionally without the use of the [atomic] bomb"[57] and also that it was ". . . no indication of any weakening in the Japa-

---

and James, *The Rise and Fall of the Japanese Empire*, 329–30. According to Mr. Byrnes, "President Truman expressed his approval of Stalin's action."

Although the available evidence is not absolutely clear, the date, July 28, is apparently not significant since Stalin told Churchill privately about the Japanese overture some time prior to July 26 and the latter, in turn, informed the President.

[56] See Millis (ed.), *The Forrestal Diaries*, 74–77 (entries for July 13, 15, and 24, 1945). Although Forrestal does not make it clear who—besides himself—knew about the deciphered cables, it seems logical to assume that the President and Secretary of State were informed. This assumption is supported by the material quoted in Byrnes, *Speaking Frankly*, 211 ff., although the latter may be based on information obtained after the war and not during it.

[57] Byrnes, *Speaking Frankly*, 262. According to Byrnes, ". . . agreement to negotiate could only arouse false hope [since Japan had indicated she would fight to the death rather than accept unconditional surrender]. Instead, we relied upon the Potsdam Declaration."

nese determination to fight rather than accept unconditional surrender."[58] Although these two statements are so worded that they do not in themselves represent any flagrant distortion, they seem either to miss or to ignore the point entirely. The mere fact that the Japanese had approached the Soviet Union with a request for mediation should have suggested the possibility that Japan, for all of her talk about "death to the last man," might accept the Allied demand for unconditional surrender if only it were couched in more specific terms than those which Washington was already using to define its meaning.[59] When Tōgō informed Satō that unconditional surrender was out of the question, he was stating the realities of the moment as they existed in Tokyo. It was not Tōgō's prerogative, either then or later, to decide whether unconditional surrender was acceptable or not, but it was his obligation, in launching negotiations with Moscow, to reveal to Satō the actual currents of opinion prevailing within the cabinet and the Supreme Council at that time. In spite of his words, therefore, the problem so far as he was concerned was not the old stand-by explanation heard time and again—face-saving—but rather it was the necessity of determining exactly where unconditional surrender ended and conditional surrender began. What Japan and her Foreign Minister needed was a *positive*, not a negative, definition of terms, with special emphasis, of course, on the future of Japan's imperial house. Had Tōgō said this in so many words, the problem might have passed through Washington in focus, but the attitude of the Japanese military and Tōgō's own concern over Allied plans with respect to the Emperor prevented him from being so explicit. Thus, what Washington received was a blurred image, albeit one that might still have produced its message had both the time and the purpose existed for a painstaking analysis.

Secretary of War Stimson has raised the question of whether an earlier surrender of Japan could have been achieved had the United States followed a different diplomatic and military policy during the closing months of the war.[60] In the light of available evidence, a final

---

[58] Stimson and Bundy, *On Active Service*, 618–19. According to Stimson, "these vague proposals contemplated the retention by Japan of important conquered areas and were therefore not considered seriously." (The Stimson quotation in the text contradicts, to some extent, the War Secretary's views with respect to Japan's susceptibility to reason. See footnote 81 below and the text corresponding thereto.)

[59] After the war, Suzuki declared that in seeking Soviet mediation Japan "was prepared to accept almost any terms in order to achieve peace." (*Statements:* Suzuki #531.) See also footnote 33, Ch. 4, above.

The question of unconditional surrender was tremendously complicated. Without a clear-cut Allied statement on the Emperor, no Japanese—not even a so-called peace advocate—could have sponsored an acceptance of the Allied formula; hence, the emphasis placed upon the unacceptability of unconditional surrender.

[60] Although American leaders were aware that a large element in the Japanese cabinet was prepared to accept, in the spring of 1945, "substantially the same terms"

answer in the affirmative seems possible, even probable. This was the setting:

In Washington, American war leaders could not decide what to do about the Emperor and consequently were unable to issue a positive statement. To a certain extent they were also unable to agree on the advantages or disadvantages of Soviet participation in the war and, hence, were divided in their efforts to get the Russians in or to keep them out. After many delays, a decision was eventually reached to define "unconditional surrender" to a point—but to maintain silence on the Emperor and to insist upon continuing the fiction that a *conditional* surrender was unconditional. At the eleventh hour a further decision was reached to prefabricate, for the Kremlin's use, a so-called legal basis for the Soviet Union to enter the war in spite of the fact that such action on her part would constitute an open violation of the Soviet-Japanese Neutrality Pact of 1941.

In Tokyo, the ruling elite was caught between desire and necessity. The government, especially its civilian members, would readily have ordered a cessation of hostilities if the Allies would have hedged "unconditional surrender" with a proviso to the effect that Japan's distinctive polity, the imperial system, would not be destroyed. Without such a guarantee there was no alternative but to fight on. At the same time the government recognized the pressing need of keeping the Soviet Union from entering the war and, in desperation, decided to employ the Kremlin as its broker. Under the terms of employment envisaged by Japan, the Soviet Union was to deliver a termination of the war short of unconditional surrender in return for a voluntary Japanese withdrawal from the Asian mainland and other adjacent areas long held in dispute between Japan and the Soviet Union.

In Moscow, Stalin was straining to commit his forces in the Far East before either Washington or Tokyo conspired somehow to make that impossible. While the Americans were piling huge spoils at the front door of the Kremlin to induce a Soviet entry into the war, the Japanese were at the back door with offerings with which they hoped to purchase continued Soviet neutrality and eventual Soviet mediation. Here was the spectacle of Washington sacrificing what it did not own but should have claimed for itself or China and of Tokyo dispensing what it had once held but no longer could maintain. Under the circumstances it could not have been too difficult for Stalin to foment plans whereby both

---

as they subsequently did, Mr. Stimson and others did not believe "that the Japanese already considered themselves beaten." At the same time, Mr. Stimson later felt that it was possible, "in the light of the final surrender, that a clearer and earlier exposition of American willingness to retain the Emperor would have produced an earlier ending of the war. . . .

"Only on the question of the Emperor did Stimson take, in 1945, a conciliatory view; only on this question did he later believe that history might find that the United States, by its delay in stating its position, had prolonged the war." See Stimson and Bundy, *On Active Service*, 628–29.

the victors and the vanquished would later have cause to regret their common folly.

Into this setting there now came the Potsdam Proclamation[61] of July 26, 1945—the Allied definition of the conditions of the "unconditional" surrender formula. Reminding Japan of Germany's "futile and senseless resistance" against the overwhelming forces brought to bear by the Allies, the proclamation ominously warned that the time had come for His Majesty's Empire to decide whether it would cross the threshold of annihilation or follow, instead, the path of reason. Here was the summons "to proclaim now the unconditional surrender *of all Japanese armed forces*"[62] or else accept the alternative of "prompt and utter destruction."

The Allies thus had here, in late July 1945, the very document which Japan finally accepted in mid-August. Had Prince Konoye, as the fully empowered personal representative of the Emperor of Japan, been permitted to travel to Moscow (or anywhere else, for that matter) and had he there been handed the text of this proclamation *prior* to its release to the world at large, he conceivably could have resolved speedily the very issues which government leaders in Tokyo spent the next three weeks in debating without result. Had the Allies given the prince a week of grace in which to obtain his government's support for acceptance, the war might have ended toward the latter part of July or the very beginning of August without the atomic bomb and without Soviet participation in the conflict. Although Stalin's price for co-operation might have been equal to what he had already been promised at Yalta, the Western Allies might at least have been spared the added burden of subsequently having the Yalta concessions flagrantly augmented manyfold by hostile Soviet action in Manchuria and Korea. If Prince Konoye had demonstrated that he was personally unwilling to entreat his government to accept the Allied terms or if the Japanese government had refused to accept the declaration in spite of Konoye's possible representations in its behalf, the bomb could have been dropped upon Hiroshima as scheduled. Since it was anticipated that the bomb might shock the Japanese into surrender,[63] its value and effectiveness in this respect would not have been impaired by a prior and secret refusal of the Japanese government to surrender on the basis of the conditions laid down

---

[61] In accordance with a distinction made by the State Department, the author has chosen to refer to the July 26 statement on Japan as the "Potsdam Proclamation" in spite of the fact that "Potsdam Declaration" (which ought strictly to be applied only to the Allied policy statement relating to Europe) seems to be in common usage. E and J texts are found in Appendix C and JFO MS: Ch. 37 (Potsudamu sengen no hasshutsu), respectively.

[62] Italics mine. It is significant that this phrase was used and not the all-inclusive, "unconditional surrender *of Japan*."

[63] See, for instance, Stimson and Bundy, *On Active Service*, 617, and Churchill, *Triumph and Tragedy*, 638–39.

at Potsdam. In truth, the Japanese government, for all practical purposes, did indeed ignore the Allied declaration until after Hiroshima
and Nagasaki had been blasted nearly out of existence.

Had the Allies decided to give Konoye a chance, they could have
dictated whatever arrangements they saw fit. They could have told the
prince, for instance, that if Japan refused to surrender at once they, in
conformity with the warning in their proclamation, would bring the full
application of their military power to bear upon Japan and would not
rest until the Japanese armed forces had been completely destroyed and
the Japanese homeland utterly devastated. Had Konoye requested a
clear statement of the Allied position with respect to the imperial institution (as he certainly would have done), the Allies could have given
him the answer which Secretary of State Byrnes ultimately sent on
August 11,[64] or they could have told the prince that the future status
of the Emperor would depend on the Japanese government's response to
their demands. This would have implied that the imperial institution
would be permitted to remain if Japan surrendered at once but would
very likely be abolished if the Japanese, by their refusal to accept the
Allied terms, forced a continuation of the war.[65] In either case, Konoye
would have had a tremendously powerful argument to level at any
opposition which might possibly have developed within the Japanese
government or among the Japanese military.

Even if Stalin had flatly refused to co-operate through fear of ending up as the loser in such a venture, there was still another alternative.
Had anyone thought of pursuing the Konoye feeler in preference to dis-
playing America's atomic achievement and in preference to seeking a
belated Soviet entry into the conflict through Manchuria, Korea, and
Sakhalin, an excellent avenue of approach existed in Switzerland where
the Dulles organization had been in touch with the Fujimura and Okamoto groups for several months. Since the United States and Great
Britain were obviously not committed to prolonging the war until Stalin
had had time to mass his forces in the Far East, there was nothing to

---

[64] The answer sent by Mr. Byrnes on August 11 read (in part): "From the moment of surrender the authority of the Emperor and the Japanese Government to rule
the state shall be subject to the Supreme Commander of the Allied powers who will
take such steps as he deems proper to effectuate the surrender terms." See Appendix E.

[65] When the Japanese government ultimately got down to discussing the Potsdam
Proclamation (after July 26), there were those who felt that the Allies would never
permit the imperial institution to remain if they were forced to spill the blood of
their men in an invasion of Japan.

In a memorandum for the Secretary of State dated August 7, 1945, Mr. Grew
wrote as follows: "I . . . am inclined to feel that if Japan refuses to heed the
Potsdam Proclamation and declines to surrender unconditionally, necessitating our
invasion of the main Japanese islands by force and the inevitable loss of life which
will occur among the Allied forces in the event of such invasion, the Emperor of Japan
might well be treated as a war criminal in order that full justice should be done." See
Grew, Turbulent Era, II, 1438.

prevent the Western Allies from attempting to bypass the Soviet Union completely. The United States could have acted upon the facts contained in the Tōgō-Satō intercepted messages even prior to the Potsdam Conference by merely informing Japan through the Dulles-Fujimura channel that no representations from *any* neutral power would be acceptable other than an announcement of Japan's undisguised willingness to surrender unconditionally. Simultaneously Washington could have transmitted the terms of the Potsdam Proclamation through Fujimura with an unmistakable ultimatum in the tone of the original: "Accept these terms now, immediately and through us, or be prepared for the consequences of your folly."

What complex of factors kept the above alternatives from being considered seriously, if they were considered at all, is not yet known, but the fact is there was at least something of an opportunity here, or perhaps a gamble, which might have yielded startling results had it not been ignored. Although this criticism may be the product of two much hindsight, it is difficult to explain why the Tōgō-Satō intercepted messages did not at least produce a logical revision of the then current draft of the Potsdam Proclamation to include some guarantee—even a qualified one—with respect to the preservation of Japan's imperial system. The pertinent question of how thoroughly the United States was wedded to a policy of getting the Soviet Union into the war has a complicated and as yet incomplete history. The content of the Yalta Agreement suggests, however, that in February 1945 Washington was anxious- -regardless of cost—to obtain a Soviet commitment to open hostilities against Japan following Germany's capitulation.

Shortly before the Potsdam Conference convened, there were those who felt that the United States could not afford to hold out any clarification of terms to Japan that might be construed as an American desire to end the war before the Soviet Union had the opportunity to enter it. This was a new twist, for up to that time a certain fear had existed that the Soviet Union would not come into the war and would thus leave the United States "committed and frozen . . . to the concept of unconditional surrender, maintenance of which might prove extremely costly . . ."

The idea that it would be much more difficult to keep the Russians out of the war than to bring them in had been broached in May 1945 by Ambassador Harriman but had not been widely accepted either then or later. On July 28, two days after the release of the Potsdam Proclamation, Navy Secretary Forrestal had a conversation with Secretary of State Byrnes in which the latter "said he was most anxious to get the Japanese affair over with before the Russians got in, with particular reference to Dairen and Port Arthur. Once in there, he felt, it would not be easy to get them out . . ."

When President Truman arrived at Potsdam, he told General Eisenhower that one of his "primary objectives" was to get Russia into the Japanese war. "Eisenhower begged him at that time not to assume that he had to give anything away to do this, that the Russians were desperately anxious to get into the Eastern war and that in Eisenhower's opinion there was no question but that Japan was already thoroughly beaten. When the President told him at the end of the Conference that he had achieved his objectives and was going home, Eisenhower again remarked that he earnestly hoped the President had not had to make any concessions to get them in."[66]

At this critical time, that is, the spring and summer of 1945, there also appears to have been no general agreement in Washington as to what underlay Japan's hopeless continuation of the conflict and her seemingly impertinent refusal to entertain unconditional surrender as a basis for terminating hostilities. There can be but little doubt that the unconditional surrender demand sparked the imagination and perhaps even fired the resolve of many people on the Allied side. What is open to question, however, is the value of the concept as an instrument of policy with respect to the enemy.

Although the communiqué issued at the close of the Casablanca Conference in late January 1943 had contained no suggestion of the implication-laden phrase, President Roosevelt subsequently told the press that the United Nations would demand "unconditional surrender" of their enemies. He also specifically asked the newsmen, in filing their stories, to refer to the Casablanca meeting as the "Unconditional Surrender Conference."[67] In an address before the White House Correspondents' Association some time later, the President declared that the only terms on which the United Nations would deal with any Axis government or any Axis factions were those "proclaimed at Casablanca: 'unconditional surrender.' In our uncompromising policy," he said, "we mean no harm to the common people of the Axis nations. But we do mean to impose punishment and retribution in full upon their guilty, barbaric leaders." American policy "toward our Japanese enemies," he added, "is precisely the same as our policy toward our Nazi enemies: it is a policy of fighting hard on all fronts and ending the war as quickly as we can on the uncompromising terms of unconditional surrender."[68]

[66] For the quotations cited in the text above and additional material relating thereto, see Millis (ed.), *The Forrestal Diaries*, 55–56; Stettinius, *Roosevelt and the Russians*, 90–91, 96–98; Stimson and Bundy, *On Active Service*, 618–19; and Sherwood, *Roosevelt and Hopkins*, 902–4. In this connection, see also Churchill, *Triumph and Tragedy*, 639–40.

[67] *Facts on File*, 1943, 25 E. For additional material and the text of the communiqué, see U.S. State Dept., *Bulletin*, VIII (January 30, 1943), 93–94. See also Sherwood, *Roosevelt and Hopkins*, 693–94.

[68] See U.S. State Dept., *Bulletin*, VIII (February 13, 1943), 146. This speech was delivered at the annual White House correspondents' dinner for the President

According to Secretary Hull, the President's announcement of this clipped formula for victory came as a surprise to the State Department.[69] Mr. Hull personally was unaware of any such decision having been reached and he was quite opposed to the principle involved.[70] In the first place, "it might prolong the war by solidifying Axis resistance into one of desperation," and in the second place "the principle logically required the victor nations to be ready to take over every phase of the national and local Governments of the conquered countries, and to operate all governmental activities and properties." So far as Mr. Hull could determine, neither the United States nor its Allies were in any way prepared to undertake such a vast obligation. Since the President had already used the phrase, however, Secretary Hull realized that the State Department could do nothing but follow it, "at least in form," while endeavoring to convince the President of the serious need for a clarification of the meaning behind the words.[71] Thus, in spite of the frequent repetitions of the unconditional surrender theme that followed its somewhat informal debut,[72] notable care was generally taken to lay a psychological basis for an eventual acceptance of the principle by the enemy majority acting in opposition to the minority—the dominant few who had "misled" their fellow countrymen into embarking on war.

With the defeat of Nazi Germany in May of 1945, a more positive revision of official thinking began to appear in terms of a limited definition of the ambiguous, yet also meaningful, phrase bequeathed by the late President to his successor. On May 8, 1945, in a statement announcing the end of the war in Europe, Mr. Truman declared,

. . . The Japanese people have felt the weight of our land, air, and naval attacks. So long as their leaders and the armed forces continue the war the striking power and intensity of our blows will steadily increase and will bring

---

(February 12, 1943). At the time, Admiral Leahy felt that the President "was promising more than he could deliver in the reasonably near future." (*I Was There*, 148.)

[69] Hull, *Memoirs*, II, 1571. Hull declares the President's promotion of the unconditional surrender formula also took Mr. Churchill by surprise. Elliott Roosevelt, on the other hand, claims that Churchill thought F.D.R.'s choice of phrase was "perfect." (*As He Saw It*, 117.) See also Sherwood, *Roosevelt and Hopkins*, 695–97.

[70] Secretary of the Navy Forrestal was also dissatisfied with the Allied formula for victory. ". . . he was aware that a policy of 'unconditional surrender' which would lead merely to the destruction of Germany and Japan would seriously unbalance the international system in the face of Soviet power." See Millis (ed.), *The Forrestal Diaries*, 24.

[71] See Hull, *Memoirs*, II, 1571.

[72] The unconditional surrender demand was reiterated as *Allied* policy in the Declaration of Four Nations on General Security (October 1943) and in the Cairo Declaration (December 1943).

The inclusion of the term "unconditional surrender" in the Four Nations Declaration was made with the approval of the President and was based on a definition of the term he had inserted in a letter to the Congress in August 1943 ("Except for the responsible fascist leaders, the people of the Axis need not fear unconditional surrender . . . they will not be trading Axis despotism for ruin under the United Nations . . ."). See *ibid.* and U.S. State Dept., *Bulletin*, IX (August 28, 1943), 124–25.

utter destruction to Japan's industrial war production, to its shipping, and to everything that supports its military activity.

The longer the war lasts, the greater will be the suffering and hardships which the people of Japan will undergo—all in vain. Our blows will not cease until the Japanese military and naval forces lay down their arms in *unconditional surrender*.[73]

Just what does the unconditional surrender of the armed forces mean for the Japanese people?

It means the end of the war.

It means the termination of the influence of the military leaders who have brought Japan to the present brink of disaster.

It means provision for the return of soldiers and sailors to their families, their farms, their jobs.

It means not prolonging the present agony and suffering of the Japanese in the vain hope of victory.

Unconditional surrender does not mean the extermination or enslavement of the Japanese people.[74]

In a new series of Japan-bound propaganda broadcasts[75] which began within two hours after the President had issued the above statement, Navy Captain Ellis M. Zacharias, speaking as the government's "official spokesman," stressed that unconditional surrender was basically a military term signifying "the cessation of resistance and the yielding of arms." In other words, the phrase referred specifically to the unconditional capitulation of the Japanese *armed forces*. It did not, and would not, mean the end of Japan's way of life or of her existence as a nation.

In a somewhat strained rebuttal to American assurances that Japan would not be destroyed if she surrendered unconditionally, Japanese broadcasters "referred to Admiral Halsey's statement about the evils of Shintoism, and his recommendation that Shinto shrines be bombed." An editorial in the *Nippon Times* assured the Japanese people that the Admiral was "typical of the mass mind of America, which will demand the destruction of Japan." One commentator was reported to have said that the enemy had overlooked the fact that all Asians, and the Japanese in particular, could stand suffering and privation far more than Occidentals. "Japan simply will not submit," he had said, "because it does not know the word defeat."[76]

In the face of such statements and attitudes as these, it would appear that what Zacharias and others had to say was not exact enough to reach the crux of the problem: Allied intentions with respect to the postwar

---

[73] Note the emphasis here upon the unconditional surrender of the *armed forces*. This "definition of limitation" was subsequently repeated in the Potsdam Proclamation.

[74] See U.S. State Dept., *Bulletin*, XII (May 13, 1945), 886.

[75] These broadcasts, done first in Japanese and then repeated in English, were known as Operation Plan 1-45. In all, fourteen broadcasts were made, the first being "released" on May 8, 1945, and the last on August 4, 1945. See Zacharias, *Secret Missions*, 342–85 and 399–424.

[76] See USFCC, *Radio Report Far East*, #79, BA 19.

disposition of the imperial house and Japan's imperial system.[77] Although there were a number of people in Washington who realized the nature of the issue at stake, there was little agreement either as to a solution or as to the proper time to make a clear-cut statement.[78] The question of the Emperor's role in the life of the nation and his relationship to the future simply produced an acrimonious debate, a sort of mental tug of war, in which each side strained to the utmost but never moved the other.

There was, however, one cabinet official who did something more than just recognize the problem or add to the confusion, and that was Secretary of War Stimson—a man whose efforts to provide a realistic and valid answer to the question were unfortunately to prove of no avail.[79] The implications inherent in the invasion plans which were approved at the White House on June 18, 1945, led Mr. Stimson to prepare a memorandum for the President, dated July 2, in which he proposed an alternative designed to secure "the equivalent of an unconditional surrender" without an invasion and to guarantee the "permanent destruction" of Japan's power "again to strike an aggressive blow at the 'peace of the Pacific.' "[80] Mr. Stimson felt that the United States and its Allies might be spared the sacrifices which would attend a full-scale invasion if only Japan were warned of what lay in store for her and were given an opportunity to capitulate.

[77] Zacharias and his associates were apparently aware of this point but were unable to get clearance to broadcast any statement on the Emperor. In a rather bizarre move prompted by Suzuki's speech to the 87th Extraordinary Session of the Diet (see footnote 44, Ch. 3), Zacharias wrote an "anonymous" letter to the editor of the *Washington Post* (July 21) in which he declared that if the Japanese wanted to know what the Emperor's status would be they should ask. (*Secret Missions*, 370–72.) In this connection, see footnote 60 above.

[78] See, for instance, Millis (ed.), *The Forrestal Diaries*, 66, and Grew, *Turbulent Era*, II, 1421–42.

[79] Assistant Secretary of War McCloy, Under Secretary of State Grew, and Navy Secretary Forrestal also deserve credit for their efforts to promote a definition of "unconditional surrender" that the Japanese could accept. See Millis (ed.), *The Forrestal Diaries*, 68–71, and Stimson and Bundy, *On Active Service*, 628–29. The material contained in these two works is in sharp contrast to a statement by Admiral Zacharias to the effect that he found Grew and his staff "most determined, first, to continue the war to Japan's total defeat, and, second, to avoid any deals with the Emperor." (*Secret Missions*, 333.) In this connection, see also Grew, *Turbulent Era*, II, 1406–42.

[80] See Stimson and Bundy, *On Active Service*, 619–24. Mr. Stimson's memorandum, which was submitted to the President on July 2, had been prepared after "discussion and general agreement" with Acting Secretary of State Grew and Secretary of the Navy Forrestal. The memorandum, which was entitled "Proposed Program for Japan," did not grow out of the problem of atomic energy but, rather, out of "the American desire to achieve a Japanese surrender without invading the home islands." The memorandum received the "general approval" of the President and was used by him and Secretary of State Byrnes as a basis for composing a draft of the declaration to be issued at Potsdam. (In this connection, see also Byrnes, *Speaking Frankly*, 206, and Grew, *Turbulent Era*, II, 1431–34.)

Believing that Japan's susceptibility to reason in the crisis facing her would be much greater than press and other current comment indicated,[81] Stimson spelled out his recommendations for an Allied declaration in specific terms, the very same which were somewhat rephrased and then released at Potsdam three weeks later. There was, however, one significant difference. Stimson's declaration contained a statement to the effect that the Allies would not exclude the maintenance of a constitutional monarchy under the present dynasty, for he felt such a statement "would substantially add to the chances of acceptance." Although it cannot be proved, it is possible that the Japanese government would have accepted the Potsdam Proclamation immediately had Secretary Stimson's reference to the imperial structure been retained. Such a declaration, while promising destruction if Japan resisted, would have offered hope if she surrendered. This was precisely Stimson's intention.[82] Before leaving for Potsdam, however, Secretary of State Byrnes consulted former Secretary Hull and found that he was opposed to the Stimson suggestion on the grounds that it was "appeasement of Japan" and "seemed to guarantee continuance not only of the Emperor but also of the feudal privileges of a ruling caste under the Emperor." Mr. Hull felt that both the Throne and the ruling elite "must be stripped of all extraordinary privileges and placed on a level before the law with everyone else." After Secretary Byrnes left Washington, Mr. Hull cabled a fuller expression of his views and subsequently received a reply to the effect that the Allied declaration, when issued, would contain no commitment with regard to the Throne.[83]

The absence of any mention of the Emperor in the Potsdam Proclamation posed a serious problem for the end-the-war party in Japan since preservation of the imperial house was the one prerequisite on which all of their efforts to date had been based. Fortunately for everyone concerned, a careful and time-consuming study of the text of the proclama-

[81] Mr. Stimson's optimism regarding Japan's susceptibility to reason was based in part on Japan's recent historical past and in part on his belief that "the Japanese nation has the mental intelligence and versatile capacity . . . to recognize the folly of a fight to the finish and to accept the proffer of what will amount to an unconditional surrender." Mr. Stimson also believed that Japan possessed "enough liberal leaders (although now submerged by the terrorists) to be depended upon for her reconstruction as a responsible member of the family of nations." (On Active Service, 621–24.)

[82] See Stimson and Bundy, On Active Service, 621–24. In referring to the Potsdam Proclamation, Mr. Byrnes states that its terms "were phrased so that the threat of utter destruction if Japan resisted was offset with the hope of a just though stern peace if she surrendered." (Speaking Frankly, 207.) (The difference between Stimson's draft, which contained hope for Japan's dynasty, and the Potsdam Proclamation, which made no mention of the Emperor, is, and was then, of fundamental importance.)

[83] See Hull, Memoirs, II, 1593–94. See also footnote 3, Ch. 9, and the text corresponding thereto.

tion subsequently convinced the peaccmakers that they could follow through with their plans without endangering an institution to which they owed the ultimate loyalty under their code of ethics. The Japanese military, on the other hand, interpreted the omission of any commitment on the Throne as evidence of the Allied intention to destroy forever the foundation stone of the Japanese nation. Here was an invaluable trump card unintentionally given them by the Allies, and the militarists played it with unfailing skill.

Both those who wanted to terminate the war at once and those who sought to continue the fighting through an invasion were basically thinking in terms of a peace with honor. For the latter, honor covered a wide field, so wide that the Allies would never have agreed to the conditions under which they might have been willing to lay down their arms. For the former, honor was simply synonymous with preservation of the national polity (*kokutai*). Out of necessity, all else had long since ceased to matter, but even these men had to be certain that they were not walking into a trap. The one thing they could not do was sign a death warrant for the imperial house. If the Allies meant to wipe out, in one stroke, an imperial institution tenaciously rooted in the mind and soul of every true Japanese, if they planned to imprison or in other ways heap indignities upon the imperial family, if they sought to deny to His Majesty's subjects the very polity upon which they rested their claims to being Japanese, then even the most ardent advocates of peace would obediently fall into step behind the fanatics rather than ever lend their support to an act so despicable that the record of it would soil their names forever and would render them the most reviled figures in all Japanese history.

7

THE MARCH OF TIME

July 26–August 9, 1945

EXCEPT for the members of the highest councils of the state, Friday, July 27, 1945, was spent in a way made common by its constant repetition. In the country, farmers took to their fields and fishermen to their boats, as yet unaware that America, Britain, and China had agreed, the day before, that Japan should be given an opportunity to end the war. In the cities, laborers, factory hands, and white-collar workers sweated through the summer heat wondering how long it would be before the sirens again howled a grim warning of approaching enemy raiders. Like their country brethren, these city dwellers were also ignorant of the fact that the historic meeting at Potsdam had produced a public proclamation challenging their leaders to accept the terms set forth by the Allies or live to see the complete destruction of the Japanese armed forces and the utter devastation of the imperial homeland.

Only at the upper level of government planning and policy making was there any of that feverish activity and strained excitement one might have expected as a result of the Allied announcement.[1] While a translation of the Potsdam terms (monitored earlier in the morning from a San Francisco broadcast) was still in progress, the Vice-Minister of Foreign Affairs, Shunichi Matsumoto,[2] took the lead in presenting to his colleagues what subsequently became the Foreign Office point of view. The Allied proclamation, he said, was a statement of the *conditions* of the enemy's unconditional surrender formula. The only way Japan could end the war was by accepting the terms as they stood. The govern-

---

[1] For the events of Friday and Saturday, July 27 and July 28, described in the text which follows, see *Statements*: Sakomizu 4/21/49, Sakomizu #62016, Shimomura #57668, Miyazaki #54478, Toyoda #57670, Yoshizumi #54484, Tōgō #50304 and #54562; Kido, "Nikki," 7/27/45; Toyoda, *Saigo no teikoku kaigun*, 202–3; Tōgō, "Shūsen gaikō," *Kaizō*, XXXI (November 1950), 133–35; Kawai, "*Mokusatsu,* Japan's Response to the Potsdam Declaration," *The Pacific Historical Review*, XIX (November 1950), 409–14; IMTFE: Tōgō, 35785–91; Sakomizu, 35607–8; JFO MS: Ch. 37 (Potsudamu sengen no hasshutsu); Shimomura, *Shūsen hishi*, 67–70; and JFO, *Present Conditions of Japan*, 1.

[2] Shunichi Matsumoto should not be confused with Shigeharu Matsumoto, wartime chief of the Editorial Bureau of the Dōmei News Agency. See footnote 44, Ch. 6, above.

ment should release the text to the people in full. Under no circumstances should it reject the Allied demand. If there had to be any compromise with the circumstances of the moment, then the only intelligent course to follow would be to say nothing at all.

Although Foreign Minister Tōgō agreed with this in principle, he apparently foresaw the difficulties which would arise in presenting the idea of acceptance to Japan's recalcitrant military, many of whom were actually quite prepared to let the blood curdle in their veins rather than surrender without first engaging the enemy on Japan's own shores. In spite of the fact that he realized the Allied terms were probably the best Japan could hope to obtain[3]—the was situation being what it was— Tōgō inwardly felt that the range of the document left considerable room for interpretation. He therefore desired, if at all possible, to seek a clarification of meaning favorable to Japan.[4] While remaining non-committal on the surface, in other words, the government should do everything in its power to promote Point III of the plan the Big Six had formulated in May and should endeavor immediately to obtain a positive answer to Japan's request for Soviet mediation. If this move proved successful, Japan might still be able to obtain more advantageous terms or at the very least a clear-cut definition of the conditions announced at Potsdam.[5] It was this argument which Tōgō presented at the Big Six meeting held later in the morning and at the cabinet session which convened in the afternoon.[6]

In many of those who participated in these deliberations, the Allied proclamation produced a bitter and unreceptive reaction. It was, after all, an order to surrender, not an invitation to negotiate: "Following are our terms. We shall not deviate from them. There are no alternatives. We shall brook no delay."[7]

Nor was this all. The terms of the proclamation gave promise of creating a cleavage of opinion that would rob the cabinet of its effectiveness and might even threaten its existence. It was perhaps fortunate, therefore, that no point-by-point consideration was given at this time

[3] This view was not shared by the army and navy authorities. See, for instance, USSBS, *Interrogations*, II, Toyoda, 319–20.

[4] See *Statements:* Tōgō #50304 and #54562.

[5] Tōgō thought that it might even be possible to arrange a meeting somewhere between Japanese representatives and an American-British delegation. See *Statements:* Tōgō #50304.

[6] At an audience with the Emperor that morning (July 27), Tōgō expressed the same views to the Throne. He also reported on the British elections and on the "progress" of the negotiations in Moscow. See JFO MS: Ch. 37 (Potsudamu sengen no hasshutsu).

According to Kido, the Emperor had entertained a faint hope, prior to Potsdam, that it would be possible for Japan to obtain a negotiated peace. After Potsdam, the Emperor resigned himself to the inevitability of terminating the war on the basis of surrender. (*Statements:* Kido #61541 and #61476.)

[7] See Appendix C.

to the document as a whole. In this way, a head-on collision was postponed until after the peace faction had gained strength from the developments of the ensuing two weeks—developments which served to undermine more conclusively than ever before the authority and influence of those who were prepared to commit the nation to self-destruction.

Although Foreign Minister Tōgō encountered opposition from the Supreme Command when he expressed the view that it would be "extremely impolitic" for Japan to reject the proclamation,[8] he eventually managed to prevail upon the Supreme Councilors and the cabinet ministers to agree that for the time being, at least, Japan should not issue an "answer" to the Allied proclamation but should merely content herself with ascertaining Soviet intentions.[9]

Had the decisions ended at this point, history might possibly have been spared the painful task of recording the consequences of one of the most unusual and contradictory actions ever taken by a government against itself. Instead, the cabinet, of necessity, turned its attention to a hitherto unvoiced dilemma. If the government attempted to withhold the text of the Potsdam Proclamation, the people might grow suspicious and restless, particularly since the press had already hinted that the Allies had discussed Japan and that a declaration directed at the Empire might be forthcoming. If, on the other hand, the government released the text, some explanatory statement or other, no matter how brief, would have to be made. In the latter event, utmost care would be required to strike a balance between the cabinet's decision not to say anything that would destroy the possibility of negotiating for better terms through Moscow and a certain necessity for it to say something that would appease the military's demand for a strongly worded rebuttal and would also satisfy the expectations of the misguided masses.

After considerable discussion, which pointedly emphasized that Japan would have to choose between unsatisfactory alternatives and dangerous ones, a compromise was reached making it possible for the newspapers to publish an expurgated version of the Potsdam text for release the following morning.[10] It was also decided, over the objections

---

[8] It would appear that it was at this time that Tōgō first stressed the change in emphasis between the Cairo Declaration (unconditional surrender of *Japan*) and the Potsdam Proclamation (unconditional surrender of the Japanese *armed forces*).

[9] In his Cable #484, dated Stockholm, July 27, 1945, Minister Okamoto reported that Russia had agreed at Yalta to enter the war against Japan within six months after victory over Germany, that during the Potsdam Conference the United States would request Russia to commence hostilities by early November, and that should the Soviet Union be unable to comply with this request the United States would ask for the use of certain areas in the Soviet Far East as bases for military operations against Japan. (IMTFE: *Analyses*, #941.) (Either this cable did not make a deep impression upon the experts at the Foreign Office or they felt that they still had no choice other than to press for a Soviet answer to Japan's request for mediation.)

[10] See the Tokyo *Asahi Shimbun* for Saturday, July 28, 1945, and the *Nippon Times* for Sunday, July 29, 1945.

Following the Allied release of the proclamation on July 26, leaflets containing

lodged by the Supreme Command earlier in the day, that the censored text would be handled strictly as news—without either editorial comment or criticism. So far so good, but from this point on the record becomes increasingly blurred until the developments of the next morning, Saturday, July 28, produce a startling clarification.

During the discussions held on Friday, the military had pressed the government to issue a strong statement in "answer" to the Allied pronouncement, but the Premier had sided with his Foreign Minister and had said that the government should simply *mokusatsu* the proclamation—literally, "kill" it "with silence," and therefore, less literally and more idiomatically, "take no notice of it," "treat it with silent contempt," or "ignore it."[11] In using this picturesque phrase, Suzuki may only have wished to pinpoint the argument for his colleagues, that is, to sum up the decision which had already taken shape, for it must have been apparent to all those present, including Suzuki, that whatever Japan said—even for home consumption—had every chance of reaching Allied ears in one way or another. The delicate balance which the better part of wisdom so clearly dictated at this time could only be achieved if the government avoided saying anything which might be construed abroad as indicating a contemptuous Japanese rejection of the Allied demand. The government could have skirted this obvious pitfall by permitting the papers, ostensibly on their own initiative and without any mention of the government, to call the Potsdam Proclamation "just another in the series of propaganda pronouncements by means of which the enemy is attempting to win the war." Although political observers abroad would have interpreted such a statement as coming from the government or at least as having its consent, such observers would probably also have surmised that the absence of any official announcement indicated that the cabinet was still in the process of deciding whether it would accept or reject the Allied terms.

Even though the Japanese military would not have been satisfied with such tactics, the only other alternative was for the government to say something so strong that the military would applaud and the Allies would declaim, "Japan has rejected the Potsdam Proclamation; therefore, she must suffer the consequences." Such a development, of course, could only result in the loss of whatever chance the government assumed it had to negotiate for better terms through Soviet good offices. So far as the people were concerned, the government could very easily have

the full text of the terms (in Japanese translation) were dropped on Japan in an effort to forestall an attempt by the Japanese government to withhold the proclamation entirely or to release only a partial text. See U.S. Navy Dept., *Psychological Warfare*, Supplement No. 2 (August 15, 1945), Leaflet #2107.

[11] *Moku*, which is also read *damaru*, means "to be silent." *Satsu*, also read *korosu*, means "to kill." In *Kenkyūsha's New Japanese-English Dictionary*, the verb *mokusatsu suru* is defined as "Take no notice of; treat (anything) with silent contempt; ignore [by keeping silence]."

refrained from saying anything so long as the newspapers nonchalantly deprecated the censored text as propaganda—all smoke and no fire. But somehow—and just how, either no one knows or cares to say[12]— the Premier's phrase, *mokusatsu*, passed out of the conference room Friday afternoon and found its way onto the front pages of Japan's Saturday morning papers. It is this point which many of the persons who were on the inside of these events either ignore entirely, blur into indistinction, or brush aside as incidental, yet the fact that *mokusatsu* appeared in the Saturday *morning* papers is highly significant and completely destroys the contentions of those who lay the use of the phrase to the demands made by the military later Saturday morning, long after the papers had gone to press.

Although the newspapers, in accordance with the instructions they had received from the government, printed only selected parts of the Allied proclamation, the people were very definitely told that the government's attitude was *mokusatsu*. "Since the joint declaration of America, Britain, and Chungking is a thing of no great value," a vernacular daily quoted *the government* as saying, "it will only serve to re-enhance the government's resolve to carry the war forward unfalteringly to a successful conclusion!"[13]

And here, in the most open-faced manner possible, is the unreasonable contradiction between what the government supposedly wanted to do and what the government actually did do. In permitting the newspapers to use the *mokusatsu* phrase and in further clarifying its meaning by flippantly characterizing the Allied proclamation as a thing of no great value, the government was not only flying in the face of the "wait and see" decision which Tōgō, in particular, had fought to obtain but was also publicly avowing that the demands made at Potsdam were *unworthy of notice* and would not cause the slightest breach in Japan's determination to continue the war, come what may![14]

[12] The possibilities are as follows: (1) In spite of its earlier decision to say nothing, the cabinet finally decided to say *mokusatsu*; (2) the Premier, who first used the term, privately gave his consent—thinking that the term expressed the actual intentions of the cabinet; (3) the chief cabinet secretary or the president of the Board of Information authorized the newspapers to use the term for the same reason as stated in (2); or (4) the military secretly forced the newspapers to print *mokusatsu* knowing that it would be interpreted abroad as a rejection of the Allied proclamation. For once at least, the latter possibility does not seem to be the case. No one, not even the most flagrant opportunist or sincere antimilitarist, has ever attempted to offer this explanation.

[13] See the Tokyo *Asahi Shimbun* for July 28, 1945: "Seifu wa Mokusatsu."

[14] The USFCC (*Radio Report Far East*, #79, BA 2 and BA 18) reported that the Potsdam terms were denounced in Japan as "ridiculous," "unforgivable," "impudent," and "insolent" and that the proclamation was construed by Japanese propagandists and publicists as "a sign of Allied weakness and war-weariness." (There were those in Washington who had argued against making a commitment on the imperial institution because they believed such a move would merely be interpreted in Japan as a sign of a weakening Allied will to fight. It is interesting to note that the Potsdam Proclamation, which contained nothing on the Emperor, was so interpreted.)

For a person who was privy to the cabinet's decision, *mokusatsu* may have conveyed the meaning of "withholding comment,"[15] but under the circumstances then prevailing the whole burden of choosing a term which not even a language-school beginner could have misinterpreted rested with the government.[16] Obviously, anything Japan said short of an expression of her willingness to accept the Potsdam ultimatum would convince the Allies that Japan had spurned the path of reason they had offered her and had chosen instead to dare them to unleash the destruction which was the promised alternative. When measured against the fact that the government actively desired to open negotiations through the Soviet Union in order to obtain a termination of the war on conditions more favorable than those released at Potsdam, the governmental announcement becomes even more senseless. Perhaps Japan meant to convey that her attitude was "wait and see," but the Allied reaction to Japan's response was based on what Japan *said* and not on what she *meant*. If this was a form of national *haragei*, therefore, it was completely lost on America and Britain.

In the years which have elapsed since that fateful Saturday in July, many persons, especially certain civilian members of the Suzuki Cabinet, have sought to blame the Japanese military for the damage done by what all agree was a most serious verbal blunder—a most prejudicial slip of the tongue. The truth of the matter, however, is that the government as a whole and not just its military branches must bear the initial and prime responsibility, since it was only *after* the governmental announcement had appeared Saturday morning that the Supreme Command stepped in and took action which resulted in a further strengthening and irretrievable confirmation of the earlier statement.

At a meeting held within the palace grounds on Saturday morning, the army and navy chiefs of staff and the War Minister called for a

[15] Although others have interpreted *mokusatsu* in this way, it is a fact that Foreign Minister Tōgō considered the use of *mokusatsu* to be a *flagrant violation* of the cabinet's decision to "withhold comment." (*Statements:* Tōgō #50304.) It should also be remembered that Premier Suzuki later reinforced the meaning of *mokusatsu* by declaring that the government looked upon the Potsdam Proclamation as "a thing of no great value" and as nothing more than a "rehash" of the Cairo Declaration. Although the term may be an ambiguous one capable of misinterpretation, the effect exerted upon the people of Japan at the time, and upon the Allies as well, was quite the contrary of ambiguity. To the man in the street *mokusatsu* meant that the government would treat the Potsdam ultimatum "with contempt"—that the government would "ignore" the Allied pronouncement and hence would "reject" it.

[16] Mr. Shimomura (*Shūsen hishi*, 69, and *Statements:* #57668) has compared the impression created by *mokusatsu* with that produced abroad by the term "Black Dragon Society" (*Kokuryūkai*). Although he has noted that the society took its name from the Amur River, which is called the *Kokuryū* (Black Dragon) river in Japanese, and should therefore have been called the Amur River Society, it should be apparent that the activities of the society did more to create a sinister impression abroad (at least among specialists in the field) than did the choice of terms used in translating into English.

positive refutation or denunciation of the Potsdam Proclamation.[17] Any other action would be untenable, they argued, in view of the effect it would have upon the morale of the troops. The single-sentence *mokusatsu* announcement which had appeared in the morning papers was not enough. Already telegrams were pouring in from front-line commanders calling for "an explicit and prompt rejection" of the Allied demand for unconditional surrender.[18]

In spite of Navy Minister Yonai's efforts to calm his colleagues, the proponents of a strong stand—Umezu, Toyoda, and Anami—remained adamant. Whether Suzuki ultimately acquiesced in their demands and then later softened the tone or whether the demands were not nearly so strong as others have claimed cannot be determined, but at a press conference held at four o'clock that afternoon Suzuki, acting as a result of what had occurred in the morning, came perilously close to sealing the nation's doom. Appended to the notes which he carried into the conference room was a prepared statement which supposedly reflected the military's point of view, or at least a modified version of it. The statement was an uncompromising reiteration of Suzuki's earlier pronouncement and, as such, was emphatically contrary to the purpose behind the decision reached by the cabinet the day before. When one of the reporters, all of whom had been told beforehand that they might ask the Premier about the Allied proclamation, turned to the planted question, the Premier glanced down at his notes and replied,

I consider the joint proclamation of the three powers to be a rehash of the Cairo Declaration. The government does not regard it as a thing of any great value; the government will just ignore [*mokusatsu*] it. We will press forward resolutely to carry the war to a successful conclusion.[19]

Two days later, on Monday, July 30, the same day on which the Premier's second statement appeared in the Japanese press, the *New York Times* informed its readers — as did other papers elsewhere throughout the United States and the world at large—that Japan had dismissed the Potsdam Proclamation with a contemptuous gesture.[20]

[17] The meeting in question was the regular weekly meeting for the exchange of information between the government and the Supreme Command. Foreign Minister Tōgō was not present (because of other duties), and apparently neither was Premier Suzuki. War Minister Anami, Navy Minister Yonai, Chief of the Army General Staff Umezu, Chief of the Naval General Staff Toyoda, and Chief Cabinet Secretary Sakomizu were the persons directly concerned.

[18] There is some disagreement over whether or not such telegrams were received. There are also strong representations by the army and navy to the effect that the military did not exert any pressure at this time. It would seem, however, that the military did exert pressure on the government on Saturday but that either the pressure was far from being as severe as some accounts say or Suzuki was able to tone it down to the level of *mokusatsu* merely by making his second reference to this phrase more pointed and clear-cut.

[19] See the Tokyo *Asahi Shimbun* for Monday, July 30, 1945: "Sangoku Seimei wa Kachi Nashi."

[20] See the *New York Times* for July 30, 1945, and July 31, 1945 (editorials).

The obvious inference, and the one drawn in Washington by the then Secretary of War, Mr. Stimson, was rejection.[21] In view of the fact that "on July 28 the Premier of Japan . . . rejected the Potsdam ultimatum by announcing that it was 'unworthy of public notice,' " Stimson later wrote, the United States "could only proceed to demonstrate that the ultimatum had meant exactly what it said when it stated that if the Japanese continued the war, 'the full application of our military power, backed by our resolve, will mean the inevitable and complete destruction of the Japanese armed forces and just as inevitably the utter devastation of the Japanese homeland.' For such a purpose the atomic bomb was an eminently suitable weapon."[22]

Although many Japanese have since declared that the United States would not have used the A-bomb and the Soviet Union would not have entered the war had it not been for the *mokusatsu* phrase, it seems obvious that *mokusatsu* was not the reason for the above developments but simply a rather superfluous justification for their occurring when they did. The Japanese contention would be tenable only if based on the assumption that the Japanese government intended secretly to accept the Allied ultimatum at once—public statements to the contrary notwithstanding. Although the government did immediately press for an answer from the Soviet Union, Japan did not take any independent action on her own initiative when that answer was not forthcoming. In fact, the government was still *waiting* for the Soviet reply when the atomic bombs were dropped and the Soviet Union invaded Manchuria.[23]

While official Tokyo was thus laying the basis for a conclusion abroad that Japan preferred death to survival, Naotake Satō, the Japanese ambassador to the Soviet Union, was culling the Moscow papers to learn what had transpired at the historic meeting in Potsdam. His experiences of the preceding two weeks combined with what he read to convince him that the Soviet Union would probably not accede to Japan's request for Soviet good offices. So far as he could see, there was only one path his country could follow at this point and that was to accept the Allied surrender demand—providing, of course, that some prior guarantee could be obtained with respect to the future position of the Emperor. At the same time he had very definite instructions and it was his responsibility, regardless of what views he personally held, to adhere to his orders and to press for an immediate Soviet response to his gov-

---

[21] "Rejection" was the inference drawn throughout the rest of the world as well. Ambassador Satō in Moscow made note of the fact that British and European newspapers declared that Japan had rejected the Allied proclamation. (Satō, *Futatsu no Roshia*, 207.)

[22] Stimson and Bundy, *On Active Service*, 625. See also Byrnes, *Speaking Frankly*, 263.

[23] See, for instance, IMTFE: Kido, 31171–72.

ernment's overture.[24] At 5:00 P.M. on July 30, therefore, he again called on Vice Foreign Commissar Lozovsky in the hope, this time, of obtaining a clear statement of Moscow's intentions. Referring specifically to the Potsdam Proclamation, Satō advised Lozovsky that although unconditional surrender was "out of the question" the Japanese government did hope to end the war "on broad terms of compromise." As Satō himself had feared, Lozovsky proved to be as noncommittal as he had been in the past. All Satō could obtain, by way of an answer, was a promise from the vice-commissar to inform Molotov that the ambassador had come seeking a reply.[25] There was nothing Satō could do but play the diplomat, and so he again left the Kremlin, still hoping for but hardly expecting a change for the better in the Soviet attitude toward Japan.

One week later, on Monday, August 6, 1945, "the source from which the sun draws its power" was turned to incredible advantage against the land of the rising sun by a single B-29 dropping a bomb having an explosive force equivalent to that which would be generated by *twenty thousand tons* of TNT.[26] In the split second of the atomic bomb's invasion of history, this hitherto little-known Japanese city achieved a fame so terrible that it stunned men the world over and made them reluctant to acknowledge the inevitable horrors of nuclear warfare.

The first report of the early morning catastrophe at Hiroshima apparently reached officials in Tokyo about noon the same day in the form of a Dōmei News Agency telegram sent from the vicinity of the stricken area, but the extent of the disaster and the manner of the attack were not made clear. Toward evening on August 6 an official telegram from the Chūgoku district superintendent general arrived stating that Hiroshima had sustained appalling damage in an attack made by "a small number of enemy planes" using what appeared to be an "entirely new-type bomb."[27] This partial inaccuracy was not corrected until dawn the next day when the vice-chief of the Army General Staff received a report which contained the truth of the matter in one cryptic, terrifying

[24] Tōgō affirms that Satō cabled his personal opinion that the only way Japan could end the war was by unconditional surrender. In reply, Tōgō cabled Satō that Japan "could surrender unconditionally without Russian assistance" but that she was "not prepared to do so." Tōgō advised Satō to "spend more time in working on the USSR" and less in sending him "such telegrams." (*Statements:* Tōgō #50304.)
See also JFO MS: Ch. 35 (Satō taishi no shūsen iken den to Arita gengaishō no jōsōbun oyobi shokanrui); Millis (ed.), *The Forrestal Diaries*, 74–77; and Byrnes, *Speaking Frankly*, 211 (in which Satō is praised as "a realist and a courageous representative").
[25] See IMTFE: Cable #1484: Satō to Tōgō, 23609–10, and Satō, *Futatsu no Roshia*, 206–7.
[26] See the announcement of the President and the statement of the Secretary of War found in the *New York Times* for August 7, 1945. See also Stimson and Bundy, *On Active Service*, 615–17 and 624–26.
[27] See *Statements:* Sakomizu 4/21/49.

sentence: *"The whole city of Hiroshima was destroyed instantly by a single bomb."*[28]

As a result of this report, a strict censorship was immediately invoked by the Supreme Command and an investigation team of experts hastily organized and dispatched by air to the scene of the disaster.[29] In the meantime, the government listening posts had picked up the news of the *atomic* nature of the attack that was being flashed from Washington in the form of a presidential announcement. With phrases that cut to the very core, Mr. Truman declared,

. . . We have spent two billion dollars on the greatest scientific gamble in history—and won. . . . We are now prepared to obliterate rapidly and completely every productive enterprise the Japanese have above the ground in any city. We shall destroy their docks, their factories and their communications. Let there be no mistake; we shall completely destroy Japan's power to make war.

It was to spare the Japanese from utter destruction that the ultimatum of July 26 was issued at Potsdam. Their leaders promptly rejected that ultimatum. If they do not now accept our terms they may expect a rain of ruin from the air, the like of which has never been seen on this earth. . . .[30]

Although here was confirmation for those who chose to believe it, the President's announcement was generally regarded, in military circles at least, as American propaganda aimed at scaring the Japanese people. Opinions varied with the individual but the trend was either to deny that an atomic bomb had been used or to minimize not only the damage which had been done but also the destruction which could be expected in the future. One initial reaction was that just from the standpoint of technique alone it would be quite inconceivable to suppose that an atomic missile had been used. Not even American technical know-how, so this argument went, had as yet developed to the point where it would be possible for sea- or aircraft to transport such an obviously "unstable" mechanism all the way across the Pacific to Japan.[31] Even after the

[28] See *Statements:* Kawabe #61539. Kawabe, the recipient of this report, suspected the atomic nature of the bomb by virtue of information he had received much earlier from Dr. Nishina, a Japanese scientist who had been engaged in atomic research.

[29] For material relating to the activities and findings of the investigation team headed by Lieutenant General Arisue, see *Statements:* Arisue #61411 and Nishina #60245 and #60246. Nishina was the only civilian scientist in the group. A separate investigation was undertaken for the navy by officers from the Kure Naval Yard.

[30] Mr. Truman received the news of the successful attack upon Hiroshima while crossing the Atlantic on board the cruiser *Augusta.* The presidential announcement, which was released immediately in Washington and subsequently dropped on Japan in leaflet form, had been prepared at Potsdam prior to the President's departure. See Leahy, *I Was There,* 418–19, 430–32; the *New York Times* for August 7, 1945; and U.S. Navy Dept., *Psychological Warfare,* Supplement No. 2 (August 15, 1945), Leaflet #2114.

[31] This view was expressed on August 7 by some members of the Technical Board who—together with representatives of the War, Navy, and Home Ministries—had been organized into an "Atomic Bomb Countermeasure Committee." (*Statements:* Ikeda #54479.)

government's investigation team arrived in Hiroshima there was considerable debate among its members over the details of the attack and the type of bomb (or even bombs) which had been dropped. Not until August 10, the day after the Nagasaki debacle, did the experts finally agree that Japan now faced the prospect of fighting an enemy equipped with atomic power. In spite of the bald story that Hiroshima and Nagasaki told, however, there were those who kept trying to evade the issue by blindly declaring that concrete buildings and white clothing would afford protection.[32] Typical of this breathlessly irrational form of thinking was the officer in charge of the Hiroshima airfield where the advance group of the investigation team had landed on August 7. Rushing up to report, the officer had presented a strange sight, for one half of his face was scorched and the other half was not. "Everything that is exposed gets burned," he had explained, "but anything that is covered even slightly will escape. Therefore it cannot be said that there are no countermeasures!"[33]

A few men, like the chief of the Naval General Staff, sought to be more sensible in their approach. They argued that even the United States could not possibly possess enough radioactive material to make a sufficient number of bombs to permit a continuation of such attacks. Moreover, they felt that world opinion would step in at once to prevent the United States from repeating such an "inhuman atrocity." It was exceedingly unlikely, in other words, that the United States would be able to command "honest sympathy" for its claim that the bomb would save thousands of lives by shortening the war.[34]

On August 8, with the intensified propaganda barrage from the United States dogging his footsteps, Foreign Minister Tōgō personally assumed the responsibility of relaying to the Emperor a detailed report of the information contained in the enemy broadcasts.[35] Since Tōgō was a sensible man who had long since recognized the inevitable, he impressed upon the Emperor the urgency of the situation and the neces-

[32] See *Statements:* Sakomizu 4/21/49 and 5/3/49, Shimomura #57668, Nishina #60246, Tōgō #50304; USSBS, *Japan's Struggle to End the War*, 8; and the Tokyo *Asahi Shimbun* for the period in question.

[33] See *Statements:* Arisue #61411.

[34] *Statements:* Toyoda #61340. On August 10 a formal protest against the use of the atomic bomb was submitted by the Japanese government to the United States government through the Swiss government. See *Contemporary Japan*, XIV (April–December 1945), 267, and the *Nippon Times* for August 11, 1945.

[35] USSBS (*Japan's Struggle to End the War*, 8) is apparently in error in stating that Tōgō and Suzuki jointly reported the news to the Emperor on the morning of "August 7." Tōgō has stated that his report to the Throne was on August 8 and that Suzuki was not present. *Statements:* Tōgō #50304.

Kido has stated that when the Emperor received the first reports of the Hiroshima disaster he spoke as follows: "Under these circumstances, we must bow to the inevitable. No matter what happens to my safety, we must put an end to this war as speedily as possible so that this tragedy will not be repeated." See *Statements:* Kido #61541 and #61476.

sity of terminating the war at once on the basis of the Potsdam Proclamation.[36] When Tōgō at length withdrew from the imperial presence, he carried with him the moral support[37] of a sovereign who, though lacking the authority to help in any way, possessed an influence which—if aided by circumstances—could exert a force "beyond measure" in terms of conventional power.[38]

While these events were taking place in Japan, Ambassador Satō in Moscow was meeting each new day with fresh hope and each passing one with greater disappointment. Finally, on August 5, upon hearing that Molotov had just returned from Berlin, Satō formally requested an interview with Lozovsky's chief.[39] Two days later, on August 7, he was notified that Molotov would be able to see him the next day, August 8, at 8:00 P.M. Somewhat later, the time was moved up to 5:00 P.M.[40] At the appointed hour, Satō, accompanied by Secretary Yuhashi, arrived at the Kremlin.[41] As he was ushered into Molotov's study, the ambassador began speaking in Russian, wishing—in Japanese fashion—to congratulate the commissar on his safe return, but Molotov quickly interrupted, saying, "I have here, in the name of the Soviet Union, a notification to the Japanese government which I desire to communicate to you." He then motioned Satō to the chair in which the ambassador had sat many times before and, himself taking a seat, began reading the Soviet declaration of war:

After the defeat and capitulation of Hitlerite Germany, Japan remained the only great power which still stands for the continuation of the war.

The demand of the three powers, the United States, Great Britain and China, of July 26 for the unconditional surrender of the Japanese armed forces was

[36] Tōgō had expressed a similar though perhaps less direct view to a group of cabinet ministers who had met to discuss the situation on August 7. See *Statements:* Sakomizu 4/21/49 and Tōgō #50304.

[37] When the Emperor said to Tōgō (as the Emperor supposedly did on this occasion): "Tell Suzuki it is my wish that the war be ended as soon as possible on the basis of the Potsdam Proclamation," the Emperor's words were merely an expression of the sovereign's desire, and not a command carrying the force of a decision of state for which the cabinet alone possessed the authority and the responsibility.

[38] In this connection, see *Statements:* Kido #61476, Suzuki #531, Matsudaira #60745; IMTFE: Kido, 31203–5 (here, *chikara*, with reference to the Emperor, should clearly be translated as "influence"—not as "authority" or "power"; IMTFE: *Proceedings*, 663–64; and Uyehara, *The Political Development of Japan, 1867–1909*, 191–95 and 200.

[39] Satō was under urgent instructions from Tōgō to see Molotov as soon as the latter returned from Berlin and to obtain the Soviet Union's reply to Japan's request for mediation.

[40] Moscow time 5:00 P.M. (August 8) was Tokyo time 11:00 P.M. (August 8). See IMTFE: Cable #1530: Satō to Tōgō, 23610; JFO MS: Ch. 39 (Soren no sansen); Satō, *Futatsu no Roshia*, 207–9; and IMTFE: Def. Doc. 1476, "Report on How the USSR Gave Notification of Opening of War Against Japan," J text.

[41] See Satō, *Futatsu no Roshia*, 207–9; JFO MS: Ch. 39 (Soren no sansen); and Def. Doc. 1476 cited in the preceding footnote.

rejected by Japan. Thus the proposal made by the Japanese Government to the Soviet Union for mediation in the Far East has lost all foundation.

Taking into account the refusal of Japan to capitulate, the Allies approached the Soviet Government with a proposal to join the war against Japanese aggression and thus shorten the duration of the war, reduce the number of casualties and contribute toward the most speedy restoration of peace.

True to its obligation as an Ally, the Soviet Government has accepted the proposal of the Allies and has joined in the declaration of the Allied powers of July 26.

The Soviet Government considers that this policy is the only means able to bring peace nearer, to free the people from further sacrifice and suffering and to give the Japanese people the opportunity of avoiding the danger of destruction suffered by Germany after her refusal to accept unconditional surrender.

In view of the above, the Soviet Government declares that from tomorrow, that is from August 9, the Soviet Union will consider herself in a state of war against Japan.[42]

Two hours later, Moscow time (1:00 A.M., August 9, Tokyo time),[43] the armies of the Soviet Union invaded Manchuria and struck with full force against the much-vaunted Kwantung army, for years the pride of Japan's military establishment but now nothing more than an empty shell. The Supreme Command's overwhelming devotion to a decisive battle in the homeland had long since robbed the garrison in Manchuria of its picked troops and war equipment and had left it stranded there with little more than the "spiritual" power to resist.[44] The Soviet entry into the war thus promised the rapid disintegration of Japan's hold on Manchuria and Korea and the equally speedy establishment of a hostile force of unlimited resources and striking power at Japan's back door.

[42] In spite of its somewhat faulty English, the author is here quoting the text of the Soviet declaration of war as it is found in USSR, *Information Bulletin*, V (August 11, 1945), 1. The text (in improved translation) also appears in the *New York Times* for August 9, 1945.

[43] See JFO MS: Ch. 39 (Soren no sansen); JFO, *Present Conditions of Japan*, 2; and the imperial headquarters communiqué in the *Nippon Times* for Friday, August 10, 1945.

[44] About May 1945 the Russian Section of the Japanese army general staff judged that the Soviet Union would enter the war against Japan in August. This was a particularly disturbing estimate since it was known that in August the Kwantung army would not only be at its weakest but also would actually not possess the power to resist. See *Statements:* Tanemura #61977 and Toyoda #61340.

The transfer of Kwantung army personnel and equipment had been in progress ever since the latter part of 1944. In addition, the army had undertaken to change its plan of operation. It had not completed this by August 1945. See *Statements:* Ikeda #54479, Miyazaki #50567, and Hasunuma #58225.

In the light of the above, the following statement (Stettinius, *Roosevelt and the Russians*, 98) is of particular interest: "At both Yalta and Potsdam the military staffs [of the U.S.] were particularly concerned with the Japanese troops in Manchuria. Described as the cream of the Japanese Army, this self-contained force, with its own autonomous command and industrial base, was believed capable of prolonging the war even after the islands of Japan had been subdued, unless Russia should enter the war and engage this army.

"With this belief, the President's military advisers urgently desired Russian entry into the war. Our casualties would be far smaller if the Japanese had to divert forces to meet the Russians in the north."

The Soviet Union's sudden debouchment into the arena of the "Greater East Asia War" at a time when she was bound to Japan by a Neutrality Pact, which—by its terms—was to remain valid until *April 1946*, sardonically shattered the last particle of doubt in Japanese minds that the Pact was then, or had ever been, anything more than a scrap of paper.[45] Although the Japanese did not know it at the time, this is what had happened:[46]

On July 17, during the course of the Potsdam Conference, Marshal Stalin discussed the question of a Soviet declaration of war with President Truman but stated that his government would not take such action until an agreement had been negotiated between the Soviet Union and Nationalist China.[47] Twelve days later, on July 29, Stalin being ill, Molotov again took up the question, this time not only with the President but with Secretary of State Byrnes as well. As Molotov saw it, the best way of handling the matter would be for the United States, Great Britain, and the other Allies to address a formal request to his government asking it to participate in the war. The hurdle in the way of such an "invitation" was the Soviet-Japanese Neutrality Pact, and neither the President nor Mr. Byrnes felt that the United States "should be placed in the position of asking another government to violate its agreement *without good and sufficient reason*."[48] At the same time, the Soviet Union was pointedly harking back to the Yalta Agreement, which envisaged a

[45] Schuman, *Soviet Politics at Home and Abroad*, 635 (footnote 23), writes as follows: "Legalists may contest the 'legality' of the Soviet action [in declaring war on Japan], since the neutrality pact denounced by Moscow on April 5, 1945, would not have expired, under its own terms, until April 24, 1946. On the other hand it can be argued, though the Narkomindel did not advance the argument, that the pact itself was a corollary of the Kellogg-Briand Pact of 1928, to which both the USSR and Japan were signatories, and that Japanese violation of the earlier instrument in declaring war on the United States and Great Britain in December, 1941, violated the treaty rights of the USSR and released it from the obligations of both instruments. The earlier Japanese assault on China, under way when the Soviet-Japanese pact was signed, was never accompanied by a declaration of war and was therefore not incompatible with the technical obligations of the Kellogg Pact."

The above argument could have a doubtful validity only if the Soviet Union had publicly *abrogated* the Neutrality Pact on or before April 5, 1945. Since the Soviet Union merely notified Japan that it did not desire to extend the pact for another five years beyond the expiration date in April 1946 and since this notification was given in accordance with and under the terms of the pact, it is clear that the Soviet Union was publicly avowing the validity of the pact under which the two countries had enjoyed neutral relations through the course of the war. The alternative is that the Soviet Union was perpetrating an act of diplomatic deceit, that is, the Kremlin was only pretending the pact was valid and was quite ready to violate the pact whenever Soviet policy could best be served by such action.

[46] The text which follows is based on Secretary of State Byrnes's account in his *Speaking Frankly*, 205–9.

[47] On August 26, 1945, the Moscow radio announced the text of this Soviet-Chinese Pact (see *Facts on File*, 1945, 272 F). This would indicate that Soviet-Chinese agreement had been reached prior to August 9 or that Stalin's statement to Truman on July 17 was taken too literally. In this connection, see also Stettinius, *Roosevelt and the Russians*, 91, and Sherwood, *Roosevelt and Hopkins*, 902–4.

[48] Italics mine. See Byrnes, *Speaking Frankly*, 205.

Soviet entry into the war in the Pacific within two or three months after victory in Europe. It was now August and Germany had capitulated in early May. The Soviet Union, moreover, was stressing its willingness to join in the conflict within the very near future.

Just why the President and his Secretary of State felt it was incumbent upon the United States to provide a fitting reply to Molotov's request for an invitation to declare war against Japan is not yet fully known, but the fact is that they did feel it necessary and that their decision in this respect produced some interesting and questionable results.

Acting upon the suggestions of one of the President's advisers, Secretary Byrnes drafted a letter which was later sent by the President to Marshal Stalin. This letter,[49] a rather amazing document, began by citing paragraph 5 of the "Declaration of Four Nations on General Security" signed at Moscow on October 30, 1943, which reads, ". . . for the purpose of maintaining international peace and security pending the re-establishment of law and order" the United States, the United Kingdom, the Soviet Union, and China will consult with each other and, as occasion requires, with other members of the United Nations "with a view to joint action on behalf of the community of nations."[50] Next, the letter referred to Article 106 of the *proposed* United Nations Charter which provided that until the Charter was ratified the four nations in question would, in accordance with the provisions of paragraph 5 of their Declaration of October 1943, "consult with one another and . . . with other Members of the United Nations with a view to such joint action on behalf of the [United Nations] Organization as may be necessary for the purpose of maintaining international peace and security." Finally—and here is the knot which tied all this together—the letter quoted Article 103 of the pending Charter which states that "in the event of a conflict between the obligations of the Members of the United Nations under the present Charter and their obligations under any other international agreement [e.g., the Soviet-Japanese Neutrality Pact], their obligations under the present Charter shall prevail."[51]

In spite of the fact that Mr. Truman did not put the matter so bluntly, he was, in effect, advising Stalin that it was the considered opinion of the United States government that Articles 103 and 106 of the U.N. Charter and paragraph 5 of the Moscow Declaration constituted a legal basis for the Soviet Union to violate her Neutrality Pact with Japan. Although the argument in the presidential letter would require the scrutiny of experts in international law to determine its validity, there are those among the Japanese who regard the content of the letter as

[49] The salient paragraphs are found in U.S. State Dept., *Bulletin*, XIII (August 12, 1945), 207, and Byrnes, *Speaking Frankly*, 208–9.

[50] *Ibid.* and *Bulletin*, IX (November 6, 1943), 308–9.

[51] See the citations in footnote 49 above and U.S. State Dept., *Bulletin*, XII (June 24, 1945), 1133.

built upon a foundation of shifting sand. Their view is that Article 103 of the U.N. Charter, stating that U.N. obligations shall prevail, cannot have been written to condone or sanction a unilateral abrogation of any treaty without the prior knowledge and consent of all of the parties to said treaty and that, even if such were the intention, Article 103 cannot be applied to the Soviet-Japanese Neutrality Pact since a pact designed to maintain peace between Japan and the Soviet Union can scarcely be construed as creating conflicts between the Soviet Union's obligations to the U.N. (a world peace organization) and her obligations toward Japan.

Some Japanese further claim that Articles 103 and 106 were "inoperative" at the time in question since the United Nations Charter had not as yet been formally ratified. "Even the President's letter had to take cognizance of this," they say, "and could only weakly suggest that ratification did not matter since the Charter had had the concurrence of the Soviet government which itself would become a permanent member of the Security Council."[52] Since those who argue against the President's letter do not accept the view that the rights and duties of an agreement, such as the U.N. Charter, are operative prior to the ratification of the agreement, they conclude that the only part of the presidential letter which cannot be contested, per se, is the reference to paragraph 5 of the Moscow Declaration. Having gone this far, they are quick to declare that paragraph 5 does not contain anything which could serve as a basis for the Soviet Union's violation of her Neutrality Pact with Japan.

Although the merits of these arguments are beyond the scope of this study, one thing is overwhelmingly clear. Stalin was immensely pleased[53] with the American thesis—so pleased, in fact, that within ten days after the arrival of the President's letter the Soviet Union commenced hostilities against Japan. How much Stalin enjoyed the helping hand of the United States is apparent in those passages from the Soviet declaration of war which read:

Taking into account the refusal of Japan to capitulate, the Allies approached the Soviet Government with a proposal to join the war against Japanese aggression. . . .

True to its obligations as an Ally, the Soviet Government has accepted the proposal of the Allies and has joined in the declaration of the Allied powers of

[52] The reference is to the following sentence in the President's letter: "Though the Charter has not been formally ratified, at San Francisco it was agreed to by the Representatives of the Union of Soviet Socialist Republics and the Soviet Government will be one of the permanent members of the Security Council." See U.S. State Dept., *Bulletin*, XIII (August 12, 1945), 207, and Byrnes, *Speaking Frankly*, 208.

[53] See Byrnes, *Speaking Frankly*, 209: "The President later told me that Generalissimo Stalin expressed great appreciation of the communication. He should have. The Soviet Government's statement announcing its entry into the war did not include a reference to Section 103 of the Charter, but our finding it for Mr. Molotov will enable the Soviet historian to show that Russia's declaration of war on Japan was in accordance with what they like to claim is their scrupulous regard for international obligations."

July 26 [i.e., has become a signatory of the Potsdam Proclamation and as a consequence thereof has joined in the war in the Pacific].[54]

To Japan, the Soviet Union's entry into the war at this time was decidedly iniquitous but not entirely unexpected. The feeling within the government and the Supreme Command was generally expressed with these words: "What had to come has come." This fatalism, however, was but a poor antidote for the shock with which Japan's war leaders viewed the situation as a whole. The blow dealt them by the Kremlin in unleashing its mechanized hordes against Japan's depleted garrison in Manchuria was all the more staggering since it followed the atomic obliteration of a vital nerve center in the very heart of the homeland itself. It was at this moment of unparalleled crisis that the end-the-war advocates crowded upon the stage of national policy previously denied them by the machinations of the fanatics. In spite of the element of personal danger which still remained, the proponents of peace were prepared to act boldly. In short, they recognized in the atomic bomb and the Soviet entry into the war not just an imperative need to give in but actually a supreme opportunity to turn the tide against the die-hards and to shake the government loose from the yoke of military oppression under which it had been laboring so long.[55]

The day of August 9, 1945, was thus the beginning of the end so

[54] See footnote 42 above. In his opening address before the IMTFE, S. A. Golunsky, associate counsel acting on behalf of the Soviet Union, added the following "footnote" to the question of Japan's request for mediation and the Soviet Union's entry into the war (Golunsky's remarks are quoted exactly as they appear in the official record, IMTFE: *Proceedings*, 7283–84):

"They [Japanese politicians and strategists] appealed to the Soviet Government to mediate. The mediation meant negotiations and negotiations with such a trump in the hand as a many million army untouched by fight could give them opportunity of gaining much by bargaining and saving much.

"But the democratic countries being taught by bitter experience stoutly defended their decision to make no bargains with the aggressor. They could agree to nothing but unconditional surrender, which the Japanese Government refused. This refusal meant the prolongation of the war for an indefinite time.

"That was why the Soviet Government rejected the request of the Japanese Government for intermediation, as having no ground and declared a war against Japan, according to the request of the allies the U.S.A. and Great Britain, being true to her duty as an ally and wishing to accelerate by all means the end of the war, during which the blood of people was shed for six years."

[55] A claim to the effect that Japan had already decided to accept the Potsdam Proclamation prior to the Soviet Union's entry into the war can be validly applied only to the *thinking* of a very few individuals. The over-all impression created by the mass of evidence is simply this: When the final news of the Hiroshima disaster reached Tokyo, the members of the end-the-war party realized that they must bring the war to an end at once. By that time—or immediately thereafter—Nagasaki had been bombed and the Soviet Union had come into the war. The feeling then was as follows: "Now, indeed, we cannot go on with this war any longer."

See *Statements*: Suzuki #531, Toyoda #61340, Kawabe #52608, Tōgō #50304; USSBS, *Interrogations*, II, Toyoda, 320; and USSBS, *The Effects of Strategic Bombing on Japanese Morale*, 99.

far as the militarists were concerned. By the time Marquis Kido arrived at the palace in midmorning,[56] the city of Nagasaki was on the verge of becoming "a graveyard with not a tombstone standing"[57] and the forces of the Soviet Union were well into Manchuria. Without wasting either time or words, His Majesty requested the Privy Seal to get in touch with Premier Suzuki and to urge upon him the need for action.[58] By coincidence the Premier happened to arrive at the palace at this very moment, thus making it possible for Kido to relay the Emperor's wishes at once.[59] Suzuki, who affirmed that he himself believed Japan's only course now was to accept the Potsdam Proclamation, promised to convene the Supreme Council and the cabinet in order to obtain the decision His Majesty desired.[60] He then left the palace in great haste.

Earlier that morning Suzuki had been confronted by an irate Tōgō insisting that valuable time had been lost by the postponement of the Supreme Council meeting which should have been held the day before.[61] Since an immediate decision to terminate the war was now more urgent than ever, Tōgō wanted the Premier to summon the Big Six at once. After leaving Suzuki, Tōgō called on Navy Minister Yonai and obtained his prompt concurrence. As Tōgō was leaving Yonai's office, Imperial Prince Takamatsu, who held a captain's rank in the navy, took the Foreign Minister aside to inquire about the latest developments and the government's plan of action. Although Tōgō promised to do his best to achieve a better settlement if the opportunity arose, he made it clear that he personally felt Japan could do nothing but accede to the Potsdam demands—with the reservation, of course, that the imperial structure

[56] In the period from 9:55 in the morning until 11:37 in the evening, August 9, Kido had six audiences with the Emperor, totaling, in all, one hour and fifty minutes. In that same period he received visits and phone calls from a number of important people, all of whom were concerned with the outcome of the discussions they knew were taking place. The Emperor's second brother, Prince Takamatsu, and the former Foreign Minister, Shigemitsu, both expressed the same thought: a conditional acceptance of the type proposed by the military would be viewed by the Allies as a rejection of their terms. A rupture in the negotiations would inevitably result. See Kido, "Nikki," 8/9/45; IMTFE: Kido, 31176; *Statements:* Shigemitsu 9/9/49; and Shigemitsu, *Shōwa no dōran*, 286.

[57] A phrase from the Nagasaki Prefectural Report as quoted by USSBS, *The Effects of Atomic Bombs on Hiroshima and Nagasaki*, 5.

[58] See *Statements:* Kido #61541 and #61476, Sakomizu 5/3/49; IMTFE: Kido, 31176–77; Kido, "Nikki," 8/9/45; and USSBS, *Japan's Struggle to End the War*, 8.

[59] Since the Emperor planned to seek the views of the senior statesmen, Kido also asked Suzuki to explain the situation in advance to the former Premiers so that they would be in a position to advise the Throne.

[60] The author believes that this promise was made by Suzuki *to Kido* (and not to the Emperor) and that both USSBS and Sakomizu are in error in stating that Suzuki was received by the Emperor at this time. See the citations listed in footnote 58 above.

[61] After his audience with the Emperor on the morning of August 8, Tōgō had rushed to Premier Suzuki to request an immediate meeting of the Supreme Council. It was found, however, that several of the councilors could not make themselves available until the next morning (August 9). See *Statements:* Tōgō #50304.

of the state would be preserved. In other words, the time for negotiations had passed.[62]

In this atmosphere of immediacy made more terrible by the uncertainty of where and when the next attack would occur (rumor had it that Tokyo would be A-bombed on August 12),[63] the Big Six members[64] of the Supreme Council for the Direction of the War met to discuss a question which threatened to become academic: should Japan accept the Potsdam Proclamation? Suzuki, as Premier, opened the session[65] by briefly declaring that the developments of the preceding three days had made it impossible to continue the war. The Council must therefore come to a decision with respect to the Allied ultimatum of July 26. Everyone listened in silence. Even after Suzuki had finished and had asked the others to express their views, the reluctance to speak continued. Navy Minister Yonai, who was noted for his reticence, finally broke the spell by tersely declaring, "We can't get anywhere by keeping silent forever." He then went on to outline the problem as he saw it. Either Japan could accept the Potsdam Proclamation as it stood, with the sole reservation that the imperial house would be maintained, or she could try to negotiate with the Allies to obtain more favorable terms. If the Supreme Council decided on the latter course, then there would have to be discussion on the questions of disarmament, punishment of war criminals, and an Allied military occupation of Japan.[66]

These points, as Yonai well knew, were the only issues at stake, for no one present—not even the War Minister or the chiefs of the Army and Navy General Staffs—was any longer opposed, *in principle*, to an acceptance of the Allied terms. The main argument, as soon became

[62] See *Statements:* Tōgō #50304. The prince had asked if something couldn't be done on the question of territory, but Tōgō had replied that even though he personally felt Allied territorial demands were a violation of the Atlantic Charter it was simply too late for negotiations.

[63] *Statements:* Arisue #61411. There was another rumor to the effect that Tokyo would be atom-bombed on August 13. A captured American airman, who had parachuted from his burning plane, was reported to have said so. Kawai MS: "Japan's Struggle to Surrender," 53 (lent to the author by Dr. Kawai, Stanford University, 1950).

[64] Premier Suzuki, Foreign Minister Tōgō, Navy Minister Yonai, War Minister Anami, Army Chief of Staff Umezu, and Navy Chief of Staff Toyoda.

[65] There is no precise or detailed record of what occurred at this meeting or the meetings which immediately followed. The text, therefore, is a reconstruction based on material contained in the following: IMTFE: Tōgō, 35786–87; Suzuki, 35593–94; Sakomizu, 35608–9; *Proceedings,* 36130–31; *Statements:* Amano #54480, Tōgō #50304 and #54562, Toyoda #61340 and #57670; Toyoda, *Saigo no teikoku kaigun,* 206–11; USSBS, *Interrogations,* II, Toyoda, 322; and JFO MS: Ch. 41 (Saikō sensō shidō kaigi kōseiin kaigi).

[66] There is still considerable debate with respect to the question of whether Yonai mentioned the above conditions—even in the indirect manner indicated. The author believes that Yonai did mention the conditions but probably not with the intention of personally supporting them. In addition to the Tōgō and Toyoda citations listed in the preceding footnote, see *Statements:* Ikeda #54479 and Sakomizu 5/3/49.

apparent, was simply how far to go in drawing the line.[67] While Suzuki, Tōgō, and Yonai were committed in varying degrees to an outright acceptance on the basis of the sole reservation, Anami, Umezu, and Toyoda felt quite differently. They naturally gave their wholehearted support to the condition pertaining to the Emperor's future position as Japan's sovereign ruler, for that was obviously fundamental. What gagged these men—all true *samurai* bred in an uncompromising tradition—were the the other points Yonai had mentioned. They wanted either to prevent a security occupation entirely or to exclude at least the metropolis of Tokyo and to restrict the number of troops and the locations occupied to a minimum. So far as war criminals were concerned, they felt it should be Japan and not the victorious enemy who must try such cases. In effect, they also wanted to accept the surrender of their own men, that is, they wanted to withdraw their forces from the occupied and combat areas and to disarm and demobilize their own troops.[68]

From the standpoint of making postwar rationalizations and of "opening up the future of the country" it was psychologically vital for the Japanese army and navy to make it appear as if they had voluntarily disbanded their military might in order to save the nation and the world at large from the continued ravages of war. If they could do this, they could very easily later plant an appealing suggestion to the effect that the imperial forces of Great Japan had not really suffered defeat at all. For this reason, too, a security occupation and war crimes trials conducted by Allied tribunals had to be avoided at all costs.

To what extent this reasoning served as a basis for the stand taken by Anami, Umezu, and Toyoda cannot be determined. Although they strongly emphasized that Japan was *not yet defeated,* their primary concern seems to have been with the present and not with the more distant future. Army Chief of Staff Umezu, for instance, pointed out that Japan's soldiers and sailors were "not permitted" to surrender, that the penal code of the services prescribed heavy penalties for those who sought to lay down their arms, and that the word "capitulation" could not be found in a Japanese military dictionary. The inculcation had gone so far as to advise Japan's fighting men that, in the last extremity when their weapons were useless and they were powerless to fight on, the only honorable outlet was to commit suicide on the spot. In view of this psychological conditioning, Umezu considered it highly unlikely that the men at the various fighting fronts would obey an order

[67] In this connection, see IMTFE: Tōgō, 35786–87; USSBS, *Interrogations*, II, Toyoda, 322; and footnote 68 below.

[68] Toyoda has stated (as has Tōgō also) that no one (including himself, Umezu, and Anami) was basically opposed to accepting the Potsdam terms *providing* certain conditions were attached. The Anami-Umezu-Toyoda coalition did not feel that their conditions were unreasonable nor did they believe that the said conditions, if proposed, would inevitably result in a disruption of the negotiations. See *Statements:* Toyoda #61340 and Hayashi #61436.

from Tokyo to cast aside their arms and surrender themselves to the enemy. If Japan were to notify the Allies that she had decided to accept their terms *unconditionally*, Allied commanders might immediately attempt to move their men into areas held by Japanese forces. The reception the Allied troops would get would be far from their commanders' expectations and quite contrary as well to the sincere intentions of the Japanese government. Should any such incidents occur, hostilities would break out all over again. In view of this, Umezu believed there was only one thing to do. Should the government decide to accept the Allied terms, it must insist upon designating the time and place of surrender in each area beforehand and it must also seek the right to take whatever other precautions might be necessary to ensure that the surrender could be successfully executed.[69]

As so often in the past, it was Foreign Minister Tōgō, an outspoken man, who took up the challenge of the occasion. Just as the War Minister and the two chiefs of staff had argued forcefully and convincingly in support of their point of view, so now did Tōgō release a salvo of equally impressive arguments designed to further his own stand.[70] His primary point—and it was one the military could not deny—was that the enemy attitude indicated that the Allies would ignore Japan's proposals and would refuse to negotiate further if she attempted to inject numerous conditions or to obtain a large number of concessions. As he saw it, the situation was so critical as to preclude all hope of victory and to make it essential for the government to sue for peace. Tōgō told his fellow councilors that their sole concern should be to obtain an Allied guarantee to respect and maintain the welfare of Japan's imperial house. He made it clear that he was not opposed to the content or range of the other conditions. In fact, he would even support them himself *if* there were any possibility of their being accepted by the Allies, but there was not, and to seek such conditions from the enemy would surely result in an immediate breakdown of the negotiations.[71] Turning to the War

---

[69] The Umezu argument in the text above is based on Toyoda's recollection of what Umezu said. Both Toyoda and Anami supported this view as they did the general position of attaching the various conditions mentioned earlier.

Umezu's argument was so convincing that Tōgō eventually did present the issue to the Allies (for their information and guidance but not as a condition) when he notified them of Japan's acceptance of the Potsdam terms (see Ch. 10). Toyoda feels that it was this factor which helped make it possible for the occupying troops to take over without incident. See Toyoda, *Saigo no teikoku kaigun*, 208–10, and *Statements: Toyoda #61340.*

[70] See *Statements: Tōgō #50304.* The evidence as a whole inspires confidence in the principal's own testimony. That Tōgō strongly refuted the arguments presented by Anami, Umezu, and Toyoda is supported by the latter in *Statements: Toyoda #61340* and in *Saigo no teikoku kaigun*, 206–10.

[71] Tōgō has since stated that he was quite concerned over the territorial problem but that he refrained from mentioning it for fear that it would only complicate matters further. The fact that no one else raised the territorial issue suggests that the Big Six had recognized the inevitability of a substantial retrogression on Japan's part. It also

Minister and chiefs of staff, Tōgō pointedly asked whether Japan could win the war if a collapse of this type occurred. To this the military heads could only reply that although they were not certain of *ultimate* victory they were *still* capable of one more campaign—a "decisive" battle in the homeland. Umezu put it this way: "If we are lucky, we will be able to repulse the invaders before they land. At any rate, I can say with assurance that we will be able to destroy the major part of an invading army, that is, we will be able to inflict extremely heavy damage on the enemy." But Tōgō would not accept this, for it was quite plain that Umezu was not at all sure of himself and that no matter how lethal Japan's blows might be some of the enemy would still succeed in landing, and in due time a second assault would follow the first. In the initial holocaust, Japan would lose aircraft and other vital weapons of war which she would be unable to replace. Thus, even if the enemy did not again use the atomic bomb, Japan would still be "practically powerless." Since the government's relative position would then be far worse than it was now, the only thing to do was to end the war at once on the sole condition that the imperial polity would be preserved. This was the most, not the least, Japan could ask.[72]

The Supreme Council meeting, which had begun about eleven o'clock in the morning, had now consumed nearly two hours. The discussions, which had grown heated and had touched the dramatic, had accomplished nothing. The Council was deadlocked, with Suzuki, Tōgō, and Yonai on the one side and Anami, Umezu, and Toyoda on the other. Although the atomic attack upon Hiroshima had made it impossible for anyone present to continue to deny the urgency of Japan's situation, it apparently had not made a deep enough impression upon the chiefs of staff and the War Minister to make them willing to cast their lot outright for a termination of the war.

While the two sides were still debating the issue, however, the news that Nagasaki had suffered the fate of Hiroshima was carried into the council chamber. There had been an interval of only two days between the two attacks. This seemed to suggest that in two more days, or three, the map of Japan might grimly sport another black-faced **X** drawn through the name of a third or even fourth Japanese city. Certainly the fact that a second A-bomb had been dropped did not offer much consolation to those who were wistfully speculating about the total number the United States might have on hand.[73] It was similarly quite

---

appears that the Anami-Umezu-Toyoda conditions were actually linked to the *spirit*—to the question of Japan's honor—and not to the issue of her material welfare. See *Statements:* Tōgō #54562 and footnote 62 above.

[72] See *Statements:* Tōgō #50304.

[73] The bombs dropped on Hiroshima and Nagasaki were the only two missiles the United States had ready for use at that time, "but others were on the way and some were expected to be even more powerful." (Byrnes, *Speaking Frankly,* 264.) In this connection, the following entry (August 10, 1945) in Millis (ed.), *The For-*

useless to suggest that the Soviet invasion of Manchuria was nothing more than an unfounded supposition. It was true, of course, that Tokyo had not as yet received any official notification of the Soviet declaration of war,[74] but it was not very likely that the official messages pouring in from Manchuria and the foreign news broadcasts being monitored in Tokyo were all part of a grand strategy of deception.

Even if the discussions within the Supreme Council had been predicated upon certain knowledge and a thorough understanding and basic acceptance of that knowledge, it is doubtful that a decision would have emerged. At heart, no one was prepared to yield to anyone. The two coalitions had evolved over a period of time and they represented a pattern which had existed for an even longer period. For months now, these men and the nation at large had watched their lost war develop. They had seen their Empire sacrificed to save their home islands. To yield at this point was to admit more than national failure; it was to accept personal defeat. Not to yield now was to come within grasping distance of the last chance to achieve a token victory, a modicum of success. Thus, conviction and resolve on the one side challenged conviction and resolve on the other, and repeated discussion invariably led to the same result: stalemate.

Since a reconciliation of views among the Big Six was a forlorn hope, the meeting was finally adjourned and the question of Japan's acceptance of the Potsdam Proclamation was, for all intents and purposes, practically hand-carried into the cabinet by the very same men who had been unable to agree in the Supreme Council.[75] As soon as

---

restal Diaries, 84, is of interest: "The President observed that we would keep up the war at its present intensity until the Japanese agreed to these terms [the Potsdam Proclamation], with the limitation, however, that there would be no further dropping of the atomic bombs."

[74] Before sunrise on August 9 the radio room of the Japanese Foreign Office and the monitoring facilities of the Dōmei News Agency picked up the news of the Soviet entry into the war from a Moscow broadcast. Thus it was that Japan learned she had acquired another enemy. A cable which Ambassador Satō had sent from Moscow in code (with Molotov's assurances that the Soviet government had no objections) never reached Tokyo.

Foreign Minister Tōgō did not receive the official Soviet notification of the existence of a state of war until 11:15 A.M. on Friday, August 10, when he met with Soviet Ambassador Malik at the latter's request. Although Malik had tried to see Tōgō on August 9, the latter had been unable to receive the ambassador because the day was crowded with the events described in the text. The above testimony, to say nothing of the time factor, indicates that Kase, *Journey to the Missouri*, 225, is in error in stating that Malik handed Tōgō the Soviet declaration of war on the morning of August 8.

For material relating to the above, see JFO MS: Ch. 39 (Soren no sansen); Satō, *Futatsu no Roshia*, 208 and 213; IMTFE: Def. Doc. 1476, "Report on How the USSR Gave Notification of Opening of War Against Japan," J text: IMTFE: Tōgō, 35785–86; Sakomizu, 35608–9; and JFO, *Present Conditions of Japan*, 2.

[75] The cabinet, which was originally to have met at noon, was unable to convene until after the Supreme Council had adjourned since four of the Big Six (the Premier, Foreign Minister, Navy Minister, and War Minister) were also cabinet

the new meeting got under way, the arguments of the morning were re-stated from the very beginning with Foreign Minister Tōgō and War Minister Anami playing the leading roles. At 5:30 P.M., with the debate still not settled, a brief recess was called. An hour later, the ministers again assembled, and round two began. It is difficult to understand exactly what could have been said that had not already been aired in maddening repetition since early morning. The long wrangling would indeed have served no useful purpose had it not been for the fact that it was the cabinet, and not the Supreme Council, which would ultimately have to place its stamp of approval upon a decision of state will. The participation of persons who had hitherto only been indirectly informed of the deliberations of the Big Six thus created an opportunity in the form of a challenge to each one of the contending sides to win the support of as many ministers as possible. One hour passed into two, and two into three, and both the meeting and the evening dragged on. Finally, shortly before the clock struck ten, Suzuki called for a consensus.

The moment had come, but conviction and perhaps even courage were lacking. Although some of the ministers supported Tōgō, several did not, and a few remained undecided. Since only unanimity and not a weak majority was the unbreakable rule of thumb, the meeting re-cessed and the ministers bowed themselves out of the chamber.

As soon as everyone had left, Premier Suzuki and Foreign Minister Tōgō conferred briefly and then went directly to the imperial palace, where they were immediately received in audience. At Suzuki's request, Tōgō gave the Emperor a detailed account of what had transpired throughout the day—an account which made it clear that a decision favorable to a termination of the war could not be expected from either the Supreme Council or the cabinet. This, as the Emperor well knew, could mean only one thing, and so when Suzuki solemnly proposed convening an imperial conference that same night His Majesty nodded agreement and gave his sanction.[76]

The time for the unprecedented was at hand.

---

ministers. Thus, the cabinet did not begin its meeting until 2:30 P.M. (August 9). For details of this meeting (it would appear that no minutes were taken), see *Statements:* Tōgō #50304; IMTFE: Sakomizu, 35608–9; Tōgō, 35786–88; Suzuki, 35593–94; Kido, "Nikki," 8/9/45; JFO MS: Ch. 42 (Dai ikkai, dai nikai rinji kakugi); Toyoda, *Saigo no teikoku kaigun,* 206–11; and USSBS, *Japan's Struggle to End the War,* 8.

[76] See the Kido, Tōgō, Suzuki, and JFO MS references cited in the preceding footnote.

Before the cabinet had met that afternoon (August 9), Foreign Minister Tōgō had foreseen the difficulty of obtaining a unanimous decision and had advised Premier Suzuki that they would have to convene an imperial conference in the event that the cabinet ministers failed to reach an agreement with respect to the Potsdam Proclama-tion. In this connection, see also *Statements:* Matsudaira #60745.

Normal procedure would have called for a resignation of the cabinet, but the situation prevailing in Japan at the time was anything but normal. That is why Suzuki was able to suggest an imperial conference.

8

CHALLENGE AND RESPONSE

The Opposing Factions and the First Imperial Conference

THE Japanese government in three and one-half years of war had never been confronted with so much visible pressure to make a quick and bold decision as that with which it was faced on August 9, 1945. For the members of His Majesty's cabinet and Supreme Council, the day had been both grueling and unsatisfactory—crowded with seemingly endless hours of fruitless wrangling. For the less important but more vulnerable people of Nagasaki, it had been infinitely more—a day of death for thousands upon thousands. Yet, strangely enough, in spite of all that had happened during the preceding ninety-six hours—the pulverization of Hiroshima, the invasion of Manchuria, the dying agony of Nagasaki— the impact of these successive crises had somehow spent its force before reaching the capital.

Reports were unable to convey more than a smattering of reality. Tokyo was flooded with events. Everything came too fast—too furiously. It was hard to think, and think clearly. Those responsible for decisions had constantly to take up one question and lay down another. Their penchant for diagnoses and evolutionary formulas of compromise dogged their efforts to agree. The sudden death of ten key men would have meant more than the instant annihilation of ten thousand subjects. Hiroshima and Nagasaki were in another world. There had to be a way out of the difficulty. Very few problems were ever without a solution, very few questions without an answer. Haste promised mistakes. Hesitation invited greater hazard.

It was a threatening phenomenon—the reaction of indecision produced in the capital by the events of August 6 through August 9, and one from whose fateful clutches escape was no easy matter. The machinery of government had ground to a halt not because it had been damaged but because it had been thrown off balance. The factors which should have urged speedy and smooth operation had engendered exactly the opposite result. In this atmosphere of impending catastrophe even the last resort—an imperial conference—was little more than an uncertain chance, but it was a chance nevertheless.

166

When Admiral Toyoda and General Umezu suddenly received a summons to the conference for which Suzuki and Tōgō had hastily obtained His Majesty's sanction, their first reaction was one of puzzled surprise. They recalled that Chief Cabinet Secretary Sakomizu had cornered them earlier in the evening with a request that they sign the petition which would permit the Premier to assemble the Big Six in the presence of the Emperor. Sakomizu had explained that there was no telling when such an imperial conference would have to be held—perhaps even in the middle of the night—and so the prerequisite signatures of the two chiefs now would save time and trouble later on.

All this had sounded like a natural and reasonable request, and both the admiral and the general, for all their insistence upon a *conditional* acceptance of the Potsdam Proclamation, were not unreasonable men. Not only they but Sakomizu and everyone else associated with the intricacies of Japanese governmental practice knew full well that standard procedure ruled out the possibility of troubling the "August Mind" of His Majesty with the details of a debate. Since the Emperor was not an arbiter or a referee but simply a silent partner and occasionally a troubled witness to official transactions, presenting him with a divided opinion was manifestly out of the question.[1]

Sincerely believing that nothing would be submitted to the Throne until the Big Six had formulated a unanimous decision on their own, the two chiefs had signed the petition with the expectation that their action would have no significance other than to speed the convocation of an imperial conference once a decision of state acceptable to all the responsible officials had been determined. But now, with unanimity not even within reach, they suddenly discovered that they were wrong.[2]

So far as Sakomizu was concerned, there was nothing underhanded about the matter at all, except perhaps a prior knowledge of what might follow once the petition had been signed. Since he hadn't made any promises, he hadn't broken any. The two chiefs had complied with his request and Suzuki had presented the petition to the Throne. It was all

[1] The cabinet and the Supreme Council were supposed to achieve unanimity before bringing anything to the attention of the Emperor. If the cabinet could not agree or reach a compromise, the cabinet was expected to resign. At all costs, the Emperor had to be kept clear of responsibility for decisions of state. The one certain way of protecting His Majesty and the imperial system was never to bring anything before the Throne that did not already have the unanimous support of the officials of state— the men responsible for all decisions. When a unanimous decision was presented to the Emperor, he was *expected* to give his sanction regardless of his own views in the matter. There was never any thought of responsibility arising out of this sanction since responsibility always accrued solely to the cabinet and the Supreme Command. In this connection, see *Statements*: Suzuki #531, Hasunuma #58225, Kido #61476, Matsudaira #60745; and unpublished USSBS interrogation #507 (Hyakutake).

[2] For the details relating to the petition incident described in the text, see Toyoda, *Saigo no teikoku kaigun*, 210; *Statements*: Sakomizu #62006; and JFO MS: Ch. 44 (Dai ikkai gozen kaigi).

really quite simple. Furthermore, everyone knew that the Emperor could personally summòn the Big Six to his presence—without either a petition or the concurrence of the army and navy chiefs of staff. It would have been somewhat unusual for the Emperor to have done such a thing, but he did possess that right and could exercise it if he were so advised.[3]

In spite of the bitter feelings it engendered, the incident served a purpose in that it permitted the Premier to take the initiative, thus preserving, in effect, the constitutional character and interpretation of the government with which the Emperor had been inculcated so many years before.[4] What was unsettling to the proponents of a decisive battle in the homeland was the manner in which the Premier had undertaken the initiative.[5] In presenting the petition to the Throne while opinions within the Supreme Council and the cabinet were still divided, Suzuki had not only broken all precedent but had also taken a tremendously significant step toward cutting the ground out from under the Anami-Umezu-Toyoda faction. Faced with the imperial summons, however, these three stalwarts could do nothing but obey, regardless of their own wishes in the matter.

Thus it came to pass that at ten minutes before midnight[6] on August 9

[3] The "rights" or "powers" of the Emperor are theoretical. They receive practical expression only upon the advice of responsible officials of state (i.e., the Privy Seal, the Premier, the Supreme Command).

[4] Count Makino, who served as Lord Keeper of the Privy Seal from 1925 to 1935, has stated that Prince Saionji, by whom the present Emperor was educated for the Throne, was always concerned with guarding the sovereign's position as a constitutional monarch. As a result, Saionji guided the Emperor (by instruction and with advice) in such a way that it would be impossible for the government (cabinet and Supreme Command) ever to shift responsibility for political action onto the Emperor's shoulders. During Makino's many years of service close to the Throne, the Emperor—in obedience to the lessons taught him by Saionji—never rejected a petition filed by the government (i.e., a petition having the unanimous approval and support of the cabinet and the Supreme Command) nor did the Emperor ever follow any political advice which did not come to him from his responsible officials (cabinet and Supreme Command). See IMTFE: Def. Doc. 2247, *Makino Aff.*, 4–5 (rejected: 31615–22); Kido, "Nikki," 9/29/45; *Statements*: Sakomizu 5/3/49; Matsudaira #61636 and #60745; and Uyehara, *The Political Development of Japan, 1867–1909*, 27 and 201.

[5] As already noted in Ch. 1, above, the idea of seeking an imperial decision in a crisis of the type facing the government had originated with Shigemitsu and Kido as early at June 1944. In his June 1945 "plan for dealing with the situation" Kido had again mentioned the inevitability of relying on an imperial decision to turn the tide. This plan (as well as Kido's more intimate views) was known to Suzuki and Tōgō. Tōgō, moreover, had advised Suzuki earlier in the day that if a decision could not be reached by the cabinet the matter would have to be placed before the Emperor. The credit for this maneuver, therefore, accrues to several men and not just to Suzuki alone.

[6] There is some discrepancy in the various records as to the exact time the meeting began and the exact time it adjourned. Kido, whose diary is very precise with respect to time, states that the conference began at 11:50 P.M., August 9, and lasted until 2:20 A.M., August 10. (IMTFE: Kido, 31177.) The other accounts all place the

His Majesty quietly entered the underground air raid shelter adjoining the imperial library, which now served as his home, to listen to the arguments and the entreaties of the Empire's first soldiers and statesmen.[7] After the chief cabinet secretary had read the Potsdam Proclamation to the assembled councilors,[8] Premier Suzuki took the floor to repeat the same story he and Foreign Minister Tōgō had privately reported to the Emperor little more than an hour before: The Supreme Council had met during the day and the cabinet as well, but neither the one nor the other had reached any conclusion.[9] Since the decision could not be postponed any longer, it was necessary to submit the matter to His Majesty and to request an imperial opinion even though it was unthinkable, indeed, to take such a step without being able to present an accompanying recommendation.[10]

Having made this apology, which was perhaps directed more toward Toyoda and Umezu than toward the Emperor, Suzuki quickly recapitulated the major points on which the two opposing factions stood firm

---

meeting within the period 11:00 P.M. to 3:00 A.M. (See the references cited in footnote 7 below.)

[7] Since apparently no minutes were taken at the imperial conference, it has been necessary to reconstruct what occurred from the material found in various sources. Although this material is either from persons who attended the conference or from those who heard the details immediately after the adjournment, there is naturally a certain amount of variation in their recollections and even in the notes which a few privately took at the time. Although specific points will be covered by individual citations, the following references contain the details presented in the text: Kido, "Nikki," 8/9–10/45; Toyoda, *Saigo no teikoku kaigun*, 210–13; *Statements*: Yoshizumi #54484, Hiranuma #55127, Ikeda #54483, Hoshina #53437, Tōgō #50304; IMTFE: Sakomizu, 35608–9; Tōgō, 35788; Kido, 31177; USSBS, *Japan's Struggle to End the War*, 8; and JFO MS: Ch. 44 (Dai ikkai gozen kaigi).

[8] In addition to the Emperor, the Big Six, and Baron Hiranuma (see footnote 13 below and the text corresponding thereto), the following persons were also present: Sakomizu, Hoshina, Yoshizumi, Ikeda (who had replaced Akinaga as a member of the Supreme Council's "secretariat"), and Hasunuma (the chief aide-de-camp, who escorted the Emperor to the conference). These latter five attended as aides and did not participate directly in the deliberations or arguments.

[9] In IMTFE: Kido, 11393, the Privy Seal erroneously declared that Premier Suzuki reported to him at 1:30 P.M. on August 9 that the Supreme Council had decided to accept the Potsdam Proclamation on the basis of the four conditions advanced by the military (preservation of the imperial house; Japan to disarm her own troops; Japan to try persons accused of war crimes; no military occupation of Japan). Kido subsequently corrected himself (IMTFE: Kido, 31175) and stated that only after he had heard the evidence presented to the Tribunal did he learn that the Supreme Council had not reached such a decision but had merely discussed the four conditions as a possible basis for ending the war.

[10] Whether Suzuki made this statement at the beginning of the conference and again at the end (or possibly only at the end) is open to question. If he did make it at the beginning, he may have done so in the hope that the councilors would bend every effort, in the ensuing discussions, to iron out their differences and thus eliminate the necessity of calling upon the Emperor to decide.

and reported that there was a 6-3-5 split within the cabinet—six supporting the sole reservation relating to the preservation of the imperial system; three demanding the inclusion of additional conditions pertaining to disarmament, security occupation, and war crimes trials; and five remaining neutral but favoring an over-all reduction in the number of conditions.

The stage was now set for the opposing groups to have what many hoped would be their last say. At a word from Suzuki, Foreign Minister Tōgō arose and began repeating the arguments he had presented at the morning session of the Supreme Council. Drawing inspiration, perhaps, from the knowledge that the Emperor secretly favored the line of action he was proposing, Tōgō clearly and plainly stated his conviction that Japan's only course lay in accepting the Potsdam Proclamation *immediately*, with the sole reservation that the national entity be maintained. As he had done so frequently in the past, Tōgō once again emphasized that any attempt to negotiate on the basis of the specific conditions mentioned earlier would be to render a peaceful solution impossible.[11]

This was too much for War Minister Anami—the nominal leader of the group dedicated to laying Japan's terms on the line. Declaring that he was absolutely opposed to the opinions expressed by the Foreign Minister, Anami reiterated his belief that the government should proceed resolutely with the prosecution of the war. If the people of Japan went into the decisive battle in the homeland determined to display the full measure of patriotism and to fight to the very last, Japan would be able to avert the crisis facing her. If peace were to be concluded, however, it must be by means of all of the conditions previously proposed. These conditions, Anami said, were the prerequisites to such a task.[12]

No sooner had Anami taken his seat than Chief of the Army General Staff Umezu arose and continued in much the same vein—taking special care to point up the military's confidence in their ability to deal a smashing blow to the enemy. Although Umezu admitted that the Soviet entry into the war had rendered the situation unfavorable, he declared that he could see no need to abandon the plan to fight a decisive battle in the homeland simply because of the new turn of events. Since many brave men had gladly fought and died for the Emperor, he said, it would be inexcusable to surrender unconditionally. Although he asserted that he personally had no objection to a decision being made to accept the Potsdam Proclamation, he, too, insisted that such a decision must include all of the conditions discussed over the past few days.

Admiral Toyoda should have been the next to speak, but in the stress

---

[11] When Tōgō had finished, Suzuki called on Navy Minister Yonai, whose only response was a laconic, "I agree with the Foreign Minister."

[12] See *Statements*: Yoshizumi #54484.

of the moment Premier Suzuki passed over the chief of the Naval General Staff and called instead upon Baron Hiranuma, the president of the Privy Council. The Baron, himself a former Premier and one who had long been associated with the ultranationalist movement, had been invited to attend the conference in order to bring the Privy Council into the picture.[13] A decision of the magnitude of the one being formulated would normally have received the Emperor's sanction only after he had consulted the Privy Councilors. The pressure of events and the fear that introducing the matter to the Privy Council would merely produce another deadlock and still further postponement made it necessary either to forget about this once-powerful group of advisers or to "railroad" the question through the council without actually having it convene. For the latter purpose, Hiranuma's presence at the imperial conference was an obviously useful and clever maneuver.

From the moment the precise and legalistically minded Hiranuma took the floor until he finally sat down, he exhibited a noble interest in the facts—and in questions and answers which would produce the facts. He wanted to know many things: What had happened to the proposed Soviet negotiations? Why had the Soviet Union declared war? Just whom did the Allies mean when they spoke of "war criminals"? Would such persons be turned over to the Allies? Would they be tried in Japan? Would the Allies agree to let Japan disarm her own troops?

It fell upon Foreign Minister Tōgō to provide the answers, and he did a fair job. He brought Hiranuma up to date on what had been going on in Moscow and, for want of something better, quoted the Soviet Union's own reasons for entering the conflict. Hiranuma broke in to ask whether the Kremlin's claim that Japan had rejected the Potsdam Proclamation was true, and Tōgō answered in the negative. "Then why do they say so?" Hiranuma persisted, and to this the Foreign Minister simply replied, "It's all in their imagination."[14]

Apparently Hiranuma had not kept up with the news, or perhaps *mokusatsu* did not convey the same meaning to him as it did to Wash-

[13] Suzuki, with imperial "sanction," had specifically requested Hiranuma's attendance. See IMTFE: Kido, 31177; *Statements*: Sakomizu #61979 and Ikeda #54479. Ikeda states that he personally suggested the idea of Hiranuma's attendance to Suzuki as a matter of procedure—since a decision of the type being considered would normally have had to be referred to the Privy Council anyway.

[14] *Statements*: Hoshina #53437. Although, at the time in question, Tōgō had not as yet received an *official* notification of the Soviet Union's declaration of war (see footnote 74, Ch. 7), he had received a copy of the contents of the declaration as monitored from a *Tass* report.

Why Tōgō quoted the Soviet declaration in answering Hiranuma is not clear. Tōgō may have been irked at having been asked such a question or he may have been anxious to avoid discussing irrelevant issues (and may therefore have chosen to let the Kremlin speak for itself).

ington, London, and Moscow. It was true, of course, that the Japanese government had not *formally* rejected the ultimatum, but that was just another "detail" which did not have any significance at the time.

Continuing with his answers, Tōgō avoided hazarding any guesses as to who would fall within the "war criminal" category but he did indicate that such persons would have to be turned over to the enemy since that had been the procedure in the past.[15] In reply to Hiranuma's final question the Foreign Minister again reiterated the view that the Allies would never permit Japan to disarm her own troops.

Satisfied in this quarter, Hiranuma now turned to the military men present. In the course of his remarks, he briefly covered all of the sore points: the daily air raids, bombardment from warships, the enemy's ability to do as he pleased without fear of retaliation, the considerable increase in uncertainty among the people and an equal decline in their fighting spirit, the destruction of transportation facilities, the scarcity of food, and, finally, the atomic bomb and the Soviet invasion of Manchuria. In short, Hiranuma wanted to know if the army and navy authorities really had any confidence in their ability to continue the war.

Neither Umezu nor Toyoda, who undertook to answer the Privy Council president, could promise certain or complete victory but they did affirm that the Supreme Command would "exert its utmost efforts in the future." Umezu said that he believed the enemy's use of the atomic bomb might be checked if proper *antiaircraft* measures were taken, and to this Toyoda added an interesting footnote. Thus far Japan's air power had been grounded in the homeland—concentrated there in readiness for the decisive battle which was in the offing. "We have been preserving our strength for future use," Toyoda declared, "but hereafter we expect to counterattack." Both Toyoda and Umezu asserted that they and the services they represented were doing their best. While this was undoubtedly true, it had become quite clear that their best was not good enough and that it had not been good enough for a long, long time.

Hiranuma, who had by now spoken at greater length than anyone else, still held the floor. He was concerned about the maintenance of public order—especially the chaos which might result from a sudden termination of the war. Although he emphasized that he believed the people

---

[15] Although he did not express the view at the conference in question, Admiral Toyoda felt that the Potsdam Proclamation did not contain anything which could be interpreted as requiring Japan to deliver her "war criminals" to the Allies. He wanted war crimes to be prosecuted by Japanese courts or tribunals. See *Statements*: Toyoda #61340.

Paragraph 10 of the Potsdam Proclamation reads, "We do not intend that the Japanese shall be enslaved as a race or destroyed as a nation, but stern justice shall be meted out to all war criminals, including those who have visited cruelties upon our prisoners." See Appendix C.

were loyal at heart, he suggested that their steadfastness might be undermined by the extremely dangerous conditions then prevailing. Suzuki quickly added a word to the effect that he agreed with the view expressed by the president of the Privy Council. He too felt, the Premier said, that if the war continued to the point where the nation could not be defended no matter how hard everyone tried the government would be confronted with "grave difficulties" with respect to maintaining peace and order.

Whether Suzuki's interruption was a hint to Hiranuma that he had taken more than his share of time is not clear, but Suzuki's brief, parenthetical comment succeeded in bringing Hiranuma around to what might be called his summation. Although he agreed with the opinions the Foreign Minister had expressed, he warned that should the national polity be placed in jeopardy by the stand taken by the Allies there would be no way out except to fight on. In the meantime, he said, the wording of the reservation to be sent to the Allies must be revised. The phrase to the effect that Japan would accept the Potsdam Proclamation *on the understanding that it did not include any demand for a change in the status of the Emperor under the national laws* was not appropriate. It was also incorrect—especially from the aspect of the true relationship existing between His Majesty and his subjects. The sovereignty of the Emperor was coeval with the very beginning of the nation. This sovereignty was not determined by the national laws. Since the Constitution was merely a public formality, the phrase in question would have to be amended to read: *on the understanding that the Allied proclamation would not comprise any demand which would prejudice the prerogatives of His Majesty as a Sovereign Ruler.*[16]

He was not convinced, Hiranuma continued, that there was no room to negotiate on the other conditions. It was up to the Foreign Minister to do his utmost in this respect. The authorities should come to a decision after thorough deliberation. Furthermore, since acceptance of the Allied terms was a very grave matter, the views of the Throne should be sought.[17]

---

[16] Hiranuma has since stated that he proposed the change in phraseology because the original wording would have resulted in the Emperor's future position being regarded as merely a matter of form. (Hiranuma also observed that the three additional conditions sponsored by Anami and others confused substance with form.) See *Statements*: Hiranuma #55127.

There are those who feel that the original wording was more satisfactory and that had Japan adhered to it the Allies might have answered differently (i.e., the Allies might have given a positive assurance that they would not tamper with the national polity).

[17] Hiranuma has stated that his desire to seek an imperial "decision" lay in the fact that the question of national polity (*kokutai*) was involved. He was acting, he said, purely as an independent agent without any prior arrangement with Suzuki. In fact, he did not know beforehand that Suzuki intended to refer the question to the Emperor. See *Statements*: Hiranuma #55127.

Then, looking toward the Emperor, the president of the Privy Council made one final observation:

In accordance with the legacy of Your Imperial Forefathers, Your Imperial Majesty is also responsible for preventing unrest in the nation. I should like to ask Your Majesty to make Your decision with this point in mind.

Hiranuma sat down, and Suzuki turned at last to Admiral Toyoda, the chief of the Naval General Staff, who had begun to despair of having a chance to speak his mind. As the surrender faction had expected, Toyoda announced his support of the position taken by Anami and Umezu and emphasized that, unless the provision envisaging the withdrawal and disarmament of the troops by the Japanese themselves received the government's sanction, he would not be able to guarantee that the navy would accept the decision quietly.[18] The admiral also declared—much as Umezu had before him, "We cannot say that final victory is certain but at the same time we do not believe that we will be positively defeated."

This argument, as Toyoda well knew, was not without justification. The Japanese military still had several million men in arms, some planes, and an assortment of materials of war. Their suicide tactics had been a serious threat at times, and that was while the fighting had been far from home. The navy had organized special attack squadrons composed of *kamikaze* submarines, explosive-laden motorboats, and human torpedoes. Because of past performance, it was logical to place great hopes in their future application—especially when their employment would be within sight of Japan's sacred shores. The expendability of the loyal and the brave, although regrettable, was still an important tactical factor.

As soon as Toyoda concluded his remarks, Suzuki once more took charge of the proceedings. He had been content to let the others express their views without personally stating which side he favored. Although his action in convening such a conference under the circumstances then prevailing gave more than a hint of where he stood, his record of vacillation in the past contained the danger that even at this late date Suzuki had not really made up his mind. The imperial conference had been in session for some two hours, and the impasse experienced at the earlier meetings seemed even more impossible of solution now that it had been repeated in the very presence of the Emperor. But the Premier, who had helped engineer this conference for a specific purpose, proved equal to the occasion. Recapitulating the obvious—the fact that the councilors had covered the same ground for endless hours and had got nowhere—

---

[18] Although others have since said that this was a veiled threat, Toyoda has denied that he had anything more in mind than the peculiar psychology of the Japanese fighting man which Umezu had so aptly described earlier in the day. Although the reference is to a later date, see, for example, Toyoda, *Saigo no teikoku kaigun*, 225–27.

Suzuki emphatically declared that the gravity of the matter left him no recourse other than to seek a "decision" from His Majesty. Turning toward the Emperor, Suzuki respectfully announced: "Your Imperial Majesty's decision is requested as to which proposal should be adopted— the one stated by the Foreign Minister or the one containing the four conditions."[19]

"Without the slightest hesitation"[20] but with visible emotion welling up within him, the Emperor arose from his chair at the head of the table. The others immediately snapped to attention and bowed in His Majesty's direction. The Emperor had already begun to speak:[21]

I have given serious thought to the situation prevailing at home and abroad and have concluded that continuing the war can only mean destruction for the nation and a prolongation of bloodshed and cruelty in the world. I cannot bear to see my innocent people suffer any longer. Ending the war is the only way to restore world peace and to relieve the nation from the terrible distress with which it is burdened.

I was told by those advocating a continuation of hostilities that by June new divisions would be placed in fortified positions at Kujūkuri-hama so that they would be ready for the invader when he sought to land. It is now August and the fortifications still have not been completed. Even the equipment for the divisions which are to fight there is insufficient and reportedly will not be adequate until after the middle of September. Furthermore, the promised increase in the production of aircraft has not progressed in accordance with expectations.

There are those who say that the key to national survival lies in a decisive battle in the homeland. The experiences of the past, however, show that there has always been a discrepancy between plans and performance. I do not believe that the discrepancy in the case of Kujūkuri-hama can be rectified. Since this is the shape of things, how can we repel the invaders?[22]

I cannot help feeling sad when I think of the people who have served me so faithfully, the soldiers and sailors who have been killed or wounded in far-off battles, the families who have lost all their worldly goods—and often their lives as well—in the air raids at home. It goes without saying that it is unbearable for me to see the brave and loyal fighting men of Japan disarmed. It is equally

---

[19] Hiranuma has stated that the only "proposal" at the imperial conference was the position advocated by Tōgō. In other words, Anami's position was not presented as an alternate plan. (*Statements*: Hiranuma #55127.) Be that as it may, Suzuki asked the Emperor to choose between the two proposals (or sides).

[20] IMTFE: Suzuki, 35593–94.

[21] After the war, some of those who were present at the conference sought to recall what the Emperor had said. In their recollections (occasionally based on brief notations made following the adjournment), areas of agreement can be found. In the absence of a "shorthand" transcript or minutes, however, it is impossible to do anything more than re-create the gist of what the Emperor said. What follows in the text, therefore, is a reconstruction of the Emperor's remarks based on the material found in the following: IMTFE: Kido, 31177–79; Suzuki, 35593–94; Tōgō, 35788; Toyoda, *Saigo no teikoku kaigun*, 210–13; *Statements*: Ikeda #54483, Hasunuma #58225, Tōgō #50304; Kido, "Nikki," 8/10/45; and JFO MS: Ch. 44 (Dai ikkai gozen kaigi).

[22] In addition to what the Emperor had learned from Hasegawa and Umezu (see footnote 13, Ch. 6, and the text corresponding thereto), the Emperor's views in this respect were greatly influenced by the information (and advice) supplied by Kido (see footnote 24 below and *Statements*: Hasunuma #58225).

unbearable that others who have rendered me devoted service should now be punished as instigators of the war.[23] Nevertheless, the time has come when we must bear the unbearable.[24]

When I recall the feelings of my Imperial Grandsire, the Emperor Meiji, at the time of the Triple Intervention,[25] I swallow my own tears and give my sanction to the proposal to accept the Allied proclamation on the basis outlined by the Foreign Minister.

As the Emperor turned from the conference table and slowly made his way out of the room, Premier Suzuki flatly declared: "His Majesty's decision *should* be made the decision of this conference as well."[26] Although each man present kept his counsel and thereby registered his assent, the real fact of the matter is that the so-called imperial decision was not actually a *decision* at all. Indeed, it was little more than an expression of the Emperor's personal desire—a play upon words whereby the sovereign had said, "If it were up to me to decide, this is what I would do." The Emperor's admonitions and injunctions were in the nature of a private opinion with no legal authority to bind the will of the state, for which the cabinet alone was responsible. The councilors

[23] The author has here departed from a translation in IMTFE: *Proceedings*, 31178, since the latter creates the impression that the Emperor, in speaking at the imperial conference, recognized and acknowledged that his ministers were responsible for the outbreak of the war and consequently were war criminals. It should be obvious that this was not the case and that the sentence quoted above, when read in context, should be translated in the manner indicated.

Some three weeks later, on August 29, the Emperor, in a private talk with the Privy Seal, returned to the question of war responsibility. Repeating that it was painful to hand over, as "war criminals," the men who had served Japan faithfully in the past, the Emperor asked whether he could not settle this matter once and for all by abdicating—thus taking the entire responsibility upon his own shoulders. To this Kido replied that the attitude of the Allies was such that they would not be satisfied by His Majesty's resignation. The Privy Seal also warned that an abdication might be interpreted by the Allies as a sign that the imperial house had been shaken from its foundations. This, in turn, could result in an Allied attempt to promote republicanism in Japan. "No," Kido concluded, "I must urge Your Majesty to study this matter further after you have had time to see what moves are made by the other [Allied] side." (Kido, "Nikki," 8/29/45.)

[24] A few of the Emperor's remarks were obviously based upon the advice offered to the Throne by Kido on *July 25, 1945*. At that time Kido told the Emperor that although the military were advocating a decisive battle in the homeland their performance in the past made it impossible to place any credence in their current contentions (see paragraphs 2 and 3 of the imperial remarks quoted in the text above). Kido also advised the Emperor that the most urgent task (for His Majesty and the Privy Seal) was to conclude peace—*by bearing the unbearable*. See Kido, "Nikki," 7/25/45.

[25] The Triple Intervention occurred in 1895 when Russia, Germany, and France forced Japan to re-cede the Liaotung Peninsula to China. Japan had claimed the peninsula as part of the spoils of her victory over China in the war of 1894–95. The crowning blow came in 1898 when Russia gained control of the peninsula by leasing it from China. Japan evened the score during her war with the Russians in 1904–5 and obtained Liaotung as a result of the subsequent Treaty of Portsmouth (1905).

[26] See *Statements*: Sakomizu 5/3/49 and USSBS, *Japan's Struggle to End the War*, 9. Suzuki's use of "should" had the implication of "ought" rather than of "must." The significance of this is developed in the text.

to whom he had stated his views, moreover, belonged to an extraconstitutional organ, and like the Emperor they, too, could merely express an opinion. Whether anything the Supreme Councilors did or the Emperor said ultimately became *a decision of state* would depend entirely upon the pleasure of the cabinet, whose approval alone could impart validity and substance to policies formulated outside its chambers.[27] Yet in the final analysis, the imperial judgment and the Supreme Council's concurrence possessed a great significance in that both overawed in *influence* what they lacked in authority.[28]

At a less critical, chaotic time even this open-sesame might have proved unequal to the occasion. In spite of the emphasis which had been placed by the ruling elite upon the supremacy of the imperial will, the concept had had very little meaning and very few adherents other than undesirable elements who used "imperial sovereignty" to further their own questionable ends. By August 9, however, the past had overtaken the present and all that might have been had already raced toward an unavoidable climax—a point of no return. In such a circumstance, the theories of former times joined with the compelling demands of the moment to give the Emperor's expression of desire the force it needed to swing the pendulum from destruction toward survival.

As those who had been present at the imperial conference began to depart, word was passed that a cabinet meeting would be held immediately at the official residence of the Premier. There, between three and four o'clock in the morning, the assembled ministers, His Majesty's responsible officials of state, unanimously approved the "imperial decision,"[29] thus legalizing the action taken by the Emperor in the presence of the Supreme Councilors little more than an hour before.

With the state thus *committed* to a positive policy, the ministers turned their attention to drafting identical notes to be dispatched to the Allied powers.[30] By the time the rest of Japan was awakening in the

---

[27] For material relating to this point, see *Statements*: Kido #61476, Matsudaira #60745, Sakomizu 5/3/49, Suzuki #531; IMTFE: Tōgō, 36138–39 (garbled but decipherable).

[28] See, for instance, *Statements*: Kido #61476. In addition to "influence," there is the point that since four of the Big Six were also members of the cabinet a unanimous decision by the Supreme Council, when passed on to the cabinet, would enjoy the support of those ministers who were members of the Council (i.e., the support of the Premier, Foreign Minister, War Minister, and Navy Minister).

[29] See IMTFE: Tōgō, 35788; *Statements*: Sakomizu, 5/3/49, Tōgō #50304, Sakomizu #62051; and USSBS, *Japan's Struggle to End the War*, 9. When the cabinet ministers were called upon to sign the formal resolution whereby the imperial conference decision became the decision of the cabinet as well, Home Minister Abe was at first reluctant to sign but was later persuaded to do so.

[30] For the English text of Japan's first surrender offer, see Appendix D. For the English and Japanese texts, as well as additional details, see JFO, *Shūsen shiroku*, Ch. 44 (Kokutai mondai ni kan suru ryōkai tsuki no Potsudamu sengen judaku dempō hassō). The latter work is the published version of the "Shūsen no keii to sono shiryō" which has been cited herein as JFO MS. The somewhat revised and abridged *Shūsen*

early morning hours of Friday, August 10, cables announcing the nation's acceptance of the Potsdam ultimatum "with the understanding that the said declaration does not comprise any demand which prejudices the prerogatives of His Majesty as a Sovereign Ruler"[31] were already on their way to Japan's diplomatic representatives in Berne and Stockholm, there to be forwarded to Moscow, London, Washington, and Chungking.[32]

On the surface, Japan's future now seemed to lie in the hands of the policy makers in the Allied camp, but the end-the-war faction in Japan, for all of its success to date, could not quite shake itself loose from a fear born not of an overactive imagination but of cold experience. The imperial conference and the Emperor's sudden emergence had taken everyone, except those responsible for the move, by surprise. It was almost as if the militarists had been caught napping; yet the stroke—although bold and swift—had left something to be desired. The trap had been baited, but there was no certainty that it would be sprung.

From 1868 on, but more particularly after 1930, the army had extolled the "untouchable" prerogatives of the Throne and had preached a never-ending sermon of emphasis upon imperial infallibility and inviolability. Yet, throughout that whole period, infiltrations from the historical record of lord and vassal relationships had rendered the imperial prerogatives subject to military control and guidance. In spite of its fervent protestations, the Japanese army had never shied from

---

shiroku, which came off the presses shortly before this study was completed, is cited in only those instances where the JFO MS was no longer available to the author. Although the numbering system has been changed slightly, JFO MS references can be correlated with the *Shūsen shiroku* by a comparison of chapter *titles* (the form of reference used herein).

[31] Toshikazu Kase, who put the Japanese text of Japan's note of acceptance into English, ran into difficulty when he came to the Hiranuma amendment. Kase states that he "experienced a moment's hesitation" when he chose the word "prerogatives" to correspond to Hiranuma's *taiken* which, literally translated, means "powers inherent in the crown." (*Journey to the Missouri,* 238 and 243.)

The then Vice Foreign Minister Matsumoto has since stated that this note of August 10 was a poor stroke. Japan should simply have said: "We accept the Potsdam Proclamation. We understand that this acceptance will not affect the position of the imperial household."

Matsumoto does not know when, how, or by whom the paragraph, "The Japanese Government sincerely hope that this understanding is warranted and desire keenly that an explicit indication to that effect will be speedily forthcoming," was added. He does state that he had his doubts about using Kase's translation ("prerogatives") of Hiranuma's term (*taiken*) but let it pass because he could not think of a more suitable expression. See *Statements*: Matsumoto #61451.

[32] The Japanese Minister in Switzerland was instructed to transmit Japan's acceptance to the United States and China through the Swiss government. The Minister in Sweden was instructed to transmit the acceptance to Great Britain and the Soviet Union through the Swedish government. See IMTFE: Tōgō, 35788, and USSBS, *Japan's Struggle to End the War,* 9.

hypocrisy nor hesitated to counteract policies with which it did not agree. As a result, no one of importance in Japan, not even His Majesty's closest advisers, had ever been free of the threat of violence and assassination. In the trouble-strewn year of 1936, both Admiral Suzuki and Admiral Okada, Grand Chamberlain and Premier respectively, had narrowly escaped death at the hands of the fanatics. Count Makino, a onetime Lord Keeper of the Privy Seal who was numbered among the Emperor's most trusted retainers, was yet another of the ruling elite who had been the object of several attacks, each of which only just failed. Others, less fortunate than these men, had paid the price of "government by assassination."[33] While the moss grew green on the stones above their heads, their attackers luxuriated in the limelight of their self-appointed mission of freeing the Emperor from his "evil, crooked, and traitorous" advisers.[34]

At times the schemes of the army fanatics and their fellow travelers among the ultranationalists had erupted on a broader scale than assassination of individuals. The military had once gone so far as to march on Tokyo, and only an imperial command had dispelled the troops and kept the blood of rebellion from flowing in the streets around the palace moat.

It was the recollection of such events as these and many more like them that invited worry right now. The men who had sparked the movement to end the war realized that they were in grave and certain danger, but there was little they could do other than take added precautions. By the morning of August 10 they had indeed accomplished a great deal, but final success hinged also upon the Allied answer to Japan's note of acceptance. It was very possible that the reply would force them into a new and more deadly encounter with the opposing faction. If the answer were unfavorable or even open to different interpretations, there could be no telling how the situation would develop.

In addition to the threat posed by the militarists, the end-the-war advocates also faced the possibility of an impasse in their own thinking. They were in agreement with the military on only one point: the nation must continue to live under the imperial system. Any final acceptance of the Allied terms must be made conditional upon the willingness of the Allies to permit Japan's dynasty to retain its nominal priority of overlordship. This meant placing the dynasty, and especially the Emperor, above any taint of responsibility or any suspicion of guilt so far as the war was concerned. If the members of the end-the-war party could achieve this, they would be willing to take their own chances in

---

[33] For an account of this period, see Hugh Byas, *Government by Assassination*.

[34] The phrase, in Japanese, is *kunsoku no kan* which literally means "the corrupt (or 'evil') elements close to the Throne" and hence, in modern parlance, those advisers of the Emperor who were following policies unacceptable to the militarists and ultranationalists.

the maelstrom of charges that threatened to engulf them in the post-surrender period. Some members of the group may even have seen in their efforts to end the war a certain expiation for their failure person-ally to have taken a stronger stand in preventing its beginning.

The immediate object was survival—national survival under the Emperor–High Priest–Father of the People. Logically these men might have been able to picture Japan without an Emperor but emotionally they could not. For this reason, they could not just have rushed blindly into surrender even if the military had not stood in the way. They had to be reasonably sure that their movement to end the war would save the dynasty, which, in their eyes, was synonymous with the state. The fate of the nation thus depended not only upon the action the military might take but upon the action the end-the-war cadre itself could take once the Allied response was received.

Among Japan's chief military figures there was no less of a dilemma. They were as faithfully bound to Japan's peculiar national polity (*koku-tai*) as were the civilian leaders against whom they were pitting their strength, but they had also to cope with the fanaticism of the younger officer group—field-grade subordinates who seemed to lead more fre-quently than they followed. The power held by this element had long since reinforced the personal inclination of the titular heads of the armed forces—men like Anami, Umezu, Toyoda—to resist, at first, any attempt to end the war and, subsequently, any effort to stop the fighting on terms other than those proposed by the Japanese military.

The revulsion with which these *samurai*-inspired men viewed defeat and surrender often made them blind to all other considerations. Their thinking processes were befuddled by the emphasis they placed upon the ability of the spirit to triumph miraculously over the power of material force. These men, who had once been the wardens of the prison in which they had confined the whole nation, had now joined the ranks of the inmates. The real significance of the explosions over Hiroshima and Nagasaki and of the Soviet dash into Manchuria was that these events produced a shock great enough to crack the walls of the prison. Even this shock did not result in an escape but it did force everyone, the guards and guarded alike, to face the full and glaring light of day—to acknowledge a fact which could no longer be denied. It was not that the military men had suddenly become reasonable in the hours follow-ing the Hiroshima and Nagasaki disasters; it was rather that they, like the machinery of government with which they had been tinkering, had momentarily been caught off balance. They were also at a loss for words which could make any lasting impression upon the end-the-war faction. Prior to the dropping of the two A-bombs they had been able to pledge their belief in their ability to meet effectively any action taken by the enemy, but now whatever they said made them look foolish and insin-cere. Their moral and spiritual position had crumbled beneath the weight of the material power they held in contempt, yet they, too, still had power at their command—the physical force of men willing to resist to the death. And herein lay the unanswerable question: would they continue to resist or would they give in?

Although Japan had just sued for peace, there was nothing peaceful about the late morning of August 10, 1945. Carrier-borne planes of Admiral Halsey's squadron subjected Tokyo to "a particularly nasty air raid" and, in addition, wave upon wave of B-29's came over the city leaving havoc in their wake. At the same time, thousands of other planes were raiding the rest of the country "in the most impressive and nerve-wracking demonstration of the whole war."[35] It was under these circumstances that Foreign Minister Tōgō received Soviet Ambassador Malik at the later's request and obtained from him the official notification of the state of war existing between the Soviet Union and Japan. After reminding the ambassador that his country not only had failed to answer Japan's long-standing request for Soviet mediation but had also commenced hostilities at a time when the Soviet-Japanese Neutrality Pact was still in force, Tōgō requested Malik to inform the Soviet government of the imperial decision to accept the Potsdam Proclamation.[36]

Now that the Allied powers had been advised of Japan's acceptance by means of the cabled notes and by direct communication with Malik, the Japanese people could hardly be kept in the dark much longer. Thus far, the government's machinations had been known only to the actual participants, but the Soviet Union's declaration of war—which appeared in the morning papers (Friday, August 10)—annihilated in a single stroke the secrecy which the government had hitherto so carefully maintained. The Soviet statement to the effect that Japan's request for mediation had lost its meaning obviously suggested, even to a casual reader, that there had been something going on behind the scenes. In view of this, it seemed the better part of wisdom to give the people some idea of what was coming.

The cabinet was again divided. Every argument in support of an immediate announcement produced a counterargument pointing up the possible consequences of such a move and stressing the advantages of maintaining silence until after the Allied reply had been received and studied. At length, a weak compromise emerged. For the time being, the government would say nothing about the "imperial decision." Should the Allies accept Japan's offer, the people could then be informed of that fact by an imperial rescript. In spite of this decision, the cabinet did realize the necessity of saying something immediately which could serve as a vague indication of the unprecedented reversal which the

[35] The quotations are from Kawai MS: "Japan's Struggle to Surrender," 35.
[36] See IMTFE: Tōgō, 35785–86, and footnote 74, Ch. 7, above.

government might soon have to present to the people on practically a moment's notice. The upshot of this was a statement which appeared in all of the morning papers on Saturday, August 11.[37] Although this admonitory appeal to the people was issued in the name of the president of the Board of Information, it actually was a product of the combined efforts of not only the Information Board president but of the Ministers of War, Navy, and Foreign Affairs as well.[38]

Containing the usual platitudes about the spirit of the fighting forces and their unflinching destruction of enemy efforts everywhere, the statement warned the people that the Allies were preparing to invade Japan. To this was added a bitter castigation of the Empire's "diabolical enemies" for their use of a "new-type bomb" with which they were ravaging the innocent, the young and the old, and Japan's fair womanhood— spreading death and destruction "unprecedented, in the history of the human race, in ruthlessness and barbarity." Only the concluding sentence had a completely different cast. Referring to the over-all picture— the coming Allied invasion, the introduction of the new-type bomb, and the Soviet entry into the war—the government statement declared:

In truth, we cannot but recognize that we are now beset with the worst possible situation. Just as the government is exerting its utmost efforts to defend the homeland, safeguard the polity, and preserve the honor of the nation so too must the people rise to the occasion and overcome all manner of difficulties in order to protect the polity of their Empire.[39]

Although this was meant to be a hint that the cabinet was preparing to end the war on the basis of the Potsdam ultimatum and that the people were expected to obey by bearing the unbearable, the wording of the statement convinced the masses that they were to ready themselves for a death-to-the-last-man stand through the length and breadth of their sacred land.

As if this were not enough, the government statement was thoroughly overshadowed by a proclamation from the War Ministry—a very brief but rampant verbal gem which the newspapers were forced to print alongside the Board of Information's oblique pronouncement. Without

[37] For the details relating to the cabinet meeting and for the Japanese text of the Board of Information statement, see JFO, *Shūsen shiroku*, Ch. 45 (Shimomura jōhō-kyoku sōsai dan to rikushō fukoku). See also the vernacular papers and the *Nippon Times* for Saturday, August 11, 1945.

[38] Strictly speaking, the draft was initially prepared by the staff of the Information Board. This draft was later revised by Anami, Yonai, Shimomura, and apparently Tōgō. There is some question as to whether or not Tōgō participated but the evidence favors the affirmative.

[39] See the references cited in footnote 37 above. The *Nippon Times* for August 11, 1945, capped the Shimomura (Board of Information) statement with the following heading: "Total Wartime Effort Asked Japanese Nation—Overcoming of Present Crisis to Defend National Polity Urged by Shimomura."

a doubt this proclamation, which was issued over the name of the War
Minister, constituted a brazen contradiction of the cabinet's true intentions and wishes, nor can there be any question but that it represented
the will of the Japanese military as opposed to the will of the Emperor's
cabinet. Significantly describing the Soviet entry into the war as a sinister design on the part of the Kremlin to subjugate and rule all of East
Asia, the "War Minister" vigorously flourished an appealing standard
for the men of the army to follow: unfaltering prosecution of the "holy
war" for the preservation of the "sacred land." "Even though we may
have to eat grass, swallow dirt, and lie in the fields," the proclamation
quoted General Anami as saying, "we shall fight on to the bitter end,
ever firm in our faith that we shall find life in death." Then came the
final appeal, carrying with it a force exclusive of all other considerations: "Follow the illustrious examples of Nanko [the symbol of eternal
loyalty to the Throne] and Tokimune [the *shōgun* who repulsed the
Mongol invasion of 1281] and surge forward to destroy the arrogant
enemy!"[40]

When the civilian members of the ruling elite heard about this blood-
curdling tirade, they were at a loss to know what to do. Some wanted
the Foreign Minister or another person in authority to countermand the
army's order to the newspapers and have the presses stopped, while
others advocated seeking an explanation directly from the War Minister.
There was a great deal of confusion at the Foreign Office, the fear of
army-inspired violence flared up anew, and in the end no one did anything. The presses rolled and the people were made to believe that they
would soon be fighting, with their neighbors, the ultimate in battles—
the one from which there would be no retreat.

Only later, when the whole incident was no longer significant, did
the story behind this striking proclamation come to light. It seems that
at approximately 9:30 on the morning of August 10, shortly after Anami
returned to the War Ministry from the cabinet meeting at which the
imperial decision to accept the Potsdam Proclamation was approved
unanimously, the word was passed among the senior staff officers of
the Ministry's various bureaus and departments that their presence was
requested in the general's office. When everyone had assembled, Anami
addressed them briefly—bringing them up to date on the developments
of the preceding twenty-four hours. His announcement of the imperial
decision to accept the Allied terms caused consternation, but he continued quietly—both reasoning with his subordinates and playing upon

[40] For the Japanese text, see JFO, *Shūsen shiroku*, Ch. 45 (Shimomura jōhōkyoku
sōsai dan to rikushō fukoku), and the vernacular papers for August 11, 1945. For the
English text, see the *Nippon Times* for Sunday, August 12, 1945: "War Minister
Exhorts Army in Stirring Call—Press Forward to Smash Enemy with Spirit of Nanko,
Tokimune, Declares Message."

the feelings of respect and confidence which he knew they held for him. In essence, he concluded as follows:

I do not know what excuse I can offer but since it is the decision of His Majesty that we accept the Potsdam Proclamation there is nothing that can be done. The really important consideration is that the army act in an organized manner. Your individual feelings and those of the men under you must be disregarded.

Since the imperial decision is predicated upon the assumption that the Allies will guarantee the preservation of our national polity, it is too soon to say that the war has already ended. The army must therefore be prepared either for war or for peace.

If there is anyone here who is dissatisfied, and who wishes to act contrary to His Majesty's decision, he will have to do so over my dead body.[41]

It so happened that among the officers listening to Anami was a certain Lieutenant Colonel Inaba, a member of the Budget Branch of the Military Affairs Bureau. With little or no thought about the consequences, Inaba decided that *until the surrender became a fact* the army—especially the forces in Manchuria—must maintain the offensive and fight on with unshakable determination. Only if the whole army were encouraged to the very last would it be possible, Inaba believed, to prevent the rise and spread of unrest and disorder once the truth became known.

No sooner was Inaba out of Anami's office than he set to work drafting a statement to fit the circumstances as he saw them. About two o'clock in the afternoon, after he had obtained general approval of his idea from Anami, Inaba showed his first draft to Vice-Minister of War Wakamatsu and to the chiefs of the Military Affairs Bureau and the Military Affairs Section (Yoshizumi and Arao, respectively). All three officers read the document through, suggested several revisions, and then affixed their personal seals by way of indicating their concurrence. Since Anami was nowhere to be found, Inaba asked Colonel Arao, who was to call at Anami's official residence that evening, to take along a hastily revised draft and to obtain the War Minister's support.[42]

Somewhat later, two rather impatient staff officers,[43] who shared Inaba's views, arrived at the War Ministry, anxious to obtain a copy of Inaba's statement so that it could be included in the evening news broadcast. Since Colonel Arao had already left with the original, Inaba and his callers fished around in the wastebasket until they found the unrevised first draft. They then made a clean copy with Inaba changing

---

[41] There is no verbatim record of Anami's remarks, but the words in the text represent his brother-in-law's recollection of what Anami said. (See *Statements*: Takeshita #50025-A.) For the sequel to the above, see footnote 8, Ch. 10, below, and the text corresponding thereto.

[42] See *Statements*: Inaba #57692 and Takeshita #50025-A.

[43] Takeshita (Anami's brother-in-law) and Oyadomari.

the wording here and there in order to bring the draft into line with the final revision which had been approved earlier in the day. Although he was somewhat concerned over the fact that Anami had thus far only approved the idea in principle and had never seen either the first or final drafts, Inaba did nothing to dissuade his friends from their plan to release the draft at once.

While these events were taking place at the War Ministry, General Anami, in accordance with the cabinet's wishes, was busily engaged in helping his colleagues prepare the Information Board announcement. President of the Board Shimomura later recalled that of those present Anami displayed "the greatest interest of all" and "was responsible for many amendments." As has already been indicated, the primary object of this government statement was to soften the blow which would inevitably rock the nation's morale once the truth became known. Anami was "fully aware of this purpose" and co-operated with his colleagues seriously and conscientiously toward that end. While this work was still in progress, Shimomura received repeated phone calls from his office beseeching him to return at once. He did not do so, however, until he, Anami, and the others had finished their task.

When Shimomura finally reached the Board of Information headquarters, he learned to his surprise that the army had ordered the newspapers to print a proclamation issued over the name of the War Minister. Although the press had asked the military to withdraw their demand, the authorities in the War Ministry had refused.[44] After hearing all the details—a rather meager sum in total—Shimomura telephoned Anami to get the facts. As soon as Anami began answering his queries, Shimomura realized that the mild-mannered War Minister actually knew nothing about the matter. Just at this point, however, Shimomura heard faintly through the receiver that someone else was talking to Anami at the other end. And then, as if he had just got hold of himself, Anami spoke up, saying, "Ah . . . are you referring to *that*? Well, *now* I understand. Please push it through somehow and have it published." Surmising that Anami was caught in a difficult position—wedged in, as it were, between the views of the government and those of the stubborn younger officers, Shimomura decided to comply with the War Minister's request lest a refusal to do so result in some unforeseen harm being visited upon the person of Anami.[45] The result of these unexpected developments followed soon thereafter. When the news broadcast came over the air that evening (August 10), the so-called "Anami Proclamation" was read first—followed by the less forceful

[44] See *Statements:* Ōshima #61059. Only one newspaper, the English-language *Nippon Times*, took a chance and did not print the proclamation, but its attempt to exert independent judgment was short-lived. The paper was forced to print the statement on August 12. (Kawai MS: "Japan's Struggle to Surrender," 41–42.)

[45] See *Statements:* Shimomura #57688.

generalities of the Board of Information, and the next morning, August 11, both statements appeared side by side in the newspapers.[46]

Although no one had been willing, on August 10, to antagonize the army openly by attempting to stop the publication of the "Anami Proclamation," the Vice-Minister of Foreign Affairs and several other Foreign Office officials had spent much of the day trying to devise some means of letting the Allied world know, quickly and accurately, the gist of the note of acceptance which had been dispatched through the rather slow-moving diplomatic channels normally prescribed for such official business. The obvious method was to broadcast the news, for a forthright announcement over the air might stop the United States from dropping a third atomic bomb. With direct hits already registered upon two Japanese cities, this was a powerful argument. Equally forceful was the theory that a radio announcement, which would filter through to the man in the street more readily than an official note, would cause such public rejoicing among the Allied peoples that their governments would have to accept Japan's conditional offer whether they really wanted to do so or not.

Although the army's eager minions, the censors, were everywhere at hand, their activities apparently did not extend to the Morse code broadcasts, which were conducted, under government authorization, by the Dōmei News Agency. The necessary arrangements were undertaken at once and on the evening of August 10 the air waves were filled with the news of Japan's willingness to surrender.[47] The army, which did not learn of this until the following morning, was furious, but there was little it could do unless it resorted to the extreme of violence. The Emperor, the Supreme Council, and the cabinet had all supported the decision to terminate hostilities and the government had drafted and dispatched a note to that effect to the Allied powers. "Why," asked the Foreign Office in response to an army inquisition, "should we not have

---

[46] Takeshita (one of the participants) was severely reprimanded by Lieutenant General Yoshizumi, chief of the Military Affairs Bureau, when the latter returned and discovered that the proclamation had been released. On the evening of August 11 Takeshita visited Anami to apologize for his action. Anami passed the matter off—saying that he had been questioned about it at a cabinet meeting and that he had replied that the *purport* of the proclamation had had his approval. Anami also told Takeshita that the Emperor had rebuked him and had asked whether the proclamation was not contrary to the policy laid down by the cabinet. According to Takeshita, Anami had replied that the army would have to continue fighting until the end (i.e., until the final decision to surrender had been made) and that the issuance of such instructions to the armed forces was necessary. See *Statements*: Takeshita #50025-A, Inaba #57692, Matsudaira #60745, and Yoshizumi #61338.

[47] Leahy, *I Was There*, 434, speaks of a White House meeting (9:00 A.M., August 10, *Washington time*) to discuss an "unofficial" Japanese broadcast stating Japan would accept the Potsdam Proclamation. This would indicate that the efforts of Vice-Minister Matsumoto and his colleagues in having the news broadcasted (on the evening of August 10, *Tokyo time*) were not in vain.

broadcasted unofficially what we have already cabled in the form of an official communication representing the gracious command of His Imperial Majesty?"[48] Since the military did not have the answer, they could only grumble and perhaps secretly plan for the day of vengeance which even then was looming large in the minds of the fanatics.

While the Foreign Office and the Supreme Command were maneuvering at cross-purposes, the Lord Keeper of the Privy Seal and the Emperor were engaged in surveying the problem from the vantage ground of the imperial court. Early in the afternoon on August 10, the Emperor received Count Makino, the former Privy Seal, and somewhat later seven of the senior statesmen.[49] All submitted their views to the Throne on the momentous events of the preceding few days. Kido was in and out of the imperial presence throughout the day and also paid a visit to Prince Mikasa, the Emperor's third brother, to brief him on the current situation. About nine o'clock in the evening, Prince Konoye called at Kido's residence to express his concern over the Anami statement, and the two men spent some time confidentially discussing the general state of affairs.[50]

Possibly because it was too early to have an answer from the Allies, everyone was on edge and ill at ease. In spite of the fact that all of the arguments on both sides had practically been exhausted, talking did help to quiet the anxiety in many minds. There was also the chance that continued discussion would bring to light some factor or other that had been overlooked in the excitement generated by the decision to accept the Allied ultimatum.

This pattern of persistent recapitulation of points of view long since grown stale was repeated on August 11—a day which seems to have been important only in so far as its long and barren hours built up anew the tensions which had been relieved somewhat the day before. As on August 10, so now on August 11, Kido held himself in readiness to answer the Emperor's every beck and call. Throughout the day, the Privy Seal was deluged with visitors: Foreign Minister Tōgō, Premier Suzuki, President of the Board of Information Shimomura, Home Min-

---

[48] See JFO, *Shūsen shiroku*, Ch. 46 (Potsudamu sengen judaku dempō no kaigai muke hōsō sochi). See also Kawai MS: "Japan's Struggle to Surrender," 41–43, and *Statements*: Sakomizu 5/3/49.

[49] See IMTFE: Kido, 31175 and 31179–80; Kido, "Nikki," 8/9–10/45. The following *jūshin* were received by the Emperor in an audience which lasted from 3:35 until 4:30 P.M. on Friday, August 10: Hiranuma, Wakatsuki, Okada, Konoye, Hirota, Tōjō, and Koiso. Abe, who was serving as governor general in Korea, and Yonai, who was serving as Navy Minister in the Suzuki Cabinet, were unable to present themselves. (Apart from the question of presence in or absence from the capital, *jūshin* who held official positions were considered ineligible to attend meetings of the senior statesmen.) Privy Seal Kido was also present at the audience.

[50] *Ibid.*

ister Abe,[51] Chief of the Metropolitan Police Machimura, and finally Premier Suzuki again. A less prominent caller was a certain Mr. Saji bearing a letter from Marquis Yoshichika Tokugawa in which the latter called for a revolution under the imperial banner. According to the marquis, the crisis threatening Japan demanded the creation of a new internal structure built around the person of the Emperor. Only thus could the state be saved.

All in all, it was a hectic day, yet Kido passed it impatiently—waiting for the Allied reply, which did not come. The Privy Seal had long recognized the danger inherent in the confusion that would reign among the people when they suddenly learned the war had ended in defeat. After considerable discussion held over a period of several weeks, both he and Imperial Household Minister Ishiwata had finally agreed that the only way to minimize the danger and the confusion would be to have the Emperor, breaking yet another precedent, relay an awesome message by radio to a hushed and bowed audience numbering in the millions. Now, on August 11, Kido suddenly decided to obtain His Majesty's reaction to this plan. When the sovereign agreed to broadcast at any time, Kido—mindful of the pressures of the moment—hastened to make preliminary arrangements against the day, drawing imminently near, when such a broadcast would be necessary.[52] In this way, the stage was set for perhaps the most important single act in the reign of the 124th Emperor of Japan.

[51] Home Minister Genki Abe should not be confused with former Premier (and the then governor general of Korea) Nobuyuki Abe.

The compiler of the index to Kase's *Journey to the Missouri* is in error in including pages 232, 238, and 247 as references under "Abe, Gen. Nobuyuki" for Kase's remarks on the above-mentioned pages refer to Home Minister Genki Abe and not to General Nobuyuki Abe.

[52] See Kido, "Nikki," 8/11/45; IMTFE: Kido, 31180–83; JFO, *Shūsen shiroku*, Ch. 47 (Shūsen no shōchoku go hōsō no kettei) ; and IMTFE: Def. Doc. 3052, *Makino Aff.* (rejected: 38931–35).

9

CURTAIN CALL

The Byrnes Note and His Majesty's Final Decision

BECAUSE of the tricks played by the international date line and the adjustable hands of the clock, the communication signifying Japan's acceptance of the Potsdam Proclamation arrived in Washington on the same day and date (Friday, August 10) and at approximately the same hour that it left Tokyo. Had Japan's ruling elite been able to guess at the problems which were thus raised in the American capital, their unvoiced fears might have multiplied manyfold. The simple truth was that American Far Eastern experts and would-be experts were still divided in their interpretations of the role played by the imperial institution in the life of the Japanese people. The "reformers," who demanded that the Emperor and his family be denied any place in the country's future, cried "Appeasement!" at those who sought the Emperor's retention as a constitutional monarch.[1] The "appeasers," on the other hand, looked upon their antagonists as utterly foolish and stubborn men who were bent upon ignoring the "ineradicable" influence of the Emperor and the Throne. When one side propounded arguments in support of its contentions, the other side countered with arguments of its own. When new evidence was not available, old evidence was rehashed until it conformed with the particular bias being expressed. Wishful thinking rode roughshod over sound judgment, making a solution even more difficult to obtain. Continued discussion merely confirmed existing prejudices and gave rise to a more determined exposition of long-held views. What was gospel to one group in Washington was nonsense to the other. What was accepted as demonstrable fact by the one was ridiculed as naïve misconception by the other.

Until August 10, 1945, final military victory had seemed a very long way off. As a result, urgency had never been a consideration in the debate. Even when the successful testing of the atomic bomb had led to the issuance of the Potsdam ultimatum, Washington had refused to com-

[1] See Stimson and Bundy, *On Active Service*, 626–27; Hull, *Memoirs*, II, 1593–94; and Millis (ed.), *The Forrestal Diaries*, 52–53.

mit itself upon the Emperor.[2] The division of opinion on this question had by then been reinforced by a fear of the political repercussions which a clear-cut statement might produce. During the course of the war so many political figures in Washington had bluntly reviled the Emperor in their public statements that "too many people were likely to cry shame" if their leaders now suddenly reversed themselves.[3]

It was with these points in mind that Secretary of State Byrnes rushed to a White House conference[4] held early in the morning on August 10 to discuss the Japanese note and to formulate a reply. Admiral Leahy, the President's chief of staff, urged a prompt acceptance of the Japanese proposal for he was convinced that it would be necessary to use the Emperor in effecting the surrender. Byrnes, on the other hand, was unwilling to go so far or to act so quickly. He did not see why the United States should retreat from its insistence upon unconditional surrender, especially since the Allied ultimatum had been lodged against Japan prior to the use of the atomic bomb and to the entry of the Soviet Union into the war. If there were to be any conditions, he wanted the United States to advance them—not Japan. The President agreed and asked the Secretary to come back later with a draft.[5]

Here was no easy task. To accept the Japanese note as it stood would be tantamount to acceding to a demand voiced by a vanquished enemy. Such action by the United States and its Allies would give aid and comfort to the Japanese people over the years to come and would constitute a bad beginning for the program of reform and regeneration to which Japan was to be subjected. At the same time, a flat rejection of the Japanese overture would carry with it the danger of a reinvigorated

[2] In a memorandum dated May 9, 1944, the State Department noted that an outside attempt to abolish the Emperor system would probably prove "ineffective" owing to the "almost fanatical devotion" of the people to their sovereign. Since the Emperor was considered "the source, sacred and inviolable, from which all authority emanated" and since dethroning him would not necessarily abolish the institution, the State Department proposed to retain the Emperor but redelegate to him "only some of his functions." In spite of this memorandum, Secretary Hull felt the Department should not make any "advance commitments" either for or against the Emperor institution. See Hull, *Memoirs*, II, 1589–93.

[3] Stimson (*On Active Service*, 626–27) says that both the President and Secretary of State felt this might happen. Although Mr. Hull's reference (*Memoirs*, II, 1593–94) is very cryptic, he apparently believed that no one could possibly know what effect a promise to preserve the imperial institution would have upon the Japanese. Should the Potsdam Proclamation fail to result in Japan's unconditional surrender in spite of an Allied commitment on the Emperor, the Japanese people might be encouraged to continue the war as a result of the very promise that had been designed to hasten their capitulation. In that event, "terrible political repercussions would follow in the United States."

[4] Present at this conference were the President, the Secretaries of War, Navy, and State, the President's chief of staff, the director of the Office of War Mobilization, and the President's military and naval aides.

[5] See Byrnes, *Speaking Frankly*, 209; Leahy, *I Was There*, 434–35; and Millis (ed.), *The Forrestal Diaries*, 82–85.

determination on the part of Japan's leaders to continue the war in spite of the risk of new and more devastating atomic attacks. Should Byrnes decide on rejection, the administration in Washington might also have to face a highly emotional though none the less effective attack from the American people. There would be a hue and cry to end the fighting at once rather than take the questionable chance that an invasion would produce a wiser and more lasting solution later on. "The Pacific," so this argument would run, "is red enough already with the blood of men who have died on their way to Tokyo."

In spite of these and similar considerations, Secretary Byrnes lost very little time drafting a reply.[6] "From the moment of surrender," he wrote, "the authority of the Emperor and the Japanese Government to rule the state shall be subject to the Supreme Commander[7] of the Allied powers who will take such steps as he deems proper to effectuate the surrender terms."

This implied that the Supreme Commander would oversee and even limit—but would not eradicate—imperial prerogatives and governmental authority. The Supreme Commander would, in effect, become a generalissimo of the same cut as the *shōgun* of old—the men who had ruled while the Emperors had reigned. The Japanese might resent the idea of their Emperor being overshadowed by a foreign occupation commander, but they would rationalize the unavoidable by arguing that, in practice, the Japanese government—and not the sovereign—would receive and execute the Supreme Commander's orders. In any case, the imperial institution—in the broadest sense—would be preserved.

But Mr. Byrnes had to be careful. He had to speak not only for Washington, which was still not united on the issue, but also for London, Moscow, and Chungking. He therefore had to avoid saying anything which might subsequently be interpreted as an American move to redefine or otherwise alter the terms of the Potsdam Proclamation. He thus also warned that "the ultimate form of government of Japan" would be established, as envisaged at Potsdam, "by the freely expressed will of the Japanese people."

Clarification, perhaps even some slight reassurance, but no commitments; this was the Byrnes answer to Japan's first offer to surrender.[8]

While the American Secretary of State was still poring over his draft in Washington, Foreign Commissar Molotov was discussing the

[6] For the text of the Byrnes reply (dispatched August 11) to Japan's offer to surrender, see Appendix E.

[7] "Both the President and the Secretary of State emphasized the fact that they had used the term 'Supreme Commander' rather than 'Supreme Command' so that it would be quite clear that the United States would run this particular business and avoid a situation of composite responsibility such as had plagued us in Germany." See Millis (ed.), *The Forrestal Diaries*, 84 (entry for August 10, 1945).

[8] See Stimson and Bundy, *On Active Service*, 626–27, and Byrnes, *Speaking Frankly*, 209.

Japanese overture with U.S. Ambassador Harriman and British Ambassador Clark-Kerr in Moscow. Molotov frankly stated that Foreign Minister Tōgō had informed Soviet Ambassador Malik that Japan was ready to accept the terms laid down at Potsdam so long as the Emperor remained the sovereign ruler of the nation. To Molotov's mind, this reservation was not in keeping with the unconditional surrender formula, and he therefore was skeptical about the wisdom of acceding to it. While the three men were chatting, George Kennan of the American Embassy arrived with the proposed Byrnes note which had just come in from Washington. On seeing the text, Molotov immediately became noncommittal—saying that his government would give its answer the following day. Since the time factor was obviously very important, Ambassador Harriman remarked that he would have to send a reply to Washington that same evening (August 10). Hoping that Molotov would co-operate, the two ambassadors and Mr. Kennan then left the Kremlin to return to their embassies. At two o'clock in the morning (August 11), Molotov suddenly sent for Harriman and Clark-Kerr to inform them of his government's concurrence.[9] Harriman's subsequent report, as well as favorable responses from Britain and China, arrived in Washington that same day. With admirable haste, the Byrnes note was immediately dispatched to Japan via the Swiss government, the route of communication originally chosen by the Japanese themselves.

The text of the Allied note was also released to the American press and radio, a move which made it possible for the Japanese government to learn the nature of the American reply hours before the official communication could reach Japan. The result was as anticipated. A radio report monitored in Tokyo at 0045 hours, Sunday, August 12,[10] gave Japan's leaders a reasonably reliable basis for preliminary discussion a full eighteen hours in advance of the arrival of Secretary Byrnes's note.

As soon as the Foreign Office staff and the Dōmei News Agency had spelled out the Morse code text of the monitored report, Vice-Minister Matsumoto, Chief Cabinet Secretary Sakomizu, and a few other officials met at the Premier's residence to analyze the Allied answer to Japan's surrender offer. No one was very pleased and several were crestfallen. The reply was considerably more stern and less concrete than their hopes

---

[9] See Deane, *The Strange Alliance*, 277–78. Deane apparently obtained the information presented in the text from Harriman and Kennan, both of whom had been his dinner guests on the evening of August 10.

Mr. Truman was prepared, in the event of a Soviet failure to reply at once, to act without the concurrence of the Soviet Union and to proceed with the occupation of Japan. See Millis (ed.), *The Forrestal Diaries*, 84.

[10] The Foreign Office radio room monitored a San Francisco broadcast of the text of the Byrnes reply at 0045 hours and the Dōmei News Agency picked up a later broadcast. See JFO, *Shūsen shiroku*, Ch. 49 (Rajio chōshu kaitōbun to gaimu tōkyoku no kaishaku oyobi yakubun no kushin).

had led them to suppose it would be. Even Matsumoto, who seems to have been rather optimistic about Allied intentions, held back at first and only later decided to urge the others to help him push the matter through on the basis of the unofficial text. After spending some time exhausting the pros and cons and mapping their strategy, Matsumoto and Sakomizu set out to convince Tōgō and Suzuki that they should fight for a forthright and unequivocal acceptance of the Allied response as drafted by Mr. Byrnes.[11]

In the meantime the staff of the Treaty Bureau and others at the Foreign Office had been wracking their brains to come up with a Japanese translation of the English text that would reflect not just the meaning of the original but, more particularly, *their* interpretation of the meaning. This was an exceedingly bold move, for if they misjudged Byrnes's phrases or if they read too much between the lines the consequences for the nation—to say nothing of for themselves—would be incredibly grave.

This action on the part of the Foreign Office staff was prompted by the assumption that the military would do everything in their power to garble the meaning of the Allied note and would probably also prepare their own slanted translation. To counteract this, the Foreign Office people had to take the chance that their special knowledge of the language of diplomacy would not fail them at this critical juncture. If they, too, came up with essentially the army-navy point of view and consequently rejected the Allied reply, they would be committing Japan to a lethal invasion and the imperial crown and person to the proverbial graveyard of kings. If they followed "common sense" and if they succeeded in dragging the unwilling elements of the government and the Supreme Command along with them, they would be the saviors of both the Throne and the people.

The military, however, were not to be brushed aside lightly. As the morning of August 12 wore on and the Foreign Office translation progressed, General Umezu and Admiral Toyoda hastened to the palace to relay to the Emperor the Supreme Command's opposition to the Byrnes note. Whether they were too excited to be convincing or whether they privately did not agree wholeheartedly with the official line they were espousing is not clear, but the Emperor "seemed to sense" that the chiefs were under pressure from their subordinates and were perfunctory in what they said. He therefore assured the two officers that the matter would be studied in detail once the official note had arrived.[12]

---

[11] See *Statements*: Matsumoto #61451 and the JFO reference in the preceding footnote.
[12] See *Statements*: Hasunuma #58225 and Hoshina #61978; JFO, *Shūsen shiroku*, Ch. 50 (Suzuki shushō no saishōkairon to Tōgō gaishō no kushin). When he heard about the audience, Navy Minister Yonai angrily demanded an explanation from Chief of Staff Toyoda and Vice-Chief Ōnishi.

Later that same morning, after having obtained imperial support for the interpretation sponsored by his staff,[13] Foreign Minister Tōgō called on Marquis Kido to discuss all that had happened since their last meeting the day before. He mentioned his fear that the national polity advocates would take exception to the Allied note—especially to the assertion that the freely expressed will of the people would determine the ultimate form of Japan's government. At the same time, Tōgō stressed his personal belief that the Allies were not demanding a sweeping change in the national polity and that the Emperor's position, although subject to some modification, would for all practical purposes remain secure. Unless Japan were prepared to see her peace efforts collapse, Tōgō declared, she should accept the Potsdam Proclamation, as clarified by the Byrnes rider, without putting forth any new conditions.[14]

But as Tōgō soon learned, this view—sound and sensible though it was—failed to take full account of the emotions and cross-purposes playing havoc with the minds of the men on whom the decision of war or peace rested. At an extraordinary meeting of the cabinet ministers held on the afternoon of August 12, Tōgō immediately became hopelessly involved not only with War Minister Anami, a natural opponent, but also with the reluctant and procrastinating Suzuki. Earlier in the day Anami and Baron Hiranuma (the president of the Privy Council) had succeeded in convincing the Premier that the Allied reply was unacceptable from the standpoint of maintaining the national polity. At the cabinet meeting in question, Anami not only pushed this line of argument but also reiterated two of the conditions which had been shelved as a result of the imperial conference decision of August 9/10—the conditions pertaining to disarmament and to the occupation of Japan proper. In reply, Tōgō heatedly declared that to add further stipulations would be "highly improper" and would merely lead the Allies to believe that Japan intended to break off the negotiations. Tōgō insisted that to revive questions which had already been resolved by an imperial decision was to show disrespect for that decision and that to advocate a continuation of the war by raising issues which would produce a breakdown in the negotiations was "to act in a manner contrary to reason."[15]

---

[13] The Emperor agreed with the Foreign Office recommendation to accept the Allied position and personally asked Tōgō to convey his wishes to the Premier. This was particularly gratifying to Tōgō who had already obtained the concurrence of Navy Minister Yonai and who now felt that Suzuki, frequently prone to vacillation, would naturally fall into line—a development which would give him (Tōgō) the advantage he needed in the cabinet and Supreme Council deliberations which were to follow. (As the text will show, Tōgō was indulging in overoptimism.) See the JFO reference in the preceding footnote.

[14] See Kido, "Nikki," 8/12/45; IMTFE: Kido, 31184; Tōgō, 35789; *Statements:* Matsumoto #61451 and Tōgō #50304; JFO, *Shūsen shiroku*, Ch. 50 (Suzuki shushō no saishōkairon to Tōgō gaishō no kushin).

[15] See *Statements:* Tōgō #50304 and Hiranuma #55127; IMTFE: Kido, 31184–85; and the JFO reference in the preceding footnote.

Shortly after he delivered this blast, Tōgō withdrew momentarily from the conference room in order to phone Vice Foreign Minister Matsumoto—possibly hoping that the latter would be able to supply him with additional arguments. Upon hearing that the outlook was extremely bad, Matsumoto strongly urged his chief to have the meeting adjourned and to return to the Foreign Office at once. As Matsumoto saw it, fighting the problem any more that day would accomplish nothing and might even serve to strengthen the opposition.

Upon re-entering the conference chamber, Tōgō found Suzuki forcefully echoing the Anami-Hiranuma view to which he had been exposed earlier in the day. The Allied reply, according to Suzuki, was unsatisfactory because it did not guarantee the preservation of Japan's polity. Furthermore, disarmament by the enemy was unbearable for a military man. Under the circumstances there was only one thing to do. Japan must seek clarification from the Allies. If they refused to concede, there would be no other way than to fight it out.

Had this been a full-dress cabinet meeting instead of an extraordinary round-table conference, Suzuki's remarks could well have been fatal. Fortunately, Tōgō was able to turn the situation to his own advantage. The Premier's remarks, he countered, were worthy of careful consideration, but at the same time Japan should not continue the war irresponsibly without paying any attention to its outcome. Unless there were some prospect of victory, Japan should negotiate for peace. "I therefore propose," he concluded, "that the meeting be adjourned and that the question be reopened after the official communication from the Allies has been received."[16] The others agreed, and the danger of a complete reversal was averted—at least for the time being.

In spite of this momentary victory, Tōgō was beside himself with anger and frustration. He cornered Suzuki in a side room and with the bluntness for which he was equally noted and disliked he declared that he could not possibly understand why the Premier—of all people—was taking such an attitude especially when the Emperor was of the opinion that the war could not go on. To this, Tōgō added a significant and extraordinary "threat": "If you persist in this attitude, I may have to report independently to the Throne."[17] What Tōgō meant but did not say was that he would not hesitate to appeal to the Emperor to "command" Suzuki to follow the path of reason.

At the same time, Tōgō realized that "serious complications" might result if he carried out his threat. He therefore decided to present the problem to Kido in the hope that the Lord Keeper of the Privy Seal could iron out the difficulties without implicating the Emperor and could

[16] Tōgō's move to have the cabinet session adjourned was not based on any expectation that the formal note would contain something new but rather was prompted by Suzuki's vacillation (and the unfavorable alignment which naturally resulted).

[17] See *Statements*: Matsumoto #61451, Tōgō #50304 and #54562; Kido, "Nikki," 8/12/45; and the JFO reference in footnote 14 above.

thereby close up the ranks of the end-the-war party. The Privy Seal, who had his own very definite ideas about what should be done and how it should be done, was thus given an opportunity to bring his powerful influence to bear.

Kido knew full well that the government could not listen to everyone. Japan would either have to forge ahead on the basis of the Foreign Office interpretation or face the possibility of disaster. It was therefore mandatory that the government be forced to accept the Allied reply; to retreat at this point by attempting to prolong or broaden the negotiations would be to court the most fearful consequences.

Kido had already tried, earlier in the afternoon, to persuade Baron Hiranuma that the "national polity" group should place its confidence in the views expressed by the officials responsible for the conduct of foreign affairs. Undaunted by his failure to impress the Baron, Kido now turned his attention to Suzuki and found, both to his surprise and to his relief, that the Premier was more confused than adamant.[18] Kido presented all of the arguments at his command and then concluded with an appeal which could scarcely have failed to touch the old admiral's heart. "If we do not accept the Allied position now," Kido said, "we will be sacrificing hundreds of thousands of innocent people to the continued ravages of war. If we do accept and internal upheaval ensues, we shall only have to lay down our own lives. Furthermore, it is *His Majesty's wish* that we advance on the basis of the views held by the Foreign Minister."

Suzuki acquiesced and Kido, a load off his shoulders, informed Tōgō that all was well.[19]

Thus, by the evening of August 12, the atmosphere had cleared somewhat. Tōgō had managed to postpone the final decision until after the receipt of the official note, Kido had succeeded in bringing Suzuki back into line, and the Emperor had resisted, as best he could, the pressure of those who sought to persuade him to reverse his earlier decision. The sovereign had also called an imperial family council and the princes of the blood had all pledged their united assistance and support.[20] The

---

[18] Matsumoto called on Suzuki (prior to the latter's conversation with Kido) in an effort to convince the Premier that the Allied reply did not endanger the national polity. He urged Suzuki to bring his "great statesmanship" to bear and to accept the Allied note as it stood. Suzuki indicated that he was in sympathy with Matsumoto's views but found himself in a very difficult position because of the strong opposition voiced by Anami, Hiranuma, and others. See JFO, *Shūsen shiroku*, Ch. 50 (Suzuki shushō no saishōkairon to Tōgō gaishō no kushin) and *Statements*: Matsumoto #61451.

[19] See IMTFE: Kido, 31184–87; Kido, "Nikki," 8/12/45; *Statements*: Tōgō #50304 and #54562; and the JFO reference in the preceding footnote.

[20] See Kido, "Nikki," 8/12/45; JFO, *Shūsen shiroku*, Ch. 51 (Kōzoku kaigi to Mikasa no miya); and IMTFE: Kido, 31187. The latter reference contains a phrase, "and [the Emperor] explained to them [the princes of the blood] the object of his decision, just taken," which does not appear in the Japanese text of the affidavit being quoted.

efforts of the military to enroll the services of two of the Emperor's brothers, Takamatsu and Mikasa, had failed. The brothers, in fact, had become a rallying point for the end-the-war party and an elusive thorn in the side of the fanatics.

Although Tōgō had left the cabinet meeting half intending to write out his resignation, the remonstrances of Vice-Minister Matsumoto and Kido's success with Suzuki induced him to continue the struggle. At Matsumoto's urging, Tōgō went home for the night nursing a rather slim hope that the new day would see the emergence of a unanimous decision to end the war on the basis of the controversial, yet fundamental, Potsdam Proclamation as qualified by the Byrnes reply.

As soon as Tōgō had left, Vice-Minister Matsumoto telephoned the chief of the Foreign Office Telegraph Section and gave him very precise instructions: In the event that the official communication arrived that evening, the Telegraph Section was to record the date and time of arrival as being that of the following morning! A few minutes later, *at 6:40 p.m., August 12*, the cable containing the Allied note reached Tokyo, and the chief of the Telegraph Section, in obedience to Matsumoto's orders, recorded the arrival as *"7:40 a.m., August 13."* This move—until recently known only to a handful of people within the Foreign Office—had one primary purpose: to provide a breathing spell during which the frayed tempers of August 12 could recover equanimity and the overworked Foreign Office staff could devise new arguments in support of the interpretation which had already been presented on the basis of the possibly inaccurate text culled from the Morse code broadcasts emanating from San Francisco and Washington.[21]

One of the issues in question was what might be called the case of small *g* versus capital *G*—a rather unusual problem of language. At the time of the drafting of the Allied reply to the Japanese note of August 10, Secretary Byrnes had used the phrase, "the ultimate form of government of Japan," and this—as already noted—had created

---

[21] See *Statements:* Matsumoto #61451 and Tōgō #54562; JFO, *Shūsen shiroku*, Ch. 52 (Rengōkoku kaitōbun ni kan suru zai Suisu Kase kōshi oyobi zai Suēden Okamoto kōshi no kōden sono ta). (Kase, *Journey to the Missouri*, 241, is in error in stating that the formal American reply arrived in Tokyo "early on the morning of August 13.")

Matsumoto suggests that he discussed the question of falsifying the date and time of arrival of the official communication with Tōgō and obtained his concurrence, but the latter does not recall anything ever having been said to him about the matter. The author saw the original transcript with the correct date and time blacked out and the new date and time (7:40 A.M., August 13) written in. When Tōgō was told of this document in November 1949, he agreed that it must be correct but said that at the time in question his understanding had been that the official communication 'had not arrived until the morning of August 13. (Since clean copies of the original transcript were made on the night of August 12, the documents used on August 13 bore no indication of any changes having been made.)

immediate opposition because of the "freely expressed will of the people" proviso with which it was linked. In deciphering the Morse code text, the Foreign Office radio room had copied out the phrase exactly as Byrnes had written it, but by the time the Dōmei News Agency had forwarded its version, the word "government" had taken on a new aspect; the small *g* had become a capita*l G*. Not only that, but when all the versions had been collected and the official communication as transmitted by Minister Kase in Switzerland had been received, it was found that in one of the documents a "the" had crept into the text so that the phrase read, "the ultimate form of *the Government* of Japan." This would have had no significance whatsoever had it not been for one fundamental problem: did the term "government" as used by Mr. Byrnes include the imperial institution and His Majesty's prerogatives as a sovereign ruler or did it refer simply to the administrative and legislative organs of the state? Did the small *g* connote the one and the capital *G* the other or did neither imply any special meaning at all? And just how did "the" fit into the picture?

So far as the experts at the Foreign Office could tell, "government" seemed to refer to the form of polity (*kokutai*) and to include the question of retaining or abolishing Japan's imperial system. "Government" or "the Government" seemed to be more limited in scope and to refer only to the administration in power (*seifu*) without any connection with the Throne.

The Potsdam Proclamation, which might have been expected to throw some light upon the matter, was actually no help at all. At one point, the phrase, "the Japanese Government," appeared prominently but at another and equally essential point the Potsdam text read: "The occupying forces . . . shall be withdrawn . . . as soon as . . . there has been established in accordance with the freely expressed will of the Japanese people a peacefully inclined and responsible government." And the very next paragraph began, "We call upon the government of Japan . . ."

After considerable discussion, the experts at length agreed to assume that "government," regardless of the *g* and "the" factors, did not include the Emperor. If they later found out that they were wrong, they would count on the loyalty of the people to the traditions of the past to preserve and maintain the imperial institution. This was, to say the least, an immensely wise choice of alternatives.[22]

From August 9 onward, posters had appeared in the tram stations and elsewhere throughout Tokyo denouncing Marquis Kido and others

---

[22] See the JFO reference cited in the preceding footnote and also Ch. 49 (Rajio chōshu kaitōbun to gaimu tōkyoku no kaishaku oyobi yakubun no kushin). The text is also based on discussions with Mr. Kurihara of the Foreign Office and on an interview with Mr. Sakomizu, Tokyo, April 6, 1952.

of the peace party as traitors who should be killed on sight. "Down with BADOGLIO!" the posters proclaimed. "Kill Lord Keeper of the Privy Seal KIDO!"[23] Since he was now subject to call by the Emperor at any time, day or night, and since to venture out was to take his life in his hands, Kido decided to await developments in his suite of rooms at the Imperial Household Ministry, situated well within the palace moat. There, at 7:10 on the morning of August 13, he received his first caller of the day, General Anami.[24]

In spite of the fact that Anami had been strenuously opposing the end-the-war movement, Kido had not changed his mind about the general. The Privy Seal looked upon Anami as an intelligent officer who, unlike so many of his fellows, was not imbued with absurd notions. Unfortunately, the War Minister was surrounded by army zealots, and this—Kido reasoned—accounted for much that he did and said. Kido was thus quite prepared for what was coming and was equally ready to counter whatever Anami might say with a forthright answer of his own— an approach which would have been impossible had Kido not had such great respect for the War Minister's character.

With the amenities over, Anami launched into a dismal monologue centering around the situation facing the nation. Japan would be doomed, he declared, if the cabinet accepted the Allied reply as it stood. Establishing the ultimate form of government by the freely expressed will of the people would mean the end of the national polity.[25] So far as he was concerned, an attitude of pessimism had never yielded good results in any war. If Japan were to make one last effort, it would not be impossible to end the fighting on more advantageous terms. The Emperor should therefore reconsider his decision so that the military could conduct a decisive battle in the homeland.

When Anami had finished, Kido promptly disagreed. As Lord Keeper of the Privy Seal he understood clearly that there was no room for any but one decision, and *that* decision had already received His Majesty's sanction. He therefore pointed out to Anami that the persons responsible for the conduct of foreign affairs had found nothing in the Allied reply that could be considered inconsistent with the aspirations

[23] See the Kido citations in footnote 24 below. For other evidence pointing to the danger of an outbreak of violence, see IMTFE: Def. Doc. 3049, *Machimura Aff.*, J text (rejected: 38935–37); *Statements:* Tōgō #50304, Sakomizu 5/3/49, and Toyoda #61340.

[24] See Kido, "Nikki," 8/12–13/45; IMTFE: Kido, 31187–88; JFO, *Shūsen shiroku*, Ch. 53 (Rengōkoku kaitōbun wo meguru saikō sensō shidō kaigi kōseiin kaigi to kakugi); *Statements:* Kido #61541 and #61476.

[25] It is doubtful that Anami thought the masses, if given the chance, would reject the imperial institution. It is probable, however, that he was thinking along the same lines as Hiranuma, who apparently believed that subversive elements might be encouraged (possibly by the Allies) to attempt to overthrow Japan's monarchial government on the basis of the "freely expressed will" clause.

of the Japanese government. They had not even objected to the clause to which Anami was taking exception. In view of the prevailing situation, Japan had no other choice than to accept. If the government were to reject the Allied note, Japan would find it difficult to support her action with convincing reasons. The Allies would be at a loss to understand why Japan had changed her mind at the last moment. Rejection would lead to criticism of the Emperor: the whole world would look upon His Majesty as either a fool or a madman. It would be unbearable to have the Emperor insulted in such a way. "No," Kido concluded, "the course we must follow is clear. We must abide by the wishes of His Majesty. We must accept the Allied reply in its present form."[26]

The discussions which followed Anami's tête-à-tête with Kido—discussions in which Anami played a leading role—were no less stubborn, no less fated to impasse, than were any of the earlier meetings of Japan's ruling elite. From about nine o'clock in the morning of August 13 until midafternoon,[27] the Big Six conferred in closed session—mired down, as before, in an inconclusive tug of war.

No matter how long or earnestly he argued, Foreign Minister Tōgō could not budge the opposition. Anami and his lieutenants, Umezu and Toyoda, simply would not, or could not, agree to the Foreign Office interpretation. The favorable response of the director of the Bureau of Legislation who had been especially called in to render an opinion on the legal aspects of the question proved of no avail. Anami merely parried with the adverse arguments of another "authority."[28] It was the

[26] See IMTFE: Kido, 31188–89; Kido, "Nikki," 8/13/45; *Statements*: Kido #61476, Sakomizu 5/3/49, Tōgō #50304; and JFO, *Shūsen shiroku*, Ch. 53 (Rengōkoku kaitōbun wo meguru saikō sensō shidō kaigi kōseiin kaigi to kakugi). Not quite forty-eight hours after his talk with Kido, Anami committed suicide. When asked about the events described above, Kido remarked, ". . . judging from what I have mentioned, I can assure you that in his heart, he [Anami] did not oppose peace." Although the time reference is not clear, see also *Statements*: Hayashi #61436.

[27] About an hour after the Big Six began their debate, a message was delivered advising General Umezu and Admiral Toyoda that their presence was desired at the palace. As soon as the two chiefs of staff were ushered into His Majesty's chamber, the Emperor began to question them on the Supreme Command's intentions with respect to military operations. Drawing their attention to the fact that diplomatic negotiations for a termination of the war were then in progress, the Emperor strongly implied that his own desire was to have as little fighting take place as possible until a decision had been reached. In reply, Umezu promised that the Supreme Command would not undertake any positive or aggressive action and that in the event of an enemy attack the Supreme Command would limit its counteractivity to passive defense—and the latter, only if absolutely necessary. The Emperor indicated his satisfaction, and the two chiefs returned to the meeting. See Toyoda, *Saigo no teikoku kaigun*, 215–16; *Statements*: Toyoda #57670; and JFO, *Shūsen shiroku*, Ch. 53 (Rengōkoku kaitōbun wo meguru saikō sensō shidō kaigi kōseiin kaigi to kakugi).

[28] See the JFO reference in the preceding footnote. Anami's "authority" is said to have been Professor Hiraizumi, a man whose philosophy earned him many disciples within military circles in general and the younger officer group in particular.

same story all over again. There was only one point of agreement: the necessity of safeguarding and preserving the national polity. So far as the steps to achieve that end were concerned, there had never been any meeting of minds and there apparently was never going to be any.

Although Tōgō was aided by Suzuki's now open support and by Navy Minister Yonai's silent endorsement of an immediate termination of the war on the basis of the Byrnes note, the Foreign Minister's cause showed little promise of progressing. Tōgō's growing feeling of hopelessness was further magnified by the views contained in an urgent cable which had arrived at the Foreign Office during the preceding night. Dispatched by Suemasa Okamoto, Japan's Minister in Stockholm, the cable described the Byrnes note as a great diplomatic victory for the United States (and, by inference, for Japan as well). America's allies, Okamoto advised, had not been prone to support Washington's position on the Emperor and the imperial institution. Any further inquiries or representations from Japan would not only result in greater war casualties and a deeper Soviet penetration of the Far East (to obtain a lion's share of the spoils) but would actually wreck the negotiations altogether.[29] What Okamoto said in his cable made sense, and Tōgō and his Foreign Office staff knew it all too well. Their problem lay not in deciding what to do but in determining the best way of doing it. And always, there was the question of the other side and the pressing need to obtain its concurrence and support.

When Tōgō tried to interpret the phrase "subject to" as conveying the meaning of "restricted by" rather than of "subordinate to," Admiral Toyoda made it clear that he could not agree. Having spent some time studying and dissecting the Allied response, the navy chief had reached the conclusion that His Majesty would be permitted to function only at the order or under the direction of the Supreme Commander. Toyoda felt that it was unnecessary for the Allies to implicate the Emperor in this way. The Supreme Commander could give his orders to the Japanese government. In case such orders fell within the Emperor's prerogatives as a sovereign ruler, the government could act in the manner required after it had obtained the Emperor's sanction. Toyoda realized that the Allies might reject such a stand on Japan's part, but he felt that now was the time to speak up since there might not be another opportunity to do so.

Toyoda was also disturbed over the "freely expressed will of the people" clause, for he looked upon such an idea as being incompatible with Japan's imperial structure and as amounting to a rejection of Japan's position with respect to her willingness to surrender. He insisted that the government should not hedge on its true beliefs but should

[29] See *Statements*: Matsumoto #61451 and Okamoto #61477; JFO, *Shūsen shiroku*, Ch. 52 (Rengōkoku kaitōbun ni kan suru zai Suisu Kase kōshi oyobi zai Suēden Okamoto kōshi no kōden sono ta).

make its views known to the Allies so that there would be no doubt about the future status of the Throne.

This was too much for Tōgō. If the government were to accept Toyoda's position, he declared, the enemy would leave Japan to her fate. Not only that, but if the military did not have confidence in their ability to defeat the invaders in the decisive battle for the homeland they should not be so bold as to propose all sorts of conditions and stipulations. But Toyoda remained adamant and continued to emphasize that the Byrnes note was unacceptable and that Japan should not hide her true thoughts and beliefs. His whole argument rested on the claim that since Japan had already shown her desire to end the war the Allies would not choose to fight rather than to negotiate simply because Japan sought further clarification and explicit guarantees.[30]

In this way the Big Six—Japan's "inner war cabinet"—once again became caught in a blind alley. Realizing that further discussion was pointless, the councilors voted to adjourn for the time being so as to permit the cabinet to try its hand at reaching agreement. Although this decision temporarily deprived Anami of the support furnished by Toyoda and Umezu, the absence of the two chiefs did not leave the War Minister without allies since both the Justice Minister and the Minister for Home Affairs supported the military's contentions. Thus, when Premier Suzuki pressed his cabinet colleagues for a clear statement of views, he was still unable to isolate Anami. Although twelve ministers sided with Tōgō's insistence upon an immediate acceptance of the Byrnes note, three opposed such a move, and one could not make up his mind what to do. Suzuki then took the floor, summarily reversed the stand he had assumed on August 12, and straightforwardly revealed his new intentions. When he had first seen the Byrnes note, he said, he had considered it unsatisfactory and had resolved to burn the nation's bridges behind Japan's valiant defenders. Upon reading the note over and over again, however, he had come to the conclusion that the Allies had not drafted their reply with any malicious purpose in mind. The heart of His Majesty, Suzuki declared, was seeking only one thing: the termination of the war and the restoration of peace. Since it was his desire, as Premier, to bow to the imperial will, he would report on what had taken place at the cabinet meeting and would once again request His Majesty's decision.[31]

In ordinary times a protracted impasse of the type the government had been experiencing for the past few days would have led to the

---

[30] See Toyoda, *Saigo no teikoku kaigun*, 216–19; USSBS, *Interrogations*, II, Toyoda, 322; USSBS, *Japan's Struggle to End the War*, 9; *Statements*: Toyoda #61340; JFO, *Shūsen shiroku*, Ch. 53 (Rengōkoku kaitōbun wo meguru saikō sensō shidō kaigi kōseiin kaigi to kakugi) ; IMTFE: Tōgō, 35789–90, and Sakomizu, 35609–10.

[31] See the JFO reference cited in the preceding footnote.

resignation of either the Premier or the War Minister, and this, in turn, would have brought the cabinet tumbling down. A new Premier would then have been designated and the army would have been asked to supply a War Minister. This the army would have done only if the candidate for the premiership and the men he proposed to include in his cabinet were army supporters who would vote the military ticket. If the army had any suspicion that the new cabinet might follow in the footsteps of the old, it would not name a War Minister until the "subversive" elements in the new formation had been replaced by men on whom the militarists could rely.

In view of the record of opposition between the army and the civilian members of the Suzuki Cabinet, why did the army permit the cabinet to continue in office? Why didn't the army withdraw War Minister Anami and thus force the formation of a new and more docile cabinet?

Many members of the government, including the representatives of the military, felt that the Suzuki Cabinet should be the "last" cabinet. Frequent changes during wartime robbed the government of the continuity it needed to be effective. The Suzuki Cabinet was the third wartime cabinet. Another change would be interpreted by the Allies as further evidence of Japan's inability to cope with a rapidly deteriorating situation. A cabinet shuffle would also be portrayed in the light of divided leadership. From a diplomatic and psychological point of view, such interpretations were highly undesirable.

Anami, although a stubborn opponent of the end-the-war party, was personally of a far different caliber from many of his predecessors. He was "a dignified, conscientious administrator." All through the many sessions of vigorous debate, he "never lost his temper . . . never resorted to ungentlemanly behavior, but . . . remained straightforward and courteous to the end."[32] Men who remembered the sharp outbursts of Tōjō could appreciate a man of Anami's character.

In spite of the fact that he was not a fanatic, Anami found it impossible to admit defeat. From the moment he became War Minister until the day he cut short his service, his determination to prosecute the war until favorable terms could be won remained constant. Even in the face of disaster, he continued to believe, and therefore to insist, that Japan could capture an honorable peace if only she had the courage to stand up to the Allies. Like Toyoda, he wanted the diplomats to propose sweeping reservations. If they would not do this, he and the men he commanded would fight with the sword. Although he was not confident of a decisive victory, he believed that Japan's military forces could inflict such telling damage upon the invading enemy that the Allies would be

---

[32] Kawai MS: "Japan's Struggle to Surrender," 2 and 68–69. For remarks in a similar vein, see *Statements*: Arao #54226, Sakomizu 5/3/49, Hayashi #61436, and Shimomura #57668. Shimomura has noted that Anami's attitude toward Suzuki was "warm and courteous"—in marked contrast to Tōjō's arrogance toward Konoye.

willing to tone down their demands for the sake of peace.[33] The best guides to Anami's thinking are the following catch phrases which he used to inspire his own determination and that of the men around him:

"A road to success will somehow be revealed to us if we carry on with strong determination."

"Simplicity represents strength."

"Morality is fighting power."

By the time Anami realized that tenacity of purpose and pure will power had lost their magic touch, Japan's situation had deteriorated so far that his withdrawal from the cabinet had become virtually impossible. The events which occurred after August 9 would have made any resignation criminal. All Anami could do then was to hold his ground and fight on.[34]

Although their positions are perhaps less clear, the two chiefs of staff, Umezu for the army and Toyoda for the navy, seem generally to have been motivated by the same reasoning to which Anami was committed. These men were not fools; they were not blind; and they were not sadists. They were victims of their own convictions and captives of a group of fanatics who may rightly be castigated for their ignorance, stupidity, and folly. The latter were the men responsible for the dissension which continually harassed the efforts of the ruling elite to reach a valid and lasting decision. Suzuki's August 13 announcement of his intention to report the cabinet impasse to the Throne made the danger of an army coup imminent. Once again the fate of the nation lay in a precarious balance with survival possible only if the end-the-war cadre could act before the fanatics learned the whole truth.

Under the circumstances, Chief Cabinet Secretary Sakomizu hastened to obtain the signatures of the army and navy chiefs of staff—the usual prerequisite for an imperial conference. In spite of their bitter

---

[33] During the summer of 1945 Anami told his military secretary (Colonel Matsutani) that he was considering the question of seeking peace but that he would not agree to any such stand as the Tokugawa Shogunate had adopted in yielding unconditionally to American pressure. (*Statements*: Matsutani #54327.)

[34] An army decision to withdraw the War Minister from the Suzuki Cabinet would normally have been made by the Big Three (which included Anami himself). Pressure for his removal could have been exerted by the rank and file had they known what was going on. By the time they found out, it was too late. On the question of a resignation by Anami, see *Statements*: Sakomizu 5/3/49, Hayashi #61436, Inaba #57692, Kido #61476, Takeshita #50025-A, and Tōgō #50304.

Premier Suzuki has been quoted as follows: "War Minister ANAMI faithfully complied with the Cabinet policy. The Cabinet would have collapsed immediately had the War Minister submitted his resignation. Because ANAMI refrained from submitting his resignation, the Suzuki Cabinet was able to attain its major goal, namely, war's termination. For this, I express my gratitude to the War Minister." See *Statements*: Ikeda #54479 (ATIS transl.). The remarks quoted here were made by Suzuki following Anami's suicide.

experience with the petition with which they had been "tricked" on August 9, both Umezu and Toyoda signed—but not without first wringing a firm promise from Sakomizu that the petition would not be used without their prior consent.[35]

Convinced that nothing more would happen until the following morning, the two chiefs conferred briefly and then sent word to Foreign Minister Tōgō that they would like to discuss the question of the day with him—in private. From nine until after eleven o'clock that evening (August 13), the three contenders rehashed the arguments of the preceding twelve hours but said nothing which they had not already voiced before. As they were about to adjourn, Vice-Chief of the Naval General Staff Ōnishi, the instigator of the *kamikaze* attacks, unexpectedly appeared on the scene. With tears in his eyes, the "father" of the suicide corps made a fantastic plea: "Let us formulate a plan for certain victory, obtain the Emperor's sanction, and throw ourselves into bringing the plan to realization. If we are prepared to sacrifice 20,000,000 Japanese lives in a special attack [*kamikaze*] effort, victory shall be ours!" Foreign Minister Tōgō countered with the obvious arguments, and the meeting then broke up.[36]

Although Lord Keeper of the Privy Seal Kido was hourly maintaining a careful check upon the uneasy pulse of the nation, there was little that he could do so long as the cabinet and Supreme Council continued to discuss the policy to be adopted in the crisis facing Japan. Only if the regular machinery of government broke down would it be possible for the Privy Seal to bring his influence to bear in the same way that he had during the uncertain period preceding the imperial conference of August 9. Suzuki's announcement just prior to the cabinet adjournment on the evening of August 13 convinced Kido that the last act was only hours away. Unfortunately, the plot of this final act and its execution were still open to question.

Early the next morning, August 14, one of the Emperor's chamberlains handed the Privy Seal an American propaganda leaflet giving the verbatim text, in Japanese, of the government's note of acceptance of August 10 and of the Byrnes reply of August 11. One look caused Kido "to be stricken with consternation."[37]

---

[35] See Toyoda, *Saigo no teikoku kaigun*, 219–20.

[36] See *Statements*: Tōgō #50304 and JFO, *Shūsen shiroku*, Ch. 53 (Rengōkoku kaitōbun wo meguru saikō sensō shidō kaigi kōseiin kaigi to kakugi). Toyoda and others have since confused this private session with a so-called Supreme Council meeting. The Supreme Council met only once on August 13—not twice.

Vice-Chief Ōnishi committed suicide on August 16, the day following the imperial broadcast announcing Japan's surrender.

[37] See Kido, "Nikki," 8/14/45; IMTFE: Kido, 31189–90; and *Statements*: Kido #61541. For the Japanese text of the Allied leaflet, see JFO, *Shūsen shiroku*, Ch. 51 (Kōzoku kaigi to Mikasa no miya); for the English translation of the same leaflet,

During the preceding three days both the army and the navy had stiffened their attitude toward the peace negotiations. Now here, just at this critical moment, were Allied leaflets invading Japan from the skies above—destroying the very secrecy which the government had striven to maintain with respect to the negotiations. Once the leaflets slithered into the hands of Japanese servicemen stationed throughout the country a great deal of confusion and indignation would result. Although many would probably dismiss the whole affair as clever enemy propaganda, it was possible that a significantly large number of soldiers (and civilians) would place their trust in the leaflets, especially since earlier leaflets, listing cities which were next in line to be bombed, had always forecast the actual fact. The question of whether Japan should now accept or reject the Allied reply would inevitably produce tensions which could easily culminate in a conflagration of death and destruction within the capital itself. Kido realized at once that the government would have to move quickly if it were to control this new situation. Failing an immediate decision within the inner councils of the state, all who had advocated a termination of the war would be hounded to their deaths, the die-hards would be vaulted into the driver's seat, and the nation, with its imperial institution, would be committed to a course which could only lead to final and irrevocable ruin.

Within minutes after reading the Allied leaflet, Kido was closeted with the Emperor, urging His Majesty to summon an imperial conference so as to inform the Supreme Councilors and cabinet ministers of his unshakable desire for an immediate termination of the war. The Emperor fully grasped the new elements in the situation and ordered Kido to make the necessary arrangements with the Premier.

It so happened that Suzuki had arrived at the palace while Kido was in audience and had patiently waited for the Privy Seal to emerge. When Kido asked him if he had made arrangements for another meeting of the Supreme Council, "a harried expression" flitted across Suzuki's face and he replied, "I am having a hard time. The army wants me to wait until 1300 hours while the navy wants me to postpone the meeting indefinitely." Kido hurriedly briefed Suzuki on all that had happened and the two then presented themselves before His Majesty.

This audience, which lasted twelve minutes, produced the desired result. The Emperor agreed to summon an imperial conference. In the event of continued deadlock, His Majesty would "command" the cabinet to accept the Byrnes note as it stood and to prepare an imperial rescript embodying this decision.[38]

---

see U.S. Navy Dept., *Psychological Warfare*, Supplement No. 2 (August 15, 1945), Leaflet #2117.

[38] See Kido, "Nikki," 8/14/45; IMTFE: Kido, 31189–93; *Statements*: Kido #61541, Sakomizu #62050; and JFO, *Shūsen shiroku*, Ch. 54 (Dai nikai gozen kaigi

At approximately 10:50 that morning, August 14, the Emperor, accompanied by the chief aide-de-camp, walked into the air raid shelter where the first imperial conference had been held five days before and took his place in front of a hushed audience composed of cabinet ministers, Supreme Councilors, and other high officials of state.[39] The meeting was formally opened by Suzuki with the announcement that the conference had been called by His Majesty so that the Allied reply could be considered in his presence and so that those who dissented from the opinions of the majority could express their views. Outlining what had taken place the day before at the Supreme Council and cabinet sessions, Suzuki apologized to His Majesty for the cabinet's inability to present a unanimous decision. Then, turning to the three leading dissenters (Anami, Umezu, and Toyoda) whom he had not actually mentioned by name, Suzuki called upon them to rise and state their case so that His Majesty could decide the issue which the cabinet and the Supreme Council had been unable to resolve.[40]

Umezu spoke first, followed by Toyoda and Anami. No one seems to remember very much of what the two generals said since they spoke very briefly, but Toyoda, the admiral without a fleet, repeated his earlier arguments at some length. All three men were in a considerably excited frame of mind and found it difficult to control their emotions.[41] When the last word had been said—and it was indeed their last—the Emperor began to speak:

I have listened carefully to each of the arguments presented in opposition to the view that Japan should accept the Allied reply as it stands without further clarification or modification, but my own thoughts have not undergone any change. I have surveyed the conditions prevailing in Japan and in the world at large, and it is my belief that a continuation of the war promises nothing but additional destruction. I have studied the terms of the Allied reply and have concluded that they constitute a virtually complete acknowledgment of the position we maintained in the note dispatched several days ago. In short, I consider the reply to be acceptable.

I realize that there are those of you who distrust the intentions of the Allies. This is, of course, quite natural, but to my mind the Allied reply is evidence of the peaceful and friendly intentions of the enemy. The faith and resolution of this nation as a whole, therefore, are factors of paramount importance.

---

to kakugi kettei). Kido's first audience with the Emperor was from 8:30 to 8:35 A.M. The Kido-Suzuki audience lasted from 8:40 to 8:52 A.M.

Shortly before the imperial conference, the Emperor summoned Field Marshals Sugiyama and Hata and Fleet Admiral Nagano and "commanded" (requested) their wholehearted support with respect to the termination of the war.

[39] See JFO, *Shūsen shiroku*, Ch. 54 (Dai nikai gozen kaigi to kakugi kettei).

[40] See Toyoda, *Saigo no teikoku kaigun*, 220–22; *Statements:* Toyoda #61340, Hasunuma #58225, Tōgō #50304; Shimomura, "The Memoirs of Mr. Shimomura at the Imperial Council, 14 August 1945" (MS); and the JFO citation in the preceding footnote. The text is also based on material obtained from Hisatsune Sakomizu during an interview in Tokyo, April 6, 1952.

[41] See Toyoda, *Saigo no teikoku kaigun*, 220–22 and 224.

I appreciate how difficult it will be for the officers and men of the army and navy to surrender their arms to the enemy and to see their homeland occupied. Indeed, it is difficult for me to issue the order making this necessary and to deliver so many of my trusted servants into the hands of the Allied authorities by whom they will be accused of being war criminals. In spite of these feelings, so difficult to bear, I can not endure the thought of letting my people suffer any longer. A continuation of the war would bring death to tens, perhaps even hundreds, of thousands of persons. The whole nation would be reduced to ashes. How then could I carry on the wishes of my imperial ancestors?

The decision I have reached is akin to the one forced upon my Grandfather, the Emperor Meiji, at the time of the Triple Intervention. As he endured the unendurable, so shall I, and so must you.

It is my desire that you, my Ministers of State, accede to my wishes and forthwith accept the Allied reply. In order that the people may know of my decision, I request you to prepare at once an imperial rescript so that I may broadcast to the nation. Finally, I call upon each and every one of you to exert himself to the utmost so that we may meet the trying days which lie ahead.[42]

Once again the Emperor had committed himself, only this time his words were final.[43]

While the cabinet wrangled over the content and phraseology of the imperial rescript announcing Japan's capitulation,[44] the Foreign Office

[42] There is no transcript of the Emperor's remarks available. The text is based primarily on the accounts subsequently written by persons who attended the imperial conference. See Shimomura, "The Memoirs of Mr. Shimomura at the Imperial Council, 14 August 1945" (MS); Toyoda, *Saigo no teikoku kaigun*, 220–22; USSBS, *Interrogations*, II, Toyoda, 322–23; USSBS, *Japan's Struggle to End the War*, 9; JFO, *Shūsen shiroku*, Ch. 54 (Dai nikai gozen kaigi to kakugi kettei); IMTFE: Tōgō, 35789–90; Sakomizu, 35609–10; Kido, 31191; *Statements:* Hasunuma #58225, Tōgō #50304; and Kido, "Nikki," 8/14/45.

[43] As noted earlier (see the text corresponding to footnotes 26–28, Ch. 8, above), an "imperial decision" does not become a decision of state until unanimously ratified by the members of the cabinet. In this particular case, the Emperor's words were "final" only because the cabinet (which met immediately after the imperial conference adjourned) unanimously endorsed His Majesty's views, began drafting a rescript to be broadcasted by the Emperor the following noon, and authorized the Foreign Office to inform the Allied powers of the "imperial decision" to accept the Potsdam Proclamation. In line with the constitutional requirements of earlier years, a full explanation of these developments was tendered by the government (Suzuki and Tōgō) to the Privy Council in a meeting of the latter body held on August 15. See JFO, *Shūsen shiroku*, Ch. 57 (Sūmitsuin ni okeru Tōgō gaishō no setsumei, gyokuon hōsō, naikaku kokuyu, Suzuki naikaku no sōjishoku).

[44] The first draft of the imperial rescript was prepared by Hisatsune Sakomizu and Michiyo Kihara on the basis of what the Emperor had said at the imperial conferences of August 9–10 and August 14 and was later revised and polished by two professors, Seitoku Yasuoka and Mizuho Kawada. This draft was then forwarded to the Emperor and the Premier, both of whom made some slight changes. The real difficulty was encountered when the rescript was presented to the cabinet ministers, for the latter—especially Anami—had their own ideas as to content and phraseology. Thus, it was not until close to 11:00 P.M., August 14, that final (cabinet) agreement was achieved—a prerequisite to the formal promulgation of the rescript (11:30 P.M.). (Interview with Mr. Sakomizu, Tokyo, April 6, 1952.) See also IMTFE: Kido, 31191–94; *Statements:* Sakomizu 5/3/49; JFO, *Shūsen shiroku*, Ch. 54 (Dai nikai gozen kaigi to kakugi kettei) and Ch. 55 (Gyokuon hōsō rokuon to Rengōkoku ate tsūkokubun no hatsuden).

hastily drafted cables to Japan's ministers in Switzerland and Sweden—the men responsible for transmitting the imperial decision to the Allied powers.[45] Everywhere within the inner councils of the state the murmur of His Majesty's pronouncement lingered on. Within hours this whisper became a world-wide roar: JAPAN HAS SURRENDERED! THE WAR IN THE PACIFIC IS OVER!

[45] The first hint that Japan was on the point of surrendering came in a Dōmei transmission beamed from Tokyo to the American zone at 2:49 P.M., August 14 (August 14, 1:49 A.M., EWT). The monitored text ran as follows: "Flash! Flash! Tokyo, Aug. 14—It is learned an imperial message accepting the Potsdam Proclamation is forthcoming soon." USFCC, *Radio Report Far East*, #80, B 3.

For the text of Japan's note of acceptance, see Appendix F and JFO, *Shūsen shiroku*, Ch. 55 (Gyokuon hōsō rokuon to Rengōkoku ate tsūkokubun no hatsuden).

10

THE AFTERMATH

Recourse to Violence

ON AUGUST 11, 1945—the day on which Secretary Byrnes dispatched the reply which culminated in the imperial decision of August 14—a small group of army staff officers gathered secretly in an air raid shelter at the War Ministry and there committed themselves to staging a coup d'état to recapture the initiative they had already lost.[1]

Their reasoning was that it would be useless for the people of Japan to survive the war if the structure of the state itself were destined to be destroyed. They did not share the Emperor's view that a time would surely come when the nation could be restored if only its roots were kept alive, nor did they indulge His Majesty's fear that the entire Japanese race would be wiped out in an invasion spearheaded by atomic bombs. All this seemed inconsistent with what they believed were the ideas and ideals of His Majesty's imperial ancestors.

Their state of mind was alive to visions: If the worst did happen, let it happen! The glorious determination of the Japanese people to preserve their national polity would stand forever in the annals of history—a sublime pageant of honor, bravery, and loyalty!

It was the phenomenon of the 1930's repeated—the perennial "justification" of the fanatics: "The Emperor is being insincerely advised by a group of traitors close to the Throne. To eliminate this evil influence we must place ourselves in temporary disobedience to His Majesty. The issue at stake is not confined to the present Emperor alone nor is the imperial system limited in scope to the reigning sovereign. Thus, even if we must oppose temporarily the will of His Majesty, the system will be preserved for posterity. To act in compliance with the wishes of the imperial ancestors constitutes a wider and truer loyalty to the Throne. In disobeying His Majesty we are not being disloyal to the imperial institution."[2]

---

[1] The coup was planned and engineered by field-grade officers in the Military Affairs Section, the Military Service Section, and the 2d Section (General Staff).

[2] This point of view is said to have been an outcropping of the influence of Professor Hiraizumi whose lectures at the Military Academy and at the Army General Staff

The plan these conspirators devised was age-old in its conception: a military government with all political power concentrated in the hands of the War Minister. For this purpose, the positive support of a majority of the army's leaders—especially those stationed in or near the capital—would be required. Yet it was here, within their own circle, where they should have been strongest, that the conspirators proved to be weakest. The commanders of the Eastern District Army and of the First Imperial Guards Division,[3] whose participation was deemed essential, turned their backs on the whole idea. Lieutenant General Mori of the Guards even phrased his refusal with bluntness and vigor: "Unless the Emperor personally commands me, I cannot and will not carry out any action contrary to the known wishes of His Majesty—even though said action is ordered by the War Minister himself." General Tanaka of the Eastern District Army, although perhaps slightly more diplomatic, was no less adamant in his determination to avoid being implicated in the conspiracy.

More serious than the Mori-Tanaka refusal was the failure of the fanatics to obtain a firm commitment from General Anami.[4] When they first approached him on the afternoon of August 12, he was just leaving his office for a cabinet meeting. Although he listened patiently, the conspirators were unable to go into detail and Anami was unwilling to give a definite reply.

The following day, August 13, the fanatics met again. The ring-leaders declared that Suzuki and the majority of his ministerial colleagues constituted a Badoglio cabinet and that the Emperor, unless given proper "protection," would fall victim to Suzuki's "treachery." To prevent this they proposed to stage a coup at midnight, round up the peace

---

College laid down the following "rule": If a man is seriously concerned about Japan's future and if he thinks that what the Emperor is sanctioning is wrong, he can still be loyal to the Throne even if he does not obey what His Majesty has sanctioned.

[3] Although the Eastern District Army had apparently been redesignated the "12th Area Army," the original name will be used throughout (as it was in many of the sources). The Second Imperial Guards Division was overseas, and the Third Imperial Guards Division was attached to the Eastern District Army.

[4] There is evidence to indicate that some of the conspirators, at least, planned to replace the Suzuki Cabinet with one headed by Anami. This was actually an idea which had become rather popular with the younger officer group very soon after Suzuki assumed office in the spring of 1945. Anami, who was aware of this movement in the army, seems to have done everything in his power to avoid any such "draft." Anami's fundamental concern, which is also the key to his dilemma, was to comply with the wishes of the Emperor. See *Statements:* Hayashi #54482 and #61436, Inaba #62083.

In this connection Shimomura has noted that in June 1945 Anami cautioned all staff members of the War Ministry against becoming involved in an anticabinet intrigue being instigated by some members of the Japanese Diet. At about the same time, Anami "earnestly tried to dissuade" Navy Minister Yonai from leaving his post. Anami solicited the aid of State Ministers Sakonji and Shimomura, and as a result Yonai did not resign. See *Statements:* Shimomura #57668.

advocates, declare martial law, and then continue the peace negotiations until full satisfaction had been obtained from the Allies on the question of the future status of the Emperor and the Throne.[5]

Again the group rushed to see Anami, but the hand of fate intervened and kept the War Minister out of reach—at least until eight o'clock that evening. Since it would then have been too late to complete the necessary arrangements even if Anami's consent were readily obtained, the conspirators sat down with the general at his official residence and leisurely yet forcefully explained their intentions in detail. When they had finished, Anami—who had listened in silence—noted that their planning was incomplete and that the over-all picture was somewhat crude. He did not say, however, that he disapproved of their idea or of the principle involved. In fact, his careful remarks suggested to the conspirators that he was really in favor of what they proposed. As midnight approached and the coup-minded fanatics bowed out of the War Minister's residence, Anami called after them: "Take care! You may be under watch tonight. You had better return in separate groups instead of all together."

Within twelve hours, this remark, which had struck the conspirators as a clear confirmation of all their hopes, had left them stranded instead. Early in the morning on August 14, War Minister Anami joined Chief of Staff Umezu in taking a firm stand—*against the coup.*[6]

The conspirators, who were quite unprepared for this development, were caught in an embarrassing situation. Having convinced themselves that Anami would side with them, they had already summoned Generals Tanaka and Mori to the War Ministry in order to give the two "recalcitrants" a last chance to participate in the coup. In the event of another refusal, the generals were to be placed under arrest and their troops employed at will.

So as not to give the conspirators away, Anami passed off the summons in the light of special instructions. Declaring that the situation might become very serious either that day or the next, he warned Mori and Tanaka to be on their guard and to take whatever extra precautions they deemed necessary. Anami also delivered a brief address to the

[5] Two separate coups were planned (one which originally was to have begun at the latest by 10:00 A.M., August 14, and the other which actually began around midnight on August 14). While the aim of the first may have been to continue the negotiations (on a basis dictated by the Japanse army), the aim of the second, which was formulated after the Emperor's final "decision" at the imperial conference of August 14, was to subvert the negotiations entirely and to fight to the bitter end.

[6] Anami's role is discussed in the text which follows. For confirmation of Umezu's opposition to the coup, see IMTFE: Ikeda, 36943. One officer has said that Anami would probably not have objected to the coup had it been supported by Umezu, Tanaka, and Mori. This same officer had "heard" that Umezu would not have opposed the coup had Anami agreed to it.

personnel of the War Ministry in which he urged his staff to strengthen their unity and to beware of any acts of insubordination.

Then, what the conspirators had feared would happen did indeed take place. The Emperor convened the second imperial conference and announced his final and irrevocable "decision" to surrender. The fanatics were thus faced with the virtual necessity of striking at once or of giving in completely. Before a majority of the group could decide which it would be, Anami returned from the imperial conference and called his officers before him. When he spoke, his words brushed sham and circumspection aside:

A meeting has just been held in the imperial presence and His Majesty has rendered his final decision in favor of terminating the war. The imperial army must act in complete accord with this decision.

Japan will henceforth face difficult times. Even though you may have to sleep on the ground and eat stones,[7] I ask you—one and all—to do your utmost to preserve the national polity.[8]

The imperial command and Anami's moral suasion turned the tide so far as most of the army's staff officers were concerned, but there were still a few who could not stomach the idea of surrender no matter how it was presented or by whom. This attitude is best portrayed by a conversation which took place at 4:00 P.M. on August 14 between one of the fanatics, a Major Hatanaka, and another officer, Lieutenant Colonel Ida. Their remarks[9] were as follows:

Hatanaka: The government and the highest military leaders have decided to terminate the war—a decision which I cannot accept as things stand now. My idea is that we should establish ourselves within the palace, sever communications with the outside, and give assistance to the Emperor in a final effort to retrieve

---

[7] This phrase is reminiscent of a passage in the so-called "Anami proclamation" of August 11 (for which, see footnote 40, Ch. 8, above, and the text corresponding thereto).

[8] The above remarks are based on the recollections of one of the officers present at the time. It would appear that Anami also repeated his admonition of August 10 (for which, see the final paragraph of the quotation corresponding to footnote 41, Ch. 8, above). In this connection, see *Statements:* Hara #50563, Ida #62348, Yoshizumi #59277, and Kawabe #50224. In the latter citation, Lieutenant General Kawabe speaks of a proclamation ("The Army will act in accordance with the Imperial decision to the last") which was drafted by himself and Lieutenant General Wakamatsu (Vice-Minister of War) and was signed by Anami, Umezu, Dohihara (inspector general of military education), Sugiyama (commanding general, First General Army), Hata (commanding general, Second General Army), and Kawabe (commanding general, Air General Army). (Care must be taken not to confuse Torashirō Kawabe, the vice-chief of the Army General Staff, with Masakazu Kawabe, the commanding general of the Air General Army.) The proclamation described here was "a precautionary step designed to prevent even the slightest error in the course of action of the entire army." Its main purpose was to reaffirm the army's unwavering loyalty to the Emperor's will. See also IMTFE. Wakamatsu, 36937–39; JFO, *Shūsen shiroku*, Ch. 56 (Gun no dōkō to hachi-ichigo jiken sono ta), and IMTFE: *Proceedings*, 36939–40.

[9] See *Statements:* Ida #62348.

the situation. I have already got in touch with the Imperial Guards Division and have made the necessary arrangements. I'd like you to take part in the plan.

Ida: Since the situation has come to such a pass, I feel that the entire army should, without question, comply with His Majesty's wishes and that the army's leaders should all commit suicide.[10] I do not mean to ignore your idea of making a final effort to save a lost cause, but the merit of your idea is beyond my power to judge. If the underlying spirit of your coup d'état plan is founded upon your firm conviction, the success or failure of the plan will depend upon the destiny ordained by the gods and therefore need not be considered. At any rate, I'll not dare to restrain you.

Hatanaka, who had hoped to obtain Ida's active support, merely nodded and said, "Well, I understand you . . . but as for myself I'll do my best and leave the rest to providence."

At approximately ten o'clock that evening, Hatanaka, accompanied by a fellow fanatic, called on Ida again. The two officers quickly explained that they had completed their preparations but needed Ida's support to persuade Lieutenant General Mori of the Guards Division to throw his weight behind the coup. Their excitement and wild schemes proved infectious. Ida became "inspired" and decided to abandon the "cherished ideals" he had entertained earlier in the day. He also reversed himself about success or failure. In the afternoon, when he had not been thinking about participating, he had said that *that* issue did not matter. Now, however, he saw the need to judge as quickly and as accurately as possible whether the coup would succeed or fail. If the latter, then it should be abandoned because, as he told his companions, "it is not our intention to cause public disorder by going to extremes." With that, the three left the War Ministry and went at once to the headquarters of the Imperial Guards Division.[11] It was about 11:00 P.M. when they arrived—almost the exact hour that the imperial rescript terminating the war was approved by the cabinet and roughly thirty minutes before the Emperor began cutting the record which was to be broadcasted the following day, August 15, at noon.

Hatanaka's idea was to confront Lieutenant General Mori at once, but the general already had a caller and so the three officers had to wait. A half-hour slipped by, then an hour, finally an hour and a half. Thus, it was well past midnight when Mori at last admitted the impatient trio to his office. Before anyone had a chance to spell out the issue, Mori began talking about his views on life. It was as if he were trying to forestall what lay in store. The three could do nothing but listen while Mori spoke on. Suddenly, Hatanaka left the room saying he would be back. Mori continued talking but finally paused long enough to permit Hata-

----

[10] Ida has noted that only 20 percent of his colleagues agreed with him about a mass suicide on the part of the army's leaders, 10 percent advocated going underground, and 70 percent remained undecided.

[11] See *Statements:* Ida #62348.

naka's companions to broach their business. As he had done several
days earlier when the matter was first brought to his attention, Mori again
stated his strong opposition to the coup. After exhausting his arguments, however, he told his two visitors that he understood their concern
and would himself go to worship at the Meiji Shrine so as to be able to
make up his own mind. He had no sooner said this than Hatanaka re-
entered the room accompanied by several of the Division's staff officers.[12]
A few minutes were spent in talking and then Mori summoned his chief
of staff and asked him what he thought. The Division chief merely shook
his head and replied that he could not venture an opinion since he was
not well informed about the plan. Upon hearing this Mori again spoke
of going to the Meiji Shrine and instructed Ida, in the meantime, to brief
the chief of staff. The latter immediately led the way out of the general's
suite and to his own office, where he and Ida began discussing the coup.

It was then about 1:45 A.M. Fifteen minutes later, a pistol barked
through the night air and a great commotion followed. The Division
chief of staff and Ida rushed for the general's office, but before they
could get in Hatanaka came walking out looking deathly pale: "Time
was running out— more and more time, so I finally did it. Please for-
give me."

Mori was dead, and Hatanaka was his assassin.[13]

While Ida and the Division chief of staff rushed to the Eastern District Army Headquarters to report, Hatanaka and the other conspirators
faked a Division order, "authenticated" it with the dead general's seal,
and in a very short time had complete control of the Guards Division
without any of the rank and file realizing that something was amiss.[14]
The stage was now set for the second and more important act.

Several hours before Mori's death, the Emperor had left the imperial residence and had driven to the Imperial Household Ministry, a
building situated a short distance away in one corner of the imperial
palace grounds. Nothing untoward occurred. His Majesty entered the
building, spoke into a recording microphone, drove back to his library
residence, and went to bed.[15]

---

[12] During his absence, Hatanaka had called upon Lieutenant Colonel Takeshita in
an effort to persuade the latter to intervene with his brother-in-law, War Minister Anami.
After a vain attempt to get Hatanaka to reconsider, Takeshita agreed to do what he
could. See *Statements:* Takeshita #56366 and #50025-A.

[13] Also killed with Mori was Lieutenant Colonel Shiraishi, who apparently tried to
protect Mori by stepping between him and Hatanaka. See *Statements:* Fuwa #62238.

[14] See *Statements:* Ida #62348.

[15] See *Statements:* Tokugawa #63366. The chamberlain's official diary (pertaining
to the Emperor's activities) reveals that the Emperor left his residence (the Gobunko)
at 2325 hours, August 14, and drove to the Imperial Household Ministry, leaving there,
again by auto, at 0005 hours, August 15. At 0050 hours (August 15) word was received
that the Emperor had retired for the night. See also IMTFE: Ishiwata, 38931–35.

Tokugawa says very little about the actual recording process except that the fol-

A few minutes later, just as one of the chamberlains at the Household Ministry was making the official entry that the Emperor had retired, an air raid alarm was sounded. For a while it looked as if everyone would have a sleepless night, but before long the word was passed that Tokyo would not be the target of the attack. As a result, His Majesty was not disturbed and the chamberlain, his duties completed, was able to go to bed. About three o'clock in the morning, however, he was suddenly awakened by another member of the Board of Chamberlains and hurriedly informed that the Imperial Guards Division was in the hands of a fanatical group of insurgents. By this time, too, almost everyone else of any importance in the Household Ministry had learned the disquieting news.[16] The Ministry personnel assumed, and quite rightly, that the insurgents would soon be arriving in search of the imperial record, the Lord Keeper of the Privy Seal, and the Imperial Household Minister. Since the record had already been deposited in a safe located in the chamber set aside for the officials-in-waiting to Her Majesty, it was considered to be beyond the reach of the searchers. Privy Seal Kido and Household Minister Ishiwata, however, were another matter. With great dispatch, and with barely time to spare, the chamberlains conducted the two marked men to an underground vault where they settled down to wait for death or deliverance.[17]

Two of the chamberlains then set out for His Majesty's residence via a short cut which took them along a newly constructed road passing the Dōkan moat. When they reached the Kaintei Gate, they were challenged by several officers and the usual sentries but were permitted to pass. Once inside the residence, they immediately reported to the chamberlain on duty and also to the head lady-in-waiting to Her Majesty. In spite of the unwelcome news they brought, a decision was reached

---

lowing persons were present: Imperial Household Minister Ishiwata, Grand Chamberlain Fujita, President of the Board of Information Shimomura, and Chamberlains Mitsui and Toda. Chamberlains Tokugawa and Irie waited outside, possibly in the room where the actual recording apparatus was set up. Additional material on this subject can be found in Shimomura, *Shūsen hishi*, Chs. 28–32.

[16] During a visit to Kido in the late afternoon of August 14, Prince Konoye mentioned a rumor to the effect that the Imperial Guards Division was in a state of unrest. Kido responded by saying he did not anticipate any trouble within the Guards Division. The Privy Seal's first intimation that something might be wrong came some time after midnight when the loud-speaker in his room, which had been reporting on a number of B-29 raids being staged throughout Japan, suddenly went dead. In spite of this possible sign of trouble, Kido dropped off to sleep. He was awakened about 3:20 A.M. by Chamberlain Toda and told what had occurred. Before taking refuge in the vault, Kido tore up all important documents in his possession and flushed them down a toilet.

[17] See the citations listed in footnote 18 below and IMTFE: Kido, 31194–99. Ishiwata recalls that Kido made the following remark to him upon entering the vault: "We don't know when we may be discovered and killed together, but history has already changed its course. Even if we are killed now it won't matter, for the war is being brought to an end." (Kido's meaning was that their mission had been accomplished.) See IMTFE: Ishiwata, 38931–35.

not to awaken either the Emperor or the Empress. After taking the added precaution of closing the iron shutters of the residence, the two chamberlains returned to the Imperial Household Ministry.[18]

While these events were taking place, Lieutenant Colonel Ida and the chief of staff of the Guards Division arrived at the Eastern District Army Headquarters where they received and readily honored orders commanding them to refrain from taking any further part in the coup d'état. After staying a short time at the headquarters, Ida returned to the palace and advised Hatanaka to withdraw the insurgents. Hatanaka gave no indication of what he would do and so Ida departed, this time to report to War Minister Anami, who was at his official residence at Miyakezaka.[19]

While Ida was thus endeavoring, in his own way, to repair some of the damage which had already been done, General Tanaka of the Eastern District Army was rushing to the imperial palace—determined to put down the uprising or die in the attempt. The fact that the insurgents had already failed in their task—both at the palace and at Radio Tokyo where another group of conspirators had been engaged in a fruitless search for the imperial record—forecast the success of Tanaka's efforts. Entering the palace through the gate near the headquarters of the 1st Infantry Regiment, the general came face to face with armed soldiers. Ignoring these, he stormed into the headquarters where he angrily upbraided the regimental commander. He also delivered a severe reprimand to one of the insurgents—a staff officer of the Guards Division—and had the man placed under arrest. With the situation under control at this point, Tanaka went on to the commander of the 2d Infantry Regiment. Whether the regimental commanders had been deceived by the false Division order, which had been forged by the insurgents following Hatanaka's assassination of Mori, or whether they were willing accomplices in the crime is difficult to determine. It is clear, however, that once the bold Tanaka arrived on the scene and delivered his harangue, the regimental commanders proved ready to follow his lead and help quell the disorder. By eight o'clock on the morning of August 15, Tanaka was thus able to report to the Emperor that there was no need to be concerned since the incident had been

[18] See *Statements:* Tokugawa #63366. Shortly after his return to the Imperial Household Ministry, Tokugawa was subjected to a thirty-minute interrogation at the hands of a small band of insurgents.

One direct telephone connection between the naval aide-de-camp's office and the Navy Ministry remained open in spite of the revolt. Using this line, palace officials made arrangements with the outside to have the insurrection quelled.

For the events of the night of August 14/15, see also IMTFE: Kido, 31196; Kido, "Nikki," 8/15/45; *Statements:* Kido #61541 and #61476; JFO, *Shūsen shiroku,* Ch. 55 (Gyokuon hōsō rokuon to Rengōkoku ate tsūkokubun no hatsuden) and Ch. 56 (Gun no dōkō to hachi-ichigo jiken sono ta).

[19] See *Statements:* Ida #62348.

brought under control. After a last-minute tour of inspection, Tanaka left the palace, satisfied that the greatest danger was passed.[20]

At approximately the same time that the "all-clear" was given by Tanaka, the curtain also fell on another drama in which the powerful yet restrained Minister of War, General Anami, was the principal actor. At 11:30 P.M. on August 14, as the cabinet was adjourning for the night, General Anami—wearing his sword and holding his cap in his hand— slowly and ceremoniously walked toward Premier Suzuki. "I should have given you every assistance in this war," Anami declared, "but I am afraid I have caused you a great deal of trouble instead." Suzuki, who was instantly moved, grasped Anami's hand and replied, "I fully appreciate your painful position. Since His Majesty is exceptionally enthusiastic about his ancestral religious services, I am sure that he will be blessed with the grace of heaven. I have not yet lost hope for the future of Japan." Anami nodded his agreement, bowed good night, and departed for his residence at Miyakezaka.[21]

An hour or so later, the fanatical Hatanaka, who had listened briefly to Mori's views on life and had then abruptly left the general's office, turned up at the door of Lieutenant Colonel Takeshita, Anami's brother-in-law.[22] Explaining excitedly that the plans to stage a coup had been completed and that the zero hour was 0200, Hatanaka urged Takeshita to use his influence to win the War Minister to their side. After a vain attempt to get Hatanaka to reconsider, Takeshita promised to do what he could. Upon arriving at Anami's residence soon thereafter, Takeshita found the general sitting in his Japanese-style bedroom writing something that looked like a will. After they had conversed for a while, Anami rather matter-of-factly declared, "I'm thinking of committing suicide."

[20] See *Statements:* Tsukamoto #63041, Tokugawa #63366, Fuwa #62238; IMTFE: Kido, 31196–97. Among the "prisoners" taken by the insurgents and released by Tanaka were Chief Aide-de-Camp Hasunuma, Board of Information President Shimomura, and the technicians who had recorded the Emperor's voice.

The ringleaders of the coup d'état committed suicide on the morning of August 15 to atone for their misdeeds. On the night of August 24, 1945, General Tanaka, who— like Mori—had served the Emperor well and faithfully, committed suicide in his private room at Eastern District Army Headquarters.

[21] The text is based on the recollections of Minister of State Sakonji (*Statements:* Sakonji #61339). JFO, *Shūsen shiroku*, Ch. 55 (Gyokuon hōsō rokuon to Rengōkoku ate tsūkokubun no hatsuden), reports Anami as saying practically the same thing to Foreign Minister Tōgō. It is possible that Anami addressed his remarks to both Suzuki and Tōgō (or similar remarks to each). It is also possible that someone has confused what is cited here with the Anami-Tōgō exchange cited in footnote 32 below. At any rate, Anami's behavior on this occasion is a key to his character. In this connection, see footnote 32, Ch. 9, above.

[22] For material relating to the events described in the text which follows, see *Statements:* Takeshita #56366 and #50025-A, Hayashi #61436, Ida #62348, Ikeda #54479, Sakomizu 5/3/49, Kawabe #52608, Yoshizumi #61338; JFO, *Shūsen shiroku*, Ch. 56 (Gun no dōkō to hachi-ichigo jiken sono ta).

Takeshita reacted calmly, agreeing that it might be wise if Anami were to follow such a course, but questioning whether it need be that very night. Anami looked relieved: "I am glad you agree; I was worried you might try to stop me. I dread hearing the broadcast of the imperial rescript tomorrow. Not only that, but this is the anniversary of my father's death. Of course, if circumstances prevent it, there is still August 20—the day on which my second son died, but . . ."

The two men turned to their *sake* (rice wine) and to talking about other things. Perhaps Anami knew what was taking place at the palace and sensed the reason behind Takeshita's visit—perhaps not. For the time being, neither said anything about the coup. Then, at 0200 hours, they heard the sound of shooting coming from the direction of the imperial palace. Takeshita started to explain Hatanaka's schemes, but Anami cut him short—saying that Tanaka's forces (the Eastern District Army) would not join in the revolt and that it would therefore collapse of its own accord.

It was about this time that Takeshita noticed how much Anami was drinking and expressed his concern that the War Minister might be unable to handle his sword properly in the elaborate disembowelment ritual of *seppuku* (*harakiri*). But Anami was not worried. "I have a fifth degree rank in *kendō* [swordsmanship]," he told Takeshita, "so I'll not fail. When you drink *sake*, you bleed more profusely. That way you are certain of dying. Anyway, should something go wrong, I want you to assist me."

About four o'clock in the morning, one of the War Minister's servants announced the arrival of the commander of the Tokyo military police. Anami turned to Takeshita and asked him to see what the commander wanted. When Takeshita returned to the room, Anami was sitting, Japanese fashion, on a narrow porch-way which ran along the outside wall of his bedroom. He was looking toward the imperial palace and his left hand was feeling the right side of his throat. His right hand was still grasping the dagger with which he had just cut open his abdomen. When Takeshita moved to assist him, Anami shook his head and plunged the dagger into the right side of his neck, falling forward, as he did so, in the direction of the palace. Blood gushed from the new wound and spread across the floor.

Moving closer to Anami's body, Takeshita discovered that the War Minister, who had not actually severed the artery, was only unconscious and not yet dead. Assuming the responsibility as Anami's chosen second, Takeshita placed his hand over Anami's, which still held the dagger, and thrust the weapon more deeply into Anami's throat. He then placed the general's bemedaled coat over his body and laid two scrolls, containing the last words Anami had written, by his side. In a sense, each was a legacy. The one (signed "War Minister Anami, Korechika") read: "Believing firmly that our sacred land shall never perish, I—with my death—humbly apologize to the Emperor for the great crime."[23] The other (signed "Korechika") was equally cryptic. Phrased as a thirty-one-syllable Japanese-style poem, it read: "Having received great favors from His Majesty, the Emperor, I have nothing to say to posterity in the hour of my death."[24]

Toward eight o'clock in the morning, almost four hours after Anami had knelt to die, the last spark of life finally flowed out of his body and even those who knew him well began then to speculate—and still do— wherein lay "the great crime."

While Hatanaka was perpetrating his desperate schemes at the palace and Anami was preparing to take the traditional way out of an insurmountable dilemma, there occurred several other incidents which also stand as a sign of the times—an indication of what might have happened had the conspirators possessed better organization and fuller support. Elderly Baron Hiranuma, a recognized adherent of the ultra-nationalist fringe of Japanese politics, was living in the Shibuya ward of Tokyo where he was enjoying the care and companionship of some relatives, including a grandniece, by the name of Setsuko, and her two children.[25] When the air raid alarm sounded shortly after midnight on August 14/15, the family left the house and crowded into a shelter located in the garden. It was 3:00 A.M. before the alarm was lifted and they could return to bed. Two and a half hours later there was a second alarm but this time the raiders were carrier planes, not land-based bombers, and Setsuko decided to stay in the house. All of a sudden she heard a great commotion and became instantly frightened. Looking out the window, she saw a gang of armed men—obviously in an ugly mood— pouring in through the front gate of the compound. She scarcely had to guess what this meant, for terror in the night was nothing new to people who moved within the inner circle of the ruling elite. Not only was her uncle such a man, but one of the police guards around the residence had already warned her several days before that something unpleasant was likely to happen. On the previous day (August 14) another guard had drawn her attention to the way Japanese army planes were circling low over the house. He had thought that they might bomb the place. Now all these fears were grim reality. Another look out the

---

[23] Isshi motte daizai wo shashi-tatematsuru, shinshū fumetsu wo shinji tsutsu." Even among those who knew Anami well, there is much speculation about the meaning of this legacy. Although *daizai* ("the great crime") was apparently multishaded in Anami's mind, it seems to have had one overpowering meaning: the army's responsibility in bringing the Empire of Japan to defeat and surrender.

[24] "Ōgimi no fukaki megumi ni amishi mi wa iinokosubeki katakoto mo nashi." There is some question as to whether Anami signed this poem with only his first name (as stated by his secretary, Colonel Hayashi) or with the words, "Army General Anami, Korechika" (as stated by his brother-in-law, Lieutenant Colonel Takeshita).

[25] See IMTFE: Hiranuma (Setsuko), 29321–26.

window told her no help could be expected from the police guards. They were lined up in a row, with their hands over their heads, staring into the guns of the mob and listening—since they had no other choice— to a stiffly worded dressing down: "Don't you know what a ——— Hiranuma is? You don't? I'll tell you! He is a traitor—a notorious leader of the pro–Anglo-American group, working to destroy our sacred land. Guarding an arch traitor! What kind of thing is that! You should be ashamed!"

This was the mob leader, an army captain by the name of Sasaki, and while he raved and gesticulated, some of his gang, which was composed of soldiers and students, began closing in on the house. Setsuko grabbed her children, ran with them to the amah's room, and then rushed toward Hiranuma's bedroom in order to help him escape. By this time the soldiers had poured gasoline everywhere, igniting it as they went. In a second the house was in flames. By the time Setsuko knew what she was doing and where she was going it was too late to get to Hiranuma's room. Choked with smoke, she experienced a moment of indecision, trying desperately to think what to do. Then she heard a member of the gang shout, "We can't find him," and another answer back, "It doesn't matter; in a minute he'll be burned to death anyway." Believing then that Hiranuma must have escaped from the house before the soldiers had gained entry, Setsuko retraced her steps to make sure that the amah had taken care of the children. When she couldn't find them, she ran outside where Sasaki and his men were still covering the police with swords, pistols, and more than one machine gun. Heedless of her own safety, she boldly asked one of the men about her two children and he replied gruffly that they had already left the house. She then made her way to the garden of a neighboring building, a structure which housed the library and offices of a cultural group, known as the Immortality Society (Mukyūkai), of which Hiranuma was president. Here she found the children and learned from a policeman that her great-uncle was hiding in the library building. Hiranuma had escaped through a garden gate which led directly into the grounds surrounding the Immortality Society. It was the only gate which the gang had overlooked.

By this time the house was in full blaze, and when all was over only a portion of the garage remained. Thinking that their target must certainly have perished in the flames, the soldier-student mob at length departed without harming the members of Hiranuma's family or any of the police.

Just why Hiranuma was attacked is a difficult question, for by August 1945 the end-the-war advocates no longer counted him within their ranks, if, indeed, they had ever done so. It was Hiranuma who had taken exception to the phrase used to state Japan's reservation in the note dispatched to the Allies on August 10. When the Byrnes reply arrived, Hiranuma was one of the first to claim that it did not honor Japan's position with respect to the Emperor. When those who favored the calculated-risk approach lost out, Hiranuma lost with them. The attempt to assassinate him, therefore, may represent a clue to commitments which Hiranuma endeavored to uphold but had to reject following the Emperor's final decision on August 14 or it may simply be the upshot of stupidity and ignorance on the part of the attackers. A third and perhaps less likely possibility is that the raid bore no direct relationship to the termination of the war at all; that is, the raiders may simply have used the opportunity of the moment to even an old score. Since there were upward of forty men in the gang, the attack may have been many things to many people.

In addition to the violence attempted upon the person of Hiranuma, there were also early-morning forays against the residences of Premier Suzuki and Privy Seal Kido. The Premier, in fact, was forced to spend several days dodging the efforts of the fanatics to bring their guns to bear upon him. The plot to ferret out and kill the Emperor's closest adviser, Marquis Kido, was equally sustained and was later discovered to represent part of a larger plan. It seems that among the jingoist groups there was a particularly strong-willed faction known as the Sonjō Dōshikai, composed of men imbued with the idea of fighting to the death, no matter what the outcome might be. The very name of their society was in itself a clue to their intentions—a combination of two characters (*Son* and *Jō*) from a four-character phrase, *Sonnō Jō-i*, used at the time of the Meiji Restoration (1867–68) to mean "Revere the Emperor and Expel the Barbarians." At dawn on August 15 a small band of the society, armed with hand grenades, revolvers, and Japanese swords, suddenly surrounded Kido's private residence in Akasaka ward. A fight ensued with the police guards, who managed to beat off the attack with no damage done to the fanatics but with one of their own number falling wounded from the swipe of a sword. About three o'clock the following morning, August 16, the would-be assassins pounded on the door of the Wada residence, also in Akasaka ward, on the hunch that Kido might be staying with his brother (Dr. Wada). Fortunately, the Privy Seal was sleeping safely and soundly within the imperial palace, the best possible of all sanctuaries. Kido's niece, Masako, who received the thugs at the entrance to the house, found them carrying a small swordlike object on top of a ceremonial set of three trays, a polite but firm suggestion for Kido to commit suicide—or else. When they were told that Kido was not in the house, the band left without harming anyone.[26]

[26] The extremists who raided Kido's residence on the morning of August 15 tried to pass themselves off as members of the special service troop branch of the *kempeitai*. The residence attacked on August 16 belonged to Dr. Koroku Wada, Kido's younger brother, who, some years earlier, had adopted the name of a branch of the Kido family

A day or two later the police learned that some twelve members of the Revere-Expel Brotherhood had fled to the top of Atagoyama, a hill in the Shiba ward of Tokyo, and had there entrenched themselves in a teahouse. Although the police surrounded the hill at four-thirty in the morning of August 18, the fanatics were so well supplied with hand grenades that they were able to keep the law from closing in. Four days passed without either side making any move. Then, at 5:30 A.M. on August 22, the police finally found the chance for which they had been waiting. In the midst of a driving rainstorm, one contingent of policemen rushed the teahouse while another group pinned the thugs down with a lethal fire. After some resistance, the "Brothers" realized that their game was up. On a given signal, they threw their hand grenades at their own feet and thus simultaneously, one with the other, paid the price of their common folly.[27]

There were incidents of another type as well. In the period following the imperial broadcast of August 15 some Japanese navy airmen flew over the Tokyo area dropping leaflets which denied the validity of the imperial rescript and called upon all true patriots to rise to the defense of the Emperor and the Throne. Other air units, both army and navy, vowed that they would suicide-attack the American naval forces when they entered Tokyo Bay to accept Japan's surrender.[28] Admiral Yonai later recalled that during his long career as Navy Minister he had probably never worried so much as he had during the period from August 14 to August 23. In spite of the minute precautions which were taken to prevent the rise and spread of disorder within the navy, Yonai could not help feeling, after it was all over, that it was the unique influence of the Emperor and the Throne—and not anything he or the

---

which had died out. Subsequent to the two attacks, the police learned that the leaders of the Sonjō Dōshikai had been in touch with Major Hatanaka, the instigator of the abortive coup d'état staged at the palace on the night of August 14/15.

See IMTFE: Def. Doc. 3049, *Machimura Aff.*, J text (rejected: 38935–37); Kido, "Nikki," 8/15/45; IMTFE: Kido, 31197 and 31200–201; JFO, *Shūsen shiroku*, Ch. 56 (Gun no dōkō to hachi-ichigo jiken sono ta) and Ch. 57 (Sūmitsuin ni okeru Tōgō gaishō no setsumei, gyokuon hōsō, naikaku kokuyu, Suzuki naikaku no sōjishoku).

[27] See the citations listed in the preceding footnote.

[28] Yoshizumi (chief of the powerful Military Affairs Bureau) has stated that he had the army's planes disarmed and their gas tanks emptied so that the extremists could not utilize them at will. The Emperor had to dispatch his brother, Prince Takamatsu, to Atsugi airfield (where General MacArthur subsequently landed) in order to pacify a group of malcontents who wanted to re-engage the Americans when they came. On August 17 Kido received a report that approximately 200 soldiers were marching on Tokyo from Mito. He rushed to his office to confer with the Foreign Minister and with the chief of the prefectural police.

See *Statements:* Yoshizumi #61338; IMTFE: Kido, 31203; JFO, *Present Conditions of Japan*, 4; JFO, *Shūsen shiroku*, Ch. 56 (Gun no dōkō to hachi-ichigo jiken sono ta); Toyoda, *Saigo no teikoku kaigun*, 225–27; and USSBS, *Interrogations*, II, Toyoda, 320.

army authorities had done—that had made it possible for Japan to pass through this difficult period without serious trouble arising among the rank and file of the services.[29]

Yonai was not just gracefully acclaiming the role of a beloved sovereign; he was citing, by implication at least, a key point. In a sense, the majority of the military, including many of the fanatics, were caught during these last critical days in a trap of their own setting. In spite of the fact that for years they had been able to blackmail national policy into furthering their own questionable purposes, they had always promoted their aggressive designs in the "name" of the Emperor and under the somewhat ethereal sanction of "imperial will." When His Majesty's civilian ministers had occasionally endeavored to pursue policies not in accord with the militarist-ultranationalist blueprint for the future, the fanatics within the services and their abettors on the outside had shamelessly accused the ministers of "insincerely advising" the Emperor and had taken steps, both within and without the law, to suppress what they hypocritically called "traitorous" activity close to the Throne. This pattern of conformity through force and persecution had continued, in varying degrees of intensity and method, from long before the war right through to almost the very end of the conflict—and this quite in spite of the extraordinary stress and strain placed upon the military by their failure to achieve victory. When, however, the Emperor *personally* announced his wishes at the imperial conferences of August 9/10 and August 14, the die-hards experienced the imperial will in a manner theretofore totally unknown to them. These two unusual expressions of imperial desire were as unprecedented in Japanese experience as they were inalterable in Japanese psychology. The otherwise adamant extremists were thus faced with the impossible situation of having to honor the will of their Emperor even though His Majesty's plan ran counter to their own estimate of the nation's requirements and capabilities. To have done anything but obey the imperial "command" would have been to lay the basis for the destruction of the imperial system. To have acted against the express wishes of an Emperor whom they had unceasingly extolled as sacred and inviolable and around whom they had woven a fabric of individual loyalty and national unity would have been to destroy the very polity in perpetuation of which they had persistently declared they were fighting—the very way of life in defense of which they were even then proposing to continue the war to the bitter end.

In spite of the demands placed upon the military by the Emperor's "emergence" during the critical days of early and mid-August, other considerations alerted government leaders to the necessity of their taking all manner of precautions to ensure a smooth and quiet transi-

---

[29] See USSBS, *Interrogations*, II, Yonai, 332.

tion from war to peace. In the period between August 15 and September 2, *two* imperial rescripts were issued to the armed forces, one on August 17 and another on August 22, enjoining the loyal and the brave to lay down their arms and to obey His Majesty's cease-fire command. So that the imperial forces overseas would truly understand and promptly obey his wishes, the Emperor dispatched several imperial princes to the principal centers abroad where Japan had been waging war—to the China Expeditionary Army and the China Area Fleet, to the Southern Area Army and the 10th Area Fleet, and to the Kwantung Army and the imperial forces in Korea.[30]

Pressure from Japanese army authorities plus the daily evidence of recalcitrant elements at work among the soldiers and the people also led the Foreign Office to agree to send still another note to the Allies. Expressing the government's concern over the unstable situation, the note requested special dispensations, by virtue of that situation, which would permit the government to soothe the wrath of the malcontents and to lull their bitter minds into a passive acceptance of the inevitable. This communication, which was forwarded to the Allies one day after the August 14 note signifying Japan's acceptance of the Potsdam Proclamation, is a most unusual document. Read against the confusion reigning in Tokyo, it makes perfect sense, yet out of context Japan's "final" note seems more like a brazen-faced impertinence. In part, the text ran as follows:

It is earnestly solicited that:

a) In case of the entry of Allied fleets or troops in Japan Proper, the Japanese Government be notified in advance, so that arrangements can be made for reception.

b) The number of the points in Japanese territory to be designated by the Allies for occupation be limited to minimum number, selection of the points be made in such a manner as to leave such a city as Tokyo unoccupied and the forces to be stationed at each point be made as small as possible.

2. Disarming of the Japanese forces, being a most delicate task as it involves over three millions of officers and men overseas and having direct bearing on their honour, the Japanese Government will, of course, take utmost pains. But it is suggested that the best and the most effective method would be that under the command of His Majesty the Emperor, the Japanese forces are allowed to disarm themselves and surrender arms of their own accord. . . .

In connection with the disarming it is hoped that Article 35 of the Hague Convention will be applied, and the honour of the soldier will be respected, permitting them, for instance, to wear swords. Further, the Japanese Government be given to understand the Allies have no intention to employ disarmed Japanese soldiers for compulsory labour. . . .[31]

[30] See *Statements:* Hasunuma #58225; JFO, *Present Conditions of Japan*, 3–4; JFO, *Shūsen shiroku*, Ch. 56 (Gun no dōkō to hachi-ichigo jiken sono ta) ; and IMTFE: Kido, 31192–93.

[31] See Appendix H. This document does not appear in any U.S. government publications relating to the surrender.

Washington's reaction to the above document is not known, nor can it be determined whether any direct reply was ever sent in answer to this communication. Perhaps no one in the Foreign Office expected a reply. It was enough that they could tell the militarists that the conditions in support of which they had fought in the councils of the state and before His Majesty's own person had at last been dispatched to the Allies in the form of "desires."[32]

On the same day on which the above note was sent (August 15), the opportunity was created for the ultimate in safeguards — "the never-before-in-the-history-of-constitutional-government-in-Japan" — to be brought into play. The old admiral, Premier Baron Suzuki, feeling sorely distressed that he had been forced to cause the Emperor so much trouble by implicating him in the business of government,[33] relinquished the post which he had been so hesitant to accept, taking with him, as he went, the whole of his cabinet, which—in accordance with his request—obediently resigned.[34] The imperial mandate[35] now fell upon Naruhiko Higashikuni,[36] who thus became the first imperial prince ever to head a cabinet in the sixty and more years which had elapsed since the first party-sponsored cabinet had risen to power.[37] It would have been one

[32] When Anami saw the draft of the cable late on the evening of August 14, he turned to Foreign Minister Tōgō and with the "utmost amiability" remarked that if he had seen the text of the cable earlier he would not have argued with the Foreign Minister so much during the day. See *Statements*: Tōgō #50304.

[33] See, for instance, *Statements*: Sakomizu 5/3/49.

[34] According to USFCC, *Radio Report Far East*, #80, B 24, the *Nippon Times* wrote as follows: "The resignation implies no political criticism on the policy or methods of the Suzuki Cabinet. It implies no lack of respect or confidence on the part of the people. It implies no opposition from any quarter to the ending of the war. . . . The resignation is a solely moral matter."

[35] The phrasing of the mandate is significant: "Respect especially the Constitution, and [on the basis of the imperial rescript of August 14] seek to solve present problems by exerting your efforts toward the control of the armed forces and the maintenance of law and order." See *Contemporary Japan*, XIV (April–December 1945), 286, and Higashikuni, *Watakushi no kiroku*, 141. It should be noted that the new Premier concurrently assumed the post of War Minister.

[36] According to Admiral Zacharias (*Secret Missions*, 335), a December 1944 intelligence report, "given in the utmost secrecy to one of our intelligence officers in a neutral capital," prophesied that General Koiso would soon resign as Premier and that Admiral Suzuki would succeed him. The report also stated that the Emperor was leading a group of influential persons desiring peace ("terms under the most favorable circumstances") and that when a peace formula could be evolved and the Allied unconditional surrender demand modified to permit the Emperor to remain on the Throne, Suzuki would resign and Imperial Prince Higashikuni would emerge to effect Japan's surrender and to "guarantee the execution and observance of the surrender terms."

[37] For the details relating to the resignation of the Suzuki Cabinet and the emergence of the Higashikuni Cabinet, see IMTFE: Tōgō, 35790; Kido, 31197–200; Higashikuni, *Watakushi no kiroku*, 117–57; and JFO, *Shūsen shiroku*, Ch. 57 (Sūmitsuin ni okeru Tōgō gaishō no setsumei, gyokuon hōsō, naikaku kokuyu, Suzuki naikaku no sōjishoku) and Ch. 58 (Higashikuni no miya naikaku no seiritsu).

Suzuki and his colleagues resigned on August 15 and the Emperor immediately

thing for the extremists to have assassinated Suzuki or to have check-mated his cabinet at every turn; it would have been quite another matter for them to have employed similar tactics against a member of the imperial family.

Nor was this all. The outgoing baron and the incoming prince, the president of the Board of Information, the Minister of Home Affairs, the president of the Great Japan Political Party, and numerous other personages in positions of authority and influence issued proclamations, made radio addresses, and did everything in their power to curb any tendency on the part of the masses to disbelieve or contravene the wishes of the Emperor as set forth by His Majesty at the two imperial conferences at which the question of war or peace had finally been decided.[38]

And always, there were the echoes from the unprecedented broad-cast of August 15, 1945—the unforgettable voice of the crane:[39]

. . . We are always with ye, Our good and loyal subjects, relying upon your sincerity and integrity. Beware most strictly of any outbursts of emotion which may engender needless complications, or any fraternal contention and strife which may create confusion, lead ye astray and cause ye to lose the confidence of the world. . . . Cultivate the ways of rectitude; foster nobility of spirit; and work with resolution so as ye may enhance the innate glory of the Imperial State and keep pace with the progress of the world.

---

instructed Privy Seal Kido to recommend a successor. Kido requested and received the Emperor's permission to consult Baron Hiranuma, the president of the Privy Council. Agreeing that no "ordinary" subject could weather the trials ahead, Kido and Hiranuma jointly recommended Imperial Prince Higashikuni to the Throne. The Prince received the imperial mandate on August 16.

Normally, the senior statesmen would have been summoned to select a successor to Suzuki. Just why they were bypassed in this instance is not clear. Since there was no law which said they had to be summoned, Kido may have wished to avoid giving Tōjō and Koiso (Suzuki's immediate predecessors) a voice in the selection of Japan's first postwar Premier.

[38] See the Tokyo *Asahi Shimbun* and the *Nippon Times* for the period in question and also Higashikuni, *Watakushi no kiroku*, 138–39 and 147–48. The following quotation from the Suzuki Cabinet Proclamation (*The Oriental Economist*, XII [July-August 1945], 257) illustrates the tone:

"Graciously and benevolently wishing the peace of the world and the welfare of His subjects, His Imperial Majesty issued an Imperial Rescript. The Imperial Decision has been made. The way for His subjects to take is in itself clear."

For the Japanese text of this proclamation, see JFO, *Shūsen shiroku*, Ch. 57 (Sūmitsuin ni okeru Tōgō gaishō no setsumei, gyokuon hōsō, naikaku kokuyu, Suzuki naikaku no sōjishoku).

[39] The crane (*tsuru*) is symbolical of the Emperor and the Throne. The phrase, *tsuru no hitogoe*, for instance, means "a word from the Throne."

EPILOGUE

The Role of the Emperor in the Termination of the War

IN mid-November 1945, some three months after he had resorted to "an extraordinary measure" to bring the fighting to an end, His Imperial Majesty, the Emperor of Japan, repaired to the Grand Shrine at Ise and to the imperial mausoleums of Unebi and Momoyama, and to the imperial Tama mausoleum, to report personally upon the nation's failure in the war and the people's fortune in its termination. Having thus paid his respects to his imperial ancestors and having prayed for guidance and assistance, the Emperor returned to the capital to resume once again the pursuit of peace to which, some twenty years earlier, he had dedicated his ironically ill-designated reign: *Shōwa*—Enlightened Peace.

His Majesty's spectacular "emergence" in August 1945 and the action pursued by him during the last critical days of the war represented an unprecedented departure from the constitutional practice typical of the new and modern—post 1867—Japan. So out of character was the role played by the sovereign in the final act of what has since been called "Japan's tragedy" that several questions spring immediately to mind.

Was this man—this "Son of Heaven"—something more than just the passive figurehead he had always appeared to be? Was he actually a concrete force to be reckoned with at all times—a leading member of the little-known yet immensely powerful group which directed, from behind the scenes, Japan's performance upon the world stage? Was this Emperor (as the Constitution declared) the source of all power, in fact as well as in name? Or was he, after all, nothing more than a convenient emblem to be brandished at the proper moment—a mere symbol behind whom the civilian and military elite selfishly and independently gambled for the stakes of power? And if the latter, as the balance of evidence suggests, what then brought this figurehead so suddenly to life in the last, bitter days of the war? Whence sprang the strength on which he drew to curb his former masters? And finally,

228

in view of the success of his action in support of an immediate surrender and his repeatedly emphasized love of peace, why had he not been able to prevent the outbreak of the war in 1941?[1]

The pre-Meiji Restoration (1867–68) history of Japan's imperial dynasty presents an almost unrelieved picture of imperial authority being exercised, and the affairs of state being directed, by strong men acting in the name of the Emperor. While the sovereign always remained the titular source of power, honor, and authority, his actual function in life became purely ceremonial. After the Restoration, this ceremonial expression of imperial sovereignty was transformed in character and the Emperor himself was theoretically restored to a position permitting him, at times, to have a voice in the affairs of his Empire. This concession to an almost forgotten past was so short-lived that it was only for a relatively brief period that the Emperor was honored with the right of limited participation in the councils of his administratively all-important subordinates. As the years passed, the sovereign was no longer allowed in any way personally to direct the affairs of state or to meddle with the machinery of government. He could question or caution his ministers and advisers on matters within their competence and jurisdiction but he could not override policies formulated by the appropriate organs of state. When there was unanimity in the civil administration and the military command, the Emperor could do nothing but approve what was obviously the will of the state. If His Majesty's ministers were unable to agree on a policy or if a decision reached by the cabinet was not in accordance with the wishes of the Supreme Command, the cabinet would fall and a new cabinet, amenable to the demands of the moment, would emerge. Under no circumstances did the Emperor ever assume personal direction of the government.

The effect and purpose of this practice was to keep the Emperor outside the dangerous arena of government and administration. His role was that of a bystander watching with interest the turmoil of political activity taking place around him but never interfering no matter how personally concerned for the outcome he might be.

When the Emperor's ministers made mistakes, their political opponents charged them with ineptness in office or with insincerity toward the Throne. When duties were well performed, praise was heaped, not on the ministers, but on the infallible Emperor, the source of all wisdom and benevolence. Success was synonymous with the monarch, the soul of the state, the father of his people; failure was linked with persons close to the Throne, His Majesty's "insincere" advisers, the perverters of the imperial will.

The Emperor's removal from an active role in the formulation of

---

[1] In the absence of evidence that would satisfy everyone, it is assumed, for the purposes of the discussion which follows, that the Emperor would personally have acted to prevent war from breaking out in 1941 had he been able to do so.

policy for the Empire of which he was the "sacred and inviolable" emblem proved to be a mixed blessing. As the Emperor, he was the symbol of national unity; as a man, he held his own convictions. Long years of training and indoctrination, however, left no doubt in the Emperor's mind that he was not to intervene in any course of action unanimously undertaken by the ministers of state. As the carefully "guided" occupant of a zealously guarded Throne, the Emperor thus had a duty toward the state which took precedence over his duty toward himself. As the symbol of the unity of the nation, he must not divide the nation by opposing policies which represented the combined wisdom of his constitutionally responsible ministers of state. He might not personally feel that these policies were correct or necessary; yet, if he were so advised by the cabinet and the Supreme Command, his duty would be clear and incontrovertible. The will of the state must be the will of the Emperor, for only thus could the urge of the nation be blessed with the imperial sanction needed to maintain the unity and further the destiny of the "one hundred million."[2]

In 1941 the Japanese military were at the height of their power. Their tentacles of control spread, octopus-fashion, throughout the government and the body politic. Although the military had thrown all of their efforts into concluding the China "Incident," their failure was attributed, not to their own incapability, but rather, to the "machinations and intrigue" of foreign powers and interests. With this as a starting point, the militarists brewed among the masses feelings of hatred and resentment against the "imperialist West" which were deftly molded into unreasoned support for a new adventure into a tremendously broader and potentially more dangerous area of operations. Whatever the more alert members of the ruling elite may have thought of the militarists' plan for the preservation of the homeland and the stabilization of East Asia, the fact is that the Japanese army, with varying degrees of navy co-operation, was able, by diverse and frequently dubious means, to silence opposition and to induce unanimity for its program in the highest councils of the state. Under such circumstances, the ultimate sanction of the Emperor was a foregone conclusion.[3]

The seeds of Japan's disaster sprouted with Pearl Harbor. Within

---

[2] See footnotes 1 and 4, Ch. 8, above.

[3] There are those who say that had the Emperor "kicked over the traces" by refusing to sanction the cabinet's unanimous decision in favor of war, every effort would have been made to convince him that he was acting unconstitutionally and in violation of the sacred trust bequeathed to him by his imperial ancestors. Had he still refused to co-operate, the imperial seals and other paraphernalia of imperial sanction would have been used at will and the Emperor himself placed under "palace arrest" until such time as he could once again be trusted to follow the path along which he had been led all his life. It has also been suggested that in the event of continued intransigence the Emperor would have been removed from the scene under the pretext of illness and an army-oriented regency established in favor of his son.

months after this illusory "deathblow to America," first one and then another of the ruling elite came to understand that Japan's grasp was considerably less than her ambition, yet through this bitter awakening the military caste, for the most part, remained immune to the harsh realities closing in on every side. Pinning their faith, at times, on nothing more than the twin ideals of "spirit and sacrifice," Japan's military masters succeeded in maintaining their oppressive control over high and low alike—thus preventing, far beyond the scope of reason, any serious or sustained effort to redirect the course of national policy. By the spring of 1945, however, the Japanese armed forces had failed miserably in their prosecution of the war and had thus brought the once proud Empire of Japan to the point where its very survival was threatened. The result of this failure was readily discernible in the disintegration of that united front of support the military had enjoyed when the war began.

It was a desperate Japan which turned to the Soviet Union in early June 1945, but it was a Japan which, theoretically at least, still preferred annihilation to "unconditional surrender." Until the Allies agreed not to eradicate the national polity, the ruling elite could do nothing but continue to endorse the "decisive battle in the homeland" strategy which the military said would bring victory and the civilians feared would bring ruin. In spite of the certainty that the longer the war lasted the more hopeless Japan's situation would become, the police-state methods of the Japanese militarists and the Allied unwillingness to make a firm commitment on the future status of the Throne inevitably postponed a termination of the war.

Had Japan's civilian leaders been more direct, at the risk of their lives, in their endeavors to curb the military's power by reasserting their own; had the peace advocates been firmly convinced of the hopelessness of achieving a negotiated peace favorable to Japan; had the Allies been amenable, early in the war, to guaranteeing the preservation of Japan's imperial system; or had the United States looked more searchingly for alternatives to using her newly found atomic power and to promoting a Soviet entry into the conflict, the war in the Pacific might have ground to a halt short of the unprecedented action with which the Emperor became inextricably linked in that fateful period from August 9 through August 15, 1945.

The atomic bombing of Hiroshima and Nagasaki and the Soviet Union's declaration of war did not produce Japan's decision to surrender, for that decision—in embryo—had long been taking shape. What these events did do was to create that unusual atmosphere in which the theretofore static factor of the Emperor could be made active in such an extraordinary way as to work what was virtually a political miracle.

The terrible burden of the cumulative effects of nearly four years of war, topped by the imminent possibility of atomic extermination and the near certainty of foreign invasion, clearly promised that, should the Suzuki Cabinet resign in disagreement, chaos would follow. This state of affairs made an imperial conference mandatory, even though the traditions and practices of the past argued against holding such a conference before a unanimous decision had been formulated by the cabinet. To convene an imperial conference prior to complete agreement, while undesirable, was preferable to internal chaos and national extinction.

When the Emperor, who had been taught to equate his own will with the will of his "advisers," was suddenly asked to resolve an otherwise irreconcilable conflict, he could do nothing but express his personal opinion. That this became an "imperial decision," and hence the will of the state, stems from the action of His Majesty's ministers of state, who immediately met in cabinet session and, after due consideration and debate, unanimously endorsed the Emperor's unofficial, and until then extralegal, pronouncement.

Although the trend of the decision should be ascribed to the personal preference of the man himself, the real significance of the role of the Emperor lies in *the influence of the Throne* and not in the authority or personality of its occupant. Despite the wording of the Constitution, the Emperor had never possessed the actual power to decide on war or peace. Even under the pressing circumstances of August 1945, the Emperor was only the instrument, and not the prime mover, of Japan's momentous decision.

Had a similar situation existed in 1941, where indecision could have been resolved only by a cabinet resignation followed by chaos or by an unprecedented reliance upon the harmonizing influence an imperial opinion would produce through the prestige of the Throne, Japan might not have initiated hostilities. But 1941 was not 1945. The cabinet was unanimous in its determination to choose war as the alternative to what the army and others called "national suicide." In keeping with the political patterns of the past, the Emperor was not given a chance to express his wishes in the matter. As the will of the state grew more apparent over the weeks and months preceding Pearl Harbor, the Emperor could only attempt to stem the onrushing tide by blindly groping for a medium through which to make his influence felt. Failing in this, His Majesty had no choice but to sanction the resort to war, saying, "It has been truly unavoidable and far from Our wishes that Our Empire has now been brought to cross swords with America and Britain."[4]

Little did the Emperor then know that some three years and eight months later necessity would create an opportunity for him to apply the prestige of his Throne in such a way as to render it practically, though

---

[4] From the imperial rescript declaring war, for which see *Contemporary Japan*, XI (January 1942), 158–59. In this connection, see also footnote 77, Ch. 2, above.

not constitutionally, impossible for the ministers of state to act contrary to his express desires.

Had Tōjō been Premier instead of Suzuki, or had a man of Tōjō's character held Anami's post in the War Ministry, even the Emperor's own words might not have resulted in an immediate termination of the war. The fact that the Emperor was forced to state his views *twice*, first on the night of August 9/10 and again on the morning of August 14, suggests that compliance was by no means automatic. It was the nation's good fortune that, in spite of the existence of a hard-headed and strong-willed corps of fanatics, the men responsible for the movement to terminate the war were finally able, under the circumstances of 1945, to give the fullest possible effect to the depth of appeal in the voice of the man who is the supreme symbol in Japanese life and thought.

On Sunday, September 2, 1945, the day on which the Instrument of Surrender was signed on board the *Missouri*, an age-old pattern emerged in a new, yet appropriate, cast. Prior to the formal proceedings attendant upon the surrender, the Japanese government, acting upon directives received from Allied headquarters, promulgated an imperial rescript containing the Emperor's "command" to his people forthwith to cease hostilities, to lay down their arms, and faithfully to carry out the obligations accruing from Japan's capitulation.[5]

The unprecedented reverted to the commonplace, and the man in the street bowed to a new master. The Emperor once more became the passive emblem, and the Japanese government the active instrument, of a new and—for the first time in Japanese history—a foreign formula of supervision and control.

Surveying the scene before him, General of the Army Douglas Mac-Arthur, the Supreme Commander for the Allied Powers, again expressed, in words of idealism, the goal toward which civilization has long been striving:

. . . it is for us, both victors and vanquished, to rise to that higher dignity which alone benefits the sacred purposes we are about to serve, committing all of our peoples unreservedly to faithful compliance with the undertakings they are here formally to assume.

It is my earnest hope and indeed the hope of all mankind that from this solemn occasion a better world shall emerge out of the blood and carnage of the past—a world founded upon faith and understanding—a world dedicated to the dignity of man and the fulfillment of his most cherished wish—for freedom, tolerance, and justice.[6]

[5] For the text of this rescript, see Appendix J. In this connection, see also footnote 4, Prologue.

[6] See U.S. Senate, *Surrender of Italy, Germany and Japan*, 92–94.

BIBLIOGRAPHIC NOTE

The basic material from which this volume was constructed falls within the following primary groupings:

1. Records, exhibits, and proceedings of the International Military Tribunal for the Far East (cited herein as IMTFE).
2. Documents and studies of the Japanese Ministry of Foreign Affairs (cited herein as JFO MS and as JFO, *Shūsen shiroku*).
3. Unclassified "interrogation" files of the U.S. Army's Military History Section, Far East Command (cited herein as *Statements*).
4. Personal interviews with the principals.

The thousands of pages of material which kept pace with the two and one-half years during which the International Military Tribunal conducted its proceedings proved rich in data applicable to Japan's decision to surrender. Since the historian must form his own judgments as to the value and the credibility of evidence, documents and affidavits rejected by the Tribunal on various legal grounds have also found their way into this record.

Whenever possible, the author carefully checked the Japanese texts of all documents originally written in Japanese and only later translated into English for the sake of the Tribunal. This was to avoid repeating the errors in translation which mar the pages of the official (English) record and to obtain fuller information in those cases where only excerpts from the originals were introduced in court.

A year of research in Japan (1951–52) yielded unusual rewards in the way of material. During the major part of his stay, the author had access to a four-volume manuscript, "Shūsen no keii to sono shiryō" (The Circumstances Relating to the Termination of the War and the Historical Materials Pertaining Thereto), prepared over a period of some four years by the staff of the Archives and Documents Section of Japan's Ministry of Foreign Affairs. Dr. Kijirō Miyake, the then chief of the Archives Section, and Mr. Ken Kurihara, who was primarily responsible for the preparation of the Foreign Office study, gave the author complete freedom to use not only the manuscript itself but also the original source material on which it was based.

The Foreign Office study was published in May 1952 as a single volume entitled *Shūsen shiroku* (The Historical Record of the Termination of the War). In both the manuscript version and the published work, the treatment is the same: a few pages of introduction and summary by the compilers, followed by official documents, cablegrams, dictated statements, affidavit and memoir excerpts, trial testimony, and similar material. References to both the MS study and the published work appear in this volume.

Citations beginning with the word *Statements* refer to unclassified and un-

234

published "interrogation" material compiled by the U.S. Army's Military History Section, Far East Command, and cover not only documents found in the four MHS volumes entitled "Statements of Japanese Officials on World War II" but also documents contained in two additional volumes designated by MHS "Interrogations of Japanese Officials on World War II." This economy in the form of citation has been dictated by the high cost of publication and by the fact that, in spite of the difference in titles, there is no difference in the nature of the material contained in the six volumes mentioned herein.

This MHS material, which was kindly made available to the author by Chief of Section Colonel Allison R. Hartman, proved especially valuable in that it frequently provided a "second look" at the views, attitudes, and recollections of persons who had played a part in the events described in this study. The checking and balancing procedure evolved between the IMTFE (1946–48) records and the later (1949–51) MHS statements was, in turn, applied against the Foreign Office studies and the data obtained from personal interviews.

The value of interviews lay not in the specific information produced by conversations with many of the dramatis personae but in the general understanding of Japanese politics and diplomacy which was the sum total of the asides, the apparently unrelated, and the seemingly irrelevant bits of mosaic in which each discussion abounded. (A list of persons interviewed appears in the Bibliography which follows.)

One other source, the diary of Marquis Kōichi Kido, the Lord Keeper of the Privy Seal, deserves special mention. Containing 5,920 entries and covering the period January 1, 1930, through December 9, 1945, the Kido diary (cited herein as Kido, "Nikki") is packed with cryptic references to the thoughts and actions of the Privy Seal's official life. The author is indebted to Mr. Takahiko Kido, Marquis Kido's second son, for permission to use a photostatic copy of the original "Nikki" (surrendered to the U.S. Army in December 1945).

BIBLIOGRAPHY

Only works to which reference is made in the text are cited hereunder. Japanese titles are given in Rōmaji with an English equivalent supplied within parentheses.

I. *Documents, Records, and Reports* (manuscript and printed).

Imperial Household Document. "Shōwa nijūnen nigatsu, jikyoku ni kan suru jūshin hōtōroku" (Record of the Senior Statesmen's Advice to the Throne in February 1945 with Respect to the Situation Facing Japan). This document, a copy of the original, was lent to the author by Takahiko Kido, second son of the former Lord Keeper of the Privy Seal.

International Military Tribunal for the Far East. *Analyses of Documentary Evidence.*

———. *Decisions of Conferences.*

———. *Exhibits* (accepted and rejected) and *Miscellaneous Documents.*

———. *Proceedings.*

———. *Summations* (Summation of the Prosecution; Summation for the Defense).

Japan, Ministry of Foreign Affairs, Archives and Documents Section. "Shūsen no keii to sono shiryō" (The Circumstances Relating to the Termination of the War and the Historical Materials Pertaining Thereto). 4 vols., unpublished MS and source materials.

———. *Shūsen shiroku* (The Historical Record of the Termination of the War). Tokyo: Shimbun Gekkan Sha, 1952. The published version of the previous citation.

Japan, Ministry of Foreign Affairs, Division of Public Information. *Present Conditions of Japan: Political Section.* Tokyo, 1951.

Japanese Government. *Dai Tō-A sensō shūsen ni kan suru shiryō* (Source Materials Pertaining to the Termination of the Greater East Asia War). Tokyo, 1945.

Kido, Kōichi. "Nikki" (Diary). Photostatic copy of the original, in Japanese; portions have been translated into English. This citation should not be confused with a small published work which, although entitled *Kido Nikki* (edited by Kyokutō Kokusai Gunji Saiban Kenkyūkai; published by Heiwa Shobō, 1947), is nothing more than the Japanese text of the affidavit presented by Kido to the IMTFE. Although the affidavit contained entries from the diary, it is not Kido's "diary." The Kido "Nikki" cited in this study is in the possession of Marquis Kido's second son, Takahiko Kido.

Takagi, Sōkichi. Letter to the author, dated August 7, 1951, Chigasaki City, Japan.

United States Army Air Forces. *Mission Accomplished: Interrogations of Japanese Industrial, Military, and Civil Leaders of World War II.* Washington, D.C.: Government Printing Office, 1946.

United States Army, Far East Command, Military History Section. "Interrogations of Japanese Officials on World War II." 2 vols., unpublished material.[1]

――――. "Statements of Japanese Officials on World War II." 4 vols., unpublished material.[1]

――――. "Translation of Japanese Documents." 4 vols., unpublished material.

United States Congress, Joint Committee on the Investigation of the Pearl Harbor Attack. *Pearl Harbor Attack: Hearings Before the Joint Committee on the Investigation of the Pearl Harbor Attack; Congress of the United States, Seventy-ninth Congress, First Session* . . . Washington, D.C.: Government Printing Office, 1945.

United States, Department of State. *The Axis in Defeat: A Collection of Documents on American Policy Toward Germany and Japan.* (Publ. 2423.) Washington, D.C.: Government Printing Office, 1945.

――――. *Occupation of Japan: Policy and Progress.* (Publ. 2671, FES 17.) Washington, D.C.: Government Printing Office, 1946.

United States, Federal Communications Commission, Foreign Broadcast Intelligence Service. *Radio Reports on the Far East.* Washington, D.C., war years.

――――. *Special Reports.* Washington, D.C., war years.

United States, Navy Department, Commander-in-Chief, Pacific. United States Pacific Fleet and Pacific Ocean Areas. *Psychological Warfare,* Part Two, Supplement No. 2 (15 August 1945), CINCPAC-CINCPOA Bulletin No. 164-45.

United States, Office of Strategic Services, Research and Analysis Branch. *Biographical Notes on the Japanese Cabinet Appointed in April 1945.* (Publ. 3045.) Washington, D.C., 21 April 1945.

――――――――――――――

[1] A list of the persons whose interrogations and/or statements were consulted follows. Asterisks indicate more than one interrogation or statement was used.

Amano, Masakazu (Maj. Gen.)
Arao, Okikatsu (Col.)
Arisue, Seizo (Lt. Gen.)
Fujimura, Yoshirō (Comdr.)
Fuwa, Hiroshi (Col.)
Hara, Shirō (Lt. Col.) *
Hasegawa, Kiyoshi (Adm.)
Hasunuma, Shigeru (Gen.)
Hattori, Takushirō (Col.) *
Hattori, Takushirō (Col.) and
  Tomioka, Sadatoshi (Rear Adm.)
Hayashi, Saburō (Col.) *
Hiranuma, Kiichirō (Baron)
Hoshina, Zenshirō (Vice Adm.) *
Ida, Masataka (Lt. Col.)
Ikeda, Sumihisa (Lt. Gen.) *
Inaba, Masao (Lt. Col.) *
Kawabe, Torashirō (Lt. Gen.) *
Kido, Kōichi (Marquis) *
Koiso, Kuniaki (Gen.)
Matsudaira, Yasumasa (Marquis) *
Matsumoto, Shunichi (Mr.)
Matsutani, Makoto (Col.) *
Miyazaki, Shūichi (Lt. Gen.) *

Nagai, Yasuji (Maj. Gen.) *
Nakamura, Katsuhei (Rear Adm.)
Nishina, Yoshio (Dr.) *
Oikawa, Koshirō (Adm.)
Okada, Keisuke (Adm.)
Okamoto, Suemasa (Mr.)
Ōshima, Taihei (Mr.)
Sakomizu, Hisatsune (Mr.) *
Sakonji, Seizo (Vice Adm.) *
Shigemitsu, Mamoru (Mr.) *
Shimomura, Hiroshi (Dr.)
Shirai, Masatoki (Lt. Col.)
Sone, Eki (Mr.)
Suezawa, Yoshimasa (Capt., IJN)
Takeshita, Masahiko (Lt. Col.) *
Tanemura, Sakō (Col.)
Tōgō, Shigenori (Mr.) *
Tōjō, Hideki (Gen.)
Tokugawa, Yoshihiro (Chamberlain)
Tomioka, Sadatoshi (Rear Adm.)
Toyoda, Soemu (Adm.) *
Tsukamoto, Kiyoshi (Maj.)
Tsukamoto, Makoto (Col.)
Yoshizumi, Masao (Lt. Gen.) *

United States, Office of Strategic Services, Research and Analysis Branch. *The Japanese Emperor and the War.* Washington, D.C., 8 September 1944.

United States Senate. *Surrender of Italy, Germany and Japan: World War II; Instruments of Surrender, Public Papers and Addresses of the President and of the Supreme Commanders.* (Doc. 93, 79th Cong., 1st sess.) Washington, D.C.: Government Printing Office, 1946.

United States, Strategic Bombing Survey. *The Effects of Atomic Bombs on Hiroshima and Nagasaki.* Washington, D.C.: Government Printing Office, 1946.

————. *The Effects of Strategic Bombing on Japanese Morale.* Washington, D.C.: Government Printing Office, 1947.

————. . . . *Japan's Struggle to End the War.* Washington, D.C.: Government Printing Office, 1946.

————. . . . *Interrogations of Japanese Officials* . . . 2 vols. Washington, D.C.: Government Printing Office, 1946.

————. *Interrogations* (unpublished). A list of those consulted follows:

Abe, Genki	Mori, S., and Hiroye, K.
Akabane, Yutaka	Nagano, Osami
Ando, Kisaburō	Nambara, Shigeru
Hayashi, Kimiyo	Nishizawa, Nobushige
Hiranuma, Kiichirō	Suzuki, Kantarō
Koizumi, S.	Tanikawa, N.
Konoye, Fumimaro	

Ushiba, Tomohiko. Draft translation of the Konoye "Memorial." This translation, which was originally prepared for the United States Army in late 1945, was lent to the author by Mr. Ushiba, former secretary and aide to Prince Konoye.

II. *Personal Interviews Conducted by the Author.* All interviews were held in or near Tokyo between February 1951 and May 1952. Asterisks indicate more than one interview.

Blakeney, Ben Bruce	Morgan, Roy A.
Furness, George Abbot*	Ōi, Atsushi*
Kase, Shunichi	Sakai, Kōji
Kido, Kōichi	Sakomizu, Hisatsune*
Kido, Takahiko*	Satō, Bunshirō*
Konoye, Michitaka	Satō, Naotake
Kurihara, Ken*	Shigemitsu, Mamoru
Matsudaira, Yasumasa*	Shimomura, Hiroshi
Matsutani, Makoto	Takagi, Sōkichi*
Miyake, Kijirō*	Toyoda, Soemu
Monaghan, Edward P.*	Ushiba, Tomohiko*

III. *General Works.*

A. *Books and Articles.*

Baldwin, Hanson W. *Great Mistakes of the War.* New York: Harper & Brothers, 1950.

Byas, Hugh. *Government by Assassination.* New York: Alfred A. Knopf, Inc., 1942.

Byrnes, James F. *Speaking Frankly.* New York: Harper & Brothers, 1947.

Churchill, Winston S. *Triumph and Tragedy.* The Second World War. Boston: Houghton Mifflin Company, 1953.

Cohen, Jerome B. *Japan's Economy in War and Reconstruction.* Minneapolis: University of Minnesota Press, 1949.

Deane, John Russell. *The Strange Alliance; The Story of Our Efforts at Wartime Cooperation with Russia.* New York: Viking Press, 1947.

Fishel, Wesley R. "A Japanese Peace Maneuver in 1944," *The Far Eastern Quarterly,* VIII, No. 4 (August 1949), 387–97.

Fujimura, Yoshirō. "Tsūkon! Daresu dai ichi den" (Bitter Remembrance! The First Dulles Cable), *Bungei Shunjū,* XXIX, No. 7 (May 1951), 106–18.

Grew, Joseph C. *Turbulent Era; A Diplomatic Record of Forty Years, 1904–1945.* Edited by Walter Johnson, assisted by Nancy Harvison Hooker. 2 vols. Boston: Houghton Mifflin Company, 1952.

Hanayama, Shinsho. *The Way of Deliverance: Three Years with the Condemned Japanese War Criminals.* Translated by H. Suzuki, E. Noda, and J. K. Sasaki; translation revised by H. Collins. New York: Charles Scribner's Sons, 1950.

Higashikuni, Naruhiko. *Watakushi no kiroku* (My Account). Tokyo: Tōhō Shobō, 1947.

Hull, Cordell. *The Memoirs of Cordell Hull.* 2 vols. New York: The Macmillan Company, 1948.

James, David H. *The Rise and Fall of the Japanese Empire.* New York: The Macmillan Company, 1951.

Kase, Toshikazu. *Journey to the Missouri.* Edited by David Nelson Rowe. New Haven, Conn.: Yale University Press, 1950.

Katō, Masuo. *The Lost War: A Japanese Reporter's Inside Story.* New York: Alfred A. Knopf, Inc., 1946.

Kawai, Kazuo. "Japan's Struggle to Surrender." MS lent to the author by Dr. Kawai, Stanford University, 1950.

———. "*Mokusatsu,* Japan's Response to the Potsdam Declaration," *The Pacific Historical Review,* XIX, No. 4 (November 1950), 409–14.

Kuroki, Yukichi. "From War to Peace Cabinets," *Contemporary Japan,* XIV, Nos. 4–12 (April–December, 1945), 182–92.

Leahy, William D. *I Was There: The Personal Story of the Chief of Staff to Presidents Rooosevelt and Truman Based on His Notes and Diaries Made at the Time.* New York: Whittlesey House, McGraw-Hill Book Company, Inc., 1950.

Millis, Walter (ed.), with the collaboration of E. S. Duffield. *The Forrestal Diaries.* New York: Viking Press, 1951.

Nakamura, Seigo. *Nagatachō ichibanchi* (No. 1, Nagata chō). Tokyo: Niyūsu Sha, 1946.

Okada, Keisuke. *Kaikoroku* (Memoirs). Tokyo: Mainichi Shimbun Sha, 1950.

Roosevelt, Elliott. *As He Saw It.* New York: Duell, Sloan & Pearce, Inc., 1946.

Samson, Sir George. *The First Japanese Constitution.* Tokyo: Asiatic Society of Japan, 1938.

———. *The Western World and Japan: A Study in the Interaction of European and Asiatic Cultures.* New York: Alfred A. Knopf, Inc., 1950.

Satō, Naotake. *Futatsu no Roshia* (The Two Russias). Tokyo: Sekai no Nihon Sha, 1948.

Schuman, Frederick L. *Soviet Politics at Home and Abroad.* New York: Alfred A. Knopf, Inc., 1946.

Sherwood, Robert E. *Roosevelt and Hopkins: An Intimate History.* New York: Harper & Brothers, 1948.

Shigemitsu, Mamoru. *Shōwa no dōran* (Shōwa: Years of Upheaval). 2 vols. Tokyo: Chūō Kōron Sha, 1952.

Shimomura, Hiroshi (Kainan). "The Memoirs of Mr. Shimomura at the Imperial Council, 14 August 1945." Manuscript lent to the author.

————. *Shūsen hishi* (Secret History of the Termination of the War). Tokyo: Kodan Sha, 1950.

Stettinius, Edward R., Jr. *Roosevelt and the Russians: The Yalta Conference.* Edited by Walter Johnson. Garden City, New York: Doubleday & Company, Inc., 1949.

Stimson, Henry L., and Bundy, McGeorge. *On Active Service in Peace and War.* New York: Harper & Brothers, 1947.

Takagi, Sōkichi. *Shūsen oboegaki* (Recollections of the Termination of the War). Tokyo: Kōbundo, 1948.

Tōgō, Shigenori. "Shūsen gaikō" (The Diplomacy of the Termination of the War), *Kaizō,* XXXI, No. 11 (November 1950), 122–44.

Toyoda, Soemu. *Saigo no teikoku kaigun* (The End of the Imperial Navy). Tokyo: Sekai no Nihon Sha, 1950.

Uchida, Shinya. *Fūsetsu gojūnen* (Fifty Turbulent Years). Tokyo: Jitsugyō no Nihon Sha, 1951.

Uyehara, George Etsujirō. *The Political Development of Japan, 1867–1909.* London: Constable and Co., 1910.

Wakatsuki, Reijirō. *Kofūan kaikoroku* (Memoirs). Tokyo: Yomiuri Shimbun Sha, 1950.

Willoughby, Charles A., Maj. Gen. *Shanghai Conspiracy; The Sorge Spy Ring: Moscow, Shanghai, Tokyo, San Francisco, New York.* New York: E. P. Dutton & Co., Inc., 1952.

Zacharias, Ellis M. *Secret Missions: The Story of an Intelligence Officer.* New York: G. P. Putnam's Sons, 1946.

B. *Miscellaneous.*

Asahi Shimbun. Tokyo, war years.

Contemporary Japan: A Review of East Asiatic Affairs. Tokyo, war years.

Facts on File. New York, war years.

Foreign Affairs Association of Japan. *The Japan Year Book.* Tokyo, war years.

International Who's Who.

Jahrbuch für Auswärtige Politik. IX. Jahrgang 1943.

Japan-Manchoukuo Year Book.

Jinji kōshinroku.

Keesing's Contemporary Archives. Volume for 1940–43.

New York Times, war years.

Nippon Times. Tokyo, war years.

The Oriental Economist. Tokyo, war years.

Pacific Stars and Stripes.

Saishin Shina yōjin den.

Union of Soviet Socialist Republics. *Information Bulletin.*

United States, Department of State. *Bulletin.*

APPENDIXES

Appendixes A through G, and Appendixes J and K are from U.S. State Dept., *Occupation of Japan*, 51–64. Appendix H is from JFO, *Shūsen shiroku*, Ch. 55 (Gyokuon hōsō rokuon to Rengōkoku ate tsūkokubun no hatsuden). Appendix I is from *The Oriental Economist*, XII (July–August, 1945), 254.

Appendix A
THE CAIRO DECLARATION

United States of America: President Roosevelt

China: Generalissimo Chiang Kai-shek

United Kingdom: Prime Minister Churchill

Statement released December 1, 1943

The several military missions have agreed upon future military operations against Japan. The Three Great Allies expressed their resolve to bring unrelenting pressure against their brutal enemies by sea, land, and air. This pressure is already rising.

The Three Great Allies are fighting this war to restrain and punish the aggression of Japan. They covet no gain for themselves and have no thought of territorial expansion. It is their purpose that Japan shall be stripped of all the islands in the Pacific which she has seized or occupied since the beginning of the first World War in 1914, and that all the territories Japan has stolen from the Chinese, such as Manchuria, Formosa, and the Pescadores, shall be restored to the Republic of China. Japan will also be expelled from all other territories which she has taken by violence and greed. The aforesaid three great powers, mindful of the enslavement of the people of Korea, are determined that in due course Korea shall become free and independent.

With these objects in view the three Allies, in harmony with those of the United Nations at war with Japan, will continue to persevere in the serious and prolonged operations necessary to procure the unconditional surrender of Japan.

APPENDIX B

THE YALTA AGREEMENT

Between the Leaders of the Three Great Powers—

The United States of America

The Union of Soviet Socialist Republics

and the United Kingdom of Great Britain and

Northern Ireland

Signed at Yalta February 11, 1945

The leaders of the three Great Powers—the Soviet Union, the United States of America and Great Britain—have agreed that in two or three months after Germany has surrendered and the war in Europe has terminated the Soviet Union shall enter into the war against Japan on the side of the Allies on condition that:

1. The status quo in Outer-Mongolia (The Mongolian People's Republic) shall be preserved;

2. The former rights of Russia violated by the treacherous attack of Japan in 1904 shall be restored, viz:

    (*a*) the southern part of Sakhalin as well as all the islands adjacent to it shall be returned to the Soviet Union,

    (*b*) the commercial port of Dairen shall be internationalized, the preeminent interests of the Soviet Union in this port being safeguarded and the lease of Port Arthur as a naval base of the USSR restored,

    (*c*) the Chinese-Eastern Railroad and the South-Manchurian Railroad which provides an outlet to Dairen shall be jointly operated by the establishment of a joint Soviet-Chinese Company it being understood that the preeminent interests of the Soviet Union shall be safeguarded and that China shall retain full sovereignty in Manchuria;

3. The Kuril islands shall be handed over to the Soviet Union.

It is understood, that the agreement concerning Outer-Mongolia and the ports and railroads referred to above will require concurrence of Generalissimo Chiang Kai-Shek. The President will take measures in order to obtain this concurrence on advice from Marshal Stalin.

The Heads of the three Great Powers have agreed that these claims of the Soviet Union shall be unquestionably fulfilled after Japan has been defeated.

For its part the Soviet Union expresses its readiness to conclude with the National Government of China a pact of friendship and alliance between the USSR and China in order to render assistance to China with its armed forces for the purpose of liberating China from the Japanese yoke.

J. STALIN*

FRANKLIN D. ROOSEVELT

WINSTON S. CHURCHILL

February 11, 1945

---

* Romanized to accord with English usage.

THE POTSDAM PROCLAMATION

July 26, 1945

(1) WE—THE PRESIDENT of the United States, the President of the National Government of the Republic of China, and the Prime Minister of Great Britain, representing the hundreds of millions of our countrymen, have conferred and agree that Japan shall be given an opportunity to end this war.

(2) The prodigious land, sea and air forces of the United States, the British Empire and of China, many times reinforced by their armies and air fleets from the west, are poised to strike the final blows upon Japan. This military power is sustained and inspired by the determination of all the Allied Nations to prosecute the war against Japan until she ceases to resist.

(3) The result of the futile and senseless German resistance to the might of the aroused free peoples of the world stands forth in awful clarity as an example to the people of Japan. The might that now converges on Japan is immeasurably greater than that which, when applied to the resisting Nazis, necessarily laid waste to the lands, the industry, and the method of life of the whole German people. The full application of our military power, backed by our resolve, *will* mean the inevitable and complete destruction of the Japanese armed forces and just as inevitably the utter devastation of the Japanese homeland.

(4) The time has come for Japan to decide whether she will continue to be controlled by those self-willed militaristic advisers whose unintelligent calculations have brought the Empire of Japan to the threshold of annihilation, or whether she will follow the path of reason.

(5) Following are our terms. We will not deviate from them. There are no alternatives. We shall brook no delay.

(6) There must be eliminated for all time the authority and influence of those who have deceived and misled the people of Japan into embarking on world conquest, for we insist that a new order of peace, security and justice will be impossible until irresponsible militarism is driven from the world.

(7) Until such a new order is established *and* until there is convincing proof that Japan's war-making power is destroyed, points in Japanese territory to be designated by the Allies shall be occupied to secure the achievement of the basic objectives we are here setting forth.

(8) The terms of the Cairo Declaration shall be carried out and Japanese sovereignty shall be limited to the islands of Honshu, Hokkaido, Kyushu, Shikoku and such minor islands as we determine.

(9) The Japanese military forces, after being completely disarmed, shall be permitted to return to their homes with the opportunity to lead peaceful and productive lives.

(10) We do not intend that the Japanese shall be enslaved as a race or destroyed as a nation, but stern justice shall be meted out to all war criminals, including those who have visited cruelties upon our prisoners. The Japanese Government shall remove all obstacles to the revival and strengthening of democratic tendencies among the Japanese people. Freedom of speech, of religion, and of thought, as well as respect for the fundamental human rights shall be established.

(11) Japan shall be permitted to maintain such industries as will sustain her economy and permit the exaction of just reparations in kind, but not those which would enable her to re-arm for war. To this end, access to, as distinguished from control of, raw materials shall be permitted. Eventual Japanese participation in world trade relations shall be permitted.

(12) The occupying forces of the Allies shall be withdrawn from Japan as soon as these objectives have been accomplished and there has been established in accordance with the freely expressed will of the Japanese people a peacefully inclined and responsible government.

(13) We call upon the government of Japan to proclaim now the unconditional surrender of all Japanese armed forces, and to provide proper and adequate assurances of their good faith in such action. The alternative for Japan is prompt and utter destruction.

APPENDIX D

JAPAN'S FIRST SURRENDER OFFER

August 10, 1945

THE HONORABLE
 JAMES F. BYRNES
  Secretary of State

SIR:

I have the honor to inform you that the Japanese Minister to Switzerland, upon instructions received from his Government, has requested the Swiss Political Department to advise the Government of the United States of America of the following:

"In obedience to the gracious command of His Majesty the Emperor who, ever anxious to enhance the cause of world peace, desires earnestly to bring about a speedy termination of hostilities with a view to saving mankind from the calamities to be imposed upon them by further continuation of the war, the Japanese Government several weeks ago asked the Soviet Government, with which neutral relations then prevailed, to render good offices in restoring peace vis a vis the enemy powers. Unfortunately, these efforts in the interest of peace having failed, the Japanese Government in conformity with the august wish of His Majesty to restore the general peace and desiring to put an end to the untold sufferings entailed by war as quickly as possible, have decided upon the following.

"The Japanese Government are ready to accept the terms enumerated in the joint declaration which was issued at Potsdam on July 26th, 1945, by the heads of the Governments of the United States, Great Britain, and China, and later subscribed by the Soviet Government, with the understanding that the said declaration does not comprise any demand which prejudices the prerogatives of His Majesty as a Sovereign Ruler.

"The Japanese Government sincerely hope that this understanding is warranted and desire keenly that an explicit indication to that effect will be speedily forthcoming."

In transmitting the above message the Japanese minister added that his Government begs the Government of the United States to forward its answer through the intermediary of Switzerland. Similar requests are being transmitted to the Governments of Great Britain and the Union of Soviet Socialist Republics through the intermediary of Sweden, as well as to the Government of China through the intermediary of Switzerland. The Chinese Minister at Berne has already been informed of the foregoing through the channel of the Swiss Political Department.

Please be assured that I am at your disposal at any time to accept for and forward to my Government the reply of the Government of the United States.

Accept [etc.]

GRÄSSLI
Chargé d'Affaires ad interim
of Switzerland.

APPENDIX E

REPLY TO JAPAN'S FIRST SURRENDER OFFER

By Secretary of State Byrnes

August 11, 1945

MR. MAX GRÄSSLI
  Chargé d'Affaires ad interim
  of Switzerland

SIR:

I have the honor to acknowledge receipt of your note of August 10, and in reply to inform you that the President of the United States has directed me to send to you for transmission by your Government to the Japanese Government the following message on behalf of the Governments of the United States, the United Kingdom, the Union of Soviet Socialist Republics, and China:

"With regard to the Japanese Government's message accepting the terms of the Potsdam proclamation but containing the statement, 'with the understanding that the said declaration does not comprise any demand which prejudices the prerogatives of His Majesty as a sovereign ruler,' our position is as follows:

"From the moment of surrender the authority of the Emperor and the Japanese Government to rule the state shall be subject to the Supreme Commander of the Allied powers who will take such steps as he deems proper to effectuate the surrender terms.

"The Emperor will be required to authorize and ensure the signature by the Government of Japan and the Japanese Imperial General Headquarters of the surrender terms necessary to carry out the provisions of the Potsdam Declaration, and shall issue his commands to all the Japanese military, naval and air authorities and to all the forces under their control wherever located to cease active operations and to surrender their arms, and to issue such other orders as the Supreme Commander may require to give effect to the surrender terms.

"Immediately upon the surrender the Japanese Government shall transport prisoners of war and civilian internees to places of safety, as directed, where they can quickly be placed aboard Allied transports.

"The ultimate form of government of Japan shall, in accordance with the Potsdam Declaration, be established by the freely expressed will of the Japanese people.

"The armed forces of the Allied Powers will remain in Japan until the purposes set forth in the Potsdam Declaration are achieved."

Accept [etc.]

JAMES F. BYRNES
Secretary of State

APPENDIX F

JAPAN'S ACCEPTANCE OF THE POTSDAM PROCLAMATION

Statement by President Truman

August 14, 1945

I have received this afternoon a message from the Japanese Government in reply to the message forwarded to that Government by the Secretary of State on August 11. I deem this reply a full acceptance of the Potsdam Declaration which specifies the unconditional surrender of Japan. In the reply there is no qualification.

Arrangements are now being made for the formal signing of surrender terms at the earliest possible moment.

General Douglas MacArthur has been appointed the Supreme Allied Commander to receive the Japanese surrender. Great Britain, Russia, and China will be represented by high-ranking officers.

Meantime, the Allied armed forces have been ordered to suspend offensive action.

The proclamation of V-J Day must wait upon the formal signing of the surrender terms by Japan.

Following is the Japanese Government's message accepting our terms:

"Communication of the Japanese Government of August 14, 1945, addressed to the Governments of the United States, Great Britain, the Soviet Union, and China:

"With reference to the Japanese Government's note of August 10 regarding their acceptance of the provisions of the Potsdam declaration and the reply of the Governments of the United States, Great Britain, the Soviet Union, and China sent by American Secretary of State Byrnes under the date of August 11, the Japanese Government have the honor to communicate to the Governments of the four powers as follows:

"1. His Majesty the Emperor has issued an Imperial rescript regarding Japan's acceptance of the provisions of the Potsdam declaration.

"2. His Majesty the Emperor is prepared to authorize and ensure the signature by his government and the Imperial General Headquarters of the necessary terms for carrying out the provisions of the Potsdam declaration. His Majesty is also prepared to issue his commands to all the military, naval, and air authorities of Japan and all the forces under their control wherever located to cease active operations, to surrender arms and to issue such other orders as may be required by the Supreme Commander of the Allied Forces for the execution of the above-mentioned terms."

APPENDIX G

NOTIFICATION TO THE JAPANESE GOVERNMENT

By Secretary of State Byrnes

August 14, 1945

MAX GRÄSSLI, Esquire
   Chargé d'Affaires ad interim
   of Switzerland

SIR:

With reference to your communication of today's date, transmitting the reply of the Japanese Government to the communication which I sent through you to the Japanese Government on August 11, on behalf of the Governments of the United States, China, the United Kingdom, and the Union of Soviet Socialist Republics, which I regard as full acceptance of the Potsdam Declaration and of my statement of August 11, 1945, I have the honor to inform you that the President of the United States has directed that the following message be sent to you for transmission to the Japanese Government:

"You are to proceed as follows:

"(1) Direct prompt cessation of hostilities by Japanese forces, informing the Supreme Commander for the Allied Powers of the effective date and hour of such cessation.

"(2) Send emissaries at once to the Supreme Commander for the Allied Powers with information of the disposition of the Japanese forces and commanders, and fully empowered to make any arrangements directed by the Supreme Commander for the Allied Powers to enable him and his accompanying forces to arrive at the place designated by him to receive the formal surrender.

"(3) For the purpose of receiving such surrender and carrying it into effect, General of the Army Douglas MacArthur has been designated as the Supreme Commander for the Allied Powers, and he will notify the Japanese Government of the time, place and other details of the formal surrender."

Accept [etc.]

JAMES F. BYRNES
Secretary of State

APPENDIX H
JAPAN'S FINAL NOTE

The Japanese Government would like to be permitted to state to the Governments of America, Britain, China and the Soviet Union what they most earnestly desire with reference to the execution of certain provisions of the Potsdam Proclamation. This may be done possibly at the time of the signature. But fearing that they may not be able to find an appropriate opportunity, they take the liberty of addressing the Governments of the Four Powers through the good offices of the Government of Switzerland.

1. In view of the fact that the purpose of occupation as mentioned in the Potsdam Proclamation is solely to secure the achievement of the basic objectives set forth in the said Proclamation, the Japanese Government sincerely desire that the Four Powers, relying upon the good faith of the Japanese Government, will facilitate discharge by the Japanese Government of their obligations as to forestall any unnecessary complications.

It is earnestly solicited that:

(*a*) In case of the entry of Allied fleets or troops in Japan Proper, the Japanese Government be notified in advance, so that arrangements can be made for reception.

(*b*) The number of the points in Japanese territory to be designated by the Allies for occupation be limited to minimum number, selection of the points be made in such a manner as to leave such a city as Tokyo unoccupied and the forces to be stationed at each point be made as small as possible.

2. Disarming of the Japanese forces, being a most delicate task as it involves over three millions of officers and men overseas and having direct bearing on their honour, the Japanese Government will, of course, take utmost pains. But it is suggested that the best and the most effective method would be that under the command of His Majesty the Emperor, the Japanese forces are allowed to disarm themselves and surrender arms of their own accord.

Disarming of the Japanese forces on the Continent be carried out beginning on the front line and in successive stages.

In connection with the disarming it is hoped that Article 35 of the Hague Convention will be applied, and the honour of the soldier will be respected, permitting them, for instance, to wear swords. Further, the Japanese Government be given to understand the Allies have no intention to employ disarmed Japanese soldiers for compulsory labour. It is sincerely hoped that shipment and transportation facilities necessary for the evacuation of the soldiers to their homeland will be speedily provided.

3. Since some forces are located in remote places, difficult to communicate the Imperial Order, it is desired that reasonable time be allowed before the cessation of hostilities.

4. It is hoped that the Allies will be good enough quickly to take necessary steps or extend us facilities for the shipment of indispensable foodstuffs and medical supplies to Japanese forces in distant islands, and for the transport of wounded soldiers from those islands.

APPENDIX I

THE IMPERIAL RESCRIPT OF AUGUST 14, 1945

To Our good and loyal subjects:

After pondering deeply the general trends of the world and the actual conditions obtaining in Our Empire today, We have decided to effect a settlement of the present situation by resorting to an extraordinary measure.

We have ordered Our Government to communicate to the Governments of the United States, Great Britain, China and the Soviet Union that Our Empire accepts the provisions of their Joint Declaration.

To strive for the common prosperity and happiness of all nations as well as the security and well-being of Our subjects is the solemn obligation which has been handed down by Our Imperial Ancestors, and which We lay close to heart. Indeed, We declared war on America and Britain out of Our sincere desire to ensure Japan's self preservation and the stabilization of East Asia, it being far from Our thought either to infringe upon the sovereignty of other nations or to embark upon territorial aggrandizement. But now the war has lasted for nearly four years. Despite the best that has been done by everyone—the gallant fighting of military and naval forces, the diligence and assiduity of Our servants of the State and the devoted service of Our one hundred million people, the war situation has developed not necessarily to Japan's advantage, while the general trends of the world have all turned against her interest. Moreover, the enemy has begun to employ a new and most cruel bomb, the power of which to do damage is indeed incalculable, taking the toll of many innocent lives. Should We continue to fight, it would not only result in an ultimate collapse and obliteration of the Japanese nation, but also it would lead to the total extinction of human civilization. Such being the case, how are We to save the millions of Our subjects; or to atone Ourselves before the hallowed spirits of Our Imperial Ancestors? This is the reason why We have ordered the acceptance of the provisions of the Joint Declaration of the Powers.

We cannot but express the deepest sense of regret to our Allied nations of East Asia, who have consistently cooperated with the Empire towards the emancipation of East Asia. The thought of those officers and men as well as others who have fallen in the fields of battle, those who died at their posts of duty, or those who met with untimely death and all their bereaved families, pains Our heart night and day. The welfare of the wounded and the war-sufferers, and of those who have lost their homes and livelihood, are the objects of Our profound solicitude. The hardships and sufferings to which Our nation is to be subjected hereafter will be certainly great. We are keenly aware of the inmost feelings of all ye, Our subjects. However, it is according to the dictate of time and fate that We have resolved to pave the way for a grand peace for all the generations to come by enduring the unendurable and suffering what is insufferable.

Having been able to safeguard and maintain the structure of the Imperial State, We are always with ye, Our good and loyal subjects, relying upon your sincerity and integrity. Beware most strictly of any outbursts of emotion which may engender needless complications, or any fraternal contention and strife which may create confusion, lead ye astray and cause ye to lose the confidence of the world. Let the entire nation continue as one family from generation to generation, ever firm in its faith of the imperishableness of its divine land, and mindful of its heavy burden of responsibilities, and the long road before it. Unite your total strength to be devoted to the construction for the future. Cultivate the ways of rectitude; foster nobility of spirit; and work with resolution so as ye may enhance the innate glory of the Imperial State and keep pace with the progress of the world.

(Imperial Sign Manual)
(Imperial Seal)

The 14th day of the 8th month
of the 20th year of Showa.

APPENDIX J

THE IMPERIAL RESCRIPT OF SEPTEMBER 2, 1945

September 2, 1945 (Tokyo Time)

Accepting the terms set forth in Declaration issued by the heads of the Governments of the United States, Great Britain and China on July 26th, 1945 at Potsdam and subsequently adhered to by the Union of Soviet Socialist Republics, We have commanded the Japanese Imperial Government and the Japanese Imperial General Headquarters to sign on Our behalf the Instrument of Surrender presented by the Supreme Commander for the Allied Powers and to issue General Orders to the Military and Naval Forces in accordance with the direction of the Supreme Commander for the Allied Powers. We command all Our people forthwith to cease hostilities, to lay down their arms and faithfully to carry out all the provisions of Instrument of Surrender and the General Orders issued by the Japanese Imperial Government and the Japanese Imperial General Headquarters hereunder.

This second day of the ninth month of the twentieth year of Syōwa.

Seal of
the   HIROHITO
Emperor

NARUHIKO-Ō
Prime Minister

MAMORU SHIGEMITSU
Minister for Foreign Affairs

IWAO YAMAZAKI
Minister for Home Affairs

JUICHI TSUSHIMA
Minister of Finance

SADAMU SHIMOMURA
Minister of War

MITSUMASA YONAI
Minister of Navy

CHUZO IWATA
Minister of Justice

TAMON MAEDA
Minister of Education

KENZO MATSUMURA
Minister of Welfare

KOTARO SENGOKU
Minister of Agriculture and Forestry

CHIKUHEI NAKAJIMA
Minister of Commerce and Industry

NAOTO KOBIYAMA
Minister of Transportation

FUMIMARO KONOE
Minister without Portfolio

TAKETORA OGATA
Minister without Portfolio

BINSHIRO OBATA
Minister without Portfolio

APPENDIX K

INSTRUMENT OF SURRENDER

September 2, 1945 (Tokyo Time)

We, acting by command of and in behalf of the Emperor of Japan, the Japanese Government and the Japanese Imperial General Headquarters, hereby accept the provisions set forth in the declaration issued by the heads of the Governments of the United States, China and Great Britain on 26 July 1945, at Potsdam, and subsequently adhered to by the Union of Soviet Socialist Republics, which four powers are hereafter referred to as the Allied Powers.

We hereby proclaim the unconditional surrender to the Allied Powers of the Japanese Imperial General Headquarters and of all Japanese armed forces and all armed forces under Japanese control wherever situated.

We hereby command all Japanese forces wherever situated and the Japanese people to cease hostilities forthwith, to preserve and save from damage all ships, aircraft, and military and civil property and to comply with all requirements which may be imposed by the Supreme Commander for the Allied Powers or by agencies of the Japanese Government at his direction.

We hereby command the Japanese Imperial General Headquarters to issue at once orders to the Commanders of all Japanese forces and all forces under Japanese control wherever situated to surrender unconditionally themselves and all forces under their control.

We hereby command all civil, military and naval officials to obey and enforce all proclamations, orders and directives deemed by the Supreme Commander for the Allied Powers to be proper to effectuate this surrender and issued by him or under his authority and we direct all such officials to remain at their posts and to continue to perform their non-combatant duties unless specifically relieved by him or under his authority.

We hereby undertake for the Emperor, the Japanese Government and their successors to carry out the provisions of the Potsdam Declaration in good faith, and to issue whatever orders and take whatever action may be required by the Supreme Commander for the Allied Powers or by any other designated representative of the Allied Powers for the purpose of giving effect to that Declaration.

We hereby command the Japanese Imperial Government and the Japanese Imperial General Headquarters at once to liberate all allied prisoners of war and civilian internees now under Japanese control and to provide for their protection, care, maintenance and immediate transportation to places as directed.

The authority of the Emperor and the Japanese Government to rule the state shall be subject to the Supreme Commander for the Allied Powers who will take such steps as he deems proper to effectuate those terms of surrender.

Signed at *Tokyo Bay, Japan* at *0904 I* on the *second* day of *September*, 1945.

MAMORU SHIGEMITSU*

By Command and in behalf of the Emperor of Japan and the Japanese Government.

YOSHIJIRŌ UMEZU*

By Command and in behalf of the Japanese Imperial General Headquarters.

Accepted at *Tokyo Bay, Japan*, at *0908 I* on the *second* day of *September*, 1945. for the United States, Republic of China, United Kingdom and the Union of Soviet Socialist Republics, and in the interests of the other United Nations at war with Japan.

DOUGLAS MACARTHUR

Supreme Commander for the Allied Powers.†

---

* Romanized to accord with English usage.
† General MacArthur's signature is followed by those of C. W. Nimitz (United States Representative), Yung-ch'ang Hsü* (Republic of China), Bruce Fraser (United Kingdom), General-Leitenant K. Derevyanko (Union of Soviet Socialist Republics), T. A. Blamey (Commonwealth of Australia), L. Moore Cosgrave (Dominion of Canada), Leclerc (Provisional Government of the French Republic), C. E. L. Helfrich (Kingdom of the Netherlands), Leonard M. Isitt (Dominion of New Zealand).

INDEX

Note: No reference is made to the footnotes in cases where the connection between the text and the footnotes is such that reference from the one to the other is a matter of course.

251

PUBLICATIONS OF THE HOOVER LIBRARY
ON
WAR, REVOLUTION, AND PEACE

———————————————☆———————————————

FALL OF THE GERMAN EMPIRE, 1914–1918. Edited by Ralph Haswell Lutz. Two volumes. $15.00

THE BOLSHEVIK REVOLUTION, 1917–1918. Edited by H. H. Fisher and James Bunyan. (Out of print.)

THE CAUSES OF THE GERMAN COLLAPSE IN 1918. Edited by Ralph Haswell Lutz. $5.00

THE TREATY OF ST. GERMAIN. A DOCUMENTARY HISTORY OF ITS TERRITORIAL AND POLITICAL CLAUSES. Edited by Nina Almond and Ralph Haswell Lutz. $7.50

OUT OF MY PAST. THE MEMOIRS OF COUNT KOKOVTSOV. Edited by H. H. Fisher. Translated by Laura Matveev. $7.50

PUBLIC RELATIONS OF THE COMMISSION FOR RELIEF IN BELGIUM. George I. Gay and H. H. Fisher. Two volumes. $10.00

THE FAMINE IN SOVIET RUSSIA, 1919–1923. THE OPERATIONS OF THE AMERICAN RELIEF ADMINISTRATION. H. H. Fisher. $5.00

THE TESTIMONY OF KOLCHAK AND OTHER SIBERIAN MATERIALS. Edited by Elena Varneck and H. H. Fisher. $5.00

A DIPLOMATIC HISTORY OF THE BALKAN CRISIS OF 1875–1878. THE FIRST YEAR. David Harris. $5.00

CHINA AND THE WORLD WAR. Thomas E. La Fargue. $4.00

ALLIED PROPAGANDA AND THE COLLAPSE OF THE GERMAN EMPIRE, 1918. George G. Bruntz. (Out of print.)

FEATURES AND FIGURES OF THE PAST: GOVERNMENT AND OPINIONS IN THE REIGN OF NICHOLAS II. V. I. Gurko. Edited by J. E. Wallace Sterling, Xenia Joukoff Eudin, and H. H. Fisher. Translated by Laura Matveev. $7.50

THE BOLSHEVIKS AND THE WORLD WAR. Olga Hess Gankin and H. H. Fisher. $7.50

THE BLOCKADE OF GERMANY AFTER THE ARMISTICE, 1918–1919. Selected and edited by Suda Lorena Bane and Ralph Haswell Lutz. $7.50

BRITISH LABOUR'S RISE TO POWER. Carl F. Brand. (Out of print.)

HISTORY OF THE UNITED STATES FOOD ADMINISTRATION, 1917–1919. William C. Mullendore. With Introduction by Herbert Hoover and Foreword and Bibliography by Ralph Haswell Lutz. $5.00

RAYMOND POINCARÉ AND THE FRENCH PRESIDENCY. Gordon Wright. $3.50

ORGANIZATION OF AMERICAN RELIEF IN EUROPE, 1918–1919. Edited by Suda Lorena Bane and Ralph Haswell Lutz. $6.00

THE LIFE OF A CHEMIST. MEMOIRS OF VLADIMIR N. IPATIEFF. Edited by Xenia Joukoff Eudin, Helen Dwight Fisher, and H. H. Fisher. Translated by V. Haensel and Mrs. R. H: Lusher. $7.50

REGIONAL CONFLICTS AROUND GENEVA. Adda Bruemmer Bozeman. $5.00

THE GOLD COAST: A SURVEY OF THE GOLD COAST AND BRITISH TOGOLAND, 1919–1946. F. M. Bourret. $4.00

JAPAN'S DECISION TO SURRENDER. Robert J. C. Butow. $4.00